Popular Newspapers, the Labour Party and British Politics

'IT'S THE SUN WOT WON IT', was the famous headline claim of Britain's most popular newspaper following the Conservative party's victory over Labour in the 1992 general election. The headline referred to a virulent press campaign against Neil Kinnock's Labour party, and dramatically highlighted one of the chief features of British politics during the twentieth century – the conflict between a socialist Labour party and a capitalist popular press. Labour's frequent complaints of the political and electoral unfairness of newspaper bias meant that some commentators considered that this dispute had a heritage as old as the party itself. Others, including the Labour leadership at the time, argued that despite past tensions, the 1992 election marked the culmination of an unprecedented campaign of vilification against the party.

Popular Newspapers, the Labour Party and British Politics assesses these competing claims, looking not only at 1992 but both back and forward to examine the continuities and changes in newspaper coverage of British politics and the Labour party over the twentieth century. The book explores whether the popular press has lived up to its claim of being a democratic 'fourth estate', or has merely, as Labour politicians have argued, been a powerful 'fifth column' distorting the democratic process. Drawing on a range of previously unexamined sources, this book offers the first original and comprehensive history of a fascinating aspect of British politics from Beaverbrook to Blair.

James Thomas is a lecturer at the Cardiff School of Journalism, Media and Cultural Studies at Cardiff University, and has published articles and essays exploring the relationship between the popular press and British politics.

British politics and society
Series Editor: Peter Catterall
ISSN: 1467-1441

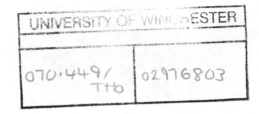
Social change impacts not just upon voting behaviour and party identity but also the formulation of policy. But how do social changes and political developments interact? Which shapes which? Reflecting a belief that social and political structures cannot be understood either in isolation from each other or from the historical processes which form them, this series will examine the forces that have shaped British society. Cross-disciplinary approaches will be encouraged. In the process, the series will aim to make a contribution to existing fields, such as politics, sociology and media studies, as well as opening out new and hitherto-neglected fields.

Poor Health
Social inequality before and after the Black Report
Edited by Virginia Berridge and Stuart Blume

Mass Conservatism
The Conservatives and the public since the 1880s
Edited by Stuart Ball and Ian Holliday

Defining British Citizenship
Empire, Commonwealth and modern Britain
Rieko Karatani

Television Policies of the Labour Party, 1951–2001
Des Freedman

Creating the National Health Service
Aneurin Bevan and the medical Lords
Marvin Rintala

A Social History of Milton Keynes
Middle England/edge city
Mark Clapson

Scottish Nationalism and the Idea of Europe
Atsuko Ichijo

The Royal Navy in the Falklands Conflict and the Gulf War
Culture and strategy
Alastair Finlan

The Labour Party in Opposition 1970–1974
Prisoners of history
Patrick Bell

The Civil Service Commission, 1855–1991
A bureau biography
Richard A. Chapman

Popular Newspapers, the Labour Party and British Politics
James Thomas

Popular Newspapers, the Labour Party and British Politics

James Thomas

Routledge
Taylor & Francis Group

LONDON AND NEW YORK

First published 2005
by Routledge
2 Park Square, Milton Park, Abingdon, Oxon OX14 4RN

Simultaneously published in the USA and Canada
by Routledge
270 Madison Ave, New York, NY 10016

Routledge is an imprint of the Taylor & Francis Group

© 2005 James Thomas

Typeset in Garamond by Wearset Ltd, Boldon, Tyne and Wear
Printed and bound in Great Britain by MPG Books Ltd, Bodmin

British Library Cataloguing in Publication Data
A catalogue record for this book is available from the British Library

Library of Congress Cataloging in Publication Data
A catalog record for this book has been requested

ISBN 0-714-65337-3

Contents

Acknowledgements

This book has been a somewhat long-drawn-out affair, so my debts of gratitude are particularly numerous and can hardly be covered in this brief note. In view of its origin as a PhD thesis I am particularly grateful for the help, encouragement and hospitality that my supervisor Peter Stead provided, while my thanks also go to the examiners of the thesis, George Boyce and the late Ben Pimlott, for their valuable input. I also owe a particular debt to Peter Catterall, both for his helpful comments on an earlier draft and also, more generally, for his generosity and help throughout my academic career. While my appreciation goes out to all (or almost all!) colleagues at Swansea, Bangor and Cardiff where I have been employed, I am particularly grateful to David Howell for all his faith in my abilities, however misguided it sometimes seemed. My warm appreciation also goes to all those who took the time and effort to talk to or correspond with me about my research, namely Robert Edwards, Geoffrey Goodman, Joe Haines, Michael Hartwell, Anthony Howard, David Hill, Trevor Kavanagh, Neil Kinnock, Terry Lancaster, Julia Langdon, Mike Molloy, Robin Oakley and Richard Stott. Neil Kinnock also kindly granted me access to his then closed archive at Churchill College, Cambridge, while Elizabeth Quadhi permitted me to consult the papers of John Strachey that she holds. My gratitude also extends to the help provided by the staff at all the libraries and archives that I consulted.

More personally, a big thanks goes to all my friends who have at times helped, and on other occasions, hindered this book's completion. All have helped teach me that the meaning of life, while elusive, does not rest in spending a sunny weekend or a long evening chasing up footnotes and triple-sourcing references. Lloydee, Skies, Sqwodga, Lis and Arakna deserve particular mention for their efforts to rescue me from such a fate. Many thanks also to my extended family in London for all their entertaining hospitality on research trips and sorry Liz, yet again, for destroying the table! Two final debts of gratitude: first to Debs for her invaluable academic help and friendship, and second, and most importantly, to my Mam and Dad for, quite simply, everything. This one's for them, with much appreciation.

James Thomas
Ystrad, July 2004

Introduction

'IT'S THE SUN WOT WON IT', claimed Britain's most popular daily newspaper following Labour's surprise defeat in the 1992 general election. Two days later Neil Kinnock appeared to agree. Announcing his resignation as Labour leader, he attacked the 'misinformation and disinformation' of a Conservative-supporting press which had 'enabled the Tory party to win yet again when it could not have secured victory on the basis of its own record, its programme or character'.[1] Notwithstanding the ever-present tensions in Labour's relations with a capitalist press, this appeared to be something new. A number of commentators considered that the dispute marked the climax of a long and concerted anti-Labour campaign of vilification unprecedented in its intensity. It was also the first time since the pre-war era that a Labour leader had seemed to blame the press for an election defeat, a view which attracted a remarkable level of support from political enemies as well as friends. Never one to credit her successor with any achievements, Lady Thatcher was for once reported as sharing the views of her old adversary. Another disaffected Thatcherite and former treasurer of the Conservative party, Lord McAlpine, also suggested that the tabloid editors were the real campaign 'heroes'.[2]

Meanwhile their response was rather more modest. Flamboyant *Sun* editor Kelvin MacKenzie was to quickly withdraw his claim following what he described as 'the biggest bollocking of his life' from proprietor Rupert Murdoch.[3] In the heated post-election debate on press power, he was to be joined by his fellow 'heroes', Sir Nicholas Lloyd of the *Express* and Sir David English at the *Mail*, in dismissing Kinnock's display of 'sour grapes', the reactions of a 'whingeing politician' who could not accept defeat.[4] They in turn found some strange allies in the shape of *Living Marxism*, Ken Livingstone, and a series of commentaries in the left-leaning broadsheets. These argued that the hostility of the tabloids in 1992 had a heritage as old as the Labour party itself and had not prevented previous election victories in the post-war era.[5] Continuity rather than change, according to these accounts, was the order of the day.

This book aims to explore the validity of these competing claims as it examines the role of the popular press in British politics since 1940. Its main body is divided into five extended chapters, each representing a different phase of political coverage. The first chapter is concentrated around the role of the popular press in Labour's shock election victory of 1945. It explores the virulent anti-Labour hostility of the emerging popular press in the inter-war period. But the rise of a centre-left popular press from the 1930s meant that, by 1945, the popular press remained individually partisan but was collectively more politically balanced than ever before, a pattern that continued throughout the post-war Labour governments between 1945–1951. Chapter 2 takes up where the previous one left off to explore Labour's treatment in the years and months prior to the 1964 general election, an occasion which formed the high-point for the party of a more general trend after 1951 towards a reduction in individual press partisanship. Chapter 3 begins by examining the early origins of the breakdown of this trend with the dramatic end of the Wilson government's press honeymoon from 1966 onwards. But its main focus suggests that it was only really from 1974–1979 that an overwhelmingly partisan right-wing press gradually emerged. Chapter 4 moves on to chart how the party's electoral and political failures between 1979–1992 were accompanied by a more relentlessly hostile press coverage than at any time in the post-war era. In particular it explores the above controversy surrounding the 1992 general election and suggests that there is some truth in the claim that it was 'the *Sun* (in alliance with the other Tory-supporting tabloids) wot won it' for the Conservatives. The final section then analyses the reasons behind the astonishing transformation of New Labour's treatment in the tabloid press between 1992–1997. It demonstrates how, in both the latter election and 2001, it was Blair's New Labour party – but not social democracy – that gained more support from the right-wing press than ever before.

It is perhaps worth outlining at this early stage what I think are the strengths and weaknesses of this book. It has been largely outside its scope to systematically examine the 'quality' broadsheet press, based on the (contestable) rationale that, given the different contents and audiences they reach, there is no logical reason why they should be grouped together. The concentration throughout has also been on daily rather than Sunday newspapers due to the greater potential power of the former and also because the 'Sundays' often merely provide a muted reflection of the political line of their daily counterparts. Perhaps a more important failing is that this book does not offer any systematic examination of how the message of the popular press has interacted with television news, even if it does provide some illustrations of this process. It also reproduces the neglect in the popular press of the Liberals and Liberal Democrats in that the main focus is on coverage of the battle between the two main parties. Nor does it offer any exploration of the political journalism that has always formed a key part of the activities of Labour party politicians. Another fundamental omission is that the book repeats the error 'in which the history of the popular press is still frequently thought of by academics and elite journalists as properly concerned with politics'.[6] The entertainment content of the popular press, which forms the bulk of what people read, is not given the attention that its potential political significance deserves.[7] This book also originated as a PhD thesis and has all the weaknesses – and hopefully the occasional strength – that such an undertaking demands. Most of this book was written within, or at least merely semi-detached from, a history department, before I eventually moved to the lush pastures of the Cardiff School of Journalism, Media and Cultural Studies. This means I am particularly conscious of its failings from the latter perspectives. The approach here is to tell the story of Labour's treatment in the popular press through a largely historical form of analysis, rather than one that utilises social science approaches and methodologies. That said, these insights have been incorporated as far as my competence allows and this book certainly aims to provide some interdisciplinary fusion between contemporary history, political science and media studies.

In the latter field, for instance, some illuminating qualitative studies of how audiences interact with media messages have led academics to radically revise their assumptions about 'the ideological effect' of media content on attitudes.[8] Again this book has many weaknesses in this area, mitigated slightly by a couple of strengths. Reconstructing the rich, complex, contradictory, fluid and multiple relationships newspapers have with their readers is difficult with the best of evidence. A half-century-odd historical framework compounds the problem and makes it very difficult to satisfactorily explore this area. At the same time this book does draw on a variety of quantitative and qualitative evidence that at least offers some rudimentary picture of the relationships between readers and their paper's politics. Other recent studies, meanwhile, have systematically examined how media content is produced within newsrooms or among political journalists.[9] Again this was not possible to do, although selected interviews, diaries, memoirs and primary documents (where available) allows for some feel of this process. Equally, the same evidence from politicians also conveys some of the reaction of those in the firing line of coverage. Finally, the large timescale that was deliberately chosen inevitably meant a selective focus, particularly around general elections, the most obvious indication of press partisanship. The rationale for a long period was simply that it was impossible to explore the validity of the competing claims made after 1992, and other more general questions as well, without a comparative examination of previous and subsequent periods. While hardly all-encompassing, this book still hopes to be comprehensive in its scope.

Such routine academic self-flagellation over, it is perhaps also worth briefly and immodestly drawing out some of the book's strengths. Given the enormous growth in media studies over the last 20 years, it is perhaps surprising that no detailed exploration has been made of the Labour party's fortunes in this area. Many academic books refer to the party's treatment by the press, but few so far have examined it in any detail. Partly this can be explained by the focus of media studies (and social science) on the contemporary rather than the past, so that history has been dubbed 'the neglected grandparent' of the discipline.[10] It also might owe something to recent trends within the field away from discussions around media power or biased content and towards illuminating the previously under-researched audience. It certainly owes something to the perceived feeling that the press is an old-fashioned subject compared with other media forms like television or the Internet. This is, incidentally, despite the fact that even in 2002 the Internet was used weekly for news by just one-fifth of the population compared with over 80 per cent who still read newspapers at least once a week.[11] The difficulty of accessing popular newspapers (this study necessitated prolonged visits to the excellent National Newspaper library in London) provides another explanation. Equally the traditional neglect from historians suspicious of anything as crude and popular as the 'philistine' (to quote G. M. Trevelyan) press may have improved in recent decades.[12] But again the media history that has been generated tends to relegate press history behind a greater focus on film and television.[13]

One particularly useful contribution from the social sciences have been the analyses of media coverage that can be found in the Nuffield studies that have quickly followed every election since 1945.[14] These have been complemented more recently by other analyses of contemporary elections that contain important sections on the media, while others have offered brief thematic overviews of the trends that these works suggest.[15] But there has been no book-length examination of the role of the popular press in British politics since 1945. This study aims to do just this with a relatively broad examination that contains primary research on every general election since 1940 (and a few more in the inter-war period), but focuses more closely on selected key elections. It also aims for a greater depth of analysis in that, while most election studies focus on one month in four years, each chapter here has a broader time scope, averaging 15 years and which particularly seeks to illuminate newspaper politics in the years immediately prior to these key elections. The main focus is on content, given both its availability as a source and my chief interest in the messages being conveyed to readers. But it aims to also offer a rather more three-dimensional picture than a simple discussion of media messages as it examines, as far as is possible, the production, content and popular reception of the politics of the popular press since 1940.

Ultimately, the book stems from a concern about the operation of media power (and by extension the nature of media content), a subject that has been endlessly debated within academia and elsewhere for three-quarters-of-a-century. Not that this has taken scholars much closer to any clear conclusions. Any attempt to place precise media effects within their broader context faces the obvious problem that there is simply no independent, pre-given world of opinion that exists independently of a media-influenced world. Examining media effects also comes up against the classic 'chicken and egg' difficulty of whether, for example, *Daily Mail* readers vote Conservative because of their paper's political line, or whether they read it precisely because they vote Tory. Determining precise cause-and-effect relationships between readers and their papers remains very difficult. For much of the post-war period the dominant orthodoxy was of a 'minimal effects' model. This argued that media messages were limited in power in that they were much more likely to reinforce opinions rather than change them (although this itself can have important effects, for example if the media is skewed in one particular political direction or works to reinforce the existing status quo).[16] Such conclusions from political science have been reinforced by recent work within media and cultural studies that have stressed the (at times seemingly limitless) power of audiences to resist and subvert media messages as traditional concerns about media power have become unfashionable, dismissed as patronising, old-fashioned and naive.[17] One media studies academic writing in 1995 about television reflected wider thinking as he boldly suggested that 'the search for direct "effects" . . . on behaviour is over, every effort has been made and they simply cannot be found'. Others within political science offered their broad agreement, or at least they would have done so if the two fields talked to each other more often.[18] But around the same time, however, another academic was referring to how the field had gone virtually full-circle with the re-emergence of a 'massive' media effects model to replace the previous 'minimal' one.[19] This provides further evidence that academics cannot even agree on the state of literature on the subject! But it also reflects a new emerging body of what has been dubbed 'new effects research'. Empirical analyses from both from media and cultural studies[20] and political science[21] have assembled a collectively impressive range of evidence that demonstrates the very considerable power of the media at times to set political agendas, construct rather than reflect sociopolitical meaning and affect attitudes, beliefs and behaviour. They also more specifically suggest that 'newspaper effects' mean that 'the partisan composition of the Fleet Street press does matter' in its power to sway enough votes to influence election results.[22]

The evidence that exists both for and against this proposition at selected historic periods in British politics is explored throughout this book. Meanwhile a recurring theme is what Harrop has argued to be an often-underestimated media effect – the negative power of the press to selectively exclude some ideas while promoting others.[23] And it remains a working assumption – and an important motivation – of this analysis that the popular press does have considerable (although far from unlimited) power to affect the UK's political culture and even, at times, its election results. To assume that it does not effectively serves to let the *Sun*s and *Daily Mail*s of this world 'off the hook of any responsibility' for any distortion of reality, however extreme, that they can come up with.[24] This book also shares the assumptions that others have argued, in opposition to some recent academic trends, that there emphatically is a real world out there that cannot be collapsed into media representations. Exploring the gap between that reality – the truth even – and the media image remains an important (although far from exclusive) area of inquiry.[25]

A number of additional introductory points are also worth making. The bare statistics that tell us that the *Mail*, *Express* and *Mirror* endorsed their chosen party consistently at every election between 1945–1997 rather suggests little need for further detailed study. Yet they need to be qualified and examined more closely as they say nothing about the qualitatively differing level of commitment offered at various times or changes in the paper's political agenda. They give no indication of the extent to which the final editorial endorsement from newspapers was reflected in their actual news coverage during elections, and, just as importantly, in the months and years prior to it. A useful general distinction here is sometimes made between the role of the press as 'spectators' and 'players'. In their spectator role, newspapers sit on the sidelines, perhaps editorially supporting one side but usually taking a broadly dispassionate and detached line. Whatever each newspaper's individual slant, such an approach concentrates on reporting the campaign rather than distorting the news for political gain. By contrast the 'players' approach sees newspapers place themselves as participants within the electoral battle, offering unrelenting commitment to their side alongside fierce hostility to their opponents. In this arena, news is not something to be reported, but a weapon to be manipulated through processes of suppression, selection, distortion, exaggeration and presentation. The first approach seeks primarily to inform while the second desires only to propagandise. It is a question, as C. P. Scott famously put it, of whether 'comment is free but facts are sacred', or alternatively, of whether 'comment is sacred and facts are selective'.

This is not to ignore the naivety of such a distinction and the limitations of such concepts as 'objectivity', 'impartiality' and 'balance', of which much has been written about in recent years.[26] The above division is certainly far less clear cut in practice. Nevertheless its central assumption remains valid in the key role which a press plays in, at best, enhancing and, at worst, distorting the workings of the democratic process in its political coverage. As distinguished liberal journalist Tom Baistow once observed, 'the fair presentation of both or various sides of a case is an essential prerequisite of a responsible newspaper's right to beat the drum of its own propaganda'. The right of access to information is enshrined as a fundamental human right and is, of course, always seen as one central element to a 'free' society.[27]

The means by which this right has been maintained over centuries in Britain has been through a libertarian form of press freedom. Its defenders suggest that a free-market untrammelled by state control ensures a press that reflects the attitudes and interests of readers, who ultimately determine its content. Newspaper proprietors, whatever their politics, are largely impotent when faced with the power of the commercial market. Critics, on the other hand, argue that owners rather than readers are fundamentally sovereign in a structure that ensures that only the few individuals or businesses rich enough to own newspapers control the information available to the many.[28] Ultimately, this book explores whether this free market system has enhanced or diminished British democracy in its political coverage, as it asks the deceptively simple questions: to what extent has the Labour party, and to what extent has the electorate, suffered a bad press over the last half-century?

1 'Vote for them'

The popular press and the 1945 general election

Throughout the inter-war years, Labour suffered a serious disadvantage in newspaper representation from a new, stridently independent and largely right-wing force in British politics, the popular press. Yet the same period also saw the beginnings of a mass-readership centre-left press. It was not, however, until the Second World War that the most important popular paper in this mould, the *Daily Mirror*, swung to the left. By the 1945 general election, Labour gained better treatment than ever before from a popular press as partisan as in the inter-war period, but which was now fairly evenly divided in its loyalties – a pattern which continued throughout the lifetime of the Attlee governments. Reflecting these trends, this chapter begins by focusing briefly on the political stance of the popular press during the inter-war period before examining in more detail the changing content, ownership and impact of coverage leading up to the 1945 election. It then concludes with a brief examination of the response of the popular press to the first Labour governments between 1945–1951.

'Red letters and savings scares': the right-wing press 1906–1935

The emergence and rapid growth of the national popular daily press from 1896 onwards, to reach a circulation of over ten million by 1939, came at the very time when the newly-created Labour party was competing for the support of the same mass electorate.[1] Commercialisation had freed newspapers from dependence on party finance and their more independent position was symbolised, if not caricatured, by the press barons who dominated the press in the inter-war period. Their vigorous independence brought severe conflict with Conservative leaders, as much as anyone else, most famously in the battle over Empire Free Trade in 1929–1931. But ultimately there was little doubt that, when the choice had to be made, the press could be largely guaranteed to 'speak with one voice if not to extol the virtues of Toryism, at any rate to proclaim the "menace of socialism"'.[2]

From the outset, Labour found itself 'severely handicapped' by a lack of press support for its electoral efforts.[3] The *Daily Mail* summed up the capitalist press' instinctive antipathy in its first ever profile in 1906. This argued that Labour's aims 'must of necessity conflict with the organisation of industrial enterprise' and would give the state an 'insane' power through 'an extension of the most evil features of the present system'.[4] Four years of 'Socialistic legislation' further hardened its stance against Labour's 'campaign of class hatred and plunder' as, not for the last time, the *Mail* won praise from Conservative leaders as their 'most potent auxiliary'.[5] Labour's gradual electoral eclipse of the Liberals during the war and post-war years was accompanied, for the press, by what one contemporary commentator described as 'the simplification of major issues into the two main elements of socialism and anti-socialism'.[6]

Representing this in most reactionary form was Northcliffe's brother, Lord Rothermere, owner of the picture paper the *Daily Mirror*, who assumed control of the *Daily Mail* on Northcliffe's death in 1922. Rothermere, a man consumed by fear of the world's imminent economic armageddon and rise of communism, saw himself in suitably negative terms as an 'anti-Socialist', dedicated to opposing a foreign doctrine that represented 'the enemy outside the gates of Britain'.[7] For the most part, Rothermere showed little faith that the country's 'feeble politicians' would do this, as even Conservative governments were denounced for the 'socialism' of their 'extravagant' social reforms. His one exception was a brief 'hurrah for the blackshirts' of Oswald Mosley in 1934, whom he hoped would defeat the threat of 'red revolution' 'cunningly concealed' by 'a mild and benevolent programme' of its Labour party 'dupes'.[8] It was hardly surprising that in the post-war elections of 1922 and 1923 the *Mail* took the hysterical line that a vote for Labour was 'a vote for Bolshevism' which would 'threaten every man's house and furniture and every woman's clothes and jewellery'. Labour were fantastically denounced as 'a wing of the German Bolshevist Sozialitische Arbeiter Internationale' – a far cry from the 'truly British reasonable and moderate ... party of ten or twenty years ago' – which would replicate 'the sweated wage, the massacres, the machine guns, the fearful famines and the pestilences' of Soviet socialism.[9]

Aside from the menace of socialism, the *Mail* had a rather more serious challenger to its commercial prosperity for, by the 1920s, its circulation dominance established by Northcliffe was gradually being eroded by Beaverbrook's *Daily Express*. The Canadian had a press baron's complex personality that could be repellent, savage, tyrannical yet also charming and benevolent.[10] Politically he was just as contradictory, as he embraced many progressive philosophies within his idiosyncratic conservatism. His anti-establishment rhetoric, alongside policies which endorsed a minimum wage, opposed intervention in the Russian civil war and supported the opening of a second front in World War Two, found common cause with some on the left who crowded around his dining table to debate with political opponents. Beaverbrook's impish love of mischief, along with his persona as a political seducer of left-wing talent, saw him employ numerous left-wing propagandists from David Low to Tom Driberg. A few of these, such as Michael Foot and A. J. P. Taylor, even came to love Beaverbrook 'like a second father'.[11] Many more on the left, however, despised the press baron and his newspapers for their hostility to 'the socialists', as they always called the Labour party. Beaverbrook's belief in Imperial Preference and private enterprise ensured that from his arrival in Britain in 1909 he almost automatically became a Conservative. And he remained true to these principles, if not to the Conservative party, throughout his life, defining the *Express* in 1923 as 'an independent organ tied neither to the Conservatives nor to the Liberal party but opposed to socialism'.[12]

Despite facing what Labour leader Ramsay MacDonald condemned as a 'gross misrepresentation and malignant suppression of facts' by 'gutter papers', the first minority Labour government took office in January 1924 amidst great fears from Rothermere that the party would shake the economic structure 'to its foundations'.[13] The rather more anodyne reality of Labour's first eight months in government failed to alter his stance. Labour's attempts to appeal to the middle-classes through the 'politics of moderation' was countered by the *Mail*'s increasingly aggressive efforts to portray a party gripped by the politics of extremism in a battle that would be repeated many times.[14] The *Mail*'s primary vehicle in 1924, the 'Red Scare', had been visible just before polling day the previous year in an alarming report: 'MOSCOW FUNDS FOR ROWDIES: LABOUR CANDIDATES SUBSIDISED: ELECTION DAY PLOT'. Two events intensified its importance by October 1924. The Labour government's diplomatic recognition of the Soviet government had been followed by a pledge of a future financial loan, while the government had resigned after its role in the dropping of sedition charges against the editor of a Communist newspaper.

Both incidents added weight to Conservative allegations of the government's subservience to Moscow and, in a virulent campaign, the *Mail* ferociously denounced that there should be 'No British Money for Bolshevik Murderers'. News columns overflowed with daily exposures of the appalling 'HORRORS A BOLSHEVIK LOAN WOULD SUPPORT' while MacDonald was depicted as the 'PREMIER UNDER THE RED FLAG' representing 'the same colour as the torturers of the Cheka use for their badge'.[15] The rest of the Conservative press strongly followed this lead, ignoring that Labour had recently reaffirmed its hostility to the Communist party by overwhelmingly rejecting its bid for affiliation and declaring individual Communists ineligible to stand as candidates.[16]

The scene was set for the *Daily Mail*'s most famous anti-Labour publication. In a dramatic seven-decked headline it reported a 'CIVIL WAR PLOT BY SOCIALISTS' MASTERS'. There followed details of subversive instructions allegedly issued to the British Communist party by the president of the Third International, Grigori Zinoviev, along with a Foreign Office note of protest to the Soviet authorities.[17] The letter had been intercepted two weeks earlier and subsequently examined by MacDonald – who was the

Foreign Secretary as well as Prime Minister – on his campaign tour. He re-wrote but did not sign a Foreign Office draft protest note which he expected to be returned to him with further proof of authenticity before publication. But he had not accounted for the *Mail*, which had obtained the letter after close contacts with Conservative Central Office. The knowledge that the paper 'was going to publish whatever happened' placed a key role in the Foreign Office's controversial decision to issue a protest without MacDonald's authorisation. Despite finding such actions inexplicable, MacDonald strongly felt that the real blame lay with the *Mail*'s detonation of a 'political bomb' obtained 'weeks ago' but exploded later to achieve maximum electoral impact.[18] These efforts were visible as the *Mail*'s editor generously hurried copies of this startling exclusive to rivals 'so editorials could be prepared on the subject for the following morning's issues'.[19]

The story dominated the front pages. Every page of the *Express*'s polling-day edition was splashed with blood-curdling red ink with the warning, 'DO NOT VOTE "RED" TODAY'.[20] The *Daily Mirror*'s front page headline – 'VOTE BRITISH, NOT "BOLSHIE"' – provided the most graphic illustration of the hysterical mood. Readers were offered the difficult choice between pictured Conservative and Liberal leaders representing 'Law, Order, Peace and Prosperity' or, alternatively, a 'vote for the overthrow of Society and ... Bolshevism' as personalised by menacing profiles of Kamenev, Rykov, Zinoviev and Trotsky, the latter having 'produced widespread bloodshed and starvation. His real name is Lev Bronstein.'[21] The issue of the letter's authenticity was hotly debated at the time and has aroused periodic controversy ever since.[22] This partly obscures that it merely detailed Comintern and British Communist party strategy, as outlined in numerous genuine intercepted communications. But it also obscures that, real or forgery, its importance lay in the way it was politically used to dramatically support earlier allegations that Labour 'tamely and humbly' obeyed 'the murderous alien despotism in Moscow'.[23]

This was the most famous illustration of the uncompromising hostility of the inter-war press towards Labour, a stance replicated seven years later following the ignominious end of the 1929–1931 Labour minority government.[24] For Rothermere the 1931 political crisis under Labour and the subsequent formation of an anti-socialist economy-seeking National Government represented his repeatedly expressed solution to a situation where 'successive governments' had 'practised squandermania as if it were the supreme function of statesmanship'.[25] Unsurprisingly in the 1931 election his newspapers fiercely denounced Labour's programme of 'unlimited taxation and unlimited expenditure' which would cause 'deaths from actual starvation'.[26] Providing the first of many illustrations that there was little dearer to the Tory press than a lapsed socialist, the *Mail* eulogised MacDonald as the 'man of destiny' with 'an unanswerable power of personality'. Where once it had found his campaign speeches greeted with cold silence, it now detected '10,000 CHEERING PEOPLE'.[27] Rothermere also made his views more directly known in an ambitious historical analysis comparing the fall of the Roman Empire with the contemporary political crisis. Alongside a suitably bizarre illustration of Romans in togas strolling along a modernised Thames embankment, he warned readers that it would be 'goodbye for ever to England's greatness' if 'the rash and ignorant demagogues of the Socialist Opposition' returned to rule.[28]

The *Express*, which by 1931 had almost as large a circulation as its rival, took a similar stance. In a speech early in the election, Beaverbrook lamented that he had 'not been a good party man' but firmly pledged his loyalty to the National Government. A few days later, some *Express* readers may have questioned this when they read of how their proprietor had led the singing of the 'Red Flag' when started by his opponents.[29] Notwithstanding his tuneful flirtation with red revolution, Beaverbrook was soon predicting that a Labour victory would produce 'the biggest industrial and financial panic the world has ever seen'.[30] His paper faithfully echoed this 'nightmare picture' under which the economy would 'crash to nothing' and destroy the 'TIDE OF PROSPERITY' already produced by the National Government.[31] Such reports laid the foundation for the notorious 'Post-Office Savings Scare'. Former Labour Chancellor Philip Snowden climaxed a series of vitriolic assaults against his erstwhile colleagues by suggesting that they had earlier borrowed substantial sums from the Post Office Savings fund to pay for unemployment benefit, creating a threat to people's savings which would return if Labour won the election. Despite bitter denials, the press strongly reinforced this last-minute scare of a 'SOCIALIST THREAT TO SAVINGS OF THE POOR' as voters were warned, 'Your Home Your Livelihood Your Savings At Stake' in the simple choice between 'PROSPERITY OR RUINATION'.[32] A grateful MacDonald was to thank both Rothermere and Beaverbrook for their help, while also hardly negating Labour's allegations of treachery by observing how it had been 'a wonderful time'.[33]

The growth of a centre-left popular press

In the face of such hostility, however, the inter-war period did see a strengthening of an alternative centre-left press. Socialists of all types had long since rated the need for an effective newspaper as a major priority. In the 20 years from 1890, almost 800 papers supportive of the Labour movement were published, but the absence of a daily newspaper remained of considerable concern to Labour leaders and was frequently contrasted with the success of the German socialist press.[34] For it was naively believed that a favourable press would almost automatically produce the triumph of socialism as the capitalist 'plot press' lost its control over 'the mind and so the policy of the nation'.[35]

It was no easy task, however, to reconstitute the successful radical press that had existed in the 1840s, given both the increased capital required to produce a newspaper and its dependence on advertising revenue which discriminated partly against the message but mostly against its low-income readership.[36] In 1912, however, two very different Labour newspapers appeared.[37] The *Daily Citizen* loyally reflected the position of the Labour party and sought to differ from its commercial rivals only in politics as it promised, 'on many pages the voice of controversy will be hushed'.[38] Not so the unequivocally political and independent *Daily Herald*, which supported the industrial militancy of the period as ferociously as it denounced the moderate Labour leadership. While the *Citizen* folded within three years of its launch, the *Herald*, contemptuous of the sterility of its rival, was to become increasingly like it after the war. After continued losses, the paper was sold to the Labour movement in 1922, although it took longer to establish control. In 1924 a stance supportive but to the left of the Labour government outraged a sensitive MacDonald who complained to the editor that it would be better if the paper 'came out honestly ... as an organ hostile to the government'.[39] There was little sign of its subversion in October 1924 as it made strident defences of the government's record and attacked the 'obvious forgery' of the Zinoviev letter. But this did not stop MacDonald ridiculously claiming that 'nothing contributed more' to the defeat than the stance of a pro-Labour paper with a circulation of just 300,000.[40]

Although the paper's editorial independence was soon curtailed, its commercial difficulties continued, a product of its political rather than newsworthy content and its inability to offer the free insurance schemes of rival papers. Key *Herald* figures advocated a less political but ultimately more effective publication that would reach greater numbers and, in 1929, this option was taken through a marriage of convenience with Odhams Press, managed by Walter Elias, later Lord Southwood. Although instinctively a Tory, Elias desired a daily newspaper for the entirely commercial reason that for six days of the week the machines printing his mass circulation Sunday newspaper, *The People*, lay idle. Under the new agreement Odhams now controlled its commercial management while the TUC and the Labour party dictated its political and industrial policy.[41] The paper was re-launched to great acclaim in March 1930, being double its previous size and more attractively packaged and designed and employing staff recruited heavily from Fleet Street.[42] Within seven months it had built up a circulation of over one million, although it was less journalism and more its tempting free gifts and insurance schemes that enabled it to pip the *Express* to become the first ever newspaper to achieve a two-million sale in June 1933.[43] Although the principal objective was commercial – 'to topple the *Daily Mail* not the Tory party' – the paper stayed solidly loyal during the party split in 1931.[44] Later claims that the *Herald* counteracted the 'complete falsity' of 'disgraceful' press coverage omitted to mention that it had much the same characteristics, as it suggested that a vote for the National Government was 'a vote against democracy ... a vote for the pinchbeck fascism of a bunch of pinchbeck Mussolinis'.[45]

Despite such impeccable loyalty and a two-million circulation from 1933, the Labour movement seemed far from content. Discontent over the way sales had been built up were added to further complaints that the *Herald* had 'lost its individuality' and was full of half-naked women rather than socialism. Yet the real commercial problem was that it still gave more space to serious news coverage than its popular, and even some more upmarket, rivals.[46] This, combined with its predictable pro-Labour stance, brought criticism from some readers who thought it was 'sometimes rather dull', while others attracted by its free gifts more bluntly dismissed its propaganda as 'a lot of tripe'. Whatever these failings, for the first time Labour had a vehicle to communicate its message to millions, many of whom could ill-afford access to an anti-socialist viewpoint as well.[47]

By the 1930s, Labour were also benefiting from the growing radicalism of the *News Chronicle*, a serious, 'popular' formed in 1930 out of a merger of two liberal papers, the *Daily News* (which had itself merged with the other liberal paper the *Westminster Gazette* in 1928) and the *Daily Chronicle*. This unity of the Liberal press stood in direct contrast to a party that was further fragmenting into three conflicting and electorally marginalised factions. The Liberal papers, like their party, had long been divided in their attitude towards the Labour party. While the *Daily News* had earlier gained Labour's gratitude for its 'sympathetic treatment', the more conservative *Daily Chronicle* had allied itself with the common battle Conservatives and Liberals were fighting against Labour's 'dominant and revolutionary wing'.[48] This was visible in the *News Chronicle*'s 1931 election coverage that managed to support both 'a strong National Government' against the Labour 'menace', while calling for a strengthening of 'the saner Labour element' and debunking the 'Savings Scare' against the party.[49] The paper's policy in the 1930s continued to reflect these wider liberal divisions, with policy determination characterised by a descending level of radicalness in an uneasy three-way relationship between the paper's trustees chaired by Lawrence Cadbury, chairman Walter Layton, and the paper's editors.

The progressive liberalism of the paper's first editor, Tom Clarke, had produced frequent clashes with the *Chronicle*'s more reactionary trustees who shared the view of one contemporary that the paper was 'so far to the Left . . . it hardly differs from a moderate Labour paper'.[50] However it was only after Clarke was replaced in 1933 by the radical Aylmer Vallance that the conflict intensified.[51] His efforts to 'infuse the paper with vigorous radicalism' brought strong protests from Cadbury and the trustees that the paper had 'abandoned Liberalism and gone Labour' as they called for 'drastic changes', even replacing the editor, to rectify this.[52] In turn, Vallance protested against this desire to swing the paper 'unmistakably to the right' by explaining that the political stance was because 'the position of modern-minded "gradualist" Labour leaders' corresponded 'most clearly with the spirit of philanthropic radicalism' enshrined in the paper's guiding principles.[53] Matters came to a head in the 1935 election. With the Liberals fielding only

159 candidates, the paper focused on the failings of the National Government. Vallance's less equivocal personal views were revealed at the election night party when, inebriated, he responded to the Liberal party's electoral disaster by loudly cheering announcements of its lost deposits.[54] As this incident illustrated, it was not only Vallance's political radicalism that had weakened his position by this time. His heavy drinking and adventurous habit of making love all over the office after hours led to complaints from those staff who retained more respect for the paper's puritan Quaker philosophy. Vallance was dismissed a month later, and it was left to new editor Gerald Barry to continue the political revolution, if not the sexual one.[55]

Yet despite such advances, in 1935 the same press disadvantage that Labour had faced throughout the inter-war period remained. As Table 1.1 illustrates, in 1924 Labour had suffered a circulation deficit of nearly 20:1 compared with the Conservative and Liberal press. In 1931, the National Government/Labour press deficit was down to about seven-to-one but the Conservative popular press now reached more readers than ever before and was even more united in its hostility. Such a pattern was also visible less spectacularly four years later.[56] The consequences of this were much commented on by the left. Labour leaders considered that the deadly 'poison gas of the capitalist press' was a key reason for their election defeats, while Rothermere also estimated that the Zinoviev letter 'altered the situation to the extent of something like a hundred seats'.[57] In reality the most famous anti-Labour press campaign of the century probably at most increased the size of Labour's defeat in 1924, with the party's actual vote going up by a million despite the loss of 48 seats. Similarly the 1931 defeat was largely the product of the party's unimpressive performance in government, its divided state, and the electoral unity of its opponents.[58] Yet the press may have been important less on its impact on particular events and more in helping support and sustain over time a conservative political agenda as it 'reinforced opposition, particularly among the middle classes, to progressive change'.[59] Some advance in countering this message had been made by the 1930s. But just as it was to take the Second World War to transform Labour's level of popular support, so the same was true of the press.

Table 1.1 Party support in the press 1924–1945

	1924	1931	1935	1945
Cons	72	71	65	52
Lab	5	13	21	35
Lib	22	16	14	13

Sources: Jeffery and McCelland, 'A World Fit to Live in', in Curran, Smith and Wingate (eds), *Impacts and Influences*; Thorpe, *The British General Election of 1931*; Stannage, *Baldwin Thwarts the Opposition*; McCallum and Readman, *The British General Election of 1945*.

'The National Socialists': the Tory press and the 1945 election

This became evident for the first time in the 1945 general election when a bitterly fought out contest between Labour and the Conservatives was reflected in press coverage which remained highly partisan, but for the first time was evenly divided in affiliations. By far the most pro-Conservative newspaper was the *Express*. Although the *Herald*'s aggressive promotional campaigns had won it the initial circulation war in the 1930s, the *Express* eventually overhauled it in 1936 as Beaverbrook devoted considerable resources to developing the paper's journalistic quality. His most inspired move came in 1933 when he appointed Arthur Christiansen as editor, who was to be as responsible for the paper's phenomenal success as Beaverbrook during the 24 years he remained in his position. Politically Christiansen was totally subservient to his proprietor. As he later wrote, 'the policies were Lord Beaverbrook's job, the presentation mine'.[60] But it was in this latter area that he excelled. He crafted a technically brilliant paper with sharp layout, attractive articles, which exuded glamour and optimism, and which had the most superior journalistic staff in Fleet Street in quantity and quality. In 1933 its circulation had been 1.7 million. During the 1945 campaign its circulation actually rose by 136,000 to reach 3.3 million, the largest sale ever recorded for a newspaper at the time.[61]

Beaverbrook's close alliance with his wartime colleague and close friend Churchill was clearly demonstrated in the *Express*'s election coverage. This gave the impression of being 'the reproduced voice of Churchill', who in turn faced campaign allegations that he was controlled by Beaverbrook.[62] Their political approach was set after the Conservative leader's famous radio attack on his former colleagues early in the election was strongly supported in lurid *Daily Express* coverage predicting a 'GESTAPO IN BRITAIN IF SOCIALISTS WIN'.[63] The press baron was widely blamed for a speech which Attlee described as 'the voice . . . of Mr Churchill but the mind . . . of Lord Beaverbrook'. These attacks were carried on the paper's front page but the limitations of its impartiality was demonstrated the headline above this text – 'THE NATIONAL SOCIALISTS'. This was the brainchild of Labour-supporting journalist Brian Chapman in what the paper's general manager

Table 1.2 Partisanship and circulation of the popular press in 1945 (millions)

Daily Express	3.3	Con
Daily Herald	1.85	Lab
Daily Mail	1.7	Con
Daily Mirror	2.4	Anti-Tory
News Chronicle	1.55	Lib/Lab
Daily Sketch/Graphic	0.9	Con

Source: McCallum and Readman, *The British General Election of 1945*.

later recalled, with some understatement, was 'sheer journalistic enthusiasm' which 'went far beyond his own convictions'.[64]

The Conservative and *Express* campaign had two main characteristics. It was highly personalised in its efforts to exploit Churchill's electoral value and was highly negative in so far as it covered the Labour party. The paper, which like others was limited to just four pages due to newsprint rationing, devoted 56 per cent of its election coverage to the Conservative campaign and just over a quarter to Labour. Nearly 90 per cent of all Labour's coverage questioned the party's democratic credentials through its attacks on the party's left-wing chairman Harold Laski.[65] Laski had given the Tories their opportunity when he rashly stated that Attlee's attendance at the forthcoming Potsdam conference could not bind the party to any agreement made. This, as Hugh Dalton observed, did touch upon the 'slightly delicate' matter of where sovereign power in the Labour party actually lay. It gave the Tories their new villain and enhanced the familiar allegation that, as Churchill put it, the far-left Labour tail 'wagged the dog'. At the *Express* Christiansen was 'carried away by the excitement' of what he thought was 'an election weapon as good as the Zinoviev letter'.[66]

The result of his and Beaverbrook's enthusiasm was that 'Gauleiter Laski' was unceasingly depicted as 'the power behind the party' who made the unthreatening Attlee 'a man in chains'. Coverage merged into an even more spectacular 'NEW LASKI SENSATION' which had him calling for 'SOCIAL-ISM – "EVEN IF IT MEANS VIOLENCE"'. A libel writ from the politician hardly stemmed the message. One ingenious *Express* front page conveyed the potential menace of the 'socialist junta' by juxtaposing the headline, 'OBSCURE LASKI CAUCUS WILL GIVE ORDERS', with pictures of an intimidating military courtroom in Moscow relating to a separate story. Less obliquely, the Beaverbrook-owned *Evening Standard* carried front page photographs of Labour's 25 national executive committee members under the headline 'DICTATORS IN SESSION' as readers were urged, 'Study their faces'.[67] This personalisation of anti-Labour coverage around Laski – from 18 June to 5 July there were no photographs of any other Labour politicians – was only matched by the overwhelming attention given to Churchill, the Conservative party's 'ace of trumps' according to Beaverbrook.[68] In April 1945 Christiansen had proposed the paper's election strategy:

> Everywhere I find that the fundamental issue is whether the socialists can put up a man to compare to Churchill in the handling of all the problems of the peace. . . . The affection in which he is held by the non-party sections of the populace, who can really swing the election one way or the other is tremendous. 'Win the Peace with Winston' is, there-fore, the best call in my view.

Beaverbrook, who his editor claims would not permit one word of criticism of Churchill in his paper, replied that he was 'very much impressed' with this strategy, duly realised in adulatory coverage of 'the greatest man now living'.[69] Despite Beaverbrook's campaign denials, supported by Taylor, that he did not 'issue any direct orders' to his newspapers, the evidence suggests otherwise, even if the press baron hardly ever set foot in the famous black glass Express building. At the start of 1944, Beaverbrook was informing Churchill that the press was 'not making a Conservative case', which he promised to 'rectify as far as the principal newspaper is concerned'. During the election he further told an encouraging prime minister of his intention 'to participate in the direction of leading articles and the determination of policy'.[70] Certainly Beaverbrook had 'the time of his life' during the campaign and was in constant touch with Christiansen, proving, in the latter's typically sycophantic thanks, to be 'wise' in putting him 'back on the right track' whenever he veered in his approach.[71]

But in any case the paper's executives hardly needed any instructions. They later revealed to the Royal Commission on the Press that the paper's stance since 1944 had been determined by a policy committee that Beaverbrook had 'never made the slightest attempt to override'. This was hardly necessary because, as the press baron freely observed, those who served on it would not have been asked to join if they did not share his views.[72] In any case, as the commission pointed out, each newspaper had a set of long-held 'unspoken assumptions' about its policy, style, tone and character. Christiansen and Robertson agreed that this was 'certainly the case on the *Daily Express*' where policy was the product of 'a sort of tradition'.[73]

Symbolising his paper's partisanship, Beaverbrook adopted a high-profile campaigning role. He denounced Laski for 'aiming at the destruction of the parliamentary system' and clashed bitterly with his old enemy in the wartime coalition, Bevin, who objected 'to the country being ruled by Fleet Street ... instead of from parliament'.[74] Beaverbrook did not, contrary to allegations, play any role in Churchill's 'Gestapo' speech. But he was consulted over the Laski affair and strongly advised in favour of a minimalist programme on domestic reconstruction, dismissing Conservative complaints that Churchill should be encouraged to show more interest in 'reconstruction and social reform'.[75] Mass-Observation's conclusion that 'the fundamental issue' framing the election was 'socialisation versus private enterprise' was certainly borne out by the *Express*. The paper constantly suggested that the basic choice lay between the vibrant spirit of free enterprise to 'GET BRITAIN GOING' or the 'shackles' of 'state direction'.[76] If there was a political consensus in existence by 1945, clearly no one had told Beaverbrook.[77]

The *Express* was again joined by the *Mail* in its endorsement, although its approach was rather more restrained than in the past. One reason was that, by 1945, Harold Rothermere's son Esmond, a moderate Conservative, had assumed close control of a paper which, after his father's destructive reign, trailed well behind the *Express* with a circulation of 1.7 million. Esmond had been a Conservative MP between 1919–1929, where he was derided as his father's poodle, before beginning his life's work managing Associated News-papers. However Harold Rothermere still retained 'active control' until autumn 1938, after which he was 'gradually given up' before his death in November 1940.[78] Like the *Express*, the paper cautioned against the 'increas-ing measure of state control or totalitarianism' implicit in Labour's revolu-tionary programme, while the damning 'inefficiencies' of Australian socialism were exposed in an article by one Keith Murdoch in an approach his son was later to emulate. Scarce pictorial resources were lavished on Churchill's tour as the paper urged readers to return 'the man who has done so much, and can do so much more, for his country and the world'. Never-theless under the less rabidly anti-socialist Esmond, the *Mail* took a more moderate position than in the past or compared with its rival. It rarely assumed the offensive in its propaganda, leading with election news on just nine occasions. Even then the paper's headlines were 'mild and tame', as it later earned *Tribune*'s praise for its 'quite unexpected ... sense of respons-ibility'.[79]

Rather more high-profile support came from the Welsh press barons, the Berry brothers, who in 1937 had divided the vast press empire they had gradually established over the previous 20 years. Lord Camrose now assumed sole control of the *Daily Telegraph* and the *Financial Times* while Lord Kemsley became proprietor of 18 of the group's newspapers, including the *Daily Sketch* and the *Sunday Times*. Camrose had long exercised close control of the *Telegraph*, and was a close friend and supporter of Churchill and the paper, as leader writer Malcolm Muggeridge recalled, 'campaigned hotly for a Conservative victory'. This was not least because his proprietor alarmingly feared that a Labour victory would signal an end to financial journalism and possibly the entire capitalist system and swiftly disposed of the *Financial Times* after the result before the more prosperous reality became clear.[80]

Much the same line was broadcast by Kemsley's tabloid *Daily Sketch*. The press baron, who could have doubled for Groucho Marx, had played no part in the editorial direction of the Berry empire until the 1937 separation. He more than made up for it afterwards, however, boasting in 1947 that he was in 'closest possible touch' with his editors and had 'every edition of every issue' of his papers 'gone through every day'. In any case, as Kemsley put it, his editors were 'all men ... with similar ideas to my own and it is quite unnecessary to tell them of my views ... they know our policy and ... I have never had any trouble'.[81] Kemsley, as one of his editors recalls, was 'a deeply conservative Conservative', whose newspapers could be depended on 'to support the party-line with Pravda-like fidelity'. Socialism, as Kemsley bluntly warned in 1946, produced 'the servile state' and would destroy 'the liberty of the individual'. Such a message was evident a year earlier and was further reinforced by the fact that Churchill had converted the peerage of the social-climbing Berry from Baron to Viscount on the promise of his support in the election.[82] Eulogies of Churchill as 'THE MAN OF THE HOUR' were combined with violent assaults on Labour's democratic credentials as it warned, 'ARE GAULEITERS TO DICTATE TO BRITONS?'[83] Kemsley's later claim that he had instructed that opponents be given 'fair and liberal representation' in his newspapers begged the question of what a pro-Conservative campaign would have looked like.[84]

'Never again': the 1945 election (2)

For the first time, however, such hostility was balanced by a considerable anti-Tory stance of nearly half the total circulation of the popular press. Partly this reflected a continuation of the pattern visible in the pre-war era. The *Daily Herald* once again offered the same diet of strident and uncritical pro-Labour propaganda. Headlines screamed, 'FRAUDS, CHEATS, WRIG-GLERS SEEKING POWER', 'More Babies Die under Tory Rule', and most interestingly, 'A VOTE FOR CHURCHILL IS A VOTE FOR FRANCO' – the latter just being pipped by the *Daily Worker*'s 'IS RIBBENTROP HOLDING TORIES TO RANSOM?' as the most inventive campaign prose. This rather contradicted later claims by senior staff that the election had been covered 'very fairly' by a paper which in fact 'hardly ever reported an opponent, except for an occasional snippet under a derisive headline'.[85]

Perhaps the most underlying theme of its propaganda was the suggestion that the electorate could not trust a Conservative party dominated by 'vested interests' and the 'old gang', comprising of 'profiteers, monopolists, landowners and speculators'. Its distinctly backward-looking coverage asked, 'DO WE GO BACK TO THIS?' Text and pictures offered a 'grim reminder of life under Tory rule' in the 1930s, characterised by 'wretched conditions', 'casual work' and skilled workers 'rotting in idleness' outside employment exchanges.[86] How valuable this support was is debatable. Party secretary Morgan Phillips praised the 'loyal, vigilant and active' support which Attlee suggested was of 'immense importance' to the result. The *Herald*'s official biography also emphasised the value of its 'consistent support to a comprehensive philosophy of change' since 1930. Camrose, on the other hand, 'heard prominent members of the party' including some former directors of the *Herald* describe it as 'very little use to them as a political newspaper'. The extremity of its partisanship and its close identification with Labour may well have rendered its coverage relatively ineffective. Even some of its overwhelmingly Labour-supporting readers considered the paper's coverage to be 'too one-sided'.[87] On the other hand, given that the *Herald* was overwhelmingly read by Labour voters who frequently cited politics as a reason for choosing it, the paper may have proved valuable in reinforcing the opinions of the converted and getting out the Labour vote.[88]

Reaching more floating Labour voters, including the key middle-class vote that was so important in swinging the election, was the *News Chronicle*. New editor from 1935, Gerald Barry, later recalled that his aim was 'to make the paper as radical as I could stretch my more hesitant proprietors – or beyond'. Such an approach was soon provoking further rumours of an imminent 'conversion to socialism'.[89] This brought renewed opposition from Cadbury, who moved even further to the right as he got older.[90] His suspicions that his editor was a socialist Trojan Horse were later confirmed by Barry's view that 'one can sometimes exert more influence from within a moderate framework than by pavement squatting or resorting to obvious political extremes'.[91]

By 1942, Cadbury was trying to muster the courage to sack Barry for his editorial insubordination, with one particular source of tension being his employment and development of the raw brilliance of left-wing Hungarian cartoonist Vicky (Victor Weisz).[92] Ironically, Barry's radical stance was made easier by the fact that, in 1936, Cadbury had bought out the most reactionary of the paper's trustees. This in turn increased the authority of Layton, whose daily presence and attempts to dictate policy 'in considerable detail' was resented by an editor who considered that it reduced him to 'a kind of dignified office boy'. Despite such conflicts, Barry survived and pushed the paper 'further to the left than Cadbury or even Layton wanted' before his 'long and finally losing battle on this score' ended in resignation in late 1947.[93]

Perhaps the high point of the *Chronicle*'s radicalism came in the 1945 election. The paper was highly sympathetic to Labour as it was, as readers recognised, 'much further to the left than the Liberal party'.[94] It sought to harness and unite the 'overwhelmingly radical and anti-Tory mood' for 'far reaching reforms' which could not be achieved by a Conservative government dominated by 'the solid lines ... of vested interests, of wealth and privilege'. By contrast there was 'much in common' between Labour and Liberal policy. While advising readers to vote Liberal, the paper suggested that 'the real issue should be the record of the Tory party between the wars and their failings ... of too little and too late'.[95] Vicky's anti-Tory cartoons reinforced this message. One, entitled 'the big three', showed Beaverbrook, Churchill and Bracken formulating their scare plans, but being dwarfed by three noble working-class giants of Housing, Social Security and Employment.[96]

Vicky's only superior as the finest cartoonist in the country, David Low, was suspiciously absent through 'illness' in the opening stages of the election. But his subsequent work for the *Evening Standard* made up for this as it reached a wider, and perhaps more conducive, audience by being reprinted in the *Manchester Guardian*. It pursued a similar line in attacking the 'Childminds' in the Tory party for their 'stunts' which clouded the real choice for the puzzled elector between 'haphazard enterprise for private profit' or 'planned development for the common good'.[97] This fitted closely with the stance of a paper that thought the chance of a Labour victory was 'pretty remote'. This led it to call not just for Liberals to vote Labour in those constituencies (over half in total) where there was no Liberal standing, but even to leave it open whether readers should vote Liberal or Labour in three-way contests.[98]

In many ways the support or sympathy of these above papers echoed the position they had taken in pre-war years, as Labour replaced the Liberals as the main hope of the progressive left. But the key change in the balance of the press came with the leftward shift of the populist tabloid *Daily Mirror*, which by 1945 had built up a circulation of 2.4 million and may have reached up to 11 million readers.[99] In 1931, Rothermere had largely withdrawn from active editorial control of the *Mirror*, but the paper continued to decline and by 1934 had reached a circulation low of just 700,000. It was then that its transformation began, directed by its editorial director Guy Bartholomew, and fellow board member, polar opposite and fierce rival, Cecil Harmsworth King, a nephew of Northcliffe. Adding to this were two brilliant new journalists, Hugh Cudlipp and William Conner (Cassandra), recruited by the paper's short-lived but influential features editor, Basil Nicolson.[100] Under them, the *Mirror* initiated a tabloid revolution based around sex, sensationalism, crime and sports coverage that aimed to appeal to a youthful working-class that had previously not read a daily paper.

As King later put it, a sub-element to this commercial appeal, 'conceived in cynicism', was that 'the politics had to be made to match' the appeal to young, low-income readers. But the readers were not that poor, at least collectively. For, giving crucial backing to the new project were American advertisers J. Walter Thompson who identified the increasingly affluent working-class market found in the South where wartime *Mirror* readers became largely concentrated. But the radical sympathies of the paper's high command ensured that, for them at least, commercial imperatives fused conveniently with political beliefs.[101] The paper's political transformation proved slower than its commercial one, but the war years, in Alan Taylor's famous words, saw the emergence of a 'brash but . . . serious organ of democratic opinion' that 'gave an indication as never before what ordinary people in the most ordinary sense were thinking. The English people at last found their voice.' Taylor's endorsement of the authentic voice of wartime Britain has been echoed in numerous journalistic memoirs from those at the *Mirror* that record how it 'regarded itself as a paper with a mission and it was accepted as such'.[102] Traditional academic accounts tell much the same story of how the paper responded to the 'new mood of radical populism' that 'had seized many in 1945' by learning to speak for and with the voice of working-class 'popular radicalism'.[103] Ensuring the effectiveness of this bottom-up pressure was the way wartime newspaper rationing freed newspapers from commercial pressures and allowed journalists to dictate content at a time of increased demand for news. This meant that the *Mirror*, previously still cautious for fear of alienating advertisers by being identified too exclusively with the less-affluent working class, was now free to develop a solidly proletarian audience where 'demotic radicalism . . . constituted the common denominator of a mass readership'.[104]

Such studies see the *Mirror*'s wartime transformation as the high-point of twentieth-century radical journalism. Yet they are arguably tinged by a nostalgia that overstates the *Mirror*'s wartime politicisation and radicalisation.[105] According to Mass-Observation, the wartime paper continued to carry a lower percentage of political reporting than any of its rivals apart from the tabloid *Daily Graphic*.[106] The apparent apathy of the bulk of the population, along with the feared commercial challenge from broadcasters, led those at the *Mirror* to see the paper's function continuing to be primarily one of entertainment. As Cecil King wrote to Hugh Cudlipp at the end of 1943:

> There is clearly going to be more and better radio after the war . . . This will entirely and obviously kill the function of the newspaper in purveying hot news, and makes all the more important the organising of a good service of the simple human kind of story which is meat and drink to the tabloid newspaper. The '*Mirror*' and 'Pic' [*Sunday Pictorial*] have sobered up quite a lot, and we are now in greater demand than any other papers . . . I believe that more people are more seriously minded than they were before the war, but there are formidable numbers, at home anyway, who are at least as feather brained as ever. I am not arguing that instruction should not be given, but that our main task is, and is likely to remain, entertainment.[107]

The paper's efforts to address its predominantly youth-based audience sometimes led it to exclude day-to-day politics and the war effort from its content in favour of a 'great preoccupation with the young . . . with the minimum about the war and politics'. The paper continued to emphasise its sensational exposures of 'A DIARY OF SINS OF A BRIDE OF MONTH', alongside the pictures, cartoons and headlines that formed its most popular parts.[108] Even at times of high political drama, the extent to which political news dominated should not be overstated, as demonstrated by the paper's limited coverage of the crucial parliamentary debate on the Beveridge report.[109]

The *Mirror*'s appeal was that it was sensational, light, bright, easy to read, while it also inspired more general disbelief in the truth of its contents than any rival.[110] Just 3 per cent bought it for its politics (compared with 20 per cent and 24 per cent for *Daily Herald* and *News Chronicle* readers) or read the editorials. Even as the paper's pro-Labour stance hardened after 1945, only 55 per cent of *Mirror* readers could correctly identify this stance, suggesting a less clear-cut political relationship with readers than other popular newspapers, where the figures were between 70–80 per cent.[111] Mass-Observation concluded in March 1942 that the *Mirror*'s 'special appeal' lay to 'the politically and culturally apathetic' as 'the most persistent trend' it discovered was 'that *Daily Mirror* readers have less opinions than others' concerning politics in all its forms.[112]

This is not to say that the paper was content merely to reinforce these attitudes, as it frequently rallied readers 'to make a personal and individual effort to fight against apathy'.[113] Such a role would appear to confirm the *Mirror*'s role in leading the way to a new participatory democracy. Yet for all the occasions that the paper could be found at the vanguard seeking to politicise, it was more often to be found at the back, reinforcing apolitical pleasures and interests. As the paper put it just before the 1945 election, 'Heaven forbid that people should forever be occupied with the asperities of politics'.[114]

For, just as the politicisation of the paper should not be overstated, neither should the extent of its radicalisation. Traditional portrayals of the Second World War as a golden era of twentieth-century radical journalism form a sub-story to more general historical accounts that have emphasised the apparent growth in popular political radicalism that culminated in the 1945 electoral revolution.[115] But in recent years revisionist historians have challenged the latter interpretation, painting a less left-wing picture of an electorate characterised more by political apathy than idealism and activism, negative and backward-looking anti-Toryism rather than positive pro-Labour sentiment, and practical, moderate concerns rather more than social-ist convictions.[116] Such writing also strikes at the basic premise that the *Mirror* offered 'firm evidence' of 'the theory that the war itself generated a new popular radicalism' and suggests the need for a re-examination of the paper's politics.[117]

Leaving aside an appeal that could work largely on an a-political level, the *Mirror*'s coverage was more centrist and anti-Tory than socialist and pro-Labour. Traditional analyses identify this process as occurring in the 1950s and 1960s with the socialist and radical 'old *Daily Mirror*' being replaced by a more centrist, intermittent and negative politics characterised by 'opposi-tion to the Conservative Party rather than positive advocacy of a socialist alternative'.[118] Yet in many ways this attitude was even more visible in 1945 than later.

During the war, the *Mirror* adopted a class-based rhetoric that spoke for 'us', 'the people' against the 'vested interests' of 'them' in 'the gentry' seeking to go 'back to the good old days of under-nutrition for millions, of millions, of unemployment, and of slums'. This articulated a vague leftist mood which, as one famous contemporary report noted, 'does not appear to be on Labour party or socialist lines but it does seem to be directed against the Conservative party in so far as this represents the so-called "Men of Munich", "the old gang", "Colonel Blimp" and similar diehard types'.[119] Such anti-Toryism was its dominant theme, but for much of the war the paper showed little love for Labour, criticising its disunity and a leadership that was 'dying on its feet', complaining that while the Churchill govern-ment was a step behind the people, Labour were 'two steps behind, not one" This was chiefly the responsibility of the failings of leaders 'more con-spicuous for character than ability' or who had 'become tainted with the pomp of personal power'.[120] By summer 1943 it was bluntly warning of the 'LAST CHANCE' for 'this party which ought to be great ... but most emphatically is not great' and 'still lacks that degree of public confidence which would make it either a successful instrument of opposition or an inevitable alternative government'.[121] And none of the opposition forces filled King with much enthusiasm as he outlined the paper's cautious, non-ideological anti-Toryism as the election approached:

> It is hard to see what we can do, beyond supporting various worthy politicians (mostly Leftish) and attacking various unworthy ones (mostly Tories). What else can we do? I can't put my hand on my heart and urge our 2 and a quarter readers to vote solidly for Attlee, or for Ackland – or for Sinclair. I should much rather go flat out for one party, but don't see how it can honestly be done just now.[122]

In some respects the *Mirror*'s politics reflected the 'movement away from Party' that occurred during the war. This was characterised by an anti-Tory, anti-party populism that only eventually and reluctantly embraced the Labour party as the only practical channel for such sentiments. It found expression in support for left-leaning independent by-election candidates and a popular, Common Wealth party led by Richard Ackland that won a series of by-elections based on an idealistic socialism in which class conflict and sectional interests would be replaced by national interest and service to the community. Most notably there was the 'non-party' appeal of independent left-winger Stafford Cripps. Cripps was a *Mirror* favourite, as it frequently praised a 'political innocent who puts his principles first … the man who millions believe to be somehow different from other politicians'.[123] The *Mirror*'s equivocation towards Labour also contrasted with a more favourable stance towards a 'much more virile' and less sectional Common Wealth party. Equally the 'indecisive and frightened whisper' of Labour MPs was compared with 'the thunder' of the Independents.[124] But ultimately the paper could not endorse the Common Wealth party or other alternatives despite declaring its 'greatest sympathy', realising reluctantly that 'in politics, as in war, it generally turns out that God is on the side of the big battalions'. Nevertheless there remained in its coverage the 'vague hope that *something* would emerge' to replace the existing political leadership as the *Mirror* considered that 'new policies cannot effectively be put into operation by old parties. At least the old parties must have new and vigorous membership, and must be animated by an entirely new spirit'.[125] In demanding this, the paper was also articulating a young against old message as it called for 'a mental and spiritual rebirth in which the gates of opportunity must be opened to the young'. All political parties were accused of being 'too greatly dominated by Old Gangs', while Labour was attacked for its 'ageing stock which can no longer make an effective show' and were alienating youth.[126]

In the end the *Mirror* did not formerly endorse Labour in the 1945 election, and this reticence was not, as has been widely suggested, simply a matter of tactics. For what the *Mirror* sought to encourage among readers, if not the parties, was 'a popular front of the left' to defeat the 'unpopular front of the right'.[127] Polls indicated that 55 per cent of the electorate supported an anti-Conservative popular front, an attitude the *Mirror* reflected in an election endorsement which, as King noted, 'came out very definitely on the Labour–Liberal side' rather than specifically for Labour.[128] While Labour were the main hope, few, including those at the *Mirror*, thought Labour could win, while the Liberals were expected to perform well after a wartime revival.[129] The result was that the 'Resurgent Liberals' were also presented as 'a helpful force in the social "liberation" of the country'. The anti-Tory policy unity of the two centre-left parties was emphasised in a message that was not that different to that conveyed by the Liberal *News Chronicle* and *Manchester Guardian*.[130] The *Mirror*'s letters pages, headlined 'Labour and Liberals', and which accounted for roughly 30 per cent of election coverage, provided the best illustration of its stance. A sample three-week period saw 40 per cent of letters urge a Labour vote, while 30 per cent were negatively anti-Tory, 25 per cent supported the Liberals and 5 per cent a Lab/Lib vote.[131]

Above all, the defining characteristic of the *Mirror*'s wartime politics was negative anti-Toryism rather than positive pro-Labourism. The *Sunday Pictorial* offered the clearest exponent of this stance as it urged readers to 'USE YOUR VOTE TO GET THE TORIES OUT', lamented the lack of an electoral alliance of the left and called on both parties to get together if Labour did not gain a clear majority.[132] Similarly the *Mirror*'s 'deeply pessimistic' coverage focused less on Labour's plans for the future and more on the threat of the 'return to the bad old pre-war days' of 'diehard Toryism' characterised by 'degradation and misery' as 'poverty and unemployment stalked the land'.[133] While such coverage may have been less radical than sometimes claimed, it was democratically reflective of the popular mood as it captured the anti-Tory common denominator of perhaps 70–80 per cent of readers rather more inclusively than an explicit appeal to vote Labour.

To qualify the *Mirror*'s political position, however, is not to understate its potential influence or lose sight of the most important point: in 1945 the Conservative press was for the first time counterbalanced by a greater degree of press support and sympathy for the centre-left than ever before. Despite objections, there is some justice in bracketing the *News Chronicle* with the *Herald* and *Mirror* given the centre-left message of them all and Labour's position, recognised by the electorate, as the only realistic alternative to the Tories.[134] This meant that the 48 per cent of newspaper circulation made up by anti-Tory newspapers was roughly equal to the remaining 52 per cent supporting the Conservatives.

Alongside this statistical balance must be noted the contrasting usefulness of newspaper propaganda. On the pro-Tory side, the stance propounded by the *Daily Express* may have done the Conservative campaign as much harm as good. The 'disappointment' and 'widespread anger' aroused by

Churchill's 'Gestapo' speech was accompanied by 'disgust' at the 'absolutely wicked' and 'dishonest perverse, ranting, reactionary badness' in the *Express* under the 'scoundrel' Beaverbrook.[135] The Laski incident was also widely viewed as an 'election stunt' and a 'red herring', while the *Evening Standard*'s 'study their faces' story, with 'its cheap insinuations about concentration camps', was seen as 'the foulest piece of election propaganda'.[136] While there was 'little criticism' of the *Mirror* among readers, the *Express* was 'most criticised all round' – its coverage was 'all Beaverbrook' which 'rammed down every way' a 'purely Conservative' line.[137] Readership feedback also confirmed to worried executives that its 'style of campaigning was indeed doing the Conservative harm' as it found the paper:

> ...falling into disfavour among people who liked it because it was an objective and fair newspaper, and who now regard it as the most politically prejudiced paper in the country.... Our adulation for Churchill and the Conservatives is being regarded by some as absurd as the constant belittlement of Labour.[138]

Beaverbrook's activities were also viewed with growing consternation within the Conservative party by those, including senior party officials, who did not share his views and saw his exaggerated propaganda as counterproductive.[139] As Churchill had anticipated, this disquiet was articulated at an October 1945 conference for defeated Conservative candidates as the press baron became the scapegoat for the poorly fought Conservative campaign. There was, it was alleged, 'no man living more detested throughout the political world' than Beaverbrook, who had done the party 'very very serious harm' by his election activities.[140] To be fair, if his paper's propaganda was not to the liking of the Tories, the fundamental blame lay with their party leader who considered its coverage to be 'admirable'.[141] Regardless of the reality, Beaverbrook's notoriety also provided a way by which Labour could indirectly attack and explain the excesses of the still-revered Churchill. As the *Mirror* explained, 'in what no doubt was a loyal effort not to let a colleague down, Mr Churchill let his party down'. The press baron appeared in more cartoons in the opposition papers than any other figure or issue. Moreover, the picture presented of a prime minister and party dominated by an irresponsible clique of political adventurers (an image he had long had within his own party) must have given further weight to Labour's accusations that their opponents could not be trusted to preside over post-war reconstruction.[142]

Most importantly, while the paper's wild propaganda echoed some middle-class resentment against restrictions, it was largely out of touch with the sober popular mood.[143] This was conveyed far more authentically and powerfully by the *Mirror*, whose campaign has been judged by a variety of sources as the most influential. One Tory cabinet minister even claimed the paper was worth a hundred seats for Labour. While a clear exaggeration, the greater numbers of politically disengaged and undecided that the paper reached may, as the *Economist* suggested, have given it an influence denied to its rivals.[144] Its message was also reinforced by the *Daily Herald*, and, importantly for the crucial middle-class vote, the sympathy of liberal newspapers.

Perhaps the most important propaganda theme of the centre-left press was their contribution to an image of the 1930s as synonymous with depressed Jarrow rather than thriving Coventry. Given the relative affluence of the majority of the population in the 1930s, the actual importance of the 'Never Again' theme seems less straightforward than is often assumed. But there can be no doubt that the potent propaganda image of 'Jarrow and the pre-war distressed areas ... as a monument to free-enterprise' played a central role in undermining the Baldwin consensus and legitimising the triumph of a new centre-left post-war political settlement.[145] It is notable that the most significant source of the Labour's victory came from the fifth of the electorate voting for the first time, two-thirds of which voted Labour, and many of whom were probably *Daily Mirror* readers. The most detailed analysis suggests that the Conservatives would have won a comfortable victory in 1945 if the electorate had been restricted to those who voted ten years earlier.[146] The radicalising impact of the 1930s on those adults who lived through the period is therefore questionable. More important may have been the impact the retrospective myth and memory of the 'hungry thirties' had on the first generation of voters in 1945, particularly after a war that had raised expectations about what governments could and should do.

Such an image had formed a central element to wartime propaganda in which the suffering of the 'hungry thirties' was juxtaposed with demands for a progressive 'people's peace'. This links with the well-established fact that, whatever the level and quality of press sympathy for Labour during the campaign, the election had already been won and lost.[147] If the press did have an influence in 1945, then its long-term effect was most important. During the war Labour, as future minister Douglas Jay noted, gained the unique experience of a relative absence of day-to-day criticism. But it was not only this, as the press actively helped set the progressive agenda that was to decisively benefit Labour in 1945. As early as April 1941, George Orwell suggested that the popular press had shifted 'noticeably left'. This was demonstrated most clearly in it's 'vanguard' role in articulating demands for post-war reconstruction, and its criticism of the Churchill government's equivocation in this area.[148] Beaverbrook was also rebuked after the election for 'the long-term anti-Conservative' effect of his 'employment ... of some of the ablest and most consistent Left Wing propagandists of the day', as his readers 'found themselves daily guided to the Left'. More generally, it may well be that the 'unique contribution' made by the wartime Tory press was 'to demonstrate that the reforming consensus that they were seeking could not be entrusted to Churchill'.[149]

But clearly one should not exaggerate the power of the press. While there was a correlation between the transformation in Labour's press fortunes by

1945, the former was as much a consequence as a cause of its electoral strength. M-O surveys also found that substantial numbers of Labour voters read Conservative papers (a third in one London constituency) and vice versa, and concluded that there were 'a relatively high proportion of readers who just do not read political news and comment'. On the other hand, it also suggested that because people read the political news sketchily and uncritically, they were likely to 'absorb its outlook and political trend all the more'.[150] Even so, it is probable that press support altered the size of Labour's victory rather than the result itself and the change has to be seen within the context of the wider wartime reforming consensus visible in publishing, the cinema and, to a lesser extent, radio.[151]

'Among the foremost enemies of mankind': the popular press 1945–1951

This 1945 pattern of a partisan but politically more balanced press continued throughout the Attlee governments. As the 'dream' of 1945 was followed by the sometimes nightmarish 'business' of government, the right-wing press fought a fierce campaign against the rationing and restrictions of the 'age of austerity', a selective image of the period which owes much to their labours. This was answered in kind by violent denunciations from some ministers. Arch-enemy Nye Bevan condemned 'the most prostituted press in the world' that was 'among the foremost enemies of mankind' while Attorney General Sir Hartley Shawcross denounced their 'gutter' campaign of 'misrepresentation and calumny'.[152] At the forefront of attacks was the government's communication supremo, Herbert Morrison, who was as sensitive and manipulative of the press as Attlee was as famously 'allergic' to it.[153] Morrison had denounced newspaper 'inventions' which constituted 'a disgrace to journalism', and singled out the 'Kemsley gramophone chain' of provincial newspapers for all faithfully repeating the views dictated from the centre. Kemsley in turn reaffirmed that his group had 'no option but to continue its policy of assailing a government so wilfully bent on placing its ideology before the nation's first necessities'. On the other hand his denial of its 'gramophone' nature was hardly strengthened by an article which contained four examples of proprietorial direction and appeared in every one of his newspapers.[154] Morrison encouraged and orchestrated demands from Labour-supporting members of the National Union of Journalists for a Royal Commission inquiry into the concentration and ownership of the press.[155]

In their detailed evidence, virtually all newspapers announced their commitment to complete accuracy, objectivity and impartiality, so that 'neither in headlines or in the text should propaganda be allowed to colour the news'.[156] The existence of such commendable sentiments was not borne out by the commission's wide-ranging examination of contemporary press coverage. It found a 'frankly partisan' approach that stemmed from an adherence to 'pre-determined party policy' which produced 'a degree of selection and colouring of news which can only be regarded as excessive'.[157] Coverage of the politically important Gravesend by-election of November 1947, for example, saw news and views become 'inextricably interwoven' as newspapers concentrated on 'spotlighting the candidate they favoured and, when not ignoring, depreciating his opponent'. The *Daily Express* and *Graphic*, for instance, reported Labour candidate Sir Richard Ackland's statement that he was 'rather proud' of 'all these government controls' without adding his explanation that they provided regular and equitable food distribution to all classes. The *Graphic*'s partisan headlines showing a 'BRITAIN TIRED OF SOCIALISM' were accompanied by 72 per cent of space devoted to the Conservative side and only 18 per cent to Labour. Kemsley defended what he saw as 'a very fair' and 'generous' balance for 'a Conservative newspaper' to give.[158] The high-sounding principles of impartiality, as Michael Foot pointed out, were now reduced to the 'generosity' with which a Conservative newspaper would treat opponents and were considered consistent with giving one side four or five times as much space as the other.[159]

The demands for an inquiry had been directed against the right-wing press. But the commission also punctured what one Conservative MP described as the myth that 'all the papers of the Left are Sir Galahads in shining armour riding in the quest of the truth while all the papers on our side are just shabby scoundrels'.[160] At least 90 per cent of the *Herald*'s political coverage was devoted to their favoured party, meaning, not surprisingly, that the Conservative view was 'inadequately' covered. One headline report of a 'NEW HOUSING RECORD' in the rate of monthly house building proved, on closer examination, to be a generous gloss. The rate of house building was actually lower than in the previous month, the only record being the increase in total houses built that the month's additions had produced. Faced with such evidence, even left-wing critics were forced to admit that distortion was 'often as bad' in left-wing newspapers which 'could give more space' to the views of opponents.[161]

Much the same 'overwhelmingly partisan' approach was evident in the 1950 and 1951 general elections, leading one American journalist to express disgust at the 'degradation of the press into unprincipled party organs' characterised by 'nothing more than a series of editorial pages'.[162] Again the popular press formed two relatively solid blocks of support for the main parties, while the Liberals continued to be substantially represented. The *Mail* climaxed its self-styled six-year 'fight' against socialism by ringingly denouncing a general record of 'failure, futility and frustration unprecedented in our annals'.[163] Meanwhile the *Daily Graphic*'s choice between Conservative 'prosperity' and 'ever broadening freedom' or 'totalitarian expedients' under Labour's 'road to serfdom' ensured Churchill's thanks to Kemsley for his 'invaluable support'.[164] While Labour in turn complained about this 'heavy barrage of misrepresentation' from opponents, they once more expressed 'warm appreciation' for the *Daily Herald*'s 'continuous support'.[165] But again more valuable was the endorsement of the *Daily Mirror*, which had dramatically increased its circulation to 4.5 million by 1951. Between elections, the paper's political coverage was 'often inadequate' and 'tended to emphasise sensational rather than important news', as the Royal Commission pointed out.[166] But, in the two campaigns, the *Mirror* joined the *Herald* in devoting considerable space to an 'I remember' theme, faithfully echoing Labour's campaign that contrasted the 'misery' of 1930s Tory rule when compared with the 'startling' advances made between 1945–1951. The *Mirror* now explicitly endorsed Labour in wholly partisan coverage, demonstrated most famously in the 'most politically disreputable feat' of the 1951 campaign, the paper's libellous 'WHOSE FINGER ON THE TRIGGER' smear of Churchill as a warmonger, which Harold Macmillan felt had lost his party 'millions' of votes.[167]

Whereas in 1945 Labour had benefited from its common ground with the Liberal press, by 1951 it had swung to the right. The *Manchester Guardian*'s hostility to Bevan led it to advocate a Churchill government as 'a lesser evil', leading an amused Christiansen to tell Beaverbrook how the paper had 'played such a fine part in putting the Tories back'.[168] In 1950 the 'radical liberalism' of the *News Chronicle* both supported Labour's 'desire for social reform' and criticised what Cadbury had described as 'the government's obsession with the doctrinaire planks of its programme'. Even after the election, the paper viewed itself as a 'candid friend' rather than a 'carping critic' of the government.[169] But a shift to an acknowledged stance which was 'less to the left in outlook' was reflected in sympathy in 1951 for the 'studied moderation' of a Conservative campaign in coverage which remained sophisticated and largely non-partisan.[170]

Most difficult of all to categorise, however, remained the *Daily Express* which functioned as the political loose cannon of the popular press between 1945–1951. Beaverbrook was out of sympathy with the entire direction of domestic and foreign post-war politics, while he was personally despised as much by his own party as by Labour. For the remainder of his life he spent the bulk of his time at his residences abroad but his close control over Express newspapers continued to be exercised by means of the telephone and his famous soundscriber dictating machine.[171] Politically, Beaverbrook remained resolutely opposed to the Labour government's 'socialisation' and 'in favour of free enterprise entirely', a belief which, as general manager Robertson noted, made his papers firmly 'anti-government'. Such a stance was to produce the resignation of Brian Chapman in 1947 due to the 'sharp conflict' between his opinions and the paper's 'utter and uncompromising hostility to the government on all issues'. It was a position which was also clearly visible in the following election.[172]

One story which the paper 'had a great time with' and which 'really infuriated the socialists', as Christiansen informed Beaverbrook, concerned German de-rationing. This was featured under headlines such as 'GERMANY – TOO MUCH MEAT', as the 'juicy steaks' consumed by the 'beaten Germans' on an 'eating orgy' were contrasted with continued British austerity as 'STRACHEY STOPS MEAT'.[173] The Tory press also portrayed the concurrent murder trial of 'spiv' Brian Hume as indicative of a socialist culture fostered by 'laws, orders and regulations' which bore 'no obvious moral sanction'. Ever the opportunist, Christiansen still hoped for 'another good murder to add human interest' to an election characterised by 'less public interest' than any he could remember.[174] Attention was also paid to the 'hopeless muddle' of Bevan's housing policy, although perhaps not enough for Beaverbrook, who, in its aftermath, was instructing:

> Tell Mr Christiansen I hope that he will make indignant attacks on the Government over the failure of their housing programme. I saw that in Glasgow the housing programme has fallen so far behind that in fact they are getting worse instead of better ... I hope Mr Christiansen you will look out for similar situations in other directions. I hope you will find cases where houses have been built with costs as high and inefficiently ... and I hope you will tear the government to bits on that account. It is the greatest scandal of the age that the housing programme should be in such a terrible condition.[175]

A similar line of attack was present in 1951. In the 1950 election the paper's editor had noted the 'extreme difficulty' in finding out where Bevan and Shinwell were speaking, alleging 'a plot on to keep the press away from these two-loudmouths'. Perhaps Transport House had good cause to be suspicious, judging by the paper's strategy for the following election. Aneurin Bevan's role as the chief bogeyman of the right-wing press had been enhanced by his high-profile resignation from cabinet in April 1950. The presence of a powerful dissenting voice of the Labour left was too good to miss in the following election as the *Express* planned its campaign around what its leader-writer called:

> a powerful exposure of the falsity of the Bevan–Attlee axis with the slogan: 'A vote for Attlee is a vote for Bevan'. To give this its maximum weight, it would be wise to lay off opinion comment on Bevan and the internal situation of the Socialist Party, but to collect as many quotes as possible from Bevan illustrating his intransigence and his implicit claim to be the spiritual leader of the rank-and-file Socialists. A short, sharp campaign of say the last three days ... should be good effect on the waverers. Obviously some new issue would be better. But we can't count on it and it might be as well to have this one ready.
> p.s. reports of Wilson, Driberg and Castle should also be scrutinised carefully.[176]

While little prominence was given in Fleet Street to the election, the *Express* proved the exception as it duly presented 'BEVAN TO "VET" SOCIALIST

MANIFESTO' and 'BEVAN "NEXT PREMIER"'.[177] The rising cost of living under a Labour government was also graphically illustrated by cartoonist Cummings in an inventive and ever-expanding tall, thin character, 'Mr Rising Prices', 'the shadow behind the socialist party'. A week after his first appearance, he had grown to occupy a full two pages of the paper's limited newsprint. Harold Wilson was to apparently tell Christiansen that, while the paper was 'politically dishonest in raising so vigorously' the issue, it was 'right on the ball if it sought to inflame anti-socialist feeling'.[178]

Such hostility was reciprocated by a party whose leader viewed the press baron as 'the only evil man' he had ever met.[179] The most famous example of this mutual conflict came in March 1950, after a furious political row followed the publication of a MaCarthyite smear by the *Evening Standard* against new Minister of War John Strachey. Strachey had been subject to previous attacks as Minister of Food (the famous slogan was 'Shiver with Shinwell and Starve with Strachey'). The paper linked his appointment with the spying conviction of Communist agent Klaus Fuchs in a front page, 'FUCHS AND STRACHEY: A GREAT NEW CRISIS', which wrongly claimed that the minister had 'never disavowed communism'.[180] It came complete with a sinister-looking picture of Strachey and was published by editor Herbert Gunn, despite the advice of the paper's news editor that the allegation was both untrue and absurd. Downing Street immediately issued a statement attacking a 'disgraceful' story that 'had no possible justification' and while this failed to satisfy the *Standard*, left-wing opinion rallied to his side.[181] The *Manchester Guardian* pointed out that Beaverbrook could be viewed with the same 'suspicion' given his statement to the Royal Commission that he did not believe in the Russian threat, with Wadsworth telling a grateful minister, 'it was the least we could do'.[182] More famously, James Cameron resigned in protest from *Express* newspapers in protest against a 'witch hunt', explaining to Strachey that 'as there is no real impact an individual can make from within, then by staying he only condones it'.[183]

The most powerful attack came from Michael Foot. On the evening the story broke, the *Express*'s Labour-supporting industrial editor Trevor Evans had, to his acute embarrassment, attended a socialist reception given by socialist peer Lord Strabolgi at the Savoy. Here he was clearly made aware of 'the depth of reaction' felt by the party as Foot 'in a frenzy' approached him and thundered that Gunn's place lay 'in jail, not skulking like a coward behind the editorial chair'.[184] In *Tribune* he was no less venomous, awarding the story 'the prize for the foulest piece of journalism perpetuated in this country for many a long year', which was even 'lower than Kemsley'.[185] The incident had a curious coda as Kemsley sued *Tribune* for what he considered to be the latest in a long defamatory 'campaign of personal vilification' against him, placing the magazine on the verge of bankruptcy. Foot appealed to Beaverbrook for help and was secretly given £3,000. When Robertson objected, his proprietor told him, 'Where else would we get our recruits without *Tribune*'![186]

Beaverbrook's employment of left-wing journalists was one factor that clouded his paper's loyalty to the Conservatives. When criticised for this after the 1945 election by Conservative chairman Ralph Assheton, he replied firmly that 'the papers were built up on a conception of freedom which gives a hearing to every Party'.[187] While the press baron is remembered for his famous confession that he ran his papers 'purely for the purpose of making propaganda', less publicised was his insistence that this propaganda should be 'all in the leader column but never, never, never in the news'.[188] Such sentiments had an undoubted fictional side, but while editors were firmly controlled, columnists and some cartoonists such as David Low were sometimes – although far from always – allowed their independence. This meant, as Robertson told the Royal Commission, that the paper contained 'views diametrically opposed' to its established policy as he added, 'You ought to see some of the letters we get from Conservatives'.[189] Trevor Evans also told how he was 'surprised and gratified' that he had 'been permitted to be as frankly pro-miner and pro-government' as he had been in his feature articles, a point confirmed by its research which also found the paper's reports on bread rationing and parliamentary debates to be 'well balanced'.[190] Beaverbrook's independence was also reflected in his frequent instructions about 'not being too anti-government and nagging' and 'identifying too closely with the Conservative point of view', even at low-points in Labour's popularity.[191] Meanwhile, Christiansen would frequently attempt to win his master's favour by contrasting the *Express* where 'praise for the Tories is very rare as you know' with the constant 'white hot opposition to the government' from the 'faking, lying, cheating' *Mail*.[192]

While this was clearly an exaggeration, at no time between 1945–1951 could the Tories rely on the uncritical support of the *Express*, nor did they sometimes even appear to want it. The *Express* was critical of the Tory acceptance of the post-war settlement. It attacked Butler's 1947 Industrial Charter, arguing that it was 'futile to fight the socialists under a socialist banner' and 'back to free enterprise should be the cry'.[193] A furious Churchill told Max Aitken that the leaders were 'plainly inspired' by his father, although the internal evidence suggests that it came without Beaverbrook's instructions, although undoubtedly with his approval.[194] Yet to present Beaverbrook as proof of the survival of a free-enterprise strand of Toryism is too simple. His maverick conservatism incorporated a commitment to full employment, increasing wage levels, the protection of small enterprises and support for the strengthening of the Liberal party.[195] Just before the 1949 Tory party conference he unveiled a ten-point election manifesto for the Conservatives which included plans for a £6 minimum wage. Amidst rumours that he had been expelled from the party, Churchill was obliged to publicly disown Beaverbrook's opinions, while Shawcross now praised his 'refreshing and stimulating independence'.[196]

This was demonstrated in the two elections that followed. In 1950 *Express* staff advised Beaverbrook not to return to London for the election, allegedly fearing a personal 'Churchill ... appeal for all-out *Express* support' when the Tories' embracement of 'a milk and water form of socialism' meant they should be supported only 'broadly as the better of two bad lots'.[197] Christiansen unsurprisingly agreed with his proprietor's advice 'not to let the papers go all out on the Tory line' and adopted an 'anti-socialist rather than ... pro-Tory' stance.[198] The paper maintained its adulation for Churchill's 'inspiring leadership' and his 'complete supremacy by an ever growing margin' as it climaxed in an appeal to vote for 'PEACE WITH WINSTON'. At the same time it considered that, without him, the rival leaderships were 'matched in ability', called for a minimum wage and urged electors to 'shun the state planners, Tory as well as socialist'.[199] In 1951, the paper's policy was even more lukewarm to the Conservatives as it once again pursued an independent programme, announcing that it shared 'precious little agreement' with the Tories. To demonstrate this, Beaverbrook did not renew his membership of the party in 1951 while in the middle of the election, the Empire Crusader that headed the *Express* front page, appeared in chains for the first time. It remained so after Churchill's victory and for the rest of the press baron's life.[200]

Conclusion

In 1925 Labour had complained about a disadvantage in press representation never suffered before by a major party, as it argued, 'Under the old two-party conditions, the falsehoods and misrepresentations of one party were promptly exposed and refuted in the national organs of the other'. By 1945–1951 such conditions had been re-established as the overwhelmingly anti-Labour press bias of the inter-war period had been replaced by a greater (although far from perfect) balance of political partisanship, which reflected the division of the electorate into two largely monolithic opposing blocks. The press now 'paralleled' the party system more closely than at any time since Labour's emergence as a major electoral force.[201] The growth in the circulation of the *Daily Herald*, the sympathy and relative impartiality of the *News Chronicle*, and above all the commercial and political transformation of the *Daily Mirror*, all gave the Labour or anti-Tory viewpoint substantial representation. On the other side, the Conservatives still retained majority newspaper support, although its largest circulation supporter, the *Daily Express*, remained very much an unpredictable and sometimes unwelcome friend. Taken individually, newspapers, as the Royal Commission concluded, still failed 'to supply the electorate with adequate materials for sound political judgement', a defect shared by the right- and left-wing popular press alike. The major difference by 1945 on previous years was that the broad circulation balance in this propaganda ensured that the press as a whole 'did adequately provide for a sufficient variety of political opinions'.[202] Individually, the popular press remained firmly rooted in an era of partisanship rather than consensus. Collectively, however, it had acquired a greater diversity than ever before.

2 'George the Third – or time for a change?'

The popular press and the 1964 general election

> The traditional complaint that Labour has had a bad press could not be raised in 1964; those who view any trend towards objectivity in the right-wing press as 'disloyalty' had more to complain about.... The reader wishing to be informed was probably better served than in any previous election by a more conscientious and more sophisticated press.[1]

The 1964 election saw Labour's return to office, by the narrowest of margins, after 13 years in the electoral wilderness. It also saw the party gain a more favourable press than even in 1945. This is an area that has been seldom comprehensively explored in the wider academic focus on Wilson's electoral impact, the party's modernising strategy and the Conservative party's many political and electoral difficulties after 1959. In so far as communications has a place in 1964, it is one that gives rather more space to detailing how modern political marketing and television were well exploited by Wilson. This chapter rectifies this imbalance by exploring the important political role played by the popular press between 1962–1964. It details how a strongly partisan Labour press at the height of its power was combined with a distinctly lukewarm attitude to the Conservatives from their traditional press allies, both before and during the 1964 election. It begins, however, by charting the important shift in press coverage that characterised the 15 years after 1951.

The decline in press partisanship 1951–1959

The chaining of the *Express* crusader after the 1951 election symbolised the beginning of a new, markedly less partisan phase in press behaviour for the next 20 years.[2] This was first evident in the restrained press coverage of the 1955 election, none more so than the *Daily Mirror*. With the polls suggesting a comfortable Conservative victory amidst increased affluence and a divided Labour party unsure of its direction, it was not an easy task to sell a left-wing alternative – and the *Mirror* certainly did not try too hard. It was 'not a close secret in Fleet Street', the directors of the *Daily Herald* later noted, 'as to how narrow was the top level decision of the *Mirror*' to endorse

Labour. Cecil King, by now *Mirror* chairman after deposing Bart in a board-room coup, had wanted to adopt the slogan, 'We are pro-Labour, but not this time', believing that the party 'was so divided and poorly led' that it could not be supported. The paper's editor in all but name, Hugh Cudlipp, along with distinguished political editor Sydney Jacobson, managed to per-suade King against this course of action, even if Cudlipp was far from a Labour loyalist, earlier asserting to columnist Richard Crossman that the paper 'should be really independent'.[3]

The *Mirror* instead moved to distance itself from its past partisanship, relieving Conservative fears of a repeat of 1951 by declaring it would 'take no part in scare campaigns'. In 'sensationally reticent' coverage, its main theme was again a demand for more youthful political leadership, a subject which it freely observed was 'not a party issue'.[4] In so far as it was, as Cudlipp admitted, it was 'more damaging to Labour than to the Tories' given that the 73-year-old Attlee presided over a shadow cabinet and party that was, on average, five years older than their Tory counterparts.[5] Rather, this decision to 'bang the drum for youth' saw the triumph of commerce over politics from a publication that advertised itself as having 'more readers under 35 than any other daily newspaper in the world'.[6] It was only in the last three days of the election that the *Mirror* came out with an, even then, half-hearted campaign that urged readers to 'Keep the Tories Tame', and deny them a 'bloated majority'.[7] In the 1959 election, the *Mirror*'s attitude was almost a carbon copy of four years earlier as it called on youth to 'shout its head off' regardless of their political views and campaigned for votes for 18 year olds.[8] Again there were rumours that the paper had only narrowly decided to endorse the party, and in the aftermath of a result cheered by its Tory-supporting journalists, Cudlipp dropped Crossman's column in the paper, explaining that 'the paper isn't going to be as pro-Labour as that'. Amidst widespread fears that Labour would never win another election, politics was temporarily abandoned in favour of an emphasis on 'youth', 'fun' and 'gaiety' and 'finding the girl with the smartest autumn sparkle'. It symbolised that the over-riding priority of the paper in the age of affluence was not so much 'Forward with the People' – the slogan also dropped after the 1959 election – as 'Forward with the Shareholders'.[9]

Predictably more loyal during this period was the *Daily Herald*.[10] But even its partisanship showed signs of waning. In the 1955 election, it led with just three main election headlines, all at the end of the campaign. This triggered another of Labour's periodic attacks on the paper, this time for the 'inad-equacy' of coverage that had done little to counteract the party's major problem of widespread electoral indifference. Such a mood had been encour-aged by a Tory press that had allegedly conspired with the Conservatives in 'keeping the election off the front page until the last few days'. The *Herald* had adopted a 'similar attitude', preferring to lead with 'trivial, sensationalised or alarmist' headlines such as 'Love Orgy Men Get The Sack', and had devoted only half of its front page column space to the election as compared to 1951.[11]

But despite Labour's allegations, the partisanship of the pro-Conservative popular newspapers was even less in evidence. Roughly half of the *Daily Mail*'s election reports in 1955 were classed by one study as neutral, while even less biased was the *Express*. where two-thirds leaned to no side.[12] Just before the campaign began, Beaverbrook had outlined his election strategy:

> The Tories are very sure of their win. If, by any chance, they don't pull it off, they will not be in a position to repeat their indignation meeting in 1945. Or if they do repeat it, the substance of their complaints will be different. Last time they complained of too much support from the *Daily Express*. This time possibly not enough assistance.[13]

This was true as the paper proved 'the most wary of all the national papers in admitting election material to its pages'.[14] What coverage it offered still contained vestiges of its earlier partisanship. Its prediction of 'a triumph of the Left Wing' within 'the socialist party' was backed up by a famous Cummings cartoon parodying Labour's election theme – 'You Can Trust Mr Attlee' – by showing a menacing looking Bevan peering through a cardboard cut-out of the Labour leader.[15] But the *Express* showed little of its earlier anti-socialism, while in 1959 it was particularly sympathetic to a Labour programme that contained 'much' that was 'good and worthwhile'. This was again combined with Beaverbrook's very individual and highly critical style of Conservatism.[16] With the *News Chronicle* proving even more unbiased – three-quarters of its 1955 coverage was neutral – it was left to the *Daily Sketch*, which had been purchased in 1953 by Rothermere, to demonstrate the only real old-fashioned press partisanship during this period.[17] In 1955 it devoted most of its coverage to exposing a socialist conspiracy to install 'PRIME MINISTER BEVAN' as head of a 'fanatically extremist' Labour government. But even left-wing observers questioned whether the call to 'VOTE TORY and keep Bevan out of No. 10' 'convinced anybody outside the lunatic fringe of its own readers'. Four years later it was warning readers of a 'SECRET LABOUR PLOT' to ban commercial television in favour of a second state service serving up 'buckets' of boring 'culture'. Providing a welcome boost to the paper's ailing circulation, 100,000 copies were bought up by the Conservative party and circulated among the London marginals to reinforce their message not to 'let Labour ruin it'.[18]

'Tories in a ferment' 1962–1963

The early 1960s had seen what appeared to be an alarming concentration of press ownership. To the horror of liberals, the *News Chronicle* was amalgamated overnight with the *Daily Mail* in October 1960, while the following year the *Daily Herald* was taken over by Mirror group newspapers. The 1961–1962 Royal Commission on the Press, set up to examine any threat this posed to press diversity, took comfort in the knowledge that newspaper political affiliations had weakened since 1945. There still remained 'a considerable range of choice' in a national press which tended 'to the right' but freely criticised Conservative governments and saw left-wing opinion 'not insignificantly expressed'.[19] Contemporary political developments were to offer graphic confirmation of these conclusions.

From 1961 onwards, a multitude of political and economic difficulties undermined popular support for the Macmillan government and also brought a sharp conflict with its traditional press supporters. Chancellor Selwyn Lloyd's unpopular 'pay pause' measures in July 1961 received, in the words of Macmillan's press secretary, Harold Evans, 'the most universally critical press I can remember for any government proposals'. However it was really in the second part of 1962 that newspaper opinion turned.[20] Macmillan's dramatic 'Night of the Long Knives' in July 1962, when he sacked one-third of his cabinet, was given a long-lasting negative image by the press (which had also influenced its decision and timing) as an act motivated by panic and desperation.[21]

But it was the Vassall affair, which began two months later, that really soured relations. Amidst a background of earlier security scandals, John Vassall, a homosexual clerk at the Admiralty who had worked in the private office of junior minister Thomas Galbraith, was found guilty of spying for the Soviet Union. A flood of press reports linking Vassall with Galbraith duly followed that implied the minister's complicity in Vassall's treachery due to a sexual relationship between them. More general newspaper denunciations of government incompetence also demanded the resignation of First Lord of the Admiralty, Lord Carrington. Amidst growing press and opposition criticism, Macmillan made two decisions that were both to subsequently prove disastrous. He announced that a powerful judicial tribunal chaired by Lord Radcliffe would investigate admiralty security and the press allegations made against the two ministers, and he also decided that Galbraith should resign.[22] The press saw the tribunal's terms of reference as a direct attack, accompanied as they were by Macmillan's fierce denunciation of 'the spirit of Titus Oates and Senator McCarthy'. As he told his press secretary, it was a stance that had made him 'a lot of enemies' in Fleet Street, although, as Evans later wrote, what followed 'went beyond any expectations at the time'.[23]

Partly this was because the inquiry cleared Carrington and Galbraith of all allegations and concluded that not one of the 250 newspaper reports examined had a basis of fact. While cabinet ministers were delighted, Fleet Street was unsurprisingly less pleased at this public exposure of a 'sordid tale of journalistic exaggeration, distortions and sheer inventions'.[24] Yet even before its publication, a rather more emotive focus of resentment had been produced in March 1963 when the tribunal had sent to jail two journalists from the *Mail* and *Sketch* for refusing to reveal their sources (some suspected that they did not have any) of stories about Vassall. Macmillan was held responsible by the press, having given the tribunal its powers on the basis that 'if those who accuse them [Galbraith and Carrington] have done so falsely out of wantonness or malice, let them receive . . . the reprobation that they deserve'. And he certainly 'shed no tears' over their sentences, a sentiment not without notice in Fleet Street at the time.[25] The journalists had been imprisoned for stories which were hardly ones of substance – they had refused to reveal their sources for information that Vassal had bought and wore women's clothes and was a known homosexual nicknamed 'Aunty' by his colleagues. But the press saw deeper issues at stake and, Macmillan noted contemptuously, treated the journalists as 'martyrs'.[26] The result was that 'war was declared by the press upon the Macmillan government', although Fleet Street saw it as the other way around, amidst fears in the aftermath of the case that the prime minister was thinking of 'doing a Baldwin on the press'.[27] The latter were in a mood for revenge and, after Radcliffe's ringing condemnations, out to prove a point. In March, then left-wing journalist Paul Johnson was to warn that the Conservatives should not only expect 'heavily pro-Labour' news coverage in the election run-up, but that any scandal involving a Conservative MP would be given 'the full treatment'.[28]

Johnson may have had in mind the rumours that had already been privately circulating about the soon to be infamous relationship between War Minister John Profumo and call-girl Christine Keeler.[29] The papers, on the defensive due to the Vassall inquiry, held back from publishing. But in mid-March an ingenious front page in the *Express* 'finally put the cat amongst the pigeons', in the words of one Conservative insider.[30] Under the banner headline, 'WAR MINISTER SHOCK', were two stories, the main one reporting that Profumo had offered to resign 'for personal reasons'. Positioned directly to its right was Keeler's picture above a report of how 'the 21-year-old model' had failed to appear as a key witness at an Old Bailey trial. Inside the paper were four more pictures of Keeler 'from which most people could readily infer her calling', as Lord Denning later put it.[31] The story led to further rumours about Keeler and Profumo and his parliamentary denial of any improper friendship, as Max Aitken wrote to his father, 'did not ring true and it has not cleared the situation'.[32] Two months later, Profumo admitted his lie and resigned, bringing a wave of press criticism against Macmillan for his poor leadership. As hysteria gripped the capital in what Evans felt to be a newspaper 'fit of morality', coverage also spilled over into a series of other salacious and not entirely unfounded sexual rumours involving unnamed cabinet ministers. It left the 'TORIES IN A FERMENT' amidst what the *Mirror* detected, with the aid of a bishop, to be a 'SMELL OF CORRUPTION AND EVIL PRACTICES IN HIGH PLACES'.[33]

Commercially the story was a highly profitable one. Stafford Somerfield, 11 years the editor of the *News of the World*, which bought Keeler's story for the huge sum of £23,000, later argued it was the greatest of his lifetime. 'It had everything – sex, intrigue, espionage, politics, high society, crime, passion, the law. You name it.' Sales went up by 250,000.[34] Culturally and politically, the revelations were viewed as symbolic of Britain's moral as well

as economic and political malaise under an aristocratic, Conservative establishment.[35] But there was also a settling of scores going on. Macmillan complained that 'every part' of the story 'was used by an exultant Press, getting
its own back for Vassall', and without this background of conflict, the story
may not have generated such hostility or gathered such momentum.[36]
Equally, Macmillan's handling of the crisis might have been more forceful
and effective without the precedent of Galbraith – where an innocent man
had been forced from office by false press reports – which the Prime Minister
had bitterly regretted and was determined should not happen again.[37]

'Sowing the seeds of discord': Beaverbrook and the *Express*

In the front-line of attacks from the Tory press on Macmillan was the
Express, which in the final years of Beaverbrook's life was at the height of its
circulation. Despite Beaverbrook's advanced age and ailing physical health,
his close editorial control showed no signs of diminishing, as he remained
what staff called 'the principal reader' almost right up to his death in June
1964. As he observed just weeks before, on the occasion of his eighty-fifth
birthday, 'We have a system you know. I speak at this end and there is a
machine at the other end and it comes out as a leading article.' Indeed
Beaverbrook's constant attacks on his staff seemed even to intensify with age
and led Max Aitken – 'weary from trying to patch up oversensitive and
deeply loyal feelings hurt by constant criticism seldom if ever tempered by a
little praise' – to write a rare rebuke to his father.[38] Politically the highly
independent and critical conservatism which characterised the paper's politics also seemed, if anything, to sharpen during this period.

Appropriately the press baron's last great campaign came against the
Conservative party on behalf of the British Empire following Macmillan's
1961 announcement of Britain's application for entry into the Common
Market. With the issue dominating British politics for the next 18 months,
Beaverbrook closely co-ordinated an intense *Express* campaign that brought
praise from dissident Conservatives and a series of secret meetings with
Labour leader Hugh Gaitskell.[39] Soon after Gaitskell's September 1962 conference speech in which he had suggested that Common Market membership would mean an end to 'a thousand years of history', he had 'a long
session' with Express leader writer George Malcolm Thompson. Thompson
informed Beaverbrook that Gaitskell 'for the first time ... plainly sought
some form of communication with the *Express*'.[40] There duly followed more
direct contact with Beaverbrook, although the Labour leader was anxious to
prevent his links with a symbol of reaction from becoming public knowledge.[41] After a lunch meeting, Beaverbrook wrote that he had instructed
Common Market correspondent Alexander Kensworthy to 'keep in touch'
with Gaitskell, 'a most excellent journalist and quite faithful to the *Daily
Express* ... He used to be on the *Daily Mail*, but he was much too good for

that paper.' Beaverbrook detected opinion against the Common Market 'hardening every day' and when the one attitude that mattered most, that of De Gaulle, produced the fatal veto a month later, the *Express*'s front page – 'Glory, Glory Hallelujah! – echoed Beaverbrook's private rejoicing.[42]

The significance of this campaign should not be exaggerated – it would have been more surprising if it had not occurred – and it was also counter-balanced by government support from the rest of the press, including the *Daily Mirror*.[43] The *Express* campaign was also conducted within the bounds of some loyalty to the Tories for, as Beaverbrook observed, 'It is the Common Market we want to destroy, not Macmillan'.[44] His residual Tory loyalty was also demonstrated in a rather more famous Fleet Street incident, the aborted resignation of *Sunday Express* editor John Junor in May 1963. Junor told Beaverbrook that he felt 'so strongly against Macmillan' that he could not 'say a word of praise of him'. As his proprietor pointed out, 'this would have resulted in great difficulties for us because of the impending election and the fact that we are an independent Tory newspaper'.[45] Yet, as Beaverbrook always stated, the *Express* was 'only faithful at elections' to the Conservatives and his earlier promise to Macmillan that he would support the government 'in everything but that blasted Common Market' was cer-tainly not kept between 1962–1964.[46]

The *Express* was to prove particularly hostile to the government over the Vassall and Profumo affairs. At the height of Conservative difficulties in March–May 1963, the *Sketch* and *Mail* contained as many front page stories hostile as favourable to the government, but the *Express* was most anti-government, with almost three times as many negative as positive front pages, and even marginally more hostile editorials.[47] Beaverbrook himself expressed his puzzlement that Macmillan appeared 'to be promoting a quarrel with the Conservative press'. But never one to shirk a challenge, he called on *Express* staff to return fire against this 'vendetta' and 'prepare at once please an article in defence of the journalists, all of them, at the Vassall Tribunal'.[48] Later in the year he was demanding of his editor, 'You have got Mr Nicholson at the *Express* office. He is a very clever young man. Please use him to prepare a brief report on the maladministration of the Tories.'[49] There duly followed a detailed 16-point critique of the Tory record that faithfully repeated Beaverbrook's detailed instructions and was turned into an article.[50] Such a critical attitude also led him to rebuke his normally reli-able leader-writer, with a typical assertion of his power in a message dictated in front of the paper's editor:

> Mr Thompson, your leader on Mr Macmillan is too sharp a turn to his support. You have been very crusty about him for some time over the Vassall report, and the attacks he made on our staff, and now suddenly you are embracing him as a dear companion ... You should restrain yourself until we see how Mr Macmillan is going to behave ... I am saying all this in front of Mr Edwards who is here.[51]

Thompson replied immediately:

> I am so sorry that you think the leader of 11th April made 'too sharp a turn' towards support of Macmillan. It was my intention to be consistent with previous leaders. It was certainly not my intention to support the Tory party, but only to suggest that Mr Macmillan is the best leader it can find! In future, we shall try to conform to the limited degree of support for the Party which you speak of. As one of the victims of the Vassall Tribunal I am certainly not anxious to embrace the Prime Minister.[52]

Again on issues that he did not feel strongly about, the press baron demanded certain standards of objectivity and balance, complaining on one occasion:

> Your front page should be packed with news, should be given over to news, instead of that you have got one, two, three pieces of propaganda on it, quite running mad, that is not going to do you any good.

Or as he observed more succinctly to his editor on another occasion, 'I wish to make it clear to you Mr Edwards, that the DX no longer engages in suppression'![53] This illustrates how Beaverbrook's strong opinions were often complemented by his mischievous desire to 'stir things up', captured by a 1945 Vicky cartoon showing an impish proprietor throwing a spanner into the works and watching for the resultant effects.[54] In the controversy following Macmillan's resignation in October 1963, the Conservative press had favoured the more popular Rab Butler and Beaverbrook's own papers strongly endorsed him as the 'THE PEOPLE'S CHOICE'. Beaverbrook formally urged the *Express* to remain 'impartial, taking no sides, just telling the story and nothing more'.[55] But when his secretary remarked, 'everybody seems to be going for Douglas-Home' Beaverbrook replied, 'then it's time for us to be going the other way'. In an incident that brought him into further disrepute with the Conservatives, Beaverbrook sung down the phone, to the tune of 'The more we are together', the instructions, 'We'll sow the seeds of discord. Of discord. Of discord. We'll sow the seeds of discord. How happy we shall be.'[56]

Nor was there much sign even in 1964 of the *Express* falling back into line under the discipline of an impending election. The *Express*'s first editorial of the year set the tone as it promised that Labour would be 'fairly judged' and regard would be paid 'to the party's good sense and moderation'. It added that it had frequently attacked the Conservatives in the past and would 'in days to come . . . have occasion to disapprove of the Tories'.[57] This latter attitude was again to predominate in the forthcoming months, most notably in Beaverbrook's campaign against the government's bill to abolish Retail Price Maintenance, pushed through by the architect of the

Common Market policy, Edward Heath. That Beaverbrook, well known for his vindictiveness and vendettas, had not forgiven Heath for endangering his sacred British Commonwealth was illustrated by his instructions in October 1963:

> Heath probably made a prophecy that the economy of Great Britain would decline if we did not go into the Common Market. In his speech on Saturday he predicted the exact opposite. I suggest that you do some research on the subject and do something.[58]

The modernising RPM measure aroused the protests of thousands of small shopkeepers, produced the biggest Conservative backbench rebellion since 1940, and prevented the party focusing its attack on the opposition. Along with these benefits for Labour, Douglas Jay has suggested that its 'real importance' was in the way it 'kept the *Daily Express* in an anti-Tory mood in the months running up to the election'.[59] The paper began its campaign against this 'ill-conceived proposal' in mid-January and there followed a three-month barrage against a 'totally discredited' and 'wretched measure' that should be dropped. Heath, the administration's 'albatross', should meanwhile resign to 'save' his party 'from destruction and damnation', the paper argued in religious prose that could only have been inspired by the press baron.[60] It was not just Heath who suffered at the hands of the *Express*. Beaverbrook's private opinion that Home had 'not made good' as prime minister was replicated in *Express* attacks on a man who 'had utterly failed to impose his leadership and authority' in the course of a 'most disappointing' stewardship of a 'racked and riven' party.[61] Beaverbrook did not share the enthusiasm that greeted the new Labour leader following Gaitskell's death in January 1963. Harold Wilson's 'whole career', he argued, had shown that he had 'not got the balance and the understanding and the steadfastness that a political leader should have'.[62] But there was little sign of such hostility in the *Express* aside from very occasional mild snipes which accused Wilson of keeping the rest of his party hidden, not clarifying policy and for his nationalisation plans on steel.[63] But the *Express* remained in predominantly anti-Conservative mood in the first four months of 1964. The *Mail* had a more underlying pro-Conservative loyalty during this time, but partly because the RPM controversy along with other dramatic airings of Conservative divisions, dominated the political agenda, the Conservative press made little attempt to turn their fire on the opposition. Both the key Tory papers were largely apolitical in the hot summer months leading up to the election and made virtually no attempt to enthuse readers behind the new Conservative administration or explain why a party they had so severely criticised was now worthy of support.[64]

Exposing the Tory 'black record': the Labour press in 1964

Yet, despite all the difficulties faced by the Conservatives since 1961, the result of the election was very far from a foregone conclusion when it was called in September 1964. On the back of economic recovery, the party had gradually clawed back the huge lead Labour had built up, and when the election was announced in September 1964, the parties were running almost level. Newspapers faced competition in supplying election news from television, a more trusted medium that now reached 90 per cent of British homes.[65] Yet newspapers were more important in circulation terms than they had ever been. 85 per cent of adults read a national daily (compared with 73 per cent in 1947) and a massive 18 million newspapers were sold every day. While viewing peaked on election day with 27 million people watching the election-night broadcasts, newspapers had a total daily campaign readership of around 40 million (although how many of these consumed election coverage remains an open question).[66] Nor should we forget, from a contemporary perspective, how rudimentary the news services were in those periods. ITV, for example, had one short service at 8.55 p.m. (*News at Ten* was not introduced until 1967) while the BBC also had just one main 15-minute bulletin that went out at 9.15 p.m.[67]

As in 1945, the principal anti-Tory campaign came from the *Daily Mirror*, which was at the height of its power with the world's biggest circulation of over five million and a 14 million readership, reaching about one-third of the entire electorate.[68] The paper's two key figures remained the unlikely duo of the chairman King, together with Cudlipp. Together they 'worked closely' in determining policy. The more aloof King dictated the overall guidelines while Cudlipp was responsible for the day-to-day direction and strategy, although ultimately subordinate to the chairman.[69] Cudlipp was widely seen at this time, in King's words, as 'unquestionably the finest journalist in the country' with a superb talent for brilliant headlines and punchy prose. Whereas he was a brash extrovert, King was a shy, aloof elitist, an extraordinarily arrogant figure, believing himself to 'have a very large fund of general knowledge, covering more ground than anyone I have ever met'. Or, as he commented on one occasion, 'I see nothing wrong with power as long as I am the fellow who has it.'[70] His oft-cited sympathy for the underdog increasingly co-existed with contempt for a 'stupid' mass

Table 2.1 Partisanship and circulation of the popular press in 1964 (millions)

Daily Express	4.19	Con
Daily Mail	2.4	Con
Daily Mirror	5.09	Lab
Sun	1.45	Lab
Daily Sketch	0.9	Con

Source: Beith, 'The Press', in Butler and King (eds), *The British General Election of 1964*.

of readers 'quite uninterested in education of any kind'. King asserted that his position gave him 'the right, indeed the duty, to exert influence' in areas he considered important and this certainly included the paper's election coverage which he always took a 'passionate interest' in.[71]

Since 1945 the paper had adopted a 'bread and circuses' approach, which saw politics carefully rationed and diluted with entertainment. This, and a less loyalist style of political coverage, allowed it to build up circulation at the expense of the *Herald*. Despite the paper's fiercely anti-Bevanite stance in Labour's bitter infighting during the 1950s, relations between King and Gaitskell had been cool.[72] King, somewhat ironically given his own temperament, found him to be 'a most difficult, buttoned up character', while the Labour leader distrusted a man he saw as too closely resembling his uncle, Lord Northcliffe. Mirror executives also felt that Gaitskell 'rather imprudently' assumed the paper's automatic support 'as if it were a popular version of the unpopular *Daily Herald*'. Other sources of conflict came over Labour opposition to Mirror group's 1961 take-over of the *Herald*, along with the group's support for Britain's entry into the Common Market.[73] But most importantly, King was not treated by Gaitskell, or by the Tory leadership that he also courted, with the importance he felt he deserved. Wilson seemed different as King saw him frequently during 1963–1964 and liked a man he considered 'a brilliant leader of the opposition' and representative of the youthful and dynamic political leadership he had long campaigned for.[74] And throughout this period, as King bluntly put it, 'Wilson was disposed to listen to advice as Gaitskell was not', and showed due deference for the *Mirror*'s support.[75] In October 1963, Wilson waxed lyrical in appreciation of the Mirror group's pages reporting the Labour conference and his famous speech about 'scientific socialism' in particular:

> They have in fact been first-class all week, but Wednesday's paper was, from our point of view, out of this world – the planning, conception and commentary of the main contributors succeeded in creating an impression far beyond the event described . . . let me say how grateful I was – and what an impression it made on all the delegates I met. The *Herald*, too, have in my view done a better job for the party than I have ever known before – a consistently high level of reporting and team work giving a more dynamic and warm-hearted picture than I can remember. But what prompted me to write was Wednesday's *Mirror*. I doubt if a single issue of any paper has ever done quite such a political job.[76]

Wilson had good cause to be grateful, not just for the paper's coverage of the speech, but for Cudlipp's contribution of one inspired mood-catching phrase. The journalist recalled:

> A private room lunch in London in the week before the party's annual conference was a tradition with Gaitskell, continued with Harold

Wilson: we would discuss the state of the nation and of the Labour Party in particular, and often, of course, the Leader's forthcoming speech. This time, 1963, with Labour out of power for 13 years, it needed to be not merely good but triumphal ... I made a mild comment, nothing earth-quaking, just seven words but Harold's eyes twinkled as he puffed at his cigar and then despatched a brandy. ... My contribution was simply the words *the white heat of the technological revolution* but they kindled a spark in Harold's imagination.

Finally admitting authorship over thirty years later, Cudlipp captured the derision with which the phrase was later viewed, if not the enthusiasm it initially inspired, when he commented, 'I hadn't the slightest idea, and still haven't, what the seven words actually meant'.[77] But such cynicism was not apparent in the heady days of 1964, as King and Cudlipp promised Wilson that the *Mirror* would campaign for Labour 'as no newspaper has ever campaigned before'. King's support even extended to ostentatiously touring London with a red flag on his official Rolls saying 'Vote Labour', although Cudlipp declined to show the same commitment with the explanation, 'My chauffeur is a Tory. I don't want to upset him.'[78] As in past years, the *Mirror* made a fairly low-key beginning, based on King's belief that 'most newspapers start their election propaganda too soon and by election day their readers ... are sick of the whole subject'.[79] Nevertheless, time was still found to describe the Labour manifesto as 'the most inspiring political document ever put before the electors of Britain', although not to reveal Cudlipp's part in helping to write it. In July 1964, Wilson lunched with King and requested 'a touch of gold dust' to the manifesto, asking him to 'go through it and add some sparkle'.[80]

It was a full two-weeks later before the *Mirror* announced its entry into the election 'with all guns firing', arguing that the years in office had reduced the Conservatives 'to confusion and exhaustion', while Labour had 'fresh men with new ideas and the energy to carry them out'.[81] The emphasis on leadership partly represented a personalisation of the dominant theme of the Labour campaign, that the country's advance was being held back by the continued dominance of an out-of-date, antiquated aristocracy. This reflected the dominant diagnosis of 'what was wrong' with the country, but also a modernised version of the us/them class theme of previous elections. A series of high-profile editions drew attention to 'the predominance of Old Etonians in the Cabinet' and asked 'Why Should Britain be Run 'By "Chaps" Mourning For George The Third?', a reference to the origins of the black uniform of Eton. Cudlipp omitted to mention that two of the chairman's sons went to the school as he juxtaposed an electoral choice between 'George The Third – Or Time For a Change'. The latter would provide the opportunity for rule by the meritocratic leadership of 'scientists and engineers and intelligent grammar-school boys' that Wilson, a 'political gladiator' with 'computer-like intellect', was presented as the almost faultless embodiment of.[82] The *Mirror*'s wholehearted support was demonstrated by a polling-day front page that simply featured a photograph of a confident, trustworthy looking Wilson, aged forty-eight, beside the slogan, 'LET'S ALL VOTE TODAY AND VOTE FOR OUR FUTURE'. Its back page showed a rather more youthful Wilson, aged 8, photographed outside No. 10 by his father 40 years earlier, under the questioning headline, 'The Most Prophetic Family Snap Ever?'[83]

King later regretted a 'hysterically pro-Labour' position but the paper was predominantly hysterically anti-Conservative, for aside from its personal devotion to Wilson it offered 'few positive reasons for voting Labour and certainly no constructive arguments'.[84] Two-thirds of front pages attacked the Conservatives rather than supported Labour and the *Mirror* clearly felt more success could be achieved in urging a negative anti-Conservative vote than in enthusing readers behind the alternative. If its reputed close touch with readers was again in operation, then this once more reinforces the argument that the election result was determined rather more by hostility to the Conservatives than positive enthusiasm for Labour.[85] In other respects, the *Mirror*'s election strategy co-existed uneasily with Labour's. Just before polling day it produced a grim eight-page 'Election Shock Issue'. Ironically entitled, 'Is This the Promised Land?', the front page showed 'a picture of a backyard . . . six feet by nine feet. No hot water. No bathroom. Just one of 600,000 slums in the Tories "affluent society".'[86] It was a bitter and powerful edition, but it caused some dismay among Labour ranks because it diverged from a strategy that aimed to appeal to the new affluent middle class or skilled working classes by emphasising a concern to tackle high rents and mortgage rates rather than poverty. As one irritated party official complained, 'It identifies the Labour party with slums.'[87]

More alarm was caused to the party by the publicity given to Conservative minister Quintin Hogg's controversial comments that there were also adulterers on the Labour front bench. There was fear and panic among the Labour leadership over the possible printing of rumours about a sexual relationship between Wilson and his political secretary, Marcia Williams. Labour asked the left-wing papers not to report Hogg's remarks, but while the *Mail* and the *Express* ignored the story, the newly-launched *Sun* reported it and the *Mirror* gave front page treatment to a 'fantastic smear against Labour Front Bench'. This, and the controversy it generated, made the paper's front page on three further occasions to become the biggest single subject of its election coverage. It also generated front page coverage in the Conservative popular press that had earlier ignored it.[88] In the event it did Labour little harm as it became transformed into a frivolous personal duel between '"HALO" HOGG AND THE WICKED, WICKED MIRROR'. Yet it was a potentially unhelpful intervention in which commercial sensationalism and promoting the paper's own self-importance were clearly of more importance than political loyalty or policy substance.[89]

Despite these qualifications, the *Mirror* undoubtedly performed an invaluable political service with a campaign that was, in some respects, superior to that fought by Labour. In retrospect, the party's 1964 campaign has developed a somewhat 'undeserved reputation for professionalism and dynamism'. The reality was a certain lack of purpose and direction as surprisingly few efforts were made to stimulate memories of Conservative difficulties since 1961.[90] It proved to be 'the *Daily Mirror* rather than Mr Wilson which sustained the Labour campaign to a polling day climax' as 'almost by itself', the paper 'tried to remind voters of why they had turned against the Conservatives' as it denounced the Tory 'BLACK RECORD' of '13 wasted years'.[91]

The election also saw the emergence in Fleet Street of a new paper, with the *Sun* emerging to replace the *Daily Herald*. Labour's opposition to Mirror group's take-over of Odhams had been overcome by Cudlipp's reluctant public promise that the paper would continue to be published for seven years. In private he was less pleased, telling King he was a 'blithering idiot' for agreeing to buy a paper where 'the prospects of success were zero'.[92] The slide in circulation and advertising revenue continued unchecked and, by 1963, a fresh start was ordered through a new paper untainted by association with the *Herald*'s old 'cloth cap' image. So, early in the campaign, the *Sun* was launched as 'a new newspaper, born of the age we live in', the product of market research that suggested that readers in the 'age of affluence' would demand more serious newspapers.[93] It aimed to appeal to the increasingly educated younger generation through a more sophisticated and impartial political line than its predecessor.[94] In journalistic terms, the paper was a flop, with critics soon deriding it as 'the only newspaper still born of the age we live in'. The Labour high command in 1964 similarly denounced it, in Tony Benn's words, as 'appalling ... a pale wishy washy imitation of the *Daily Mail* and ... it won't be as much of a help to us between now and polling day as we had hoped'.[95] But there was never any doubt, whatever its defects, of the paper's endorsement, if only because over three-quarters of readers were going to vote Labour. Living up to its original brief, politicians from all parties were given space to advance their case, while Labour's 'bleakly negative' attitude to Europe was criticised.[96] Yet, from its first edition, the *Sun*'s sympathies were clear as it attacked the lack of leadership, drive and decision-making of a government whose 'sole aim has been to stay in office' in a country 'desperately needing leadership, drive and a new sense of national purpose'. There followed 'first-rate support' for Labour in the campaign's final stages as the paper, like the *Mirror*, declared that it was 'time for a change'.[97]

'Nominally Conservative': the Tory press in 1964

Such support for Labour also contrasted notably with the muted position of the Conservative popular press. The chief rival to the *Mirror* was again the *Daily Express* which, appropriately in the year of Beaverbrook's death, was also at its circulation peak. Its 4.2 million purchasers and a readership of over 11 million encompassing all social groups meant it was again the mass-circulation newspaper most important to the Conservatives. But to their dismay the paper 'surprised both readers and writers by its lively but impartial coverage'.[98] Little of the *Express*'s past anti-Labour rhetoric was visible, even in editorials which 'often occupied themselves with the virtues of democracy or the failings alike of all parties'.[99] The *Express* unambiguously declared against only one Labour policy – its nationalisation plans – but even here it found little to arouse any real hostility, exploring the subject in just one restrained editorial and no front pages.[100]

The editor behind this stance was Robert Edwards, a left-wing socialist who had been a Labour candidate in the 1955 election and editor of *Tribune*, before following the path of many of its journalists and joining Beaverbrook newspapers soon afterwards. He had first been *Express* editor between 1961–1962 before being sacked and then re-appointed by Beaverbrook in 1963 in an incident considered bizarre even by Fleet Street's eccentric standards. Edwards was, he recalls, 'a great fan' of Wilson and remained a paid up member of the Labour party.[101] Junor suggested that the 'less than white-hot enthusiasm' that the *Daily Express* showed for the Tories later produced his dismissal by Max Aitken (who inherited ownership in June after his father's death).[102] Certainly Edwards did not get on personally or politically with Aitken, whom he viewed as 'a drearily conventional Tory' and who in turn viewed him as a political 'Trojan horse'.[103]

His proprietor's suspicions could hardly have been helped by the appointment of another former Labour candidate, Terry Lancaster, as political editor immediately before the election. He replaced the equally pro-Labour Ian Aitken, who had resigned to avoid the potential political horror of working for the *Express* during an election. Lancaster had similar doubts but was enthusiastically urged on by Wilson who told him, 'it's much better if they start distorting your words than if they started distorting somebody else's'.[104] In any case Lancaster was assured by Edwards 'that not one word of my copy would be altered, and it wasn't, and that the paper would not take part in any scaremongering against Labour as it had done in the past'. During the election the paper was, according to editor and journalist, 'pro-Conservative but in a purely nominal sense' in 'fair and wonderfully independent' coverage. Meanwhile Max Aitken 'sat glowering upstairs' but exerted no pressure for a more pro-Conservative line.[105]

One early indication of the paper's attitude came with its coverage of Labour's manifesto, which, like its Tory counterpart, was given front-page-headline prominence under the uncritical heading 'FROM ME TO YOU', with an accompanying cartoon depicting Wilson as Santa handing out presents. Positive coverage of its details dwarfed a Tory 'counter attack' which was confined to just a few column inches at the foot of the page, while even an editorial displayed little hostility. After a lukewarm endorsement of the Conservative manifesto, the paper considered that, because there were so 'few differences between the parties', the over-riding question was, 'Who was fittest to rule?'[106] Such an emphasis hardly inclined the paper to the Conservatives in 1964, particularly given its generous coverage of the 'extremely capable' Wilson where 'more often than not a note of respect, even warmth, was heard'.[107] A profile of Wilson's 'great success' in dealing with Tory hecklers with 'wonderful fluency and urgency' at a Birmingham rally symbolised an uncritical tone in which the main 'trouble with Harold' seemed to be that he was 'impeccable, unruffled, coolly confident and just too good to be true'.[108] Even more remarkably, the cartoons of hardline right-winger Cummings tended to be independent or against all parties. When they made partisan points, they were as often anti-Conservative. One, for instance, supported Labour allegations that the Tories were hiding a coming economic crisis, as well as ridiculing Home as the 'matchsticks' economist (based on an infamous remark he had made), by featuring him rebuking Wilson, as 'Scaremonger: I've been conferring with my matches and all is well'. His alarmed opponent points to the Prime Minister's back pocket where his 'balance of payments' matches blaze out of control.[109]

The only real help to the Conservative campaign from Express newspapers came in the revelation that Labour deputy-leader George Brown had appeared to commit Labour to a halving of the mortgage rate to 3 per cent. The press had been closely following the unpredictable Brown, his reputation as a potential Labour liability having increased following a deeply embarrassing American TV interview on the day of John F. Kennedy's assassination from the drunk Labour deputy-leader.[110] The story of 'BROWN'S BOMBSHELL' originated in the considerably more pro-Conservative *Sunday Express*. It appeared to have 'all the ingredients of a political disaster' in that it seemed reminiscent of similar attempts by Gaitskell to 'bribe' electors in 1959.[111] The resulting Conservative 'BLITZ' on Labour's alleged fiscal irresponsibility was then given front page treatment in the *Express* two days running (although even here there was only a mild editorial attack) and left Brown complaining of misrepresentation and Wilson wearily dismissing a 'somewhat typical *Sunday Express* stunt'.[112]

With this one exception, however, the *Express*'s heart did not appear in the electoral battle and, until polling day, its reservations about the Tories appeared greater than its usual opposition to Labour.[113] Indeed there were times when the paper actively supported Labour's campaign agenda, most notably following the most exciting day of events during the election (30 September). At a morning press conference, Wilson foolishly responded to an unofficial dispute at the Hardy Spicer car components factory by suggesting that strikes were being deliberately fermented at election time to aid the Tories. It was his 'one colossal blunder of the campaign' and was widely ridiculed.[114] But the day got rather better for Wilson when the release of quarterly balance of payment figures showed a unexpectedly high deficit of £73 million. As Home later recalled, it was a gift to Labour given their allegations of an impending crisis.[115] Wilson duly launched a stinging attack on the Conservative leader, whom he compared to recently bankrupt washing machine magnate John Bloom. Newspaper editors that night had the choice of two leading, politically opposing election stories. Predictably, the *Mail* led with 'WILSON'S GAMBLE' on Hardy Spicer and the *Sun* asked, 'HAS SIR ALEC DECEIVED THE NATION?' The *Mirror*, putting commerce before politics, relegated Wilson's speech to page two in favour of a non-political story.[116] Most surprisingly, the *Express* devoted most of its front page to Wilson's attack on the Conservative leader under the headline, 'WILSON LETS FLY: Home? Just like Bloom living in make believe he thunders.' Reinforcing this point was an accompanying Cummings cartoon portraying Home according to Wilson's description.[117] The paper placed its main account of the Hardy Spicer affair, which it recognised as Wilson's 'biggest blunder yet', on the inside pages. Lancaster, who wrote the main story, recalled that the decision to lead with what the paper called 'these highly embarrassing statistics' was because:

> Wilson had made the speech in the evening, Hardy Spicer had been running since the early morning press conference and we thought frankly that this enormous attack on Home was the bigger news angle, though I must say that we didn't mind the fact that it was a big attack on Douglas Home by Wilson.[118]

This incident was symbolic of an objective, news-based approach that also gave prominent space to undoctored coverage of Labour speeches. One brutal attack by Wilson on Home not only made the front page, but its most powerful section was italicised to emphasise his savaging of *'a political illiterate, failed in economics, who cannot make a speech for himself, cannot read one when it is handed to him, and cannot understand it when he reads it'*.[119] News values rather than political loyalty were also evident when the *Express* produced the one real newspaper election exclusive. The paper's journalist, George Gale, interviewed the notoriously indiscreet Conservative minister Rab Butler who did not disappoint as he predicted that 'things might start slipping in the last few days' away from the Conservatives. This by itself was something of a coup as it was hardly customary for ministers to acknowledge the possibility of election defeat. But there followed so many further indiscretions about the shortcomings of the Prime Minister and his colleagues that Edwards checked twice that Butler was aware the interview was on the record.[120] The interview caused a minor sensation, enraging cabinet colleagues and Home, who attributed it as a crucial cause of defeat and later winning Gale the 'Granada Interview of the Year' award.[121]

The paper's impartiality even extended to its polling-day front page. Headlined 'FIGHTING FINISH', the text simply gave a balanced summary of statements of the party leaders. Finally the editorial concluded that the Conservative performance was 'an impressive one' and there were 'strong reasons for preferring the Tory record to the Labour champion' who was 'a man of high ability and untested powers'. The endorsement was made, according to Edwards, both 'half-heartedly and too late to have any influence', and such coverage led an aggrieved Conservative party vice-chairman, Oliver Poole, to complain to Aitken 'that they would have won if he had not had a socialist as editor'.[122]

There was little more comfort for the Tories from the *Daily Mail*, where Esmond Rothermere remained in control. A businessman rather than a journalist, his uncertain and uninspiring control had seen the paper's sales continue to trail two million behind its much better directed and more lavishly financed rival. Rothermere was a shy, remote figure whose only visible eccentricity seemed to be a preference for those who drank martinis, and he largely ruled through his managers and editors. The awkward silences that could accompany his conversations with journalists would often be filled by reference to their proprietor's obsession with news of the British climate – leading to one anecdote that an ill-informed junior reporter had responded to Rothermere's phone call after Macmillan's famous 'winds of change' speech by telling him that it was about the weather. 'What, all of it?' the proprietor queried.[123] Despite his aloofness, Rothermere was in daily touch with his editor, who would make his 'compulsory call' to him at 5.30 every evening. This would last for 5–15 minutes and would see the proprietor either accept a verbal outline of an unwritten lead article or insist that it be read for his approval later in the evening.[124] Rothermere was 'a fairly liberal Conservative', and a trend to a moderate editorial line was also reinforced by the absorption of the *News Chronicle* in 1960, which raised the question, as one journalist recalled, of 'were we a Tory newspaper or not?'[125]

In a constant search for the quick fix to the *Mail*'s problems, Esmond had pursued something of 'a revolving-door policy' for his editors, while the paper's political uncertainty was also reflected and influenced by his most recent choices. William Hardcastle, editor from 1959–1963, faced complaints from the Prime Minister's press secretary about the paper's coverage, while Macmillan once greeted him with the words, 'It's nice to meet the editor of an opposition newspaper.' Hardcastle, the paper's fifth editor under Esmond's control, was sacked in 1963, with his proprietor famously commenting that having tried a short, fat editor without much success, he was now going to appoint a tall, thin one.[126] Politically, new editor Mike Randall reflected the thoughtful liberalism of the *News Chronicle* where he had worked before the 1960 take-over. He had captured his proprietor's imagination with his ambitions to shift the paper upmarket into 'an intelligent, authoritative newspaper which spells out the facts ... never twisting them, getting them wrong or avoiding them'.[127] The Labour-supporting editor aimed to modify what he saw as the *Mail*'s 'absurdly Right wing Tory line' and 'nudge, if not steer it stealthily towards the centre'. He curiously believed that Rothermere was really a liberal, not a Conservative, sympathetic to these changes.[128] When appointed editor in April 1963, he wrote to his proprietor stating:

I believe that we are agreed that politically the *Daily Mail*, while being a paper of the Right and a supporter of the Tories; will not make the mistake of upholding the outdated ideas of outdated men; will not assume that everything Tory is good and everything Labour is bad; will welcome new thinking and new men from whatever quarter; will not shut its columns to those who oppose its policies; will not take up automatic positions to events.[129]

One symbol of what the editor described as a new 'objectivism' in the paper's political coverage was his innovation of what was called 'the split lead' to the main front page story, a less sensational approach which was intended to show that the chosen subject could have two different sides. Randall's introduction of such unfamiliar viewpoints was not without internal opposition. The leader-writer on the paper for the past 30 years, George Murray, was nicknamed 'Gunboat' for his robust pro-Conservative views. Asked if he had ever written a leader that contained one word of praise for Labour, he replied, 'Good God, No. Who do you think I am?' Nevertheless, Murray's professionalism allowed Randall 'to incline his column at least a few inches to the Left'.[130]

During the election, the paper proved more firmly committed to the Conservatives than the *Express*, as Murray's editorials frequently warned that it was 'no time for a change' to a narrow and introverted Labour philosophy that would undermine continued Conservative prosperity.[131] Such a position sometimes extended to the news columns. Most notably, the 'serious error' of Labour's 'blues under the beds' allegations at Hardy Spicer was covered in greater detail than in any other paper.[132] But in general the Mail 'tried hard to be fair', and even the above-story, headlined 'WILSON'S GAMBLE', was relatively restrained. It was further balanced by front page space, under the headline 'Home has "Bloom's delusion"', to Wilson's accusation that the Conservative leader was guilty of 'hiding from the nation the shock facts of the economic crisis facing Britain'.[133] Editorials also lacked aggressive hostility and did not generally seem to influence news coverage, Labour's manifesto was covered in much the same positive way as the *Express*, while the paper devoted considerable space to balanced summaries of party policies.[134] Judged on front pages, only three of its 14 election headlines could be classed as anti-Labour or pro-Conservative and even they – 'CHUCK IT WILSON', 'Don't Risk It' and 'WILSON'S GAMBLE' – hardly offered evidence of strident partisanship.[135] Half of the front pages were simply devoted to commentary on the election and its outcome. Opinion-poll stories were particularly prominent, with the paper giving attention on four separate occasions to Labour's progress in reducing the Conservative lead suggested by earlier polls.[136] The preference for news rather than propaganda was also illustrated by its one lead pro-Labour headline – 'Wilson's Challenge' – a well-timed call by the Labour leader for a television debate which, as intended, deflected attention from the Conservative manifesto launch.[137]

A rather more spectacular pro-Labour contribution came from the pen of Bernard Levin. He was one of the new anti-establishment satirists of the early 1960s, seen as 'the thinking man's columnist', and his employment was viewed as symbolic of the increased seriousness of the paper under Randall. Unknown to Rothermere, Levin's contract gave him complete freedom of expression and in the final week of the campaign he wrote four consecutive articles on the election.[138] This climaxed in a polling-day article which, according to Randall, outlined the case for Labour 'in a manner more convincing and in prose more eloquent' than the paper's own pro-Tory endorsement.[139] The journalist bluntly asked, 'What after all has Sir Alec Douglas-Home to do with the twentieth century or the twentieth century to do with Sir Alec Douglas-Home?' It was Wilson 'alone', who, like Lloyd George in 1916, had 'the requisite will, understanding and capacity' to meet the challenge of the age. He rousingly concluded:

> we dare not risk another Conservative administration, nor trust them to do what they have so conspicuously failed to do in thirteen years – to carry out the radical transformation of our country ... The Conservatives both in men and ideas are exhausted, and there is no possibility of their regeneration while they are led as they are at present. I think it's time to make this clear. Let's go.[140]

This, with the last phrase even echoing the party's manifesto title, 'Let's Go With Labour', was perhaps the most pro-Labour election comment ever sanctioned in the *Mail*. Rothermere, demonstrating the limits of his liberalism, was furious about this 'intolerable' article, possibly, suggests Randall, because 'somebody convinced him that, but for Bernard Levin and the *Mail*, Harold Wilson would not have scraped through to No. 10'. In a letter to the paper's managing director, he complained that 'for the first time in the history of Associated Newspapers, a member of the editorial staff has given his political opinions in the columns of the *Daily Mail* without the consent or even the knowledge of the proprietor.' It demanded 'the resignation of everyone concerned'.[141] In the event, no action was taken, but proprietorial rage at the pro-Labour bias of his paper was a fitting symbol of the fairness of the *Mail*'s coverage in 1964.

With these highly qualified endorsements, it was left to the *Daily Sketch* to provide the only partisan support for the Tories in the popular press. If the *Mail* was in a poor state, the position of its tabloid sister paper was desperate. Lack of resources made it impossible for it to compete against Cudlipp's *Mirror*, which mocked 'the only known case of a carbon copy costing more than the original'.[142] But it did its best to make up for its limited circulation with strident partisanship. All ten election leads were unambiguously anti-Labour or pro-Conservative. Prominent attention was given to Conservative costings of Labour's spending at £1,200 million a year,[143] and the economic threat of a Labour government that would produce 'less prosperity, with a plunge in savings and a sharp rise in taxes'.[144] But its main theme was a concerted attack on the leadership of 'this man of the Left, this man who has been wrong so often'.[145] This stance was also accompanied by strong support from the *Daily Telegraph*, although Labour also fared well in the broadsheet market with support, sympathy and impartial treatment from the *Guardian*, *Times* and the *Financial Times*.[146]

A press wot lost it?

In 1964 the popular press proved more favourable to Labour and lukewarm to the Conservatives than ever before. The party received very strong backing from the *Daily Mirror*, along with the less strident endorsement of the newly emergent *Sun*, giving it 43 per cent of the circulation of national newspapers. The remaining 57 per cent officially backed the Conservatives, but unofficially proved rather less keen. The *Express*, which accounted for over 25 per cent of total circulation, cannot be classed as an active Conservative supporter, while the *Mail* was also comparatively passive. Both placed their predominant emphasis on news rather than propaganda as they seemed rather more interested in reporting the election than attempting to influence the result. Overall, Labour received favourable or fair coverage in four popular newspapers that reached 93 per cent of the newspaper-reading population, not to mention a background both of anti-government press hostility and relatively uncritical coverage of the Wilson alternative. The Tory party's only wholehearted backing came from the *Sketch*, and its effects were limited, with 49 per cent of its tiny readership voting Labour and only 38 per cent supporting the Conservatives. The diversity of the press at this time, as between 1945–1951, was also further enhanced by the fact that roughly half its readers tended to consume more than one paper. Roughly 61 per cent of *Sketch* readers, 29 per cent of *Express* readers and 26 per cent of *Mail* readers also took the *Daily Mirror*, which had a higher sole readership figure than any other paper.[147]

A number of reasons, both long-term and short-term, explain these favourable conditions. General trends at this time seemed to be inclining the popular press towards what Cecil King called an 'increased seriousness'. It is only in retrospect that the 1960s has been characterised as the 'golden age' of British popular newspapers. Journalists at the time were much more likely to refer to a newspaper 'crisis'. But the high sales, genteel competition and high-minded efforts to raise standards in the absence of any real down-market pressure all suggest its 'ultimate flowering' before the onset of decline.[148] It is certainly the case that the Vassall and Profumo affairs provided numerous illustrations of newspaper misconduct. Yet other contemporary findings detected a new-found responsibility of the press, visible in more sophisticated and objective election coverage than ever before.[149] A variety of factors helped contribute to this trend. The increased importance attached to election polls played their part, as the *Mail*'s coverage illustrates most clearly. They may have taken 'the poetry out of politics' in the post-war era, as Nye Bevan famously commented, but they also helped take the partisanship out of the press. The spread of television may have convinced editors that they could not credibly depict their opponents in the same partisan light as previously.[150] Equally, the increased size of newspapers, which had doubled or even trebled in size from the rations of the immediate post-war period, also made more impartial and sophisticated coverage possible.

Beaverbrook's death also seemed to mark an era in which press ownership had increasingly shifted from press barons to businessmen such as Rothermere and Aitken who were apparently concerned more with profits rather than propaganda. In this situation the balanced coverage in the Tory popular press in particular may have stemmed from an increased awareness of, or concern for, their more politically diverse readership. Whereas 64 per cent of *Mirror* readers voted Labour, and only 22 per cent Conservative, just under half of *Mail* readers supported their paper's favoured party and one-third voted Labour. In the *Express*, 46 per cent of readers voted Conservative in 1964 – just 6 per cent more than the number who backed Labour. Both papers were also competing for disenfranchised *News Chronicle* readers.[151] Beaverbrook was also well aware of this constraint on his propaganda and, if he was, so were his journalists. As he wrote in 1963:

> I think we ought to support the Tory party, we ought however to be non-political as far as possible. Remember 32 per cent of our readers are opposed to us ... Therefore we are not going to run an out and out political paper to please the people that are hostile to us.[152]

A year later the *Mail* and the *Express* were, in a situation unique in Fleet Street history, both edited by Labour supporters and in conditions where there seemed an equally unusual limit to proprietorial direction. Perhaps most importantly, from the 1955 election, consensus politics had served to blunt press partisanship. With the number of people seeing little difference between the two parties rising from 34 per cent in 1959 to 49 per cent five years later, it was more difficult for the press to take a partisan line. This was most clearly reflected in *Express* coverage, which repeatedly suggested that there was 'no difference of principle' between two parties who were like 'Tweedledum and Tweedledee'.[153]

Given this situation, and in the context of the dominant mood, the issue of leadership was also important. Marcia Williams conceded the truth of later complaints from journalists that they had been used by Wilson 'as instruments of his propaganda' during a press honeymoon, which, as Paul Johnson noted in March 1963, had been 'far more favourable than even the most optimistic supporters could have anticipated'.[154] It was not only Tory opponents who were complaining about it. In the course of a violent attack on Wilson, Anthony Crosland was apparently to tell British journalists 'that the newspapers shocked him by their toadying attitude to the new leader and that it was time the political correspondents came out and ... denounced him for the shifty fellow he is'.[155] Shifty or not, within the context of a widespread press boredom and disillusionment with a seemingly directionless Macmillan government, the Labour leader filled a void. He was new and newsworthy, while personally 'the press was ... fascinated by Wilson, by his accessibility, his confidence that he could move mountains and the candour with which he enjoyed political manoeuvres'.[156] His famous Scarborough speech supplied the vision and 'made a profound impact on the press' at the time.[157]

The Labour leader also proved adept at exploiting the conflict between the Conservatives and their press supporters, allying Labour on the latter's side over the Vassall affair in a way the loyal Crossman considered had 'done more for our press relations than Gaitskell ever did'.[158] Wilson also made extensive efforts to court the press. Macmillan and Home would personally see the lobby, which at this time had few university graduates, about twice a year and 'patronise them something rotten, regarding them as a kind of servants' hall'. As Oliver Poole once famously remarked, newspaper journalists were all very well but 'hardly the sort of people you would ask to the country for the weekend'. By contrast the Labour leader accorded them far greater respect and status than ever before. He saw the lobby frequently, attended press parties, flattered with amazing skill as he called them by their first names and sent Christmas cards to them and their wives signed 'Harold and Mary'.[159]

Politically too the contrast in leadership could not have been greater. Given the mood of the time, the Conservatives could hardly have chosen a less suitable candidate than Alec Douglas-Home if they had tried. As their research in January 1964 on voter attitudes recognised, the party's 'weakest point' was 'modernity ... a problem shared by its leader'.[160] For the opposition papers, the choice of 'the ghastly amateur' was 'a gift beyond price', with the *Mirror* scathingly suggesting that 'Caligula's appointment of his horse as a consul was an act of prudent statesmanship compared with this gesture of sickbed levity from Mr Macmillan'.[161] On the other side, the Conservative-supporting press had, like the public, overwhelmingly favoured Butler and its welcome to the new leader ranged from lukewarm to icy. The *Telegraph* considered he would be 'too nice, too slow, too gentle' to take on Wilson, the *Mail* expressed surprise at the way Butler had been overlooked, while *Express* hostility to 'a bad, bad decision' was also visualised as Cummings portrayed Home putting a sword through 'Tory election hopes'.[162] The background of fierce criticism, together with the dominant mood, meant that the press could have rallied strongly to their party only if it was possible to portray a clear, forward-looking change of course. But the choice of a continuity candidate made such a strategy as difficult for the Tory press as it was for their party.

Much the same contrast continued to be evident during the election, as Wilson's popularity and visible strengths over Home served to further reduce press partisanship. Their tendency to report the election as a presidential contest between the rival party leaders helped Labour, and undermined the Conservative strategy of emphasising their 'team'. Party chairman Michael Fraser noted how 'it was clearly in our interests to play the "presidential" issue down'. He felt that despite some initial success, 'as soon as the press and television got bored . . . and started reporting the election largely in terms of the two leaders, we were on a loser'.[163] In a situation where the political motivation behind newspaper stories was blunted, newspapers were naturally drawn to the dynamic, entertaining Wilson rather than to Home. As one senior *Express* journalist put it, 'We played it for news and laughs', and in both these respects Wilson and Labour came out on top. Wilson's 'very cordial' press relations improved further during the campaign. Journalists enjoyed his at times brilliant campaigning style, rousing speeches, ease and skill when dealing with hecklers and chatty, intimate and entertaining manner at press conferences.[164] The evident sympathies of political correspondents were reflected in favourable profiles of Wilson in Conservative as well as Labour supporting newspapers. Cyril Aynsley, writing in the eve-of-poll *Express*, suggested that the election had been 'all about the emergence of Harold Wilson as a formidable platform speaker, a master of repartee', a view shared by Keith McDowell in the *Mail*:

> To watch his confidence grow over the past two weeks . . . to watch the Commons debater develop into the master public speaker; to observe him leaning on the rostrum, wag a finger and toss away the neat notes obviously enjoying it all now, has been to watch Wilson the Man emerging. I think the sheer Wilsonian ability . . . has come through stronger and stronger as the days have passed.[165]

Further proof of what *Mail* journalist Walter Terry dubbed 'the Fleet Street branch of the Harold Wilson appreciation society' was demonstrated on polling day. The political correspondents presented him with a gift to thank him for his co-operation and help in an unprecedented occasion that demonstrated 'the very real affection for Wilson among the many journalists who had reported him'.[166] All this contrasted markedly with the unfavourable press view of his less-accessible Conservative rival. It was difficult in the extreme to praise Home's frequently disastrous election performances on a whistle-stop tour that developed few themes, was rarely newsworthy and saw him shouted down by hecklers. Indeed the unimpressive Conservative campaign also left their newspapers searching for suitable copy, with Terry Lancaster suggesting that it was so bad that the *Express* was 'actually looking for pro-Conservative stories purely to get balance'.[167]

These differences in leadership also symbolised how wider political developments from 1961 temporarily skewed the general reduction in partisanship in Labour's favour. On the one hand, the poor performance of the Conservatives since 1961, together with Labour's revival, was reflected in the *Daily Mirror* – and Wilson's courting ensured further magnification. The election was the only campaign in the newspaper era of bi-partisanship between 1955–1970 when the *Mirror* took a highly partisan line. Equally the difficulties of the Conservative government, along with their more direct conflict with the press, muted the partisanship of their traditional supporters still further. On a deeper level, the transformation of the political, cultural, intellectual and social climate in the early 1960s certainly contributed to the lack of enthusiasm for a discredited Conservative old-guard, whose archaic amateurism was widely perceived to be the root of 'what was wrong with' the country.[168] And the general mood towards the questioning of all authority must have impacted more on press coverage of the government than the opposition. Conversely, the forward-looking, youthful dynamism of Labour and its leader appeared for once to be part of the solution rather than the problem.

Whether any of this mattered in electoral terms is, as always, debatable. The clear limits to newspaper power are demonstrated above by the substantial percentages of readers voting at variance with their instructions. Nevertheless the 1964 contest could hardly have been closer, for 900 altered voters in key constituencies would have produced a Conservative victory. The election was 'the one that got away' for the Tories in which almost anything could have swung it in their favour and the popular press was one factor that helped to swing it against them.[169] Wilson apparently agreed with *Mirror* executives who considered that their campaign had a 'decisive' effect, saw King as his first luncheon guest and offered him a peerage.[170] But as important was the behaviour of the Conservative press. The key to the result was the sharp drop in the Conservative vote by six percentage points. This may not have been primarily the result of press coverage, although it is conceivable that without its hostility, the events of 1962–1963 would not have been quite so damaging. There is evidence that newspaper criticisms in 1962–1963 'demagnetised' readers from their traditional loyalties, while the failure of the Tory press to rally enthusiastically behind the Conservatives in the run up to the election may also have prevented the full recovery of the Tory vote. Conservative research on voter attitudes also found the *Express* and the *Mail* had 'exceptionally heavy readerships' – 38 per cent and 22 per cent of former Conservative voters who had switched their support since the last election. Whether this demonstrates causation, correlation or both remains unclear, although the latter is the most probable.[171] For if Labour's victory in 1964 'owed much to the way in which its propagandists had characterised the preceding Tory regime', it was a picture given no small assistance by the stance of Conservative newspapers.[172]

This raises a more general question of what the press *did not say*, a media effect that is, as the introduction notes, often mistakenly ignored. For, on this occasion, the distorted newspaper mirror refracted the Labour party in an unusually favourable light. Despite the mythology surrounding 1964, only 44 per cent of the electorate actually voted for the party, a level of support little changed on its performance in the two previous elections (the Liberals, who doubled their support to 11 per cent, were the only party to gain). As pollster Henry Durant argued at the time, to talk of a 'swing' to Labour in 1964 would be 'rather like saying that a vehicle which is going backwards is really going forward solely because a contiguous one is going backwards at a faster rate'.[173] There were certainly visible weaknesses in Labour's position which the press could have chosen to attack had they so desired. As in the 1992 election, the key issue, as one Conservative observed in 1964, was 'time for a change versus fear of change'. As Butler and King wrote:

> many voters were torn between a desire to bring an end to a period of Conservative government which had brought with it economic recession ... and on the other hand, their doubts about the Labour party's past disunity, its financial competence, and its administrative capacity.[174]

Polls showed that 47 per cent believed the Conservatives would be better at maintaining prosperity, as against 34 per cent for Labour. 44 per cent thought Labour were promising plans that the country could not afford, compared to just 22 per cent for the Conservatives. Labour's post-election report also recognised the electoral problem of 'the "Who is going to Pay?" question'. The result, determined by 'massive Tory abstentions', was 'not altogether satisfactory' and much remained to be done 'to convince the majority of the electorate of the ability of the Labour party to govern'.[175] Yet despite these popular doubts about Labour's economic credibility, financial competence and fitness to govern, the press made few attempts to help the Conservatives in highlighting these themes. Wilson's modernisation rhetoric, judged by these figures, had left Fleet Street rather more spell-bound than the wider public. Conservative attempts to cost Labour's pro-gramme as a 'menu without prices' were given little backing from the popular press, with the exception of the *Sketch*.[176] The latter's stance demon-strates how a highly partisan Conservative press would have covered the election, highlighting the cost of Labour's plans, the left-wing past of its leader and the failings of past administrations – a very similar approach to that advanced with some success twenty-eight years later. By contrast, in 1964, 'time for a change' narrowly triumphed over 'fear of change' and both the Labour and Conservative popular press played their parts in aiding this result.

3 Towards the 'Winter of Discontent'

The popular press and the road to 1979

While Labour's complaints about a hostile press have littered the post-war period, it was only from the mid-1970s that there was a marked shift to the right in the politics of the popular press. This was first characterised by an intensification of the partisanship of the traditional Tory press, visible to some extent in the *Mail* and *Express* in the 1974 election, and to an even greater extent by the turn of 1979. By this time they were also joined by a powerful new propaganda ally, as the rapid commercial success of Rupert Murdoch's new tabloid *Sun* newspaper was accompanied by its slower political transformation into a stance fiercely hostile to Labour. This meant that, by the time of their election defeat at the hands of Margaret Thatcher's Tories, Labour was suffering a more hostile press than at any time in the post-war period. Such a position was, however, to some extent prefaced by the growing conflict that emerged between Wilson and the press from 1966 onwards.

'From honeymoon to divorce': Wilson and the press 1964–1970

Wilson's relatively favourable press treatment continued into the 1966 general election, which saw their behaviour characterised by a 'less than wholehearted commitment even than seventeen months before'.[1] The *Mail* and the *Express* again took a moderate stance. As in 1964, Bernard Levin was permitted to outline his support in the *Mail* for a Labour landslide against a Conservative party 'not only manifestly unfit to govern, but unfit even to contemplate voting for'. And the clearest demonstration of his paper's position came in its restrained coverage of the so-called 'Noose Trial', an incident that saw eight workers fined by colleagues for failing to take part in an unofficial dispute, with a noose being hung in the room where their 'trial' occurred. It offered a classic illustration of intimidatory union behaviour that the *Mail* was later to lovingly publicise. On this occasion, however, it was concerned to stress that such 'aberrations should not be made an election issue' and would 'exist regardless of the party in power until we modernise our thinking'.[2]

The *Express* also took a similar position on this issue, even if both papers undertook a rather more critical scrutiny of Labour than in 1964 as they attacked the party's 'disastrous mistakes' and 'wasted months' in government. Wilson, meanwhile, was already being derided as a 'master of gimmickry' but little else.[3] Nevertheless, in 1966 the *Express*'s support for the Conservatives was blunted considerably by two elements central to its philosophy. Its continued opposition to entry into the Common Market placed it more in sympathy with Wilson's sceptical approach, as against the clear enthusiasm displayed by the Conservatives to this key election issue.[4] In addition, the basic *Express* philosophy, as Beaverbrook earlier instructed, was to be 'an optimistic historian', a position that directly contradicted Conservative electoral allegations that the country was in serious economic trouble. So when a 'sententious' *Times* leader suggested 27 reasons 'Why the £ is weak', which was reprinted by the *Mirror*, the *Express* castigated the gloom-mongers for not looking at Britain's 'shining achievements' and 'unprecedented prosperity'.[5]

On the other side, the *Sun* proved the least partisan of the populars, despite having a higher percentage of politically committed readers, as it offered a balanced and detailed 'Election Probe' of the main issues before a lukewarm endorsement of Labour.[6] The main change in coverage came from the *Mirror*, in a shift in emphasis that one commentator considered 'the most significant in a generation of British political journalism'. Its stance, King noted, was 'as critical of the government as any paper' as it aimed 'to break loose from any close connection with the Labour party'.[7] King's sharp, private disillusionment with Wilson's 'lack of qualities needed in a prime minister – particularly foresight and administrative ability' had been publicly visible in the *Mirror* from at least mid-1965.[8] King's pro-Europeanism and his dismay at the 'horrible trouble' ahead economically was reflected in concerted campaign criticism of a man who had shown 'something less than leadership' on Europe and been 'less than candid about the real economic situation'.[9] As the *Mirror* called for 'an end to this malaise of government by half truth', its stance was viewed as so hostile that it had to deny speculation that it had threatened to completely withdraw its support for Labour. Its reluctant conclusion that there was 'no alternative' to another Labour government could hardly have been more grudging as readers were urged to 'GIVE MR WILSON A GOOD MAJORITY. So that this time there can be NO ALIBIS.' Wilson, who made no contact with the *Mirror* in 'contrast to the almost tearful requests for help last time', estimated that its campaign lost Labour 750,000 votes.[10]

What one observer described as the continuing 'passionate love affair between Mr Wilson and the press' was clearly already under strain. Some commentators argue that it was 'downhill all the way' after the election, as Wilson's badly received allegation about the 'tightly knit group of politically motivated men' behind the seamen's strike in May 1966 was followed by the economic and political 'July crisis'. But even after this, Wilson had 'continued to treat, and be treated by, many journalists with unusual friend-liness'.[11] The real turning point was the D-Notice affair, which effectively did for Wilson's press relations what the Vassall affair had done for Macmillan's. It began in February 1967 when Chapman Pincher, the fiercely anti-socialist *Daily Express* defence correspondent, was informed that all copies of overseas cables were vetted daily by MI5. He contacted Colonel 'Sammy' Lohan, the secretary of the D-Notice committee, which presided over a 'voluntary' form of self-censorship by sending out 'Defence Notices' if it was judged a newspaper story affected national security and should not be published. Chapman believed that he was 'categorically' assured that there was no D-Notice to interfere with publication and there followed an *Express* splash of a 'Big Brother' style 'CABLE VETTING SENSATION'.[12]

The story would have ended there – all it did was inaccurately describe a system that had operated unchanged since 1920 – but for Wilson. He had also been 'categorically assured' that the *Express* had been informed that the story breached D-Notices and was 'outraged' by its behaviour. The next day Wilson 'gratuitously' (in his own later words) attacked 'a sensationalised and inaccurate story', published 'despite the fact that the newspaper concerned was repeatedly warned that it would be contravening the notice'.[13] The Labour leader set up an inquiry but this concluded that Lohan 'did not manage to convey to ... Pincher' that the story was covered by D-Notices, and that 'it would not be right to say that the article amounted to a breach' of them.[14] But the Labour leader refused to accept this verdict and instead issued his own White Paper rejecting its findings. The result was two acrimonious parliamentary debates and what King estimated as 'the worst press any PM has had in my day' as Wilson was criticised from all sides for behaviour which had left his reputation seriously diminished in stature.[15] It was a classic instance of Wilson acting, as an 'appalled' Barbara Castle once noted, in a 'quite pathological' manner 'about the press'. On reflection he admitted to a 'self-inflicted' wound which was 'one of the costliest mistakes' of his government. As Marcia Williams recalled, the impact on press relations was 'disastrous'.[16]

This new situation became evident when Wilson's whole philosophy of economic modernisation collapsed in ruins with the government's forced devaluation of November 1967. While the above wounds may have healed in time, this episode had much more far-reaching consequences. Wilsonian modernisation was revealed to press and public alike to possess no clothes save for the old rags of the past, and the credibility gap that had already developed between the government's words and political deeds now widened into a chasm. Such a shift was further exacerbated in the negative response to Wilson's almost criminally over-complacent devaluation broadcast, which almost seemed to suggest that devaluation was a success he had been working for throughout his political life. Newspapers now turned to the new story and 'began with relish' to detail the government's very real failures.[17]

Moreover the mythical Wilson comment that 'the pound in your pocket has not been devalued' (it was never uttered – Wilson explicitly claimed that prices would rise – although it did symbolise the tone of the broadcast) was to be frequently used to attack stories of price increases over the following months and years. It symbolised the shifty and untrustworthy image that now became attached to the Labour leader. The 'cynicism and contempt' with which many political journalists, including Labour supporters, had come to view the Prime Minister by this stage arose from a strong feeling that they had been manipulated and misled by him, and been far too naive in believing his earlier rhetoric. This was part and parcel of a personal souring of relations. In the aftermath of the 1964 election, Wilson had continued to build up friendships with many journalists. This brought short-term gain for Labour but when the government fell into serious difficulties it placed both sides 'in an intolerable position'. The sensitive Wilson 'regarded criticism as betrayal' while the journalists, now wearing their new-found independence as badges of pride, saw his efforts 'to divert them or discriminate between them as improper or vindictive'.[18] On a political and personal level, the press had turned against the Prime Minister for reasons that almost represented an inverse to those explaining his earlier honeymoon and his relations, 'once so unnaturally good, became unfairly and unnaturally bad'.[19] By the early part of 1968, with the government deeply unpopular and the country in deep recession, the Conservative press were calling for the resignation of a government and prime minister who was 'not merely distrusted' but 'actively disbelieved'. Cudlipp later considered that such denunciations were of unprecedented hostility and 'came near to breaking his spirit'. Yet by far the greatest damage came from his own paper.[20]

King and Cudlipp's disillusionment with Wilson had only intensified after the 1966 election and as early as June 1966 the chairman was pressing for an all-out public attack. In private, King was less restrained as often over lunch with members of his cabinet – or indeed to anyone who would listen – he contemptuously denounced a man who was 'quite out of his depth . . . an even worse PM than Alec Home . . . a failure'.[21] Throughout these years, King and Cudlipp shared 'wide agreement' of an impending apocalypse that was as profoundly disturbing as it seems in retrospect utterly bizarre. A 'financial holocaust' would soon engulf the nation, the government would 'disintegrate in panic and desperation', and in the midst of bloody civil war, the only answer would be a new coalition government led by 'a man of courage and impartiality'. Incredibly, kept in King's desk was a frequently amended list of potential saviours, which most significantly included Lord Mountbatten, while the tycoon also clearly expected to play a key role in this new emergency administration.[22]

It was not only in private that these thoughts were expressed. The paper's flirtation with the idea of a coalition government had begun as early as July 1965. But it was really a year later that there began a tirade of magisterial and deeply pessimistic criticisms of government failings in editorials that often graced the *Mirror* front page and sometimes stretched to four pages. The ghost of Rothermere, it seemed, had returned to haunt the paper. In the 1966 'July crisis', for instance, the paper denounced the 'TWO MORE WASTED YEARS' under Labour, while by September 1967 it was conducting a three-day 'ruthless analysis' of the government's failings of 'too little, too late'.[23] By the end of the year, the *Mirror* was close to a 'Wilson must go' campaign, but Cudlipp managed to temporarily persuade King against this. Instead, the paper began building up King's current favourite, new Chancellor Roy Jenkins, 'the most important politician in the country' whose success the future stability of the parliamentary system rested upon.[24]

By February King was telling a bemused Tony Benn that he expected a coalition government before the end of the year and that 'there may well be a larger part for you to play'. Benn reported the conversation direct to an agitated Wilson, who replied that King was 'mad'.[25] At a policy meeting with the paper's senior executives in early March, King evoked his nightmare of impending doom in which 'money would lose its value and we should have to live by barter'. His comments were not greeted uncritically. Political editor John Beavan told King that he could survive for years on his fabulous collection of old silver. Columnist George Gale mockingly envisaged King engineering his coup d'état by turning up at the Palace in a charabanc with his maverick political allies and telling the Queen, 'Ma'am, here we are, your new Government of National Reconstruction.'[26]

By the end of March, King had gone public. This was despite the more general opposition of senior executives to a 'Wilson must go' campaign that 'would only strengthen his position', damage the *Mirror* commercially and leave it politically 'high and dry' with an 'impotent anti-Tory stance'.[27] In a BBC interview with Robin Day, he was asked if he was seeking to exercise 'power without responsibility'. King ominously took the view that Rothermere and Beaverbrook 'would have performed a great public service' if they had succeeded in toppling Baldwin. King's same sense of public duty was revealed the next day in a front page attack on a man whose continued leadership would produce 'the death of democracy' and whose replacement would 'probably be the least damaging course'.[28]

This almost represented a dress rehearsal for the following month, which also saw the culmination of King's private efforts to construct a coalition against Wilson. This took the form of the famous 'Kinnerton Street' meeting in which King, accompanied by Cudlipp, met with Mountbatten and called on him to head 'a new administration to restore order'. After his friend Sir Solly Zuckermann condemned King's 'rank treachery', the meeting broke up in what has been sensationalised as part of an abortive military coup to overthrow the Wilson government.[29] The rather less secretive climax to the affair came two days later in the form of a front page piece by the press baron which argued that 'ENOUGH IS ENOUGH' from a government that had 'lost all credibility: all authority'. Cudlipp, cannily, got King to sign the piece, which given his position as a part-time Director of the Bank of England, concluded with the potentially destabilising, if deeply misleading, words:

> We are threatened with the gravest financial crisis in our history. It is not to be removed by lies about our reserves, but only by a fresh start under a fresh leader. It is up to the Parliamentary Labour Party to give us that leader – and soon.

King's 'intention and expectation', Cudlipp recalled, was that 'the authority of his pronouncement and its timing', and his more specific efforts to ferment a financial panic, would bring Wilson down in favour of his long-planned coalition government. Military strategies were simply an irrelevance, because the self-styled 'man of destiny' confidently believed that he could topple Wilson through what he had recently described as 'easily the most powerful paper in the world'.[30] As predicted, however, the attack only served to strengthen Wilson's less-than-secure position within the party as Labour MPs queued up to denounce an inherited case of 'power without responsibility'.[31]

King's initiation of this last hurrah of the old-style press barons was partly political, as he felt let down by a man he had placed so much faith in. More personally, Wilson no longer appeared to be listening or recognising his power and had failed to provide a government position or honour of sufficient weight. Attempts to appease him with a junior position at the Board of Trade were viewed as 'a bitter insult', while repeated offers of a life peerage were rebuffed as King would only accept a hereditary honour equivalent to those of his rivals.[32] The attack also reflected King's constant world view of the gross incompetence of virtually all existing political personalities save for himself and a chosen maverick few – so, in this sense, the motivation was 'melancholia rather than megalomania'.[33] Yet this last factor, the old occupational disease among proprietors, was also important, as King began talking about 'my newspapers', 'my editors' and 'my readers' – not to mention 'his' coalition government. But King was 'a press baron in all but security of tenure' and the result was another boardroom coup at the *Mirror* that saw King dismissed for an excessive personal preoccupation with national affairs.

This may have prevented a total breach between the *Mirror* and Labour, but it made little short-term difference as Cudlipp publicly made 'absolutely clear' his agreement with King's political views and told him that he intended 'to be no more friendly to Wilson than ... in the recent past'.[34] There was certainly a marked change of emphasis to what Cudlipp ambiguously described as 'realism with pessimism to realism with optimism', which in practice meant a reduction of the long doom-laden front page editorials and a retreat away from British politics.[35] But the underlying tone remained unfriendly. Subsequent analyses spoke of the 'dangerous malaise' under Wilson's indecisive leadership and again supported a coalition as the 'inevitable' outcome of 'the gathering crisis' under a government that had 'lost its capacity for leadership'.[36]

As the more general pattern of press hostility continued well into 1969, Wilson claimed that the attacks had 'probably been worse than any other prime minister has had to face'. The deterioration of government–press relations was also remarked upon by the more impartial Press Council.[37] Yet despite these bitter conflicts, the 1970 election saw the press recover some of its balance. Fifty-seven per cent of the press supported the Conservatives and the remainder endorsed Labour, giving Labour as much support in the press as in the country. These figures were unchanged since 1964, although, unlike then, they provide a roughly accurate representation of the press advantage of the Conservatives.[38] Alongside the continued partisanship of the ailing *Sketch*, the *Mail* strongly denounced 'the worst government this century', presided over by a man whose 'dishonesty' was without parallel in British history. As in 1966, the paper strongly supported Conservative allegations about an impending economic crisis under Labour, most graphically in a polling day front page headlined, 'Devalue With Labour!' So, in contrast to its earlier optimism, did the *Express*, while Cummings also resurrected his anti-Labour creation of the 1940s, 'Mr Rising Prices'.[39]

On the other side, Labour still managed to retain the support of the *Sun* despite its change of ownership in 1969 (see below, pp. 72–3). Like the *Sun*, the *Mirror* waited until the last moment to declare its support after campaigning on the slogan, 'Man for Man, who would you put your money on?', which featured predictably favourable comparisons of Wilson's ministerial team with their Conservative rivals. Despite this, and a strongly presidential Labour campaign, it was notable that the *Mirror* could not bring itself to make *any* textual comparison of the far more popular Wilson over Heath, or run any article praising Wilson at all, apart from an eve of poll endorsement of 'WILSON AND HIS TEAM'.[40] Following Labour's shock defeat, a clutch of resolutions were submitted for consideration at the party conference blaming it on 'the sustained scurrilous attacks on the party leader by the right-wing press'. They also suggested that 'the lukewarm and belated support' received from the *Mirror* and the *Sun* demonstrated 'the pressing need for a Labour daily paper'.[41] Yet, just as the skewing of coverage in Labour's favour in 1964 stemmed from newspaper dissatisfaction with the government's performance, so the balance of coverage in 1970 reflected similar influences. It was not yet apparent that there had been any underlying shift in the balance or approach that the press had taken since 1955.

'Smears and forgeries' 1974: political reorientation (1)

A clearer demonstration of an increasingly partisan press came after four turbulent years of Tory rule climaxed in the bitter February 1974 election, initiated by Heath on the question of whether the striking miners or the elected government 'governed Britain'. Within the popular press it offered a return to 'full-blooded campaigning partisanship greater than at any election since the 1950s'.[42] Most partisan was the *Daily Mirror*, which greeted the election's announcement with a front page edged in black like a mourning card. Beside a picture of a superior-looking Heath, its only words were: 'AND NOW HE HAS THE NERVE TO ASK FOR A VOTE OF CONFIDENCE.' This early declaration was not without internal opposition from those who thought it journalistically premature, while the paper's chairman, Sir Don Ryder, also expressed his worry about a totally committed pro-Labour paper.[43] But by 1974 it was no longer the case that the group's central policy was imposed by the Chairman, who behaved 'like a constitutional monarch' and left editors largely free to edit the papers within the paper's centre-left tradition. On this occasion a key role was played by Hugh Cudlipp's successor as editorial director, old *Mirror* and Labour stalwart Sydney Jacobson, who persuaded Ryder on this line of attack.[44] The paper went on to fight its most committed campaign since 1964, with good relations with the Labour high command but rather less friendly ones with Heath, who complained about unfair coverage which climaxed in an unequivocal seven-word appeal: 'FOR ALL OUR TOMORROWS VOTE LABOUR TODAY.'[45]

Much the same trend also seemed visible as the Conservative press greeted a Labour programme more radical than any since 1945 with traditional scare stories that under 'a docile prime minister' dominated by 'reds', Labour would put '£4,000 MILLION ON YOUR TAXES'.[46] A particularly notable intensification of partisanship had occurred at the *Daily Mail* where, from 1971, control had shifted to Esmond Rothermere's son, Vere. Derided by some critics as a buffoonish and idiotic 'Mere Vere', the paper's new controller immediately took the step that was to reverse the steady decline under his two predecessors. An internal report in 1970 had revealed the dire state of a company with estimated losses of £32 million over the next five years and recommended merger with the *Express* as the only viable solution. Rothermere, however, was determined not to go down in history as 'the man who lost the Harmsworth inheritance'. He closed the *Sketch* and launched what he described as an entirely new paper, a 'respectable' tabloid *Daily Mail*, or 'compact' as he preferred to call it.[47] It was a widely seen as a highly risky move that could prove the ailing publication's final blow. But by 1988 the *Mail* had overtaken the *Express* after nearly 50 years behind it, and although by dint of a slower circulation decline, it still represented a huge success. As proprietor, Rothermere took close interest in his newspapers and determined their broad strategy. But he also gave editors substantial latitude, often comparing himself to an admiral in charge of a fleet who 'doesn't tell any individual captain how to sail his ship, but he does tell him in which direction he should head'.[48]

In large part the success of the new paper was the work of the 'captain' Rothermere appointed, David English. The editor, the son of a Bournemouth accountant who had earlier edited the *Sketch*, was later described by Rothermere as 'the perfect *Daily Mail* reader', meaning he was aspirational, enterprising, conservative and family-minded. He gradually refashioned the paper very closely in his own image in the course of his 21-year editorship. It displayed little of the uncertain direction of previous years as it set out unequivocally to appeal to the fears and aspirations of the conservative middle classes through a passionate and angry production that one rival executive later described as 'in a permanent state of outrage'.[49] Such an attitude increasingly informed its political coverage, and the *Mail*'s tabloid nature, together with its tendency to luridly highlight features less prominently displayed in the still-broadsheet *Express*, made it markedly more partisan than its rival. For example, in comparison with the *Mail*'s front page '£4,000 MILLION ON YOUR TAXES', the *Express* relegated the story to the eighth column of the front page and reported it less sensationally.[50]

The same general pattern of press behaviour was repeated in October 1974. The tabloid *Mirror*'s strident propaganda offered a virtual carbon copy of its February endorsement.[51] Meanwhile the Conservative press gave prominence to the new theme that a Labour government would be 'PUPPETS ON A UNION STRING', alongside the more traditional emphasis on the 'sinister elements' within the party that made a Marxist triumph 'a very real menace'. Both themes featured prominently in Cummings' again strongly anti-socialist cartoons in the *Express*. A polling-day caricature on the front page updated his anti-Bevan cartoon in 1955 with an extremist Tony Benn, complete with devil's tail and horns, hiding behind the moderate face of Wilson.[52] Another old theme of the economic cost of Labour was juxtaposed besides positive coverage of an 'unshakeable promise' by the Shadow Environment Minister Margaret Thatcher to reduce mortgage rates.[53]

Perhaps surprisingly for a year that witnessed two elections, it was coverage between rather than during them that aroused most Labour complaint in 1974. Immediately after the February election, Castle had expressed her hope that Wilson would not 'renew that vendetta with the press'. Soon, however, the Labour leader was locked in a bitter personal conflict with them over what became known as the 'Land Deals affair'. This centred around the property dealings of Marcia Williams' brother, Terry Field, who had been Wilson's office manager between 1971–1973. In 1967, Field had purchased some slag heaps at Ince-in-Makerfield and subsequently sold the site, generating profits of £110,000. He then joined an (unknown to him) corrupt businessman, Robert Millhench, to exploit a surrounding area. Millhench in turn tried to further his dealings with a forged letter written on House of Commons notepaper from Wilson. Williams was a sleeping partner in the original venture and the high profits laid her open to charges of land speculation and Wilson to claims of hypocrisy in employing individuals who profited from a practice current party policy was pledged to eradicate.[54] Williams had long since excited media interest and found herself besieged at her London home in the intense coverage which followed. The *Mail*, and again to a lesser extent the *Express*, gleefully questioned whether a prime minister who had 'repeatedly attacked land speculators' should employ people who had profited from a process the party condemned as 'irresponsible, anti-social and immoral'. Coverage headlined 'YARD CHECK ON WILSON STAFF', 'WILSON MET LAND DEALERS' and the *Mail*'s constant heading, 'WHO FORGED WILSON'S SIGNATURE?', all, according to the Labour leader, aimed to suggest that 'there was something nasty in the woodwork if only Fleet Street could print it'.[55] Wilson's press relations, according to press secretary Joe Haines, were 'never worse' than during an incident he considered was motivated by the wider aim of discrediting the government.[56] The following October, further attacks highlighted allegations by the widow of Wilson's former principal private secretary that his fatal heart attack had been brought on by the strains of working with the tempestuous Williams. The most graphic of these was a *Mail* story unequivocally headlined 'How No. 10 Killed My Husband'.[57]

Such coverage had also precipitated Wilson's badly received allegation that 'cohorts' of journalists had been 'combing parts of the country with a mandate to find anything, true or fabricated, for use against the Labour party'.[58] He subsequently suggested that the press had 'sought to influence the result of the two general elections' through 'the deliberate and painstaking exploitation of the smear technique'.[59] His advisers similarly recalled the handicap of campaigning in a situation where the *Mail*, *Express* and *Sun* 'were effectively being published from Conservative Central Office' and were 'more virulent than at any time since 1945'.[60] But this exaggerates the imbalance against Labour by 1974. Although statistically biased towards the Conservatives, the press in both elections actually unwittingly helped the Labour campaign by 'progressively defining the issues in non-Conservative terms'.[61] In February, election coverage failed to stick to the Conservative agenda of 'Who governs' after the first week of the campaign, but shifted to Labour's agenda emphasising prices and inflation.[62] More wittingly, the *Mail*, and to an even greater degree the *Express*, did not completely abandon the impartiality they had frequently demonstrated since 1955. They proved 'much more even-handed' than the *Mirror* in their assessments of the strengths and weaknesses of the two parties. They were also prone, with one eye on the circulation, to flirtation with the Liberals, who after recent by-election successes increased their vote by four million in February 1974.

One *Express* front page in the middle of this campaign headlined, 'HAROLD WILD ABOUT TED: Fury as Heath rejects pit plan', simply offered an even-handed, detached account of a campaign dispute between the two leaders beginning: 'Peace in the Pits? It was back to an election slanging match last night as Mr. Heath flatly rejected a new plan from Mr. Wilson – who in turn attacked the Premier for being "patronising" and "deciding everything himself".'[63] The same is also true for the *Mail*, despite its sharper degree of bias. For instance, in February the paper's exposure of the cost of Labour's programme as estimated by the Chancellor, Anthony Barber, was soon qualified the following day. A sceptical paper called on him to reveal his figures, while Healey was prominently featured attacking 'the most disastrous Chancellor since the war' for, in the words of the headline, 'seeing double' in his original estimates. Nor did the *Express* and *Mail* make much effort to play down news unfavourable to the Tories. As the campaign entered its crucial last week, both gave front page attention to the 'GREAT PAY PIT BLUNDER' – the revelation, which seemed to question the whole reason for the election, that the miners were actually paid less than the national average. This was quickly followed by an even more damaging publication of the 'Trade Gloom for Tories', as a record £383 million trade deficit was given similar prominence just before polling day.[64] The *Express*'s partisanship had certainly hardened by the following October but even then its final appeal – 'NOW IT'S UP TO YOU' – was a model of restraint in comparison with later years, with a balanced textual summary and headline quotes from all three party leaders.[65]

Meanwhile Heath's remoteness towards journalists, his embarrassing incapacity for small talk and photo opportunities had long made him unpopular with the journalists themselves, while, as prime minister, he had neglected the importance of the media and inspired little enthusiasm. Some commentators were even accusing 'once ferociously Tory newspapers' of having 'laid down with the lambs' in the electoral battle while also giving Heath a 'stinking' press.[66] At the *Mail*, English later agreed that he was 'very mistrustful' of the Conservative leader and 'gave him little support', a stance visible in attacks on the 'appalling mess' caused by the Prime Minister's economic incompetence.[67] By the end of the second election, left-leaning press critic Anthony Howard, far from detailing any anti-Labour bias, was expressing surprise at 'the remarkable lack of ardour' a capitalist press had brought to opposing the party, especially given the alternative prospect of a right-centre coalition.[68]

It is also worth noting that, despite Labour fears and the apparent intentions of Peter Wright and sections of the Conservative party, no last-minute 'Zinoviev' press scare actually transpired in either of the elections.[69] Equally the 'Land Deals' affair was not simply an anti-Labour smear, even if this was one element to it. As Alan Watkins wrote at the time, it was 'a matter of legitimate public interest' when anyone made £100,000 in property dealings.[70] The escalation of the story was partly due to an intense circulation war between the *Mail* and *Express*. The contemporary American exposure of Watergate, set alongside complaints about Britain's 'half-free press', also emboldened the press not to be silenced by writs from Wilson and Williams.[71] As over the D-Notice affair, Wilson's over-reaction hardly helped as he made the semantic distinction that Field had been engaged in 'land reclamation' rather than speculation. His comments were treated with the derision his advisers had anticipated. English, for instance, wryly suggested that the only difference he could detect between the two 'appeared to centre around whether you were or were not a friend of Wilson and played golf with him'.[72] It also appears that 'contrary to Labour suspicions of a plot by Tory newspaper magnates', there was little enthusiasm for pursuing the story further. Rothermere had postponed publication just before election day in February and remained concerned of a backlash if the *Mail* appeared to be 'gunning' for Wilson, while Aitken similarly wished to avoid allegations that the *Express* 'did not appear to be giving the Labour government a fair chance'.[73] It may well be, as Watkins suggested at the time, that the incident obscured 'a lot of goodwill for the government . . . in the press'.[74]

In their 1974 behaviour, the *Mail* and the less-partisan *Express* represented something of a hybrid, showing hints of the full-blooded partisanship of earlier and later years along with the rather more restrained coverage of recent elections. Neither reached the levels of partisanship of the *Mirror* and Wilson's complaints once again illustrated the 'classic double-standards' in Labour's attitude to press bias.[75] In any case the real key to the broad balance of the popular press in the 1970s was Rupert Murdoch's *Sun*. By 1969 the Mirror group paper, under-resourced and virtually ignored by Cudlipp, had fewer readers and bigger losses – 12.7 million in four years – than even the old *Daily Herald*. Cudlipp sold the paper to Rupert Murdoch in what, in retrospect, was perhaps the biggest error in newspaper history. Murdoch believed, with some justification, that the *Mirror* had become too highbrow for its readers in the 1960s, with the worthy Mirrorscope innovation, a four-page pull-out that examined world affairs, said to be often discarded unread. Together with the paper's first editor and former *Mirror* journalist Larry Lamb, he set out to produce a downmarket alternative that was explicitly based on an updated version of their rival's irreverent approach of previous decades. Coverage of sex, television, a cheeky anti-establishment edge, combined with aggressive and expensive marketing offered the key to the paper's rapid success, as it attracted 1.5 million readers within its first 100 days.[76]

Politically the vision was far less clear and hardly on the top of Murdoch's priorities. During his student days at Oxford University, the press baron, whose room displayed a bust of Lenin, had been something of a champagne socialist of the kind so later derided by his newspaper, and his father had once expressed concern to Cudlipp about his son's 'alarming left-wing views'. In the early 1970s Murdoch remained vaguely on the centre-left, possessing what one contemporary biographer could describe as an 'inbuilt sense of neo-socialism'. The tycoon defined himself as 'friendly' with Wilson, who contributed an article for the paper's first edition and hosted a number of visits Murdoch made to Chequers.[77] In his first election as proprietor in 1970, the *Sun* endorsed Labour because of their shared concern for 'social justice, equality of opportunity, and the quality of living' – although perhaps more important was a shared concern to attract Labour voters.[78] Nevertheless the paper covered the election in a more impartial manner than any of its rivals and, despite the contempt shown in Fleet Street for 'Rupert's shit-sheet', devoted one-third more column inches to the election than the *Mirror*.[79]

In February 1974, the *Sun* again contrived to pick the election loser as it called for a Conservative vote on polling day. This meant that the Conservatives were technically supported by 70 per cent of national newspapers, leading a number of commentators to suggest that this began an 18-year imbalance against Labour.[80] But this confuses a massive qualitative difference between a polling-day endorsement and active support of the type visible in later elections. On this occasion, the *Sun*'s coverage was highly impartial and 'more than any other of the populars, made a serious attempt at policy analysis distinct from party propaganda'. The paper proved solidly resistant to attempted Conservative Central Office manipulation in favour of the anti-union theme, declaring against 'a single-issue election on the Tory theme of '"Who Rules"'.[81] Until polling day it seemed to be edging towards Labour in headlines such as 'WILSON BLASTS "TV LIES" BY THE TORIES', and 'HEATH WILL FREEZE PAY, WARNS HEALEY'. Even its final-day declaration for Heath in the choice 'BETWEEN THE DEVIL AND THE DEEP BLUE SEA' could not, as the headline suggests, have been more grudging. It was further counterbalanced by an article from political correspondent John Akass explaining why he would vote Labour. The front page editorial also provided clear evidence of a still-centrist political line. It suggested that it might endorse a Labour party led by James Callaghan or Roy Jenkins, and argued that the Conservatives looked 'less likely' than in the past 'to lose sight of justice, fairness and social democracy' to explain why the party 'just' got the paper's vote.[82]

Much the same approach was demonstrated in October as the *Sun* advised readers to vote for the best candidates and suggested, 'ALL our instincts are left rather than right and we would vote for any able politician who would describe himself as a Social Democrat.' While the Heath government had 'failed', the prospect of a 'doctrinaire Socialist government' under Wilson could not be endorsed either.[83] Notwithstanding its attacks on 'BENN THE BOGEY MAN', for the most part the paper, even more than in February, would have no truck with the Conservative campaign agenda. Quintin Hogg's typically colourful comparison of a Labour Britain with the Soviet system was dismissed as 'frankly ludicrous'.[84] Heath was viewed bluntly as 'an electoral liability', while his eventual successor aroused little more affection as the *Sun* veered towards Labour in dismissing her promise to reduce mortgages as an electioneering stunt.[85] It is likely that the paper's position between 1970–1974 was as much the product of Murdoch's over-riding commercial objectives to appeal to its, and the *Mirror*'s, traditional Labour readers along with those from Conservative-supporting newspapers as well.[86] But whatever the motivation, its behaviour reinforced Regan's 1975 conclusion that 'one of the healthiest things' about Murdoch was the way his position balanced an otherwise right-wing dominated press. The press baron's contribution to the political plurality of the British media was, however, to prove rather short-lived.

'Sun shine and hate Mail' 1974–1978: political reorientation (2)

While it is often suggested that Murdoch found his true political supporter in Thatcher after she became Conservative leader in early 1975, the *Sun*'s political conversion was actually a more gradual process. The relationship between the two did not exactly begin harmoniously. In between supporting the miners against the Heath government, the paper's vicious attacks on its Minister of Education had allegedly reduced 'the most unpopular woman in Britain' to tears as she was dubbed 'Maggie Thatcher, Milk Snatcher' for her abolition of free school milk. 'Is she human?' the paper asked in a question later repeated by both admirers and enemies. Unlike the *Mail*, the paper did not support Thatcher during her leadership challenge to Heath and subsequently hoped that the new leader would employ his talents to the full.[87] Throughout 1975, the *Sun* was critical of Labour, but there was a distinct lack of enthusiasm for an 'L-plated Shadow Government' who were 'split right down the middle' and had 'failed to make themselves look like an alternative' worth voting for. Meanwhile Thatcher had yet to demonstrate that she could 'knock the skin off a rice pudding' in the course of an 'erratic', 'eccentric' and 'haphazard' leadership.[88]

A continued centrist stance led the paper to express reservations about the Conservative party's right-wing shift to 'the message of the day before yesterday's men'. It failed to detect 'much difference between the Tory extremists, trying to stifle THEIR middle-of-the-road men and the Labour knifegrinders' of the left. In a sympathetic 'Meet the unions' series which would have been unthinkable four years later, the *Sun* was also anxious to counter 'union bashing' by highlighting their role in 'training their members to be more useful in their jobs' and looking after the sick and unemployed.[89] Unsurprisingly, readers were unaware of any political shift in their paper. Polls taken in the second half of 1975 found that 57 per cent thought that the *Sun* did not support any one party, while for all other popular newspapers the figure was much lower, at around one-third of their readership. Among the 18 per cent of readers who thought that the *Sun* did not give fair coverage, 11 per cent thought it was unfair to the Conservatives, 9 per cent to the Liberals, and just 3 per cent thought the paper was anti-Labour.[90]

It was really only from 1976 that the paper's tone against Labour hardened as it denounced the growing influence of the Labour left in the party, led by 'the Trotskyites' friend' Tony Benn, who aimed 'to make Britain a land fit for Marxists to live in'. Meanwhile the package of cuts that followed the IMF crisis was 'the price of one of the most shameful periods of economic mismanagement in living memory', as the paper hoped the affair would topple an 'inept, inadequate government'.[91] The answers to the country's apparent 'ungovernability', it now frequently argued, were cuts in state spending and direct taxation. Yet this Thatcherite agenda did not, for the moment, incline the paper to the Conservatives. As the paper argued in its penultimate editorial of 1976, while Labour was 'disintegrating under ever-increasing pressures from the unions and the Trots, MRS THATCHER'S TORIES still do not begin to look like a convincing altern- ative'.[92]

The rather confused conclusions of the Royal Commission on the Press in 1977 reflected the degree to which the politics of the British popular press were in a state of transition. The Labour party expressed their concern about a 'marked political imbalance' of a national press that was 'well to the right'.[93] They found some unexpected support for their view in May 1977 when the *Daily Mail* spectacularly revealed a 'WORLD-WIDE BRIBERY WEB AT LEYLAND'. The paper claimed that the nationalised car industry had established a multi-million pound 'slush fund' that was 'paying bribes and conspiring to defraud foreign governments on a massive scale in a des- perate effort to attract overseas orders'. A letter allegedly written by Lord Ryder, head of the National Enterprise Board, to the Leyland chief execu- tive, indicated that the government had approved an arrangement that dra- matically illustrated 'the hypocritical face of socialism'.[94] Amidst Labour mutterings of 'another Zinoviev Letter', the story was quickly revealed as a forgery, the work of a British Leyland executive who had been paid £12,000 for the documents. English apologised unreservedly for 'a grave journalistic error' and offered his resignation to his proprietor, who refused it.[95] The exclusive had been published 'after weeks of research' which had somehow omitted to check the allegations with Ryder. English should have been alerted to its dubious authenticity when he asked the sub-editor dealing with the story whether he had ever seen anything like it. His perceptive response was that it reminded him of an earlier much ridiculed *Daily Express* story by the same reporter, Stewart Steven, which claimed to have located the whereabouts of Nazi war criminal Martin Bormann.[96]

Labour leaders, past, present and future, lined up to condemn the *Mail*. Callaghan accused English of a 'contemptible' attempt to 'smear the Labour government and bring down a nationalised industry', Wilson returned to battle against 'a peddlar of forgeries' since the 1920s which had published three such anti-Labour documents in the same number of years. Meanwhile a rising Labour backbencher Neil Kinnock set the scene for future conflict when he accused English of 'incompetence' and predicted that his editorship would be brief. English fired back against a campaign of 'intimidation and fear', while undeterred by a mere forgery, ran two further front pages detail- ing a government 'SLUSH MONEY PROBE'. Showing a power of prophecy little better than Kinnock's, English asked his critics, 'Does anyone truly believe that if we had had a Tory government for the past three years, this paper would have been a sycophantic lapdog, silently adoring our rulers with moist and worshipping eyes?'[97]

Callaghan also reported the case to the Royal Commission, which rather more ambiguously suggested that while the *Mail* had long been 'polemical and politically partisan', what was new was 'the extreme lengths to which the paper was prepared to go in an attack on the government based on inadequately checked information'. On the other hand this was contextualised as merely the latest 'lamentable' illustration of persistent attempts to discredit a party that had been 'unfavourably reported by a majority of the press . . . over most of the century'. It suggested that the contemporary press was 'less partisan' than the left alleged and the balance against Labour was not currently 'a strong one' – a belief based on its view that, while the *Mail, Express, Telegraph* and *Mirror* were 'strongly partisan', the *Sun* was not.[98] The cloudy uncertainty of the commission's findings was further demonstrated when two of its members, David Basnett and Geoffrey Goodman, refused to sign the above conclusions. Instead they issued a minority report that expressed 'surprise' at the 'complacency' of the above view in the face of 'a manifest political imbalance in Britain's national press' which threatened 'the functioning of a healthy democratic society'.[99]

It was their verdict that showed rather more foresight. Ironically it was in 1977, just as the government was beginning its recovery from the previous year's nadir, that the *Sun*'s political stance hardened considerably as it denounced a 'tattered, discredited, disastrous government . . . bogged down by incompetence . . . drifting, rudderless' and increasingly dominated by 'the Fascist left'. Yet scepticism about the Conservatives still remained. Backtracking on some of its earlier rhetoric, the paper warned of the 'political madness' of forcing a showdown with the unions or behaving 'like an economic Jack the Ripper' in reducing public spending as it alarmingly asked of the Tories, 'will they smash the welfare state?'[100] But 1978 saw two defining moments for the paper, commercially and politically. Legend had it that Murdoch had told Cudlipp that the *Mirror* would touch a four million circulation before the *Sun*, but they would do it on the way down while the *Sun* would do it on the way up. The situation did not quite evolve as predicted but, on 9 May 1978, the *Sun* officially became Britain's most popular daily. Two months earlier the paper had revealed its first explicit change of political affiliation when, at the Ilford North by-election, it called on readers to 'deliver a resounding verdict on four years hard Labour by giving a thumping majority to the Tory candidate and showing this limping government the door'. The subsequent Conservative victory was proof, the *Sun* argued, 'that it is Margaret Thatcher, not Jim Callaghan, who speaks for Britain these days'.[101]

This political shift partly reflected the close attention that was paid to the tabloids, and particularly the *Sun*, by Conservative strategists who saw it as the key to reaching the C2 voters identified as central to electoral success. Tim Bell and Gordon Reece met quite frequently with Lamb prior to the 1979 election, usually in the evenings after the paper's first edition had gone to press. Lubricated by large quantities of champagne, they would 'discuss each other's plans and seek advice' and Lamb would be rewarded for his support with access to inside political information and gossip as well as praise for his allegedly unique insights into public opinion.[102] Thatcher was also a regular visitor to the paper's headquarters in Bouverie Street where she would flatter Lamb's vanity by encouraging him to expound his 'just marvellous' thoughts on the nation's problems, while she also met Murdoch on several occasions.[103] But the Conservatives were pushing at an open door. Lamb explained that the paper's political shift reflected a change in both his and Murdoch's views in the face of 'the ever-leftward drift of the Labour party' and the increasing power of the trade unions, particularly in Fleet Street. Murdoch also later recalled, 'We were all Labour-inclined when we started the *Sun* but I think we grew pretty disillusioned with the rest of the country.'[104] Most accounts point to the tycoon's 'slowly evolving' right-wing views throughout the 1970s. The first of many episodes which made him the international bogeyman of the left occurred in 1975 when his *Australian* newspaper was publicly burnt by striking journalists protesting about its anti-Labor election bias, and Murdoch became involved in bitter public exchanges with the Labor Prime Minister, Gough Whitlam.[105]

But initially in Britain it seems that the driving force was Lamb, who was given certain latitude by Murdoch in editing a paper he once dubbed 'Larry's baby'. His proprietor was more worried about alienating a pro-Labour readership and, as late as 1978, used to complain: 'Are you still pushing that bloody woman?'[106] Notwithstanding this caution, from September 1978 Lamb had a series of meetings with Thatcher at her Chelsea home, discussing 'the kind of campaign she planned . . . and which members of her team we should stick close to'. By now the *Sun*'s political line was further hardening as Callaghan's 'voyage to nowhere', in charge of an extremist Labour party, was contrasted with uncritical publicity for the alternative. In late December the paper came close to an advance election endorsement of the Tories on the basis of their commitment to 'tax cuts, swinging reductions in bureaucracy, and dramatic curbs in public spending'.[107] It was soon to announce its political conversion in suitably more sensational style.

'A winter's tale' 1979: political reorientation (3)

Running parallel with the *Sun*'s transformation was also a gradual intensification of the loyalties of both middle-market newspapers. As the 'Slush Fund' story illustrated, the *Mail* was anxious to topple a government that English viewed as 'disastrous – the sooner we get rid of it the better'.[108] The editor recalled how, from the outset, he had been a committed Thatcherite and a 'huge admirer' of Thatcher, who shared a similar lower-middle-class provincial background. In many ways the fortunes of Thatcherism and the *Mail* were intimately linked. Both appealed to a middle class seeking to reverse their apparent 'decline and fall' in the 1970s in the face of an over-mighty state and an increasingly militant and powerful Labour movement. This, Thatcher and the *Mail* agreed, could be achieved through a 'common sense' conservative social and political ethos under which the middle-class virtues of free-enterprise, hard work, independence and initiative would 'make Britain great again'. The *Mail* was the only paper to support Thatcher in the 1975 leadership contest and she came to regard English as one of her closest and most reliable Fleet Street friends, knighting him soon after the 1979 election for his loyal 'services to journalism'.[109]

While the *Express*'s coverage in 1974 had been more restrained, its partisanship was also intensifying. A similar political revulsion against the Labour government no doubt played a part, but also important were two significant changes to the paper in 1977. Following the *Mail*, the *Express* had shifted its format from broadsheet to tabloid and, shortly after, it was sold by Max Aitken to Trafalgar House, chaired by self-made businessman Victor Matthews. In his proprietorial direction if nothing else, Matthews proved a fine heir to the Beaverbrook tradition, as he declared, 'By and large editors will have complete editorial freedom as long as they agree with the policies I have laid down.' Politically Matthews was a committed Thatcherite, indeed so right-wing that he once had to be restrained from ordering a call for a nuclear first-strike on Moscow 'to rid the world of communism'. His company donated £40,000 to the Conservative campaign in 1979 and, shortly after receiving the customary knighthood a year later, Trafalgar was among the companies to resign from the CBI after its leader promised 'a bare-knuckle fight' against the government's monetarist economic policies.[110] Unsurprisingly Matthews considered Labour's principles to be 'completely offensive' – not least because, as he would frequently complain to his editor, the Labour government had personally cost him £7 million in taxes.[111]

The first major illustration of the political shift in the popular press came in January 1979 when the government's voluntary incomes policy with the unions collapsed into a series of damaging industrial disputes involving low-paid oil-tanker drivers, road haulage workers, lorry drivers and public service unions. Even the weather conspired against the government as snow and ice covered ungritted roads. A Labour Britain was presented as 'UNDER SIEGE' from 'the tyranny of the pickets', dominated by 'THE RULE OF FEAR' and reeking of 'sheer gangsterism'. There were 'MILES OF MISERY' and 'CHAOS ON ALL SIDES'.[112] This was the inevitable result of a government that had 'neither the will or the capacity to challenge the overweening power of the union barons', and was led by 'AN OSTRICH PRIME MINISTER' whose only response was to saunter off on his 'junket in the tropics' in sunny Guadeloupe (where he was attending a summit meeting).[113] The image of government inaction climaxed in Callaghan's disastrously over-complacent manner at the press conference on the return to Britain, as immortalised in the *Sun* headline: 'CRISIS? WHAT CRISIS?' The paraphrase was soon being reported as a direct quote, although it had actually first been used by the *Mail* three days before Callaghan had arrived back.[114] Ironically, Callaghan's unwise response partly reflected his 'irritation' and 'demoralisation' at a press he felt had ignored a highly successful meeting in favour of devoting all their efforts into photographing him sunbathing.[115] As the industrial conflict continued into February, the tabloids continued their attack on the 'complete absence of leadership or action', asking angrily: 'Is ANYONE running Britain?', 'WHAT THE BLOODY HELL'S GOING ON, JIM?'[116]

By far the most emotive aspect of the 'Winter of Discontent' was the strike of badly paid public service sector workers, a 'war against the sick' that handed the tabloids their most effective propaganda weapons. 'NO MERCY – if it means lives lost then that is how it must be', was the almost identical tabloid response to an alleged 'decision by ambulancemen not to man life and death services'.[117] It was, argued the *Mail*, 'NO MERCY TILL FURTHER NOTICE'. This prediction appeared to be barbarically confirmed at the start of February as the tabloids drew attention to the 'fabulously horrible' gravediggers' strike in Liverpool. The possibility of dead bodies in 'a state of putrefaction' was, to the *Mail*, the final act of outrage by 'vicious vindictive' strikers and a system so paralysed by union power that it even meant 'THEY WON'T EVEN LET US BURY OUR DEAD'.[118] Interestingly, despite the press's retrospective wallowing in rat-infested rubbish as a key horror of the 'Winter', this received little prominence and on the rare occasions it did, was presented as an almost frivolous and comic aside to the real crisis facing Britain.[119] These public sector disputes combined some of the most blatant incidents of union excesses with some equally shocking examples of press partisanship. In January, for example, it was reported that cancer patients in Birmingham had 'had to be sent home from a hospital blockaded by strike pickets'. Union denials as 'totally untrue' that they were preventing such treatment were given little weight in headlines such as 'LIFE OR DEATH PICKET', 'WHAT RIGHT HAVE THEY GOT TO PLAY GOD WITH MY LIFE?' and 'PICKETS HIT CANCER WARDS'. It was, the press reported, yet another example of 'premeditated trade union cruelty ... in cold blood and without a shred of justification'.[120] Union leaders subsequently claimed that, for two months, the unions were subjected to an unprecedented and 'unending series of attack and abuses'.[121] TGWU leader Ron Todd recalled one such incident:

> I remember one of the tabloids running a story about the T&G jeopardising a woman's life on a renal dialysis machine. I phoned the hospital, spoke to the woman responsible for RD and said, 'What's your problem?' She said 'nothing really – I'm most embarrassed. I told the reporter that if the strike went on for six to eight weeks and I ran out of basic salt we could be in trouble'. Hence the headline 'T&G Puts Woman's Life in Jeopardy'. Salt was despatched.[122]

In a similar incident, Liverpool's Chief Medical Officer, Duncan Bolton, was 'horrified' by the reporting of the gravediggers' strike. In response to persistent press questioning, he insisted there was no short-term threat to public health but eventually conceded that if the dispute continued for months then burials might have to take place at sea. The next day the *Sun* and the *Telegraph* were united in headlining how 'Bodies may be buried at sea'.[123] Nor were the effects of the strikes anywhere near that predicted. In a series of apocalyptic headlines, the *Sun* had predicted a 'Famine Threat' in which 'Food stores could empty in days' and '1000 old "may die each day"', while industrial paralysis meant that '3 million face the dole queue' as 'Food Factories Face Shutdown'. To prove beyond doubt that there 'really is a crisis', it even relegated the usual delights of 'Page 3' further inside the paper.[124] Notwithstanding this view of the gravity of the situation, the reality, as the *Economist* noted at the time, was rather less dramatic. Only 200,000 people had been laid off by the end of January and the supermarkets remained well-stocked. Ironically the largest number of days lost to industrial disputes in 1979 came, not in January or February, but in the engineering strike later in the year under the Thatcher government.[125] Despite the many allegations that people would die due to the closure of hospital wards, the only death it was possible to relate to industrial action was that of a picket who died under the wheels of a lorry. There were no reports of people *actually* going short of food, or, with one exception, any evidence of picket-line violence. This concerned a *Mail* story headlined 'M-way Pickets Attack Driver', which began:

> A lorry driver was hauled from his cab and beaten with wooden clubs yesterday by four mobile motorway pickets who had followed him for 100 miles. As they shouted 'scab bastard', he fought them off with an iron bar. Last night a 24-hour police guard was mounted on 26-year-old David Field's home.

The story was examined by Christopher Hitchens who, after checking with the victim, found there were eight major inaccuracies in this first paragraph alone. The victim was not chased down the motorway or 'hauled' from his cab, the words 'scab bastard' were not uttered, there was no '24-hour police guard' placed on his house. Most strikingly of all, as the detective in charge of the case stated to the *Mail* before publication, there was no evidence to suggest that the men were pickets, striking lorry drivers, or even members of any union. In short, Hitchens concluded, 'the only reliable and accurate' detail on the page 'was the date'. Despite a vigorous defence against Hitchens' own selectivity, the paper was forced to admit that it could not substantiate its key point about picket-inspired violence.[126]

All this suggests that the 'Winter' was experienced second-hand as a mediated crisis rather than more directly as a 'real' one. As one cabinet member, Bill Rodgers, argued, the 'dramatic' media images 'had much more impact on opinion than the public's own direct experience of the strike'. For most people, life continued largely unaffected.[127] Derek Jameson, then editor of the *Daily Express*, recalled, 'we pulled every dirty trick in the book; we made it look like it was general, universal and eternal when it was in reality scattered, here and there, and no great problem.' As Peter Jenkins later observed:

> The crisis . . . was nothing like as serious as the one which Heath had to deal with in 1974; then the power supplies of the nation were in jeopardy and workers had to be put on a three day week . . . The nation was brought nowhere to its knees; people were not even seriously inconvenienced. Outrageous acts there were but many fewer than legend would have it. Not many emergencies were turned away from hospitals . . . and only in parts of Lancashire were the dead unburied.[128]

None of this is to ignore the events of the Winter, the 'suicidal lunacy' of the labour movement, or indecisive leadership which saw Callaghan bluntly admit, 'I let the country down.'[129] The directly partisan motives of the right-wing press should also be contextualised within a dispute that merely intensified routine anti-union media coverage of 'the scapegoats of relative economic decline'.[130] The *Mirror* was at times indistinguishable from the Tory press in its partiality, so much so that in polls taken the following April, more people thought the paper to be biased towards the Conservatives.[131] Union complaints were aroused by a *Sunday Mirror* report of a 'Supersparks' who had earned £738 in one week. It eventually emerged that this was for five exceptional weeks' overtime on 24-hour call out, but the figure was widely used by a press anxious to undermine any public sympathy for the low-paid strikers.[132] While the 'Winter of Discontent' was primarily a self-inflicted wound that played a key role in the subsequent election defeat, press coverage ensured that the wound became fatal.[133] In the short term, the highly exaggerated portrayal of a 'crisis Britain' allowed for a very effective attack on a discredited, leaderless and union-controlled government unable even to guarantee the most basic needs of its citizens. More fundamentally, as each individual event was presented as part of a wider picture of 'Crisis Britain', the press played a key role in interpreting the strikes as symbolic of the utter bankruptcy of an ungovernable, union-dominated and over-extended state form.[134] The left-wing myth of the 1930s, which had played such a key role in inaugurating the centre-left post-war settlement, now gave way to a right-wing myth of the 1970s that both heralded the Thatcherite project and subsequently helped sustain it. Press coverage ensured that symbolically 1979 was seen as 'the moment when the Old Order crumbled'.[135] Even more importantly, it was to provide the most potent popular image by which social democracy throughout the 1980s (and after) could be so effectively condemned as offering 'no alternative'. It may well be 'a point in which the influence of the media, perhaps more than at any other point in post-war British history, was crucial'.[136] More narrowly, it dramatically illustrated the re-orientation of the press in a firmly anti-Labour direction.

This was made abundantly clear in the election coverage that followed in April/May 1979. Both middle-market newspapers fought extremely committed and similar campaigns that strongly emphasised the traditional charge that behind the reassuring, avuncular Labour leader lay 'THE RED FACE OF LABOUR', personified by Callaghan's 'likely successor' and 'messiah' figure, Tony Benn.[137] When Labour-supporting Jameson had been offered the position of *Express* editor, he had raised the 'problem' of his political views, to which Matthews had responded, 'You wouldn't be daft enough to turn it into a Labour rag.' Jameson agreed and recalled proudly that he 'never once let him down on politics'.[138] This was certainly true in the election as the *Express* abandoned its erstwhile moderation of 1974 in favour of a blatant partisanship demonstrated by one headline which simply said 'DON'T VOTE LABOUR'.[139] Coverage rivalled the *Mail* as it detected a 'RED PLOT TO CAPTURE LABOUR'.[140] Adding a further visual dimension, often to the front pages, were Cummings's now violently anti-Labour cartoons which, as Jameson recalled only half-jokingly, were 'slightly to the right of Attila the Hun'.[141] This propaganda climaxed dramatically as an eve-of-poll photograph showing a manic-looking Benn asked, 'Would you like this man to run Britain?' It was followed by a front page that urged, 'DON'T FORGET LAST WINTER' beside the symbolically loaded picture of rubbish piled up outside Labour's headquarters. This was, the editor subsequently noted, 'nothing more than a Tory election poster – so much so that it was later framed and put up on a wall at Conservative Central Office'.[142]

The *Mail's* coverage was similarly to give 'the impression of wanting a Tory victory even more desperately than Mrs Thatcher'. Its most original anti-union contribution was a front page 'BROADSIDE AT LABOUR' from former police commissioner Sir Robert Mark, who had suggested in an obscure magazine that the relationship between the unions and the Labour government was 'not unlike the way the Nazi party seized power'.[143] The economic devastation under Labour's 'swingeing new taxes' were outlined by the paper, which even had a government minister taking the unusual step of admitting on its front page, 'YOU'LL BE WORSE OFF WITH US!' This contrasted with the utopia conjured up by it and the *Express* in response to Thatcher's promise to 'CUT CUT AND CUT AGAIN' taxation and to

Table 3.1 Partisanship and circulation of the popular press in 1979 (millions)

Daily Express	2.46	Con
Daily Mail	1.97	Con
Daily Mirror	3.78	Lab
Sun	3.94	Con
Daily Star	0.88	Neutral

Source: Seymour-Ure, *The British Press and Broadcasting Since 1945.*

bring 'the end of union tyranny'. She was, they argued, 'THE WOMAN WHO CAN SAVE BRITAIN'.[144]

Such a stance provided an interesting contrast with the traditionally anti-Labour *Telegraph*. While editorials suggested a similar line as they found a Labour manifesto with 'a mandate for . . . a totalitarian socialist state', such sentiments failed to predominate in the paper's news columns, which demonstrated both scrupulous fairness and a notable lack of enthusiasm for the Conservatives.[145] One reason may have been because the absence of *The Times*, closed in a dispute over union opposition to the introduction of new technology, encouraged the other broadsheet papers to emulate its alleged function as a journal of record. There was also a certain coolness in relations between Thatcher and the paper's owner, Lord Hartwell, and particularly his wife, strong-willed socialite Pamela Berry, who felt she had not afforded them due respect and attention. Despite the close friendship that editor 'Dear Bill' Deedes shared with the Thatchers, he also considered that editors should 'keep a hygienic distance between rulers and themselves' and adopted an 'ungracious stand of independence' from what Pamela Berry disdainfully called 'that leader of yours'.[146] For whatever reasons, Labour may have been pleasantly surprised to find its manifesto reported factually under the pro-Labour headline 'LEFT YIELDS TO CALLAGHAN'. The paper played down the controversy surrounding Labour's imposition of an approved candidate on its troublesome left-wing Newham constituency party and a later campaign warning from Lord Denning about union power.

By contrast, these were luridly headlined in the *Express* and *Mail*.[147] But the prize for the most incredibly partisan election front page went to the *Mail* for its 'devastating exposure' of 'LABOUR'S DIRTY DOZEN . . . 12 lies designed to frighten voters into staying with a bankrupt Labour government'. The entire article, with nothing more than a slight re-juggling of the order, reproduced a Conservative Central Office handout of a speech by party chairman Angus Maude exposing 12 'Labour Lies'.[148] One of these claimed that the Conservatives would double the existing 8 per cent rate of VAT. Shadow Chancellor Geoffrey Howe later revealed there was 'no difficulty in denying' this because the intention, duly realised in the first budget, was only to raise the rate to 15 per cent. Omitting this detail, the Tories reproduced the *Mail*'s front page as an election poster providing an 'independent' rebuttal of Labour smears. It was only later that the story's anonymous author, respected journalist Anthony Bevins, recalled that, despite allegations of collusion with the party, it had simply originated in the initiative of an eager, young journalist producing the anti-Labour copy required by his seniors.[149]

Similar professionalism was no doubt in existence at the *Mirror*, even if Michael Molloy, the paper's editor from 1975, had a particularly close working relationship with Callaghan and served on his campaign committee.[150] After Cudlipp's retirement in 1973, senior executives had decided to make the paper rather more overtly loyal to Labour and it did its utmost for the cause. Profiles of 'MAGGIE'S WILD AND BITTER BRITAIN' contrasted with 'JIM'S JOBS BOOST', while the paper proved as guilty in playing down the strength of the Labour left as its opponents were in magnifying it.[151] Showing the highly traditional politics typical of the sharp leader-writing skills of Joe Haines, who had joined the paper in 1977, it juxtaposed the choice between continuing to build 'a fair and decent society' begun in 1945 or a 'return to a society of privilege and inequality' which predated it. Its polling-day edition rekindled on old *Mirror* slogan to suggest that it was 'EITHER BACK TO THE TORIES OR FORWARD WITH THE PEOPLE'.[152]

The above coverage highlights the first major change in press partisanship since 1974, an intensification of the partisanship of the *Mail* and *Express* to now match that in the *Mirror*. According to one content analysis, 61 per cent and 71 per cent of *Mail* and *Express* coverage was biased, with two-thirds of this being negatively anti-Labour, a pattern that was reproduced within the three-quarters of *Mirror* coverage judged to be slanted. Such negative campaigning also demonstrated a shift in the *nature* of partisanship as compared to earlier years, when it had tended to be positive in favour of the party supported.[153] But perhaps even more significant was the second change from 1974, that of the *Sun*'s position, which was essentially similar in devoting 72 per cent of its political coverage to anti-Labour or pro-Conservative material and giving two-thirds predominance to the former. The paper made its support for Thatcher clear from the outset, although it did not provide her with the best of starts. Labour, behind in the polls but with a far more popular leader, accepted an invitation for a televised debate between the leaders and leaked the news to the *Mirror*, which dutifully splashed the story.[154] But Conservative strategists were not keen to make this debate the central election issue and Thatcher declined the offer just as Lamb had suggested she would be 'foolish beyond belief' to do so in a front page leader which delighted Labour as much as it depressed the Conservatives.[155]

With this exception, however, the *Sun*'s coverage was similar to that of its new political allies in Fleet Street in closely following Conservative strategy with profiles of 'Labour's wild men' led by the ever-scheming Benn.[156] Lamb also headlined, for the first time and with no apologies to Shakespeare, the phrase 'Winter of Discontent', over a centre-page spread reminding readers – 'Lest we forget' – of those 'long cold months of industrial chaos that brought Britain to its knees'.[157] This public service was also complemented by private help. Lamb was an important influence on Bell in the long hours they spent discussing Saatchi and Saatchi's advertising strategy, advised Thatcher about popular communication and even wrote some of her election speeches. His paper similarly waxed lyrical in support of 'Maggie's master plan to make Britain great again' and featured a series of articles by former Labour figures, including George Brown and the zealous convert Paul Johnson, explaining 'How Labour left me'.[158] The culmination of the *Sun*'s position as 'Mrs Thatcher's missionary outpost to the working-class voter' came in a mammoth 1,700-word two-page polling day editorial. This called on readers to 'VOTE TORY THIS TIME' and, like the paper's entire cover-age, specifically sought to address its large number of traditional Labour supporters. The wording of its opening, in clumsy non-tabloid prose such as 'hitherto' and 'so to do', gave the impression of 'a newspaper nervously clear-ing its throat'. This was certainly true of Murdoch, who had 'significant reservations' about the leader and substituted 'THIS TIME' for Lamb's pref-erence of 'TODAY', so as to suggest less of a long-term Tory commitment. Nevertheless, the leader remained 'totally unequivocal' in presenting the choice for 'a nation in crisis' as 'between freedom and shackles', as it urged, 'Vote Tory to Stop the Rot. There may not be another chance.'[159]

Quite what influence this had is, as always, difficult to assess. The length of the paper's final editorial had caused some amusement among its journal-ists who had often been treated to Lamb's boast of his genius in brevity. There were jokes about readers' lips wearing out as they struggled through the dense text which completely covered page two. Polling evidence sug-gested many paid little attention. 52 per cent of *Sun* readers voted Labour in 1979, a level of support that had remained virtually constant since 1976, despite the paper's political shift. One-third of *Sun* readers actually thought the paper still supported Labour, with only the same number correctly iden-tifying its affiliations. This did, however, represent something of a shift from two years previously when nearly half thought the paper was pro-Labour and just 7 per cent considered it Conservative supporting.[160] This offers clear evidence of the very substantial limits to the *Sun*'s political influence and the lukewarm nature of its readers' embrace of Thatcherism, which in any case was visible only in muted form at the time.

At the same time, readership ignorance about the paper's affiliations may have given it opportunities for influence denied to rivals, especially as the *Sun* was seen as impartial by more of the electorate than any other popular newspaper. 45 per cent of its readers thought the paper was unbiased, com-pared with one-fifth to one-third of readers of the other tabloids.[161] Nor should it be assumed that television had rendered newspapers politically impotent, even if it did give readers a more impartial and trustworthy alternative. One election study found that newspapers remained a key 'rival for television', with substantial majorities of readers spending at least 10–30 minutes reading election coverage. Nearly three-quarters of *Mail* and *Express* readers and 60 per cent of *Sun* and *Mirror* readers rated their paper's political coverage as useful, not far below the 75 per cent rating for television. Other research also demonstrated that twice as many people read British news-papers than watched television news, each consuming roughly twice as much material as that offered by broadcasters in the average day.[162]

More specifically, the *Sun* was read more widely than any other paper among the skilled and unskilled workers who swung substantially to the Tories, by a massive 21 per cent among the 18–24-year-old males who predominated amongst the paper's readership. Never one for modesty, false or otherwise, Lamb considered it 'distinctly possible' that the appeal to a 13 million audience swayed enough votes to have a 'critical, if not decisive' influence on the result. Thatcher 'certainly . . . thought so' and thanked her 'Larry' in 'a charming letter' and then a knighthood, while Bell also rated the paper as 'one of the biggest influences' in 1979.[163] And the evidence does not completely disprove these claims. For, while support for Labour remained constant at around 50 per cent, the Conservatives increased their support among *Sun* readers from 27 per cent in November 1978 to 38 per cent by April 1979. This tentatively suggests that, while the paper made few inroads against its traditional supporters, it may have had rather more effect on the undecided and politically apathetic, a point supported by later studies.[164]

A 'sea-change' in press coverage

A few months before his general election defeat, Callaghan had told press proprietors and editors assembled for a 'What the Papers Say' awards dinner:

> We don't grumble that your leader writers write Conservative editorials – they have the privilege of the freedom of their columns. But we do complain if Fleet Street is going to allow editorial policies to colour both its presentation of its news and its selection of what it gives prominence to.[165]

Despite undoubted periods of strong anti-Labour coverage, the press had remained collectively well balanced, as well as individually more muted in partisanship, for much of the post-1951 period. Viewed from the perspective of 1979, Labour may well have wondered what they previously had to complain about. To judge by both of Callaghan's criteria, partisanship was more skewed against Labour by the beginning of 1979 than at any time since before the war. Between 1945–1951 a strongly partisan press had largely cancelled each other out but now, as the Royal Commission Minority Report had anticipated, there was 'no balance of political irresponsibility'.[166] The *Sun*'s political conversion, combined with an intensified hostility from the *Mail* and *Express*, meant that 70 per cent of newspapers now actively and strongly opposed Labour and unequivocally, if with lesser emphasis, endorsed the Conservatives. Only the *Mirror* offered an alternative, equally partisan approach. The extent of the electoral and political revolution towards the Conservatives in 1979 has perhaps been exaggerated. But a more decisive 'sea-change' against Labour, in Callaghan's famous words, had undoubtedly taken place in the position of the popular press.[167] It was to both persist and intensify over the next 12 years.

4 A 'Nightmare on Kinnock Street'

Labour and the Tory tabloids 1979–1992

On 9 April 1992, the *Sun* rounded off a comprehensive electoral assault on Labour by placing the Labour leader's head in a lightbulb beside the words, 'If Kinnock wins today will the last person to leave Britain please turn out the lights.'[1] This, and the fierce debate such coverage generated after the Conservative victory, marked a symbolic climax to a period between 1979–1992 when Labour faced the sustained opposition of a popular press more hostile than at any time in the post-war period. This chapter begins by exploring this briefly in relation to 1979–1987, before going on to assess in more detail press behaviour and its impact on the 1992 election.

A 'loony left': from Foot to Kinnock 1979–1987

After 1979, the press quickly emerged as key supporters of the Thatcherite experiment in the face of severe divisions within the Conservative government and cabinet.[2] Simultaneously, press hostility to Labour hardened considerably with the party's leftward shift and the outbreak of a bitter, internal civil war. The process culminated spectacularly as Labour's electoral humiliation in the 1983 election was accompanied by the worst press the party had received for over 50 years. The most astonishingly partisan coverage came from the *Daily Mail* where David English remained firmly in control. The paper's most innovative newspaper contribution to the Conservative campaign was an exclusive front page that firmly predicted '35,000 JOBS LOST IF FOOT WINS'. A Nissan 'leading official' told how the Japanese car firm was to 'scrap plans for a £50 million British plant' if a Labour party committed to leaving the Common Market won the election. What one former editor described as the 'most misleading headline of the campaign' was quickly picked up by broadcast news. It was followed by a further front page prominently quoting the less than impartial source of Industry Secretary Patrick Jenkin to support its story, but burying on page two Nissan's more authoritative denial that a Labour government 'would not substantially affect' their proposals.[3] Labour complained to the Press Council, which, unusually quickly, ruled that the story was not a fabrication but was 'likely to mislead readers' as it 'presented conjecture as fact and omitted the vital distinction between a Labour victory and withdrawal from the EEC'. It also found that 'insufficient prominence' had been given to the car manufacturer's statement the following day. The paper buried this ruling on an inside page under the headline, 'Nissan: *Daily Mail* did not make it up', after giving further front page coverage to a 'grim warning' from Thatcher of 'THIS THREAT TO JOBS'.[4]

Responding to left-wing attacks against right-wing 'propaganda sheets more interested in selecting news than in reporting it', the *Mail*'s hired polemicist Paul Johnson was to insist that policy was determined democratically 'by editors and the general consensus of senior staff, themselves influenced by rank-and-file journalistic opinion'.[5] Such an analysis was soon found lacking on his own paper where a union meeting of at least 60 *Mail* journalists voted by 6–1 in favour of a motion condemning their election coverage as 'too one-sided in favour of the Conservative party'. It requested that 'the editor give more space and a fair degree of prominence to unbiased factual reports of the positive proposals made by other political parties'. The rebellion was unprecedented in Fleet Street and stemmed from professional rather than political objections even among Conservative-supporting journalists to the paper's coverage. But it had no effect on the paper's stance – although English's retort that it was 'unacceptable' for anyone to interfere with his control must, as Tom Baistow observed, have been a rather nasty shock to his proprietor.[6]

Only slightly less partisanship was demonstrated by the *Daily Express*, edited now by another Tory knight, Larry Lamb, which announced it stood 'four-square and 100 per cent behind Mrs Thatcher'.[7] The most notable illustration of this came in the paper's efforts to discredit the 'People March For Jobs' from Glasgow to London, organised by the TUC to highlight the high unemployment levels under the Thatcher government. Under the headline, 'Work Galore But The Job Marchers Just Pass By', the paper detailed how 'Hundreds of jobs were yesterday offered to 74 demonstrators marching on London to protest about unemployment. But the marchers turned down every one of the openings offered by the job centre manager.' But the jobs had not been 'offered' in this way at all, but by an *Express* reporter who approached the marchers in what the Press Council condemned as 'a serious lapse from acceptable journalistic standards' in an 'inaccurate' and 'misleading' story. It also ruled that an offer of a brief, censored letter of reply to the protesting organisers 'did not fully correct this or give an adequate right of reply'.[8]

More restrained was the *Express*'s sister paper and Fleet Street newcomer, the *Daily Star*. Launched in November 1978 as a Manchester downmarket tabloid – editorial director Derek Jameson was quoted as saying it would be 'all tits, bums, QPR and roll your own fags' – it quickly built up a circulation of nearly a million. For commercial reasons if nothing else, Jameson and editor Peter Grimsditch wanted to inject a pro-Labour subtext amidst the supply of naked flesh.[9] Matthews, who once declared that he would not have the new paper in his house, was also less keen on its political stance, so the paper began taking a broadly centre-left line on social issues but never explicitly endorsed the party editorially.[10] In 1979, the *Star*'s election coverage was apolitical and neutral in that order. The paper told readers that it would be 'presumptuous' to insult their intelligence by telling them how to vote, but seemed to think they would be more insulted if the election was covered at all as it allocated just a quarter of the front page space given by the *Mirror* and *Sun* to the campaign.[11]

The *Star*'s uncertain political direction initially continued after 1979. But after the installation of new editor, Lloyd Turner, in November 1980, it seemed for a time to be the nearest thing to a loyal press supporter Labour could count on. Turner and managing director Jocelyn Stevens also believed that its political stance should be left of centre and now managed to persuade a reluctant Matthews to this effect. The *Star* was the only national newspaper to support Michael Foot in the Labour leadership election as a man who could provide the 'crusading spirit' and 'flaming passion' for 'a non-stop attack on the miseries of Thatcher's Britain'.[12] The paper's subsequent high-profile campaigns on behalf of the unemployed and pensioners brought praise from Labour leaders, which was reciprocated when it called for a Labour vote in the May 1981 local elections.[13] Less impressed was the Prime Minister. She complained to Matthews, who dutifully ordered that the paper 'must not attack Mrs Thatcher' despite Stevens protesting that this entailed 'a fundamental change of policy'.[14] In the 1983 election, the *Star* provided the most balanced, if conservative-tinged, tabloid coverage before finally declaring that it could not support a left-dominated Labour party in a decision which brought more complaints than support from the paper's predominantly left-of-centre readers.[15]

Far less equivocal was the *Sun*, where Larry Lamb had been succeeded in late 1981 by a young, brash and brilliant sub-editor Kelvin MacKenzie. He crudely terrorised and entertained his staff as he fashioned a paper that was to prove to be more outrageous, opinionated and irreverent than anything ever produced in Britain. Whereas Lamb's *Sun* was cheeky and had an element of restraint and balance, MacKenzie's paper, like its editor, was downright offensive at times in politics as in much else. MacKenzie's strategy to 'shock and amaze on every page' blurred the already murky distinctions between news, views and entertainment to an extent greater than ever before. This was demonstrated most famously by its jingoistic coverage in the Falklands war, satirised by one *Private Eye* spoof front page as 'Kill an Argie, and Win a Metro'.[16] In domestic affairs, the *Sun* led the way in a vicious press smear campaign against the left-wing gay rights activist 'Red Pete' Tatchell, which culminated in Labour's loses of its safe Bermondsey seat in a bitter by-election of February 1983.[17] While its subsequent election coverage was slightly more muted, it was never less than wholly partisan.[18]

Given the Labour party's shift to the left after 1979, it was predictable that the tabloids would pay particular attention to the 'sinister Marxist forces' apparently now dominating the party and ensuring that Labour's 'doctrinaire socialism' was virtually indistinguishable from Communist party policies.[19] As in 1979, the favourite leader of the red revolution was the 'dedicated ruthless' Tony Benn who remained 'bent on the destruction of Britain as we know it'.[20] The *Express* earned top marks from Tory Central Office with a 'Spot the Trots' feature of 70 'extremist' Labour candidates. Listed alongside Neil Kinnock and Robin Cook was left-wing MP Robert Hughes, described as a member of three Communist 'front' organisations.[21] Hughes denied any involvement with these bodies, two of which he had never heard of. But it took eight months for the Press Council to condemn 'a politically malicious and unjustified slur on Mr Hughes which should have been withdrawn'. It also found the paper guilty of having 'failed to either substantiate or withdraw its allegation that most of the 70 Labour candidates it named were "cold doctrinaire advocates of the all-powerful state"'.[22]

The biggest illustration of tabloid partisanship in 1983 came in their attitudes to political leadership.[23] This was captured most tellingly by one memo apparently from the *Sun* and *Express* to freelance reporters at a rally the Labour leader was visiting. There were, it stated, to be 'no pictures of Foot unless falling over, shot or talking to militants'.[24] Foot had long been derided by the tabloids for all manner of political and personal shortcomings, the most famous example of the latter being the alleged disrespect he had shown in attending the 1981 Remembrance Sunday service at the Cenotaph in what was wrongly mythologised as a donkey jacket.[25] In the election, the *Sun* proved perhaps most contemptuous of a Labour leader who was 'as dead as a stuffed dodo', as it asked, 'DO YOU SERIOUSLY WANT THIS OLD MAN TO RUN BRITAIN?' The *Mail* was rather more representative of the general tabloid attack on a 'sincere and sometimes confused idealist' who had already proved a 'lamentable leader'.[26] In the *Express*, meanwhile, the paper's two columnists appeared locked in a sharply escalating rhetorical war. Jean Rook's description of Foot as 'pathetic, outdated and washed up' was rather shaded by George Gale's polemic against a man who was 'half socialist . . . half ranter, half raver, half baked and half gone'.[27] On the other side, his fawning for Thatcher as 'the sun around which all politicians orbit' was faint praise compared with Rook's amazing journey 'up, up and away with superwoman . . . an astonishing woman bird. A plane in itself.'[28] Such a message climaxed in the final endorsements as the three Tory tabloids all agreed that 'in the end it all comes down to her', 'a lady with more fire and conviction than a whole parliament'. 'NOW IS THE HOUR', they eulogised, 'MAGGIE IS THE MAN'.[29]

The only popular newspaper dissenting from this verdict remained the *Mirror*. The emergence of the SDP in 1981 had placed its affiliations in some doubt, a point demonstrated when Lord Cudlipp announced his defection to the new party because of Labour's growing 'militancy'. Some initial equivocation saw a vote of the paper's executives only narrowly decide to continue its support for Labour, despite the fact that its centre-left tradition had more in common with the politics of the SDP. But thereafter the *Mirror* stayed solidly loyal – at least until the readers said otherwise – and demonstrated this in strongly anti-Tory election coverage which involved 'some distortion of conventional news values' in its refusal to address Labour's weaknesses.[30] Press coverage in general showed a marked polarisation in 1983, with the quality newspapers demonstrating a greater level of sophistication and detailed analysis than ever before.[31] By contrast the tabloids treated their readers to a diet of unadulterated propaganda throughout the news columns which frequently 'amounted to a rejection of any professional standards of journalism'.[32]

The virulence of this attack did reflect the underlying reality, albeit one highly exaggerated in the tabloid hall of mirrors. Labour had entered the campaign after a three-year period in which it had, as Denis Healey noted, 'acquired a highly unfavourable public image based on disunity, extremism and crankiness and a general unfitness to govern'. It was also led by a leader who was seen as the least plausible candidate for prime minister for 50 years and featured a manifesto that one Labour MP complained was 'not fit to be given that name'.[33] To make matters worse, Labour lost the election 'as no party has ever lost a campaign before' dropping eight percentage points in four weeks to produce the worst result in its history.[34] It was symbolised by Foot's habit of waving his stick on his morning walk 'like an escaped loony', as one sympathetic newspaper despaired.[35] Aside from this, a series of spectacular own-goals made one suspect the presence of a Saatchi and Saatchi fifth column in Walworth Road. Callaghan's 'Rocket' attack on Labour's defence policy was quickly upstaged by his predecessor's decision to explain to the *Daily Mail* 'WHERE MY PARTY HAS GONE WRONG' in an interview a furious Foot justly felt could have been approved word for word by the editor.[36] Party chairman Jim Mortimer then falsely suggested that the campaign committee had felt it necessary to issue 'an extraordinary vote of confidence' in Foot. The campaign climaxed as intemperate comments from Healey and Kinnock about the Falklands provoked fierce press condemnation and only drew attention to the Conservative party's strongest issue. If Foot really was 'the man who saved the Labour party', as his biographer maintains, then he had a funny way of doing it.[37]

These shortcomings also reflected inept campaign management that seemed positively hostile to sullying its purity through contact with the media, a shortcoming all the more notable given their opponent's effective communications strategy. As a Labour press secretary recalled, 'If a miracle had happened and Fleet Street had suddenly come clamouring to Walworth Road for pro-Labour material, they would have been sent away with a copy of the manifesto each.'[38] But perhaps the greatest illustration of partisanship in the election was that, faced with Labour's manifest weaknesses, and where a Conservative triumph was never in any doubt, the tabloids still found it necessary to distort their material.

Such coverage also set the tone for Neil Kinnock's treatment throughout his eight-and-a-half years as leader. Even before his election in October

1983, his allies were detecting newspaper 'attempts ... to vilify Neil'. Kinnock found himself dismissed as 'Foot Mark 2' and the party was consigned 'to the dustbin' of history under a man who lacked the necessary weight, experience or depth.[39] Later internal analyses suggested that a 'persistent and unyielding ... press barrage of criticism and questioning' had continued throughout Kinnock's first two years as leader. But it was from autumn 1986 that an 'unremitting campaign of vilification' really began in the right-wing tabloids.[40] In late December, a *Daily Mail* smear on 'Glenys the Menace' led the leadership to conclude that there was no possibility of building cordial relations with most of the press. It left Kinnock suggesting that 'even veterans say they can't remember such consistent distortion and nastiness'.[41]

Throughout 1986 the tabloids had conducted a sustained attack against the 'loony-left' equal opportunity policies pursued by London Labour councils. They reported how, for example, black dustbin liners and the rhyme 'Baa Baa Black Sheep' had been banned as racist, alongside sexist words such as 'manhole'. Academic analysis concluded that not one of these or other similar stories were true and they had served 'to distort public perceptions of London councils'.[42] Whatever their accuracy, such attacks also linked up with the theme of socialist extravagance to fund such minority causes, and singled out for particular criticism was Ealing Labour council where Kinnock was a resident rate-payer. His qualified endorsement of a rate rise of over 60 per cent in March 1987 was offered as proof of Labour's support for costly, extremist policies. O, as one *Sun* headline succinctly put it, 'Kinnock admits – I back loonies.'[43] By this time the more general theme of extremism was rearing its head, with the *Sun* arousing Labour's protests for a highly imaginative 'Horrific 100 Days Under Kinnock' – with Tony Benn in charge of Britain's defence, economic crisis, street riots and mass immigration.[44]

This theme also merged seamlessly into national politics in the Greenwich by-election of February 1987. During this, one tabloid myth became self-fulfilling after a nursery teacher banned a five-year-old handicapped child for singing 'Baa Baa Black Sheep' – after reading in the tabloids that this was council policy.[45] Left-wing Labour candidate Dierdrie Wood, chosen by her local party despite leadership opposition, had privately promised Kinnock, 'I won't drop you in it', to which he had responded, 'It's not you it's those bastards out there', referring to the Tory press.[46] The 'bastards' duly lived up to their reputation as 'Dreadful Dierdrie' faced a sustained press vilification of her political and personal life. Labour's efforts to present Wood as 'a hard working local woman with sensible policies' were countered immediately after her selection by a *Daily Mail* centre-spread reporting how she was living comfortably with a militant shop steward who was not the father of her children. The *News of the World* followed this with a series of widely-condemned personal attacks that revealed that the alcoholic father of the 'hard left feminist, anti-racist and gay-rights supporter' had died alone in a hostel. While this provoked sympathy, a more credible and damaging image came in the press portrayal of Wood as an IRA sympathiser who wanted to twin London schools with PLO camps and had lived in a council house for two years while owning her own home. As the Labour leadership later noted, the damaging 'loony left' image produced a huge swing in support to the SDP as Labour disastrously lost a seat that it had held since 1945.[47]

Kinnock's personal image was hardly much better, and singled out for concerted attack were a series of foreign visits made by the leadership. 'Kinnock in Blunderland', announced coverage of his first trip to Washington in February 1984 as his 'bid to be an international statesman ended in disaster', in a story that was to be re-told on many more 'trips of shame' abroad.[48] One illustration of the worsening press relations came when Kinnock returned to America at the end of 1986 to explain the party's unilateral defence policy. The Labour leader's suspicion that the accompanying journalists were out to trip him up rather than looking for genuine stories was confirmed by one editor who told his reporter that it was time to 'do some knocking'.[49] The tensions only deepened during the visit, as the tabloids made much of a series of perceived snubs for Kinnock's 'Mission Impossible' on 'a journey that would inevitably end in rebuff and humiliation'.[50] The American PR company that handled the visit was clearly both unprepared and shocked by what it called 'the difficulty of the British press' whose 'attitude was to find fault and print it' regardless.[51]

This was only a prelude to a much more controversial and disastrous visit to America in late March 1987. As the Labour high-command recognised, the Tories were preparing to use it for a pre-election attack on Labour's unilateral defence policy which would be 'backed by the US administration . . . and British press' and contrasted with 'extremely favourable' coverage of Thatcher's 'triumph of world statesmanship' on a parallel visit to Moscow. Given this, some advisers wanted to postpone the visit and avoid 'the press presenting another Kinnock trip as a disaster'.[52] When it went ahead, a tale of the expected was duly told by a press with 'a clear agenda' as they searched for 'snubs, any snubs'.[53] Kinnock's meeting with Reagan was preceded by an intense front page onslaught from the *Mail* on the 'major political gaffes' allegedly conveyed by the Labour leader's expressed disagreement with American foreign policy. Other tabloids headlines predicting, 'Reagan Gives Kinnock a 20-Minute Brush Off' were all the more intriguing given the controversy that followed.[54]

Both Kinnock and Healey felt that their meeting with the American President had been a success and told what they detected to be a disappointed press corps as much.[55] However an alternative version was quickly provided by Reagan's press secretary Marlin Fitzwater – who had not been present at the meeting. This suggested that Kinnock had been humiliatingly rebuked for a policy that would 'undercut' the West's negotiating position and ignored the lessons of appeasement. Despite Labour's forceful public and private protests over the 'significant inaccuracies' of this briefing, the Americans, in Kinnock's words, had 'said just enough to allow the British press to get the row story they had come for'.[56] With at least one tabloid reporter stating that he would not be filing any Labour's denials, the tabloids told a clear story of how an 'Angry Reagan Flays Kinnock' as he was warned, 'Your Policies are Putting Europe At Risk'.[57]

As Labour wrote in protest to the US administration, the impression conveyed by the British press was one of 'total conflict and bad feeling', along with the 'very damaging charge' that Kinnock 'had been deliberately misleading' in his press briefing. While this approach contrasted with American media coverage, where the incident 'was not blown out of all proportion', this offered little consolation as the dejected party returned to Britain.[58] *Daily Mirror* reporter Alastair Campbell, disgusted by the behaviour of his colleagues, broke ranks to denounce 'the US plot to stitch Kinnock ... hatched with the help of a cynical, cowardly and corrupt Tory press'. Meanwhile a bitter Labour leader refused to talk to the assembled journalists on the flight home, stating, 'If I thought for one minute they were interested in the truth I would. But they're not', and anticipated the 'Kinnock whingeing' headlines if he did.[59] All this stood in marked contrast to the 'MAGGIE MANIA' conveyed in press coverage of 'SUPERMAG' in the Soviet Union as she was 'mobbed in Moscow'. In contrast to Kinnock's treatment, the tabloids failed to report the scene in a monastery, described by one journalist as 'unseemly', when Thatcher found that she had no money and had to borrow some from an aide to ensure that she lit her much publicised 'FLAME FOR FREEDOM'.[60]

As this partisanship only intensified as the 1987 election approached, press secretary Patricia Hewitt was among others considering abandoning completely the daily press conferences as 'they allow the newspaper journalists to set the agenda ... and we know where they stand'.[61] In the campaign, all three of the Tory tabloids devoted a greater proportion of their election material to attacking Labour than even under Foot. The *Sun*, which in 1983 had roughly balanced its praise for the Conservatives with its attacks on Labour, now favoured attack over defence by a margin of over 3:1.[62] In March, a further character assassination from the *Sun* as 'Twisted, Evil, Treacherous' had led Benn to observe how it had been some time since he had suffered 'that degree of abuse'.[63] By this time, however, he had been replaced as the tabloid leader of the Opposition by 'Red Ken' Livingstone, previously the target of a concerted, if not particularly successful, press campaign as leader of the GLC between 1981–1986.[64]

The *Express*, in particular, 'took extremism to extremes' with a front page – 'OUR CONSPIRACY BY RED KEN' – that predicted an imminent left-wing 'takeover' of the party. Furious denials generated another front page – 'NEIL DENIES TRUTH ABOUT LEFT PLOT'.[65] The *Mail* similarly revealed 'THE ICEBERG MANIFESTO', a headline courtesy of a Thatcher soundbite. Kinnock's dismissal of 'a fictitious nightmare' was strengthened by the fact that none of 'the chilling list of demands' from the left which the report featured, such as withdrawal from Europe, punitive wealth taxes and abolition of the monarchy, was Labour policy.[66] The *Sun* rounded off its similar election coverage with a centre page explaining 'WHY RED KEN IS THE REAL LEADER OF THE LABOUR PARTY' to any readers baffled by the attention commanded by a first-time Labour candidate.[67]

In the tabloid world, rule by 'Red Ken' was only marginally preferable to the 'political nightmare' which would ensue if the 'inexperienced, ignorant' Kinnock was entrusted with the nation's leadership. To support this, the *Mail* even ingeniously contrived to turn the kidnapping and beating of a British diplomat in Iran into an attack on Kinnock's alleged temperamental inability to deal with such situations.[68] All this offered a contrast with Thatcher, 'the best prime minister since the war'. The extremes, although less visible than in 1983, were again best captured by Jean Rook, as she continued her love affair with 'Mega Maggie – the kind of neighbour who, if the roof fell in would hold up the ceiling with one hand while she dialled emergency with the other.' On the other hand, she speculated whether Kinnock would 'turn out to be one of those cheap red roses you find half-dead next morning, with a shrivelled little head on a bared and bent-over neck', in a vicious profile which unsurprisingly brought a successful libel action from its subject.[69]

Throughout these years, the bulk of the press, while not uncritical of the government, could be relied upon to faithfully set and follow a political agenda highly favourable to the Conservatives (as the Robert Maxwell-owned *Daily Mirror*, bought by Maxwell in 1984, did to less effect for Labour). As a key Labour strategy review noted, 'A main medium of communications for key target groups appears to be tabloid newspapers, dominated by the Conservatives.' Labour's campaign manager in 1987, Brian Gould, argued that his opposite number, Norman Tebbit, had the key advantage that he 'could pick up the phone whenever he wanted and launch a story, however unfounded, on the front page of half the nation's newspapers'.[70] Two 'gaffes' by the respective leaders in the 1987 election provide at least some illustration of this. Labour had dominated the early campaign agenda while the lacklustre Tory opening had produced complaints from their press allies and a strategy meeting at the end of the first week responded by shifting towards a more negative campaign.[71] A day later, an opportunity to attack Kinnock came when he answered a hypothetical question on television's 'Breakfast with Frost' by suggesting that the Soviets would never invade Britain because they would find any occupation untenable. His response was unwise and unclear, but any slip was not immediately obvious. As one television journalist observed, 'We didn't think it was a story.' Nevertheless Labour's opponents seized the initiative with strongly worded attacks, while privately Tory officials worked hard on sympathetic newspapers. The following days' headlines brought ample reward in their savaging of 'DAD'S ARMY KINNOCK', 'THE MAN WITH THE

WHITE FLAG'. A full five days later the attack on 'WHEN THE RED ROSE TURNS YELLOW' was still *Sun* front page news.[72] Labour's weakest issue of defence dominated the news agenda for a week as its salience rose dramatically from 20 per cent to 60 per cent, while Kinnock's image as a man who would stand up to the USSR declined by twice as much among the electorate if they read a right-wing paper.[73]

Almost the inverse service was provided on the issue of the health service, on which the Conservatives were as vulnerable as their opponents on defence. A carefully planned Labour press conference personalised the question of hospital waiting lists around the case of a child who had been waiting 15 months for a heart operation.[74] At the subsequent Conservative conference, Thatcher was diverted from her campaign agenda to comment, with brutal insensitivity, that she used private healthcare so she could go to hospital 'on the day, at the time and with the doctor I choose'. A delighted Labour immediately set about publicising the quote and television news and the *Mirror* led with the story. As one Conservative campaign insider later noted, the 'struggle to dominate the media with the "next" issue looked like slipping from the grasp of the Tories'.[75]

The Tory tabloids, however, remained impervious to such agenda-setting. They ignored the offending quote and inverted the story to illustrate either Thatcherite compassion – 'Mrs T To Aid Heart Boy' – and/or Labour's heartlessness as 'Kinnock puts sick heart boy in front line of voters fight'. Perhaps most generous was the *Telegraph*'s headline spin, 'Thatcher: I don't jump NHS queues.'[76] A concerted counter-attack also followed with a series of revelations, based on the tried and tested theme of socialist hypocrisy, of the alleged fondness of Labour politicians for private healthcare treatment.[77] Most spectacularly, the *Sun* rehashed an old story of how Denis Healey's wife had had a private hip operation two years earlier. Although Healey denounced it as 'full of lies', it set and legitimised the wider broadcasting agenda and he became involved in a furious breakfast television confrontation with presenter Anne Diamond when she raised the subject after assurances that it would not be mentioned. This in turn produced further tabloid attacks on the 'foul language and boorish behaviour' of 'HEALEY THE HYPOCRITE' in an incident that one post-election verdict from *Mirror* executives considered had done 'enormous damage'.[78] These two respective stories provide a clear demonstration of the advantage the press gave to the Conservatives in the 'competition between rival agenda-setting' which, as Mandelson and Hewitt noted, lay 'at the heart of election campaigning'. Indeed, their contrasting courses are all the more notable given that polls demonstrated that, while defence was the most prominent media issue, only 7 per cent of the electorate rated it as a subject that 'should be discussed' and an overwhelming majority favoured a focus on social and economic issues.[79]

Was it the press wot won it? The 1992 general election

In some respects the 1987 election marked the peak of sustained press hostility towards Labour. Despite the post-election controversy in 1992, for much of the campaign the Labour high command were expressing surprise at the 'relatively muted' nature of tabloid attacks and their ease in combating them.[80] Former Fleet Street editors were among those suggesting that the tabloids were merely going through the motions. This was variously attributed to a loosening of the close press–party connections of the Thatcher years, the ineptitude of the Tory campaign alongside their apparent electoral unpopularity, and the way their opponent's electioneering had been so tightly controlled that the press had found it difficult to get fresh knocking copy.[81] Yet in other respects press partisanship showed little change from 1987.[82]

Disaffected Thatcherites later joined Labour critics by suggesting that the tabloids fought a better campaign against Labour than their party. In the view of Lord McAlpine, former Tory party chairman, they 'exposed, ridiculed and humiliated . . . doing each day in their pages the job that the politicians failed to do from their bright new platforms'.[83] One example was when the failure of the Conservatives to effectively counter Labour's shadow budget did not stop the fierce press assault on 'the highest tax demand in history'.[84] David English even held back for a day a world exclusive about the Duke and Duchess of York's divorce for a comprehensive multi-page assault on Labour that warned: 'IF YOU MAKE IT THEY'LL TAKE IT.'[85] A similar service had followed in the response to Labour's controversial election broadcast on health, which was based on a real-life case. In 'the battle of Jennifer's ear', the press acted as the front-line troops for the Conservatives, as the *Mirror* did to less effect for Labour. Conservative Central Office put the consultant in the case in touch with the *Daily Express*, which denounced 'LABOUR'S SICK NHS STUNT' and claimed that the featured girl's operation had been delayed due to administrative errors. Then, with the Conservatives floundering after admitting making the girl's name public, this was obscured by a ferocious tabloid onslaught on Labour's 'BIG LIE'.[86] All this ensured that, however unwise Labour's choice of this particular case was, the

Table 4.1 Partisanship and circulation of the popular press in 1992 (millions)

Daily Express	1.52	Con
Daily Mail	1.67	Con
Daily Mirror	2.90	Lab
Sun	3.57	Con
Daily Star	0.81	Con
Today	0.53	Con

Source: Harrop and Scammell, 'A Tabloid War', in Butler and King (eds), *The British General Election of 1992*.

fact that the programme was accurate in claiming that the girl's operation had been delayed due to lack of money was largely overlooked.[87] The same could be said for the last, possibly crucial, few days of the campaign. David Hart, a former Thatcher aide, suggested that 'what we saw was the tabloids come out in front of the party, develop their own line, and take a lead in popularising the Conservatives'.[88] The result was an attack on Labour and Kinnock, the sheer scale and ferocity of which was to stun party strategists.[89]

Such an attack also, according to one media analyst, left 'serious evidence for the first time in election history that the Tory tabloids . . . influenced how the nation voted'. MORI evidence showed the final tabloid attack was accompanied by a Conservative swing among their readers of between 2–4 per cent, while Labour's post-election report estimated a swing of nearly 400,000 readers. This may have been enough to turn a potential Labour victory to defeat in many target seats.[90] On the other hand, the fact that there was a swing of 2.5 per cent among *Mirror* readers would rather suggest that 'the late swing was a national, not a newspaper phenomenon'.[91] As in previous elections, a substantial minority of readers completely ignored the political advice of their newspapers. One-third of *Mail*, *Express* and *Mirror* readers failed to vote with their papers, while 55 per cent of *Sun* readers and 69 per cent of *Star* readers failed to vote Conservative.[92] But it would not have taken much of a shift in votes to dramatically affect the result. What made the role of the popular press potentially much more crucial in 1992 compared with previous elections was the sheer closeness of the result, at least in terms of seats. If 1,241 Conservative voters had voted for the party that came second in key constituencies, this would have produced a hung parliament.[93] So even if they influenced 1–2 per cent of readers, argued Labour, the tabloids helped win the election for the Tories. Even while protesting their innocence, *Express* editor Nick Lloyd and his rival David English were not far from this argument as they suggested that they had 'some influence' on their readers and 'helped swing a number of people' to vote with their papers. Murdoch later conceded that, while overstated, the *Sun* gave him 'some power . . . to focus people's attention on certain issues'.[94]

More detailed academic analyses are, however, no more conclusive. Martin Linton's analysis estimated that there was a swing during the three months before the election of 8 per cent to the Conservatives from *Sun* and the *Star* readers, 5 per cent from readers of the *Mail*, but no swing at all from *Mirror* readers. The *Sun* was particularly important, recruiting 435,000 readers in the final three months before election day, which accounted for 49 per cent of previously undecided voters that supported the Conservatives. During the actual campaign, the greatest swings to the Conservatives came from readers of the *Daily Mail*, of 14 per cent, and the *Daily Express*, at 8 per cent. On the other hand, other analyses have argued that Linton established a correlation rather than causation and found that the most influential paper was not the largely politically impotent Tory tabloids, but the *Mirror*.[95] Linton's argument has been supported by another academic study that suggested that the Tory press 'did indeed help to win the 1992 election for the Conservatives'.[96] This was because reading a paper consistent with your viewpoint made it more likely that you would support that party in 1992, while reading a paper at variance with your politics made it less likely that you would support your chosen party. And those with no fixed party allegiances tended to vote with their paper even more closely than those who agreed with their paper's politics. It also found that reading a paper that reinforced your political attitudes made you much more likely to vote, while people whose political views contradicted with their paper's politics were more likely to resolve this dilemma by not voting.[97]

'A double whammy': taxation and the economy

Given any statistical impasse that might arise from the differing findings above, it is also worth considering more qualitative evidence about the impact of the press. Perhaps the main component of Labour's post-election complaints of what Kinnock called 'misinformation and disinformation' concerned their taxation plans. Such coverage, and Labour complaints about it, had begun in January 1992 when the Conservatives launched their near-term campaign with the claim that Labour's taxation policy would cost the average taxpayer £1,000–£1,250 more. This was hotly disputed by Labour who claimed that 90 per cent would be better off. But the tabloids, according to the party's communication director, David Hill, ensured that 'for most of the people there wasn't the possibility of having the tax position presented to them in a fair way'.[98] Robin Cook captured the core of his party's complaints when he quoted a Conservative waverer who had contemplated voting Labour but had stayed loyal after reading the details of Labour's tax plans in the *Daily Mail*. But, as Cook points out, the paper never actually published this information:

> What the *Daily Mail* did publish was a version of Labour's tax plans, prepared by Conservative Central Office. It is perfectly legitimate for the *Daily Mail* to publish the Conservative version of Labour's tax plans; it is not legitimate for the *Daily Mail* to publish that tax table without attribution to the Conservative Central Office, leaving the reader with the impression that it was Labour's tax plans.[99]

The *Express*, *Sun*, and *Star* all did much the same thing, while the two middle-market tabloids fought a persistent and high-profile campaign unequivocally reporting the '£1000 A YEAR COST OF LABOUR'.[100] The *Mail* aroused particular alarm within the party in January by its inventiveness in keeping the spotlight on 'LABOUR'S CRAZY TAX PLANS'. The above story, for instance, quoted the chairman of Ford, Ian MacAllister, as saying that a Labour government spelled 'economic suicide'. MacAllister wrote immediately to Kinnock denying the story but by this time the

Conservatives had taken up these alleged comments and it had made the broadcast news.[101] Two days earlier, the paper's report of a 'LABOUR SPLIT ON TAXATION' between John Smith and Roy Hattersley also aroused protest. The report stemmed from a lunch between Hattersley and journalists from the *Sun*, *Mail* and the *Independent*, with the latter supporting the deputy-leader's denials that any discussion of a split occurred. Just as the story was appearing, Conservative press officer Tim Collins was witnessed in the Commons press gallery depositing press releases on the desks of favoured reporters that 'revealed considerable prior knowledge' of the report and was intended to provoke follow ups in later editions. Its subsequent penetration of the television agenda also led Hattersley to register Labour's first complaint of the election as he detected 'a serious democratic problem when one newspaper can tell a lie and the BBC can report it as fact'.[102]

This long campaign continued into the election proper, with the *Mail* devoting 40 per cent to front-pages exposures of the 'insanity' of Labour's economic plans.[103] The tabloid collusion with the Tory party similarly continued. The draft Conservative party election war book pointed out that a '*Sun* double page spread on impact of tax rises' would accompany their attack on Labour on this issue. There duly followed a report on the economic 'Nightmare on Kinnock Street', with the headline later recycled in the paper's eve of poll onslaught. Joining this attack, two days before polling day, the *Mail* offered a dramatic front page editorial 'WARNING' that a Labour victory would immediately 'lead to higher mortgage payments'. On polling day, the *Express* even reprinted in its news columns a Conservative party advertisement detailing the costs of Labour's tax plans.[104] By the end of the campaign, 49 per cent of voters believed that they would be worse off under Labour, with 5 per cent shifting in the final day, figures some commentators see as decisive in the result.[105] This at least partly reflected the success of a tabloid agenda focusing on how 'LABOUR VOTES TO TAX POOR'. Canvassers cited unemployed men and pensioners in old peoples' homes, some on a disposable income of £9 a week, agonising over the prospect of a £1,250 tax rise under Labour. One exit poll also reported individuals who were nowhere near the £21,060 Labour tax threshold claiming that Labour would put up mortgages and taxes.[106]

Complementing this economic bad news for Labour was good news for the Tories in the tabloid emphasis of the economic prosperity that only a Conservative government could ensure. Voters' information about economic conditions tends to be formed, first, from their own experiences, but second, from 'a mixture of impressions gained from television, radio and the popular press'.[107] The latter can be especially important if the former is unclear, as it was in 1992 with the country promising, as the Tories claimed, to emerge from recession, but never quite managing it, as Labour pointed out. This highly imperfect media market in 1992 clearly favoured the former interpretation. And while most voters in 1992 had a poor view of the economy's past under the Tories, crucially there was more optimism about the future with consumer confidence about the national economy, household economies and inflation all 'at a five year high'.[108]

This return of the 'feel-good' factor coincided with a press emphasis on economic good news which 'probably played a part in helping to generate this increased sense of optimism'.[109] In February, Labour trade and industry spokesman Gordon Brown was to point to the contrast between this optimistic coverage in the tabloids and the pessimism of their companies' internal reports. While the *Mail* was telling readers that 'It's looking good for Major' at the same time, Rothermere was informing shareholders that the UK economy did not show 'any grounds for optimism that a market-led recovery will occur in the following year'. The *Express*'s report of 'Economy Up' contrasted with the company's annual report that 'contrary to the optimism of government ministers', detected 'few tangible signs' of recovery in the advertising agency. Meanwhile the *Sun*'s optimism – 'It's looking good', 'We're OK in the UK' and 'If that's depression let's have more of it' – was at variance with News International's annual report, published in September 1991 which noted that 'Economic conditions as they affect the media are not expected to improve during the next year'. Such a divergence created a situation, according to Brown, where 'the public gets the good news that isn't real. Only the shareholders get the real news that isn't good.'[110] This theme continued throughout the election as the *Express* rejoiced and warned, 'WE HAVE LIFT OFF – recovery is here, don't throw it away', while a *Star* exclusive told of 'Major's Big Tax Cut Vow to Poor'. The *Mail* also claimed that interest rates would fall soon after a Conservative victory, even if its headline – 'MAJOR: WE'LL BRING DOWN MORTGAGES' – did raise the problematic question of 'who put them up?'[111]

Other evidence suggests a press influence. The Conservative Research Director in 1992 later noted how 'immigration . . . played particularly well in the tabloids' and this was evident during the last week of the campaign after the Home Secretary, Kenneth Baker, made an alarmist speech about Labour's policy on asylum seekers. Taking their cue, the *Express* told of 'BAKER'S MIGRANT FLOOD WARNING', the *Mail* cautioned against 'Migrant Madness', while the *Sun* carried a xenophobic centre page graphically illustrating the 'human tide' of 'bogus refugees' who would flock to Britain in the event of a Labour victory.[112] The result, according to Labour MPs, was an upsurge in interest on the doorsteps about immigration. This exposure of roughly half the electorate to lurid 'fear' stories playing on racist attitudes also offers one explanation of both the late swing and the failure of the polls to predict a Conservative victory.[113]

The focus on any possible last-minute effect should not obscure a potentially much greater impact. Labour spin doctors argued that much more important than actual election coverage was the persistent 'day in day out' tabloid hostility since 1983. Many of the themes of coverage in 1992 were, as the party's post-election report noted, merely 'the culmination of activity of many years'.[114] Academic studies have also suggested that, given that most elections – even possibly 1992 – are won and lost long before the announcement of polling day, this longer-term coverage may be more important in affecting voter attitudes.[115] Again there is some supporting evidence. From spring 1990 there was a swing to the Conservatives of 19 per cent among *Daily Star* readers, 16 per cent among *Sun* readers and 15 per cent among readers of the *Daily Mail*, although even among *Mirror* readers the swing was 9 per cent. At the *Sun*, whose uncommitted voters swung by an even larger 25 per cent, the lead Labour enjoyed among its readers in 1990–1991 was replaced by April 1992 with a nine-point advantage for the Conservatives.[116] This evidence shows close similarities with a change in voter attitudes in the year prior to the 1987 election, which saw the Conservative lead increase by 10 per cent overall, but by 17 per cent among *Express/Mail* readers, 34 per cent among *Sun/Star* readers and only 2 per cent among *Mirror* readers. The effect on politically uncommitted readers was particularly astonishing, as the Conservative lead went up by 28 per cent of readers of the middle-market tabloids and a massive 50 per cent among *Sun/Star* readers. By contrast, there was no drift at all among uncommitted *Mirror* readers.[117] It is also necessary to take account of the fact that overt anti-Labour coverage was merely one component of the general right-wing political, social and cultural values that dominated the tabloid press throughout this period.[118]

The Sun says ... 'Why I'm backing Kinnock, by Stalin'

In 1992, as throughout the Thatcher decade, it was the *Sun* that gave the Conservatives the decisive advantage in the press battle. If the best-selling newspaper had endorsed Labour, then the imbalance in press support would have been reversed. The paper's importance was further enhanced by the fact that, whereas a high proportion of *Mirror*, *Mail* and *Express* readers were politically committed voters, *Sun* readers more closely mirrored the national electorate in their voting habits. They were also potentially easier to influence, being more electorally volatile, politically ignorant, undecided and disinterested than readers of any other paper.[119] And to add to its potential power, the paper had a high readership in the growing towns of the South East and the key marginals, in contrast to the *Mirror*, whose biggest circulation was in the traditional Labour strongholds of the South Wales valleys. In the 1992 political barometer of Basildon, for instance, the *Sun*'s circulation was 50 per cent.[120]

One of the most important political effects of the *Sun*, particularly under MacKenzie's editorship, was how it further redefined the nature of political coverage towards entertainment. Small-scale qualitative surveys of *Sun* readers in the late 1980s showed how their paper was enjoyed for its catchy headlines and a humour not thought to be found among rivals with the entertaining 'way they put things' being much admired. It also found 'an overwhelming rejection' of the relevance or attraction of political coverage amongst all readers and a strong conservative apolitical self-identity.[121] These findings illustrate the possibility of a considerable degree of power of the paper over its readers in the determination of the paper's politics. They are also worth remembering when assessing an election strategy that was based around Goebbels's maxim that the most effective form of propaganda was entertainment. In 1992 the *Sun* was unique among the tabloids in its comparatively apolitical and even anti-political stance, with more than one-third of its front pages being devoted to non-political stories. Political coverage, meanwhile, often had a very light-hearted formula. In 1987, for instance, the paper employed a psychic to ascertain the voting intentions of dead celebrities. As well as adding a whole new meaning to McLuhan's famous proposition that 'the medium is the message', it also produced one of the most inventive and outrageous political headlines of the century – 'WHY I'M BACKING KINNOCK, BY STALIN.'[122]

In the following election a similar message was conveyed in a ten-page special, 'Nightmare on Kinnock Street', eve-of-poll edition. Conservative supporters included Elvis, Churchill and Queen Victoria, who was 'not amused at all' by 'the ginger jester'. Joining Stalin in his conversion to democratic socialism were Mao Tse Tung and Trotsky, while Robert Maxwell showed his loyalty from the grave as he 'observed', 'I see a lot of me in Neil Kinnock.' The one rather surprising Labour supporter in the form of John Lennon was because the editor's instructions for Lenin had been appar-ently misunderstood by a younger executive! Other attempts to link politics with entertainment included reports of how famous celebrities would leave Britain if Labour were elected, and a daily election mastermind competition composed of propagandist questions. The paper's polling-day front page had much the same frivolous tone, and was reinforced by a page-three profile of 'roly poly Pat Priestman' under the headline 'Here's How Page Three Would Look Under Kinnock' (referring to campaigns by the left to ban the feature). There were frequent elements of fantasy to the paper's coverage which really transcended the description of them as 'untruths'.[123] It is pos-sible that this outrageousness, approaching self-caricature, may have reduced its impact. Equally, the paper's coverage may have been effective as it drew closely upon its more general relationship with readers by satisfying their demands 'for a laugh' in its election coverage while, at the same time, con-veying a serious political message.[124]

A 'nightmare on Kinnock Street'

Perhaps the central element to tabloid coverage alongside attacks on Labour's economic policy was a persistent questioning of the competency and fitness of Neil Kinnock to be prime minister. Coverage showed a strong emphasis on leadership, particularly the leadership of the party that the paper opposed. In practice this meant that, while the *Mirror* had nothing positive and everything negative to say about John Major, 42 per cent of the

Mail's coverage centred around the question of leadership, chiefly that of Kinnock's. The *Sun* also devoted 25 per cent of its front page news to attacking Kinnock as weak, ineffective, uncaring and leading a divided party.[125] The *Sun*'s coverage of the 'Jennifer's ear' controversy, for example, was simplified into the question of 'If Kinnock will tell lies about a sick little girl, will he ever tell the truth about anything?'. The paper's eve-of-poll edition headlined 'A QUESTION OF TRUST' argued that the crucial question was who readers trusted to run the country. Major was 'a solid, dependable man with a cool head'. Kinnock was 'a novice with no experience of running a government . . . no great intellectual . . . someone who could be drawn into a punch up in a curry house.'[126]

This, as we have seen, was merely the culmination of what Robert Harris described as 'one of the most poisonous campaigns of vilification ever waged by the British press'. The result, according to Roy Hattersley, was that the tabloids 'destroyed' Kinnock's chances of becoming prime minister and ensured an 'extraordinary warped public perception' of him.[127] To many close to him, the Labour leader's public image seemed to confirm the classic proposition that 'the response is to the image, not to the man'. Kinnock's two press secretaries, for instance, have both regretted their failure to convey the 'real' Kinnock.[128] Certainly popular attitudes to the Labour leader were seemingly an important cause of Labour's defeat in 1992. Poll evidence, used to good effect by the press, suggested he was by far the most frequently cited reason for not voting Labour, which would have been in a superior electoral position if John Smith had been leader.[129] While this has been disputed, the fact that 40 per cent could cite Kinnock as the main reason for not voting Labour illustrated the extent to which the question of his leadership competence had become a public issue.

As some of the above coverage demonstrates, there was also an ethnic element to these attacks. During the election, one Tory poster featured their opponent robbing the people of their savings under the distinctly unsubtle question, 'Taffy was a Welshman, Taffy was a. . .?' This attack – on Lloyd George in 1910 – illustrated the extent to which the Labour leader was but a new face to a much, much older story of centuries-old English stereotypes against the Welsh. Also in 1910, Arthur Tyssilo Johnson's 'the Perfidious Welshman' was published, and its references to 'the wild Welshman' of 'inferior intellect, excitability, deceitfulness' and 'appalling ignorance' almost perfectly predicted Kinnock's portrayal as 'a weaselly Welsh windbag'.[130] Throughout his leadership, his nationality was constantly depicted in a way that was inconceivable had he been English, much less Black or Jewish, as he was told, 'Get lost. Go spout to the valleys, boyo.'[131] Again the climax came in the 1992 election as the 'You can't trust Kinnock' theme was complemented with a subtext of 'You can't trust Kinnock because he's Welsh'. At one Conservative press conference, Swansea-born Michael Heseltine adopted a thick Welsh accent to convey the message: 'Neil Kinnock: he's a windbag!; he's stupid!; he's two-faced!; he's *Welsh*!'[132]

Such attacks entertained the watching journalists, who offered their own profiles of 'Taff the Lad', 'this brawling how's-yer-father boyo from the Welsh valleys' who 'finds it all trem-e-e-e-e-ndous, lu-u-uvly, gre-e-e-at'. The choice, as the *Mail* put it on polling day, lay between 'Major or Kinnock. The bank manager or the boyo.'[133]

Kinnock's cautious complaint that there may remain 'an innate antago-nism to Welsh people and the things that are Welsh' around the old stereo-types has been supported by a diverse array of political commentators and politicians as well as some more substantial evidence.[134] Canvassers found a particularly negative reaction to Kinnock on the doorsteps in England.[135] More detailed research also discovered widespread 'racial stereotyping and prejudice' in English attitudes towards Wales, especially in the South East, around the view that the Welsh were 'not to be trusted'. Popular percep-tions also linked with the more general, negative image of Labour in 1992 in seeing Wales as remote, outdated, industrial and populated by militant, anti-business collectivists.[136]

'A siege mentality': the effect on Labour and Kinnock

So far, the debate has focused, as it has a habit of doing, on the media and public opinion. But perhaps as significant was the impact a hostile press had on Labour's campaign, the party and its leaders.[137] Partly because of the dif-ficulty of dealing with 'The Beast', as Labour dubbed the hostile press pack, their 1992 campaign was 'vacuum sealed', a safety-first, no-risks strategy. Kinnock spent the election, in his words, as 'the only man wearing a bloody corset over his mouth'. Labour acknowledged that this was successful in giving 'little opportunity for the media to exploit perceived splits or gaffes'.[138] Yet other commentators and politicians believed that this strategy reduced the Labour leader's potentially vote-winning appeal by failing to make the best use of his qualities, such as his passionate oratory, powers of persuasion and campaigning strength.[139] Instead the stifling straitjacket put around him by all-powerful spin doctors meant, as David Hare's play *The Absence of War* argued, that the only message a defensive Kinnock could now convey was: 'Oh God, I hope I don't drop a bollock tonight.'[140]

Such a strategy may have reduced some of the worst excesses of the tabloids, but it made no difference to their fundamental hostility. During the campaign Kinnock refused interview requests from the *Sun* and the *Daily Mail*. The latter's response was to print a list of hostile questions along with blank spaces where Kinnock's answers should have been and then attack his 'arrogant' refusal to respond. The *Sun* did the same but simply made up what they thought Kinnock's replies would have been.[141] Labour's strategy also allowed the press to supplement their 'You can't trust Kinnock' theme as they portrayed the Labour leader as a man protected by his minders due to his own incompetence, afraid and unable to answer ques-tions from the public.[142] Equally it is difficult to see much alternative given a pre-determined tabloid agenda that, as one journalist half-jokingly observed, was looking for one or both of two stories: 'the gaffe story in which Mr Kinnock forgets a colleague's name, and the Mask Slips story in which Mr Kinnock talks warmly of Albanian economic policy or is seen meeting former members of the Stasi in a Cardiff pub'. For, as Chapter 5 notes, when the *Mail* did something similar to Blair in 2001, he answered the questions but the paper still refused to print his comments.[143]

More importantly, fear of press attacks certainly encouraged a wide degree of defensiveness about Labour's campaign and about policy pronouncements throughout 1983–1992 out of the fear that 'the Conservative tabloids would punish its slightest mistakes and would seize on the hint of anything that could be presented as "looney leftism"'.[144] David Hare, who attended Labour's campaign meetings, provided a small but revealing insight into the siege mentality that a hostile press produced. Both Roy Hattersley and Jack Cunningham were instructed to watch the six o'clock news to hear the exact words John Smith was using to reply to a question on the budget, so they could repeat them in later interviews. When asked if this was really all necessary, Kinnock replied that if only three words were different in the answers then 'the press will say there's a split'.[145]

In a more general way these attacks may have affected the confidence of the party. Kinnock repeatedly stressed during his leadership that the press bred party disunity and conflict, as he considered that the 'one basic fault' of his party was the way 'it denounces the capitalist press on the one hand and yet on the other it accepts what it reads in it'. As one adviser to the Labour leader put it, 'It is not the press which is damaging. It is when the party starts to believe what the press says.'[146] Some of Kinnock's closest advisers suggest that some colleagues 'appeared to accept the version of Neil presented in the tabloids', which in turn had a 'terribly undermining' effect on Kinnock throughout his leadership.[147] Similarly, Alastair Campbell, Kinnock's closest ally in Fleet Street, argued:

> While I never fully subscribed to the theory that the Tory press won the election they played a part. They ensured that Kinnock was rarely seen as he is, but through a prism of hostility which made *him* defensive, his colleagues concerned, and his opponents cheerful.[148]

Part of the problem was that Kinnock had benefited from relatively favourable reporting in his rise to the Labour leadership and had particularly good relations with journalists. He now found it 'a painful and dangerous experience' when the press turned against him. As Healey bluntly summed it up after one particular press smear, 'It's all right for us, we've been up to our eyes in shit for years. He's not used to it.'[149] But in the context of Kinnock's electoral unpopularity, and taken alongside internal doubts about his competence, the attitude of the tabloids left Labour open to aggressive and destabilising attacks on his leadership. One such example came in autumn 1991 when the *Express* and the *Mail* launched a ferocious attack on Kinnock's 'unremitting failure' as leader. This provoked wider media and political talk of a leadership crisis and Kinnock felt obliged to defend the competency of his captaincy – to which the *Sun*'s irreverent response was, 'that's what the skipper of the Titanic said'. This was, as one senior Tory admitted, a blatant attempt to 'demoralise and destabilise' Kinnock. As he commented, 'He's like everyone else. He reads the paper and it can't be very pleasant to wake up to that every morning.'[150] The Labour leader and his colleagues have testified to the effectiveness of these continuous attacks in undermining his own at times uncertain confidence and leaving him 'beleaguered and depressed'.[151] While impossible to measure precisely, this suggests that the press can be as, if not more, influential in their effect on politicians as on the wider public.

Tabloid agendas

Whatever the precise effect of the Tory press in 1992, there can be no doubt that it provided effective propaganda because it was credible. The 1992 election was Labour's third worst result since 1945 and the party was defeated by a decisive margin of 7.6 per cent of the popular vote cast. The result was only close in terms of seats because the pro-Labour bias of the electoral system would have produced a hung parliament despite leaving the Conservatives over 6.5 per cent ahead.[152] And as time healed the tabloid wounds, Kinnock and other Labour figures acknowledged that there were deeper causes of Labour's defeat than newspaper misrepresentation. Their assessments, along with more neutral analyses, detected an underlying electoral distrust, a simple feeling, in the words of campaign manager Jack Cunningham, that Labour was 'too much of a risk'. The widespread doubts in 1992 about Labour's economic competence, tax plans and leadership were crucial to explaining the party's defeat and were symbolic of a wider fear of the party that it failed to overcome.[153] Labour has claimed that it did not matter what their taxation proposals actually were because the tabloids were determined to distort them regardless. Roy Hattersley, supported by more neutral analyses, has argued:

> It was the *Sun* wot won it (sic) not John Smith who lost it. If Labour had promised an all-round tax cut of 20 per cent, the poster hordings would still have screamed about 'the double whammy' and both the *Daily Express* and the *Daily Mail* would have published Conservative Central Office handouts as if they were reputable pieces of economic analysis.[154]

Yet the tabloids could only say what they liked on this issue because, as Labour's communication specialists acknowledged, the 'invention and grotesque misrepresentation' fed into this 'deep and long standing' fear of Labour as a high-tax party.[155] The fact that nearly half the electorate believed that they would be worse off under Labour's tax plans can in part, but only in part, be related to tabloid distortion.[156] Similarly the 'Kinnock factor', the shorthand term for the Labour leader's alleged political and personal shortcomings, fed into serious doubts about his leadership, among colleagues, the public and Labour voters.[157] Perhaps most importantly, even the Labour leader's very successes worked against him, given that he had been almost as closely associated with the leftward shift of the party prior to 1983 as he was with its slow repositioning rightwards during his leadership. This gave opponents considerable ammunition to profile the 'deceit and misjudgement' of 'a man with at least two faces, both of them wrong' who had changed his mind on every aspect of policy to win power and could not be trusted.[158] All this gave weight to a press attack in which, as Kinnock argued, 'every cough was turned into pneumonia, every scratch was made to look like an amputation, every stumble was made to look like a fall from the top of the Empire State Building.'[159]

Perhaps the one area where all these alleged weaknesses came together was in the single most effective propaganda theme developed by the Tories and their press allies in the 1980s, the media memory of the 'Winter of Discontent'. During the 1992 campaign numerous references were made in the popular press, 'Lest We Forget', to the 'nightmare' of 1979, when 'Britain ground to a halt, held to ransom by greedy unions'. The *Mail*'s coverage was typical in offering 'a warning from 13 years ago' when 'the sick were turned away from hospital, streets were piled high with rubbish, and the dead could not be buried'. Such texts were invariably accompanied by pictures of cancer patients pleading with strikers, closed hospitals and schools, and, most popular, rat-infested rubbish piled high in the streets. All were cited as proof that 'we cannot afford another Labour government'.[160] Such attacks merely repeated a story emphasised repeatedly in Tory propaganda since 1979. Hill was to argue that the image of the Winter of Discontent had a 'monumental' impact in the long term, while during the campaign party canvassers also discovered people had strong 'memories' of 1979. Notwithstanding the existence of the 'events' of 1979, it is clear that popular memories of it have as much to do with selective reporting at the time and even greater selection subsequently. Indeed, some focus groups suggested that the 'memory' of 1979 was stronger among the younger groups that could not remember it rather than the older ones who could.[161]

This thorn-tinted perspective on a decade where 'all kinds of things just fell apart' obviously omits much from the story and historians have challenged the big, popular picture of the 1970s with a whole variety of 'little facts'.[162] In any case there was no logical reason for the press in 1992 to concentrate on these thirteen-year-old events at all. Kinnock had not even been part of government, nor did Labour have any intention of restoring the trade-union powers that had allegedly precipitated the event. But myths should not simply be debunked but remain 'central to the common sense and to the history . . . of the period in which they hold sway'.[163] Popular images of the past matter rather more, in political terms, than unpopular academic analyses. As Orwell once famously pointed out, 'Who controls the past controls the future. Who controls the present controls the past.' The key to controlling the perception of the 1970s was the Tory party and their press allies, who ensured that Labour not only had 'a history to offset', as Kinnock later recognised, but a history that was largely written by its opponents.[164]

For a politician who believed that 'there was no alternative', Mrs Thatcher spent a lot of time positioning Thatcherism as the antithesis and nemesis of a series of negative alternatives – social democracy, consensus, corporatism, decline.[165] These all found their most powerful expression in the myth of the Winter of Discontent. The essential sequel to this winter's tale was a rather more uplifting press history in which a new ideology and strong leadership had made Britain great again, economically, politically, internationally. But this could only continue if no return was made to days so dark that 'even the dead could not be buried'. 'Do we REALLY want to go back to all this?' asked the *Mail* in 1987 as it reminded readers of 'the nightmare that has faded since the Tories came to office'. 'These memories must never be forgotten', it pleaded, for 'they are the lessons of history'.

In a fascinating argument mainly about America but also touching on Britain, Justin Lewis points to the way that right-wing regimes in the 1980s were able to construct electoral majorities despite the widespread support in both countries for more centrist economic and social policies. There was an appearance of popular support for Reagan's policies rather than the reality and the media were more influential and successful in winning support for abstract political ideas (such as hostility to 'big government' and the 'liberal elite') than in winning popular support for specific policies.[166] Much the same could be said for Britain where the myth of the Winter helped to ideologically 'structure feelings' throughout the 1980s, giving Thatcher a negative 'symbolic majority' in discrediting all alternatives in the popular imagination. Social democracy, socialism, trade unionism, corporatism all became 'bad things', tried, tested and failed, despite the fact that in practical terms there existed widespread support for many of the key policies associated with these ideologies.

Such a point also demonstrates something of the complexity of popular, political attitudes during a time when at least half the electorate were floating voters without fixed party loyalties. And to say that the press merely reinforced and worked on certain Labour weaknesses tells only half the story. For, by focusing on certain agendas, the media can help influence and crystallise certain popular attitudes and feelings at the expense of other latent viewpoints potentially damaging to the other side. One survey of the 1992 election, for instance, found that Labour supporters who read a Conservative paper had a higher opinion of Major and a lower opinion of Kinnock than Labour identifiers who read a Labour paper, while similar results were reported for earlier elections.[167] And while highlighting and magnifying

Labour's weak spots, the tabloids were simultaneously downplaying or obscuring Conservative ones. For, to move back to the 'little facts', this time of Thatcherism, the negative popular image of Labour's past also helped keep the agenda away from a Conservative present that, in some respects, seemed as bad, if not worse. As Newton points out:

> if we are to go back to 1979 and the Winter of Discontent, why not go back a little further to Heath and the three day week? And why go back to 1979 rather than 1980/1? And why go back to 1979 rather than the first quarter of 1992?

One wonders what the consequences would have been if the Tory press had supported Labour's campaign agenda that: 'the Conservatives have produced two recessions in ten years, xxx business failures, 2.7m unemployed and a growth rate lower than Labour's. They are the economically incompetent party'? Or would only 4 per cent of the electorate have blamed John Major's government for the economic downturn – perhaps the key to explaining the result – had the press emphasised his 'personal responsibility for the recession as Treasury Minister, Chancellor and Prime Minister'.[168] The same alternative agendas can be applied to tabloid attacks on Labour as the party of high taxation. These clearly contain an element of truth, both historically and regarding party policy in 1992, although again it is intriguing to speculate what would have happened if they had taken their agenda from the *Financial Times*. The paper followed its headline 'Smith says Plan would benefit "Eight out of Ten"' with an editorial claiming that there was little difference between the tax plans of the rival parties.[169] Regardless of this, by juxtaposing the choice between 'tax cutters' and 'tax addicts' the tabloid agenda (excepting the *Mirror*) ignored the fact that, while income tax had been reduced since 1979, the overall tax burden had actually risen. Respected political journalist Anthony Bevins forced an embarrassed John Major to admit this very fact at one press conference but the tabloids, charitably, decided not to publicise the matter.[170]

Similarly there is an interesting contrast to be drawn between Kinnock's coverage and that given to Thatcher when she was leader of the opposition. Like him she was seen as a liability to her party, uncertain under pressure with a tendency to make 'gaffes', was much less popular with the electorate than Callaghan, who easily dominated her in parliamentary debate. Polling evidence suggested that the Conservatives would improve their support if someone else (Heath) was leader. Unlike Kinnock, however, the heavily pro-Conservative press never made her leadership an issue.[171] It would have been easy for a sympathetic press to have presented the Labour leader as a bold leader who had saved his party from electoral destruction – the perspective that retrospect has largely bestowed on him. Perhaps most notably, one wonders what would have happened if the bulk of the press had echoed the *Mirror*'s alternative political and social agenda that during the election focused most of its attention on social and economic issues and little on taxation or leadership. This is not to engage in endless counter-factual questioning but merely to illustrate that, as important as what the tabloids emphasise, is what they do not.[172] The result of such a selective focus is 'not so much that the media misrepresent the "true" nature of a more left-leaning public' but they limit the possibilities that complex and contradictory public attitudes suggest.[173] And they do this in a way that helps sustain right-wing political and ideological dominance.

'Always a bad press?' Continuity, change and the reasons for press bias

On one level press behaviour in 1992 showed marked continuities. As the party complained:

> Policy invades the news columns and by selection, presentation, suppression and emphasis, the controller conveys to the reader that impression of the facts that will square with his leading article of the policy he desires to introduce.[174]

Nearly three-quarters of a century on from this allegation, many specific themes also showed little change. A modernised Zinoviev Letter had been crafted by the *Sunday Times* in February 1992 when it had hyped routine links between the Labour leader and the Soviet Embassy under the banner headline 'OFFICIAL: KINNOCK'S KREMLIN CONNECTION'. An internal memorandum added, 'the subject matter is most timely as speculation surrounding the election is gathering apace and our revelations could have a dramatic effect on events'. Press attacks on Labour's economic proposals in 1992 merely represented the latest in a long line of 'saving smears'. Even before the party took office in 1924, one sympathetic newspaper was deriding the Tory press for 'the old taint that the Labour party is unfit to govern'.[175] And to point out that the *Mail* and the *Express* strongly supported the Conservatives, and the *Mirror* likewise for Labour, in 1992 hardly seems evidence of a startling new trend in press behaviour.

However, in quantitative and qualitative terms, the press was more anti-Labour between 1979–1992 than at any other time in the post-war era. Roughly 70 per cent of the press opposed Labour and did so in an unprecedentally ferocious manner as emphasis was increasingly shifted from news to opinion and political guidance. Adding to the monolithic nature of the popular press was the fact that individual readership of more than one daily newspaper – very common in the past – had now virtually died out.[176] A number of reasons have been advanced to explain this. For all Labour's complaints about the media throughout the century, it had largely accepted the prevailing definition of press freedom. This viewed it as a property freedom that came naturally from the operation of economic forces, rather than something which had to be actively guaranteed and improved by state intervention.[177] But, in the early 1980s, the party adopted a much more active media policy.[178] Part of this involved an intensification of the sporadic demands from the labour movement for the establishment of a national newspaper to counter media hostility. However, the example of the *News on Sunday*, whose three editions in 1987 cost a total of £6.5 million, offered little encouragement in a failure made all the more depressing by the simultaneous success of the soft-porn *Sunday Sport*.[179] Of more worry to established newspapers was Labour's adoption of a variety of plans for media reform. In 1992, these included a pledge to refer media concentration and cross ownership to a strengthened Monopolies and Mergers Commission, a threat to introduce statutory and independent regulation of the press, a right to reply and a law on privacy.[180] For Murdoch's News International, which had spent 1990–1991 fighting off the threat of financial bankruptcy, the prospect of a victorious Labour implementing its pledges was particularly bleak. The company would have been forced to give up either its British newspapers or its half share in BSkyB, so 'arguably no other company stood to lose as much from a Labour victory as did News'.[181] All this may have exacerbated the usual business hostility towards Labour, although it is probable that party policy was more the consequence than the cause of press hostility.

More generally, it would also be wrong to see the anti-Labour shift of the press from 1979 onwards as solely an editorial/proprietorial conspiracy. It was partly a reflection of the implosion of the Labour party in the early 1980s, while as for Kinnock, there was a press timelag to recognising his achievements. This partly reflected the central ambiguity of whether his reforms were aiming at a New Labour modernisation or an Old Labour restoration – whatever the similarities between the two. More personally, there remained serious doubts about his fitness to govern amongst even politically sympathetic journalists. Edward Pearce articulated these in December 1991 when he called on the Labour leader to resign and argued, 'I can't think of a colleague in the Gallery or Lobby who thinks Mr Kinnock adequate.'[182] The Labour leader believed that 'the extra layer of antagonism' towards him came from what colleagues viewed as the 'overweening snobbery' and 'appalling condescension' he suffered from what has been controversially dubbed the 'Oxbridge conspiracy'.[183] In his particular case the attitudes of a journalistic elite were undoubtedly influenced by what Roy Hattersley, correctly in sentiment if inaccurately in detail, calls 'the nonsense about "a pass degree in Sociology in Swansea in a bad year"'. This legitimised profiles of 'a man who took five years to do a degree which brighter students do in two'. The Labour leader's alleged inability to master economics in the 'enterprise' 1980s, along with his uneven political performances, reinforced the perception of him as an 'intellectual pygmy' – or what even a politically friendly journalist could deride as 'the unbearable lightness of being Mr Kinnock'.[184]

The hostility with which Kinnock reciprocated such profiles has also produced suggestions that he was responsible for his bad press.[185] Certainly the Labour leader, like Wilson before him, initially proved an obsessive and over-sensitive scrutiniser of newspapers and would often arrive at his office fulminating against the 'cowardice' and 'sycophancy' of much of what he read. Kinnock responded to this with frequent angry phone calls and long letters of complaint, before retreating into a refusal to agree to repeated requests from the Tory tabloids to talk to them.[186] To suggest that this offers an explanation for Labour's poor press, as several editors claimed after 1992, rather ignores the operation of cause and effect.[187] The implacable hostility of the *Sun* was demonstrated when, shortly after the end of the year-long Wapping dispute (see below, pp. 114–15), Kinnock gave an interview to the paper in what was obviously a peace feeler. He may have wondered why he had bothered. A series of hostile questions was accompanied by an editorial drawing attention to the alleged power of his wife, an allegation that was known to particularly annoy Kinnock, alongside a savage attack the following day on his 'lamentable' performance.[188] Whether greater cultivation could have softened hostility alongside Labour's rightward policy shift after 1987 remains an open question, although it is doubtful given the legacy of bitterness, the still centrist nature of Labour's programme in 1992, and the 'Thatcher factor' discussed below (pp. 114–16). But despite the urgings of his aides and fellow politicians, Kinnock's antipathy to the press ensured that this was not even tried and relations remained 'frozen'.[189]

At best these serve as marginal explanations. Far more important was the combined impact of longer-term trends to a more negative, personalised and aggressive style of coverage (see Chapter 6) with the political changes in British politics from the later 1970s. The reduced press partisanship between 1955–1974 was in part the product of the existence of, if not a post-war consensus, then a relative amount of political agreement and the subsequent political polarisation in the late 1970s/early 1980s was reflected in tabloid coverage.[190] Most fundamentally, in the intense conflict between capital and labour that characterised the Thatcher decade, there was little doubt which side the capitalist press was on. This was particularly so given that press ownership had shifted in the post-war period to large business conglomerates, which meant that the press, rather than having other business interests, had in fact 'become a subsidiary of other industries'.[191] As David (soon, predictably, Lord) Stevens, head of United Newspapers, which purchased Express newspapers in 1985 and who, on his own admission was 'quite far out to the right', argued:

> I think it would be very unlikely that I would have a paper that would support the socialist party. That isn't what some people would call press freedom, but why should I want a product I didn't approve of? I believe it is in the best interests of United Newspapers in terms of its profits and shareholders to support the Conservatives.[192]

In the midst of the breakdown of the post-war settlement, Labour's shift to the left alarmed editors and owners as much as the Conservative party's move to the right enthused them. The apparent increasing power of the trade unions on a national level was also more than reflected in Fleet Street, where their behaviour seemed to embody all that was most greedy and corrupt about them.[193] Larry Lamb argues that 'the Fleet Street print unions could probably claim to have unmade more socialists than all Labour's prime ministers put together'.[194] Most importantly, there was an undoubted 'Thatcher effect' on a popular press which, as Ian Gilmour pointed out, 'could scarcely have been more fawning if it had been state controlled'.[195] The Prime Minister kept a formal distance from the press, delegating day-to-day responsibility to the highly effective news management of her spokesman, the 'blunt, sometimes thuglike' former Labour-supporting Bernard Ingham.[196] Behind the scenes, however, she strongly courted newspaper owners, editors and journalists. The era saw the emergence of a highly personalised 'special relationship' between Thatcher and the bulk of the newspaper elite, many of whom were viewed as 'one of us' and shamelessly rewarded with honours as well as flattery for their support. Loyalty to this particular vision generally took precedence over impartiality or balance as journalistic ethics were sacrificed for the greater good of the revolution.[197]

One of those knighted, *Sunday Express* editor John Junor, illustrated this when he approvingly noted Thatcher's 'consternation' after *Sunday Times* editor Frank Giles had the cheek to respond to the compliment of an audience with the Prime Minister by arriving 'with a long list of questions'.[198] The fact that this ideology coincided with the commercial interests of the press made it all the more attractive. Most importantly, the changed climate of industrial relations in the 1980s allowed a successful attack to be made on the power of the print unions. This combination was undoubtedly true in the case of Thatcher's most valuable, and perhaps most intimate supporter, Murdoch. The tycoon was and is a highly political animal who had acquired committed and very right-wing views by the early 1980s, to the extent that he even ludicrously considered his first editor of the *Sunday Times*, Frank Giles, to be a Communist. He had the utmost contempt for the 'pissing liberals' within the Conservative party and editors were made fully aware of such views, in which the Labour party in the 1980s stood far, far beyond the pale.[199] In the last resort the tycoon has proved willing to compromise such beliefs to safeguard his commercial interests. But in Thatcher he found the best of both worlds in a 'symbiotic relationship' so close that Murdoch was dubbed 'Mr Prime Minister' by one favoured editor of *The Times*. It was demonstrated in the 1987 general election when go-between Woodrow Wyatt informed Thatcher of Murdoch's intention to use the *Sun* for two-days of anti-Labour propaganda in the 1987 election. She responded effusively, 'Rupert is marvellous.'[200]

As far as Murdoch's business interests were concerned, the long-obstructed move to new technology at Wapping in January 1986 was only made possible by Thatcher's trade union legislation, anti-union stance and the backing of the government throughout the crisis. In turn the defeat of the print unions, as well as more than tripling the value of Murdoch's four London papers, was an important contribution to the success of this aspect of Thatcherism.[201] Conversely, Wapping involved Labour in a bitter year-long public dispute with News International. Like the miners' strike, it was electorally damaging in associating the party with civil disobedience, picket-line violence and union power. Kinnock's bitter public denunciations of 'Stalag Wapping' and 'Schloss Murdoch' were complemented by his party's refusal, officially at least, to talk to News International journalists.[202] The parliamentary lobby refused to accept such 'conditions' on their meeting and withdrew Kinnock's invitation to speak to them, which suggested to the Labour leader 'that solidarity in the profession is not dead, merely selective'. He now held the weekly meetings, minus News International journalists, in the shadow cabinet room.[203] As far as News International was concerned, it meant, to quote Murdoch, that 'we became the public enemy of . . . the Labour party'. Murdoch became more hated by the left than perhaps anyone apart from Thatcher, an attitude later demonstrated by Dennis Potter's famous comment that he called his cancer 'Rupert'. All this exacerbated a personal bitterness on both sides still in evidence in 1992.[204]

Murdoch's support was also rewarded by a series of highly favourable government decisions which saw Thatcher, according to former *Times* editor Harold Evans, acting as Murdoch's 'poodle'. His acquisitions of *The Times* and *Sunday Times* in 1981 and *Today* in 1987 were both, controversially, not referred to the Monopolies and Mergers Commission. Even the anodyne Press Council was moved to comment in 1987, 'There could hardly be a more obvious case of concentration than acquisition of a fifth national newspaper by a group which already owns four.'[205] One of Mrs Thatcher's last services to the country before her resignation in November 1990 came when she did nothing to stop the illegal merger between Sky and BSB. The government was forced to admit to parliament that the law had been broken with the advance knowledge of the Prime Minister, who had met Murdoch and discussed the deal a few days before it was announced. The final payback to the party came in the 1992 general election. All five of Murdoch's British papers, which he had earlier claimed had 'widely divergent views', endorsed the Conservatives.[206] By this time the tabloids had lost their heroine in the Tory leadership election of November 1990, despite their fierce efforts to bludgeon the 'GUTLESS TRAITORS' in the party into voting for 'MAGGIE THE LIONHEART'. In their final act of devotion, they were to join her in embracing John Major as the man who would ensure that 'while Mrs Thatcher may have gone, Thatcherism must not be allowed to die'.[207] Press coverage of Major and the Conservatives in the run-up to the election was less adulatory than that of his predecessor, but wholly uncritical. The party's October 1991 conference and Major's perceived negotiating triumph at Maastricht in December brought praise for 'THE PEOPLE'S PREMIER', a man 'made of steel'.[208] For the time being, the press had bought into the 'Thatcher Mark II' story and it was not until after the election that the special relationship with the tabloids was to end so disastrously for the Conservatives.

Conclusion

Of course the relationship between the Tories and their press allies was echoed in the *Daily Mirror*'s 'extremely close' links with Labour in the 1992 election and throughout this period.[209] Political editor Alastair Campbell was given exclusive previews of both the Labour shadow budget and manifesto and its final editions even carried the party's slogan, 'IT'S TIME FOR CHANGE' and a reproduction of the Labour red rose.[210] After the election, Labour was once more guilty of hypocrisy, being quick to condemn the excesses of the Conservative press, but less willing to recognise the distortions of their own side. There was little to choose between left- or right-wing partisanship in terms of their subversion of journalistic standards. But on a practical level, it counted for more in the Tory press throughout 1979–1992 simply because there were far more of them with a greater circulation and a wider collective power to affect the television agenda and the nation's political culture. It has been tentatively estimated that the Conservatives received a net advantage of up to £37 million worth of free advertising through press support in the election.[211] There was actually little point in the party incurring sizeable advertising costs (£33,550 for a full page in the *Sun*) in a series of newspapers which, as Hill pointed out, 'could devote fourteen pages for free to Neil Kinnock being the nearest thing we have seen to Judas Iscariot!' Indeed the *Express* not only re-printed Conservative adverts for free in its news columns, its owners in 1992, United Newspapers, actually donated £41,000 to the party.[212]

The second main defence from the press after the election was to accuse Labour of the old mistake of blaming the messenger for the message. English suggested that 'every time Labour loses an election they blame the Tory press ... the fact of the matter is that it was Labour's policies that helped swing the election to the Tories'.[213] While there is some truth in this point, its basic flaw is that the tabloids misrepresented the message according to their preconceived political stances even before readers had a chance to make a judgement on it. The message was bad even when the news was good and the electorate

> weren't just lied to, they were systematically denied the facts on which to form a sensible judgement. Hostile interpretations did not just accompany the reports of Labour's policy announcements; the hostile interpretation ... was the report.[214]

The extent to which this affected the final outcome of the election will always be open to dispute and should not be exaggerated. Nevertheless a strong case can be made that 1992 was the only occasion since 1945 when the popular press has decisively influenced the result of an election in favour of the Conservatives. Even if one assumes only a marginal impact and concedes that there were deeper reasons for Labour's defeat, the press campaign still may have been enough to make the substantial difference between a Conservative victory and a hung parliament. As usual, the *Sun*'s claim that it was the press 'wot won it' told some, if not the whole, of the story.

5   'Vote conservative – vote Blair'

Labour and the popular press 1992–2003[1]

> The Tories' ruthlessness, combined with their special appeal to people's baser instincts, mean that they are the beneficiaries of crude political debate. A party that relies on prejudice will always have more chance of getting the *Sun* leader writer on board than a party which preaches tolerance.
>
> (Peter Mandelson, 1995)[2]

It is difficult to understate the transformation that occurred in Labour's electoral and newspaper support between 1992–1997. In the aftermath of the 1992 defeat, many commentators were again predicting that Labour could never win power in its present form. Not entirely unconnected for some was the way the election and its acrimonious aftermath had also graphically illustrated the state of virtual war between the party and press since 1979.[3] But by 1997 the situation had changed to an extent unimaginable five years earlier. Labour's landslide victory of May 1997 saw the election of a record number of Labour MPs in the biggest electoral swing for 50 years.[4] The shift in newspaper support appeared just as spectacular as the party gained a higher percentage of press support than ever before, chiefly by winning the endorsement of its once bitter enemy, the *Sun*. This was also accompanied by an increased sympathy from the rest of the Tory press which, from September 1992 onwards, displayed an intense and sustained level of hostility towards a government it had helped elect. This chapter explores the reasons for this change before ending with a brief examination of press coverage of the Labour governments from 1997.

'Nightmare on Major Street': an anti-Conservative press

After their 1992 victory, the Conservatives formed a government that could effectively 'do no right'. Economic crisis, bitter party divisions, the emergence of the many-sided issue of 'sleaze' and criticism of John Major's leadership produced an administration that eventually became more unpopular than any since records began.[5] The press not only responded critically to these Conservative difficulties, but also played a key role in magnifying and even creating some of them. The key event in the breaking of their 1979–1992 loyalties was Britain's enforced departure from the ERM in September 1992. The collapse of the cornerstone of government economic policy destroyed the traditional Conservative superiority over Labour as the party of economic competence and a roughly equal level of support for both parties was replaced with a commanding Labour lead which never disappeared.[6] It had an equally dramatic effect on the Conservative party's press relations.

Even before this, there had already been signs that the long period of alliance was breaking down, with the *Sun* increasingly looking like 'the paper wot won it and now wished it hadn't'.[7] The enforced resignation of 'Minister of Fun' David Mellor after the tabloids revealed his adulterous relationship with an actress and other personal misjudgements set an important precedent and encouraged the press in pursuit of later victims.[8] But his departure was a side issue to the economic disaster when Britain was forced to suspend its membership of the ERM on 'Black Wednesday', 16 September 1992.[9] The deep disillusionment of the press with the government was demonstrated most memorably when Major, anxious to find out the response of Britain's most popular tabloid, had phoned up Kelvin MacKenzie, to be told, 'Well John, let me put it this way. I've got a large bucket of shit lying on my desk – and tomorrow morning I'm going to pour it all over your head.' Major, uncertain whether this was a joke, lamely responded, 'Oh Kelvin, you are a wag.' But MacKenzie was more than true to his word and the *Sun*'s front page the next day simply read, 'Now we've ALL been screwed by the Cabinet.'[10]

Worrying signs of independence were visible at Associated Newspapers where David English had become editor-in-chief, to be succeeded as editor by Paul Dacre, who was both a Eurosceptic and 'not too keen on Major personally'. There soon followed a rapid cooling of previously warm relations as Dacre outlined his plans to take a 'slightly more independent' stance reflecting the economic 'agony and pain' of readers.[11] By mid-October, the *Sun* was also warning ominously, 'We're running out of time and patience.'[12] Three days later this deadline expired in 'THE GREAT MINE DISASTER', when Trade and Industry Minister Michael Heseltine announced plans to shut down 31 of the remaining 50 pits in Britain, making 30,000 miners redundant.[13] The ensuing crisis saw the bizarre spectacle of the entire British press orchestrating a wave of public outrage supporting the previously reviled miners' leader, Arthur Scargill.[14] The *Mail* denounced 'just another 31,000 jobs lost' in the context of a 'near-terminal slump' under a 'woefully out of touch' government while the *Sun* forged a close alliance with the miners in its 'Campaign for Coal'.[15] Mirroring the contempt MacKenzie had earlier conveyed in private, the paper offered Major a taste of its infamous savaging of England manager Graham Taylor as another policy reversal was portrayed in a front page headline and picture of Major as 'U-TURN-IP'. But the *Sun*'s most hostile act placed a tiny picture of Heseltine in the centre of an otherwise blank front page with the words, 'This page contains *all* that Michael

Heseltine understands about the worries and fears of ordinary working people in a depression-hit Britain. Nothing. Absolutely Nothing.'[16] This coverage offered a graphic highlight of the almost unanimous tone of press coverage, which former Fleet Street journalists felt was without precedent. The most distinguished of them all, Hugh Cudlipp, claimed it was 'the first time in half a century in newspapers' that he had 'witnessed the Praetorian guard of the Tory party in open mutiny'.[17] Much of the subsequent attack was initially directed at Chancellor Norman Lamont, which peaked following his 'budget of broken promises' in March 1993. As the Conservatives now dropped their very own 'tax bombshell', press attacks on the 'Nightmare on Norm Street' echoed earlier anti-Labour coverage. They denounced 'a breathtaking rewriting of history' and printed earlier quotations from Lamont and Major to highlight their broken promise not to extend VAT on domestic fuel.[18]

The climax of press hostility followed Major's ill-fated attempt to regain the political initiative at the October 1993 party conference when he launched his 'back to basics' campaign. Accompanying attacks on single-parent families from right-wing cabinet members, along with the clear spin put on the speech by Major's press secretary Tim Collins, ensured that it was widely interpreted as a 'war against permissiveness'. This was despite the fact that the leadership were well aware that any moral skew would justify the exposure of any Conservative who violated it.[19] It was perhaps only surprising that it took three months before the *News of the World* revealed that married Environment Minister Tim Yeo had fathered an illegitimate child with his mistress, a Tory councillor.[20] Yeo hardly helped his case by insisting he had done nothing wrong while giving the media he was desperately trying to avoid a picture of him 'cowering on the back seat of a car with a blanket over his head – like a convicted child-molester, not a Minister of the Crown'.[21] Major fuelled renewed doubts about his leadership by again first supporting his beleaguered minister and then demanding his resignation when the media pressure became too intense. The press were outraged, not least by Major's insistence that 'back to basics' was never intended to have been a moral crusade.[22] The *Mail* condemned the 'abysmal failure of the Prime Minister to react with convincing authority', while the *Telegraph* attacked a government 'mired in sleaze' and 'incapable of shame'.[23] Most notable was a *Sun* editorial which Peter Mandelson advised Labour to 'put aside . . . and turn into a party political broadcast' at the next election.[24] 'What fools we were to believe this lot', lamented a paper whose eyes were now 'wide open' to the 'immorality, deceit, incompetence and hypocrisy' of a government led by a man showing 'all the leadership of the lemming'. Its message to readers was simple – 'We have been conned.'[25]

Soon the *Sun* and *Mail* were among those being accused by the Tories of conspiring to bring down their government in the face of what one of the few remaining loyalist editors compared to 'a medieval bloodlust' from the tabloids.[26] By early 1994 the essential dilemma faced by the Tory press, as

Andrew Neil pointed out, was that 'its systematic and effective disembowel-
ment of the government' was making more likely a Labour government
which it certainly did not want. He suggested that the press was likely to
conclude that the only way out of this dilemma was 'Mr Major's head'.[27]
After a further year of multiple disasters for the government, this duly
occurred in June 1995 when Major announced he would seek re-election as
party leader and told party opponents that it was 'time to put up or shut
up'. To his surprise, the challenge was taken up by a cabinet member John
Redwood whose argument that 'no change' equalled 'no chance' in the next
election found strong support in the press. The *Daily Mail* urged, 'IT'S
TIME TO DITCH THE CAPTAIN', the *Sun* similarly believed that Major
was 'damaged, desperate, dead' and 'could not lead a cinema queue, let alone
a country', as did the quality Tory press.[28] To their despair, two-thirds of
Conservative MPs failed to take this virtually unanimous advice, even if
Major's 'victory' owed more to a rare presentational triumph given that the
number of votes he gained fell short of the 'convincing margin' previously
estimated to be necessary for him to continue in office.[29]

Labour: from Smith to Blair

Yet despite this anti-government hostility, Labour's press support initially
seemed to get even worse rather than better after 1992, as the party faced
serious worries over the continued loyalty of the *Daily Mirror*. After
Maxwell's death, and the subsequent collapse of his financial empire in late
1991, the banks had assumed overall control of Mirror newspapers. In
autumn 1992 they appointed former Murdoch editor David Montgomery as
chief executive, a man described by one former colleague as 'the only guy
I've ever known who can walk into a room and reduce the temperature by 10
degrees' and another as a 'Thatcherite bastard'. His initial promise that there
would be no dismissals was quickly followed by the sacking of 100 journalists and three editors and an apparent move from a 'too strident' and
'abusive' past political stance, in favour of a 'more balanced' and 'more intelligent, less doctrinaire' approach.[30] Paul Foot and Alastair Campbell were
among the high-profile journalistic resignations, while Labour peer Lord
Hollick departed from the board.[31] Over 100 of the paper's journalists
responded with a motion of no confidence in Montgomery. Meanwhile over
150 Labour MPs signed an Early Day Motion protesting that such developments, in Kinnock's words, 'compromised the independence of the *Mirror*' –
although the real fear was that it demonstrated it.[32] More lukewarm support
seemed confirmed in May 1993. The *Mirror*'s low-key coverage of what it
termed the Conservative party's 'worst disaster at the polls for 100 years'
contrasted notably with the *Sun*'s front page publicity to the local election
'NIGHTMARE FOR MAJOR'.[33] At this time there was even an 'uncom-
fortable feeling' within the Labour party and the newspaper world that by
the time of the next election Labour could be without any press support at

all.[34] Subsequent high-profile coverage of Labour's local election victory a year later helped ease this worry, although observers considered this to be accompanied by a continued more general loosening of relations.[35]

By May 1994 attacks on the Tories were overshadowing those against Labour but the fundamental press position remained little different. Despite a marked improvement of personal relations on the Kinnock years, the *Sun*'s intense hostility to the Conservatives was periodically outdone by its contempt for Labour. While the Tories had put up taxes, Labour's 'barmy' plans under its 'dead loss' leader John Smith were 'even worse' and demonstrated how 'hardline socialists' would return Britain to the 'closed shop, pickets and strikes'. It was hardly surprising, therefore, that media analysts believed it was most unlikely that the *Sun* would endorse any other party in a general election.[36] The paper was still urging a Tory vote in the May 1994 local elections against Labour councils who 'hand out YOUR cash to barmy politically correct causes like lesbian and gay clubs'. It had 'no doubt that a Tory government would be best for Britain – if only we had one'.[37] A more implicit endorsement came a month later when it urged voters in the European elections not to use the vote 'just as a protest against John Major', but against growing interference from Europe.[38]

The caution of the latter editorial may have reflected the change in British politics that followed the sudden death of John Smith in early May. Tony Blair quickly emerged as the expected successor amidst strong press backing for a man with 'the looks, style and message that could appeal to disenchanted Tory voters' and make Labour 'a truly modern left-of-centre party'.[39] Given a party backlash against 'being bounced ... into making decisions' by 'an unelected and unrepresentative elite' of anti-socialist journalists, press support for Blair may have been 'as much of a handicap as an advantage', as his close ally Campbell argued.[40] But the intense media agenda-setting in the first week after Smith's death, when the contest was effectively won and lost, was of critical importance in the view of the 'defeated' Brown camp. Coverage emphasising Blair's 'southern appeal' was quickly followed by early opinion polls showing him the overwhelming public choice.[41] Blair's subsequent anointment as Labour leader was accompanied by qualified press enthusiasm towards 'a young, intelligent, attractive leader ... genuinely committed to social democracy', whose policies 'in areas like crime and welfare dependency' were remarkably similar to those of the Conservatives.[42] Despite his popularity as the man most likely to 'slaughter the sacred cows of socialism', his press honeymoon should not be exaggerated. A full 60 per cent of *Sun* appraisals during the leadership election were negative and already newspapers were questioning whether 'Mr Blur' could 'control the malign influence of the left', 'resist the trade unions who still effectively control the Labour party' and keep down spending.[43] Such criticisms did, however, represent a significant improvement on coverage of past leaders as they did not automatically start from a position of blanket anti-Blair coverage.

'Winning a place in the Sun': Labour's media campaign

Almost as important a part of the policy-modernising 'project' begun by Kinnock, but taken to qualitatively new levels by Blair, was the complementary importance the party attached to effective media-management. Perhaps the key change to the party's communication strategy under Blair was its attempt to improve relations with the Tory tabloids. The apparent impact of their propaganda in the Kinnock years reinforced the imperative, while their subsequent disenchantment with the Tories gave Labour, according to Blair's new press secretary, Alastair Campbell, 'a chance to cultivate ... the big numbers ... in a way that would have been futile in the last election'.[44] These views fully accorded with Blair's, who was one of the few Labour figures prepared to take the message to the enemy in the 1980s.[45] Blair had impressed his hosts at the *Daily Mail* during regular lunches where he 'radiated frankness and honesty' in outlining the extent of his apparent agreement with the Thatcher government.[46] English had been seen 'applauding enthusiastically' Blair's 1994 conference speech in which he had pledged to abolish Clause 4.[47] A year later he mischievously revealed a discussion with his proprietor about whether the papers could back Labour in which Rothermere had concluded that 'it certainly would not be impossible' for at least 'some' to do so.[48]

Labour made even more strenuous efforts to court Murdoch. His paper reached the largest and most important tabloid audience while he was also more likely to change allegiances than the other more conventional Tory proprietors, as confirmed by his carefully phrased observation in August 1994 that he could 'even imagine ... supporting Tony Blair'.[49] Soon after Blair – or more accurately Campbell – made the first of many appearances as a guest columnist in the Murdoch press as he outlined to *News of the World* readers how Labour would 'not hit successful folk with tax rises'.[50] Murdoch and Blair met for the first time in mid-September when he and other Labour figures attended a reception given by the tycoon, which was followed by a private dinner with the Blairs.[51]

Murdoch's first concern was, as always, to protect his business interests under a future Labour government and confused signals were now emerging over the party's support for cross-media restrictions on ownership. In July 1994 Shadow Industry Secretary Robin Cook had pointed out that an enquiry into monopolistic trends was triggered by a 25 per cent market share. Murdoch was 'already well over' this and controlled a monolithic press which was 'right wing and conservative in political views, intolerant and judgmental in social views'.[52] But other leading Labour figures were appealing for new policies to reflect a new global media environment 'so vast as to be beyond the old traditional regulatory system'. Shadow Heritage Secretary Mo Mowlam was to outline her support for the 'loosening' of the party's stance as she argued that 'to legislate for the past would be criminal'.[53] But party critics detected a more pragmatic motivation as they considered that there should be 'no deal' with a man whose 'foul paper' had helped 'poison British society' and for fifteen years had 'waged war on the Labour party'.[54]

Such tensions were played out publicly in the summer of 1995 when Blair went on a 50-hour round trip to address News International's tri-annual conference in Australia. In a speech designed to appeal to Murdoch, he presented New Labour as heir to the anti-establishment Thatcherite spirit. Blair conceded that while previous relations had been 'poor', the 'changes on both sides' meant that 'the past should be behind us'.[55] The visit provoked further internal unease over whether Labour had the policies 'to deal with press barons who determine the agenda', while Blair attacked the 'ridiculous' arguments that the party 'should refrain from putting our case to any section of the press'. He maintained that 'no policy was traded'.[56] But insiders felt that this was not the full truth. Neil's view that there was 'no explicit' trade off but 'an implicit understanding, never openly talked about, between the two men, but an understanding all the same', is impossible to prove. But it has been supported by short-lived Labour Blairite spin doctor Joy Johnson as well as 'everyone' she had spoken to at News International.[57] While this meeting attracted most publicity, Blair, Mandelson and Camp-bell also established a whole network of contacts and friendships with senior News International executives, visiting the old battle ground at Wapping on a number of occasions, while Blair would regularly see Murdoch during his visits to London.[58]

In 1995 Murdoch had suggested that the electoral affiliations of his paper depended on finding out 'the difference between Mr Blair and Mr Major' – which one rival immediately alleged concerned their differing policies on media ownership.[59] It was soon apparent that he had little to worry about in this area. Both parties were condemned for their 'spineless' commercial appeasement as they, in Conrad Black's later words, began 'vying with each other for the honour of being the most obedient trained seal' of Murdoch. Labour's new-found credentials in what Black called the 'jumping and yelping' area were demonstrated notably in their stance on the 1996 Broad-casting Act, which relaxed existing rules on cross-media ownership.[60] In a stance that astonished media figures, the leadership opposed the govern-ment's proposal that newspaper groups with over 20 per cent of circulation should be debarred from holding a television franchise, which excluded not only the Mirror group but a furious Murdoch. The party instead tabled an amendment calling for total deregulation. Murdoch was no longer con-demned as a threat to media diversity but now hailed by Labour's media spokesman Lewis Moonie as a liberating 'visionary' who had opened up new media markets when 'no one else was prepared to'.[61] An independent analy-sis published later in the year concluded that there had been such a seachange in Labour's media policy that News International was now classed as one of the main beneficiaries of a Labour victory.[62]

But the Conservatives were old hands in 'jumping and yelping' for press support and made what Stuart Higgins, *Sun* editor from 1994, described as a number of 'very, very determined' attempts to win back the paper. Higgins was more pro-Major than his predecessor, while the paper's influential political editor, Trevor Kavanagh, was personally on the Eurosceptic right. They told No. 10 that they were 'working hard to put Murdoch off' backing Labour.[63] Higgins arranged lunches with the two party leaders on successive Mondays in the first half of 1996, attended by the same ten senior staff who were 'in many ways … more impressed by Major' who came across as 'more assured and convincing'. Major also enlisted Thatcher's help but this was less successful in what was, even by her high standards, a spectacular display of her disloyalty towards her successor, if Andrew Neil's story is accurate:

> Murdoch and Thatcher, his heroine, had this dinner, talking about British politics, and it was Murdoch who expressed a reservation about Blair. He said, 'Well, I'm not quite sure.' To which Thatcher said: 'Don't worry about Tony. He's fine, he's a patriot.'[64]

'Like him, shame about his party': press coverage of Labour 1994–1996

Despite this, Murdoch's support still remained in the balance in October 1996, as he articulated the fundamental dilemma of the Tory press throughout 1994–1997. A deep contempt for the existing Conservative government and Major personally competed with an attraction to Blair, alongside continued suspicion of Labour.[65] This ambiguity was soon demonstrated at the October 1994 party conference. Talk of a press second honeymoon was provoked by favourable verdicts of Blair's 'remarkable speech … full of devastating criticism of Tory failures', while his pledge to abolish Clause 4 was hailed as 'liberating Labour from its past'.[66] This was quickly dampened by later coverage which proved 'decidedly chilly, hostile even' towards a party committed to 'Marxist socialism' and 'a high-tax, highly regulated economy'.[67] Labour's welcoming of what David Blunkett hailed as Murdoch's 'conversion on the road to Damascus' proved distinctly premature as the *Sun* suggested that 'the REAL face of Labour' still savoured a policy of 'hard-line socialism'.[68] By the turn of the year, Labour's press coverage had taken a further dip, as the considered verdict appeared to be, as the *Express* put it, 'like him, shame about his party.' This stance was evidenced in a distinctly grudging response to the abolition of Clause 4 in May 1995, depicted as a 'mere charade' that obscured the continued power of old Labour.[69]

In the attention given to the anti-Major press coverage during the Conservative leadership contest that followed, it was rather overlooked that its entire premise was based on their even greater hostility to Labour. The *Mail*, while 'not impervious to the charms of Mr Blair', considered that 'only a Tory government' would 'defend rather than dilute the reforming achievements of the past 16 years'. Similarly the *Sun* 'passionately' outlined its

support for 'the policies of a Conservative government' as it called for 'a young fresh leader' to 'alert the country to the perils of voting Labour'.[70]
. This says something about the politically schizophrenic line taken by the tabloids, particularly the *Sun*, throughout this time. On occasion the paper was positively indignant in countering claims that Labour were not fit to govern from a governing party that could not be trusted to 'run a raffle'. When the Conservatives launched their 'New Labour New Danger' attack in mid-1996, the *Sun*, in a soundbite repeated by the Labour leader, argued that the real problem was 'Same Old Tories, Same Old Claptrap'.[71] Blair's pronouncements were often greeted favourably. His 1995 Labour conference speech, for instance, was eulogised as 'the most remarkable speech ever made' at such an event, which the paper defied 'anyone' to 'not want to vote Labour' after hearing.[72] On other occasions, however, the paper would revert to pre-1992 mode. The same conference reported how Labour 'would hammer voters with tax hikes' and, not for the first or last time, detected 'a distinct lack of substance' to a New Labour project that was dividing the party.[73] At heart, the Conservative tabloids continued to articulate a reactionary political and social ethos. The *Sun*'s attacks on 'Loony Lottery' handouts 'to lesbians, gays, prostitutes, rent boys, junkies and asylum seekers' brought back memories of its 'loony left' coverage of the 1980s. It was proof of the paper's continued belief, as it noted on another occasion, that 'As Ever, Maggie knows best'.[74]

'The press backs Blair': the 1997 general election

Nothing better illustrated how the tabloids were caught 'between fear and loathing' of Labour and the Conservatives respectively than the 1997 election.[75] For the *Mail* this produced 'a Tory paper fed up with the Tories' but still 'deeply suspicious of Labour'.[76] While the paper recognised that Blair had 'rendered Labour electable for the first time in a generation', it had little else positive to say about New Labour.[77] This was surprising given its earlier flirtations and because Rothermere had noted early in the election that while the *Mail* had always supported the Conservatives because Labour's policies were 'not acceptable', there was now 'the most original situation' where party policies were 'not terribly different'. English also declared in favour of a 'passionless' stance and the very fact that the paper's allegiance was even in question was historically unique.[78] But editor Paul Dacre evidently felt differently and misjudged the electoral mood to the extent of even, according to one senior executive, preparing a dummy paper based on a Conservative majority of thirty. It was a miscalculation epitomised by his despairing comment on hearing of the loss of Thatcher's former Finchley constituency, 'What the fuck is going on? These are fucking *Daily Mail* readers.'[79]

With this in mind, the *Mail* prominently highlighted stories linking Labour with union power, causing the first stumble of Labour's campaign with a lurid front page reporting how '63 FIRMS ON UNION HIT LIST' would 'be dragooned into recognising a union' under Blair.[80] Not even the 'CONSPIRACY OF SILENCE' of the 'union barons' could prevent the *Mail* from revealing how 'LABOUR'S BULLY BOYS' had offered a 'chilling hint' that a crippling 'summer of discontent' could once again hit Britain.[81] Other traditional coverage centred around 'LABOUR'S BROKEN PROMISES' and 'POLICY U-TURNS' while Blair was attacked for 'political kleptomania on a grand scale'.[82] Labour's most serious electoral discomfort was also caused when the paper splashed a leaked eight-week-old party document that insisted Labour 'completely opposed' the privatisation of air traffic control, a policy it was now refusing to rule out.[83]

Yet this approach was diluted by a new-found balance of attack that displayed 'an astonishingly critical attitude' to the government and especially Major. The *Mail* began the election questioning whether the electorate could 'once again trust a jaded, fractured and rudderless party that broke its word on taxation and betrayed the values of its core voters'. And it ended by declaring that it held 'no torch' for an administration marred by 'incompetence' and 'weak' leadership. Detailed content analysis concluded that the paper had 'appeared to support the Tories by default' as it had carried more unfavourable than favourable coverage about them, while Major even received almost the same proportion of negative coverage as Blair in editorials.[84] Meanwhile the intervention of James Goldsmith's Referendum party, while electorally insignificant, helped exacerbate Conservative divisions on Europe, which the *Mail* gave considerable publicity to in a dramatic 'BATTLE OF BRITAIN' campaign against the single currency. This gave a daily list of the increasing numbers of candidates who joined its 'great revolt' against official party policy.[85] This climaxed in a polling-day endorsement which listed 308 Tory candidates who had 'overturned' official government policy and called on voters to 'however reluctantly vote Conservative' on the basis of its greater Euroscepticism. It offered the climax to a campaign that demonstrated that 'with friends like the *Daily Mail*, the Conservatives hardly needed enemies'.[86]

Another unreliable ally was the *Daily Express*, which endorsed the Conservatives 'in so distant a manner that it could have been mistaken for neutrality'. Until mid-1995 the paper, edited by Major's close friend Nicholas Lloyd, had been the government's one press supporter. As late as October

Table 5.1 Partisanship and circulation of the popular press in 1997 (millions)

Daily Express	1.20	Con
Daily Mail	2.12	Con
Daily Mirror	2.39	Lab
Sun	3.93	Lab
Daily Star	0.66	Lab

Source: Scammell and Harrop, 'The Press', in Butler and Kavanagh (eds), *The British General Election of 1997*.

1995, it was being denounced by Labour for the 'fiction, invention and lies' of its political coverage.[87] By this time Lloyd's successor, Richard Addis, had been told by proprietor Lord Stevens that he was willing for him to take a more independent stance. Stevens' views were in any case increasingly eclipsed from early 1996 when United Newspapers amalgamated with the conglomerate MAI, controlled by the Labour peer Lord Hollick – a change of tone symbolised by the removal of Stevens' bust from the paper's lobby.[88] Hollick, who defined himself as 'an extremely committed' Labour supporter, was a former adviser to Kinnock (who made him a peer) and was the prime mover behind a 1997 pre-election report by British business outlining its confidence in the party's fitness to govern.[89] Unsurprisingly, a marked change in the paper's political approach soon became visible. To Major's dismay, Hollick confirmed a move away from a past 'slavish' position to a stance which would 'give Labour a fair show' and would be 'small-c conservative – like the leaders of both the main parties'.[90] The final decision would be the editor's choice, but the *Express* would report 'accurately' and 'not engage in sheer propaganda and invention . . . for political advantage'.[91]

By this stage the paper was attempting to cast away 'the barnacles of old allegiances and look at the key issues facing Middle Britain'.[92] The continuity in its formal affiliations masked a dramatic rupture with the full-blooded anti-Labour partisanship of recent elections. Its balanced approach was demonstrated by opposing articles written by the paper's two proprietors.[93] One content analysis that estimated partisanship by the subject as well as the slant of press reports concluded that the *Express*'s coverage was slightly biased towards Labour. Even editorials were balanced, factual and did not even cover the issue of trade unions that the *Mail* devoted eight leaders to.[94] The paper's almost tortuous equivocation even extended to the final front page editorial – 'NOW IT'S UP TO YOU' – which showed no sign of an endorsement until the last of its 18 paragraphs ended on page six. Finally, with what Addis described with some understatement as 'a less than ringing confidence', it concluded that the Conservatives were 'more likely to run Britain on the lines' which it approved of.[95]

But the most spectacular change of press alignment came on the first day of the campaign when Murdoch ordered a self-styled 'historic' announcement: 'THE SUN BACKS BLAIR.' In retrospect the paper's declaration reads as surprising given that coverage in the previous three months had unmistakably anticipated a 'better the devil you know' endorsement of the Conservatives.[96] By December 1996, the paper appeared to have come off the political fence to argue that 'the real election issue' was the creation of a 'Brussels socialist superstate', opposed by '99.9 per cent of the Tories'. The Labour leadership were also angered by a 'BLAIR VOWS: I'M BACKING BRUSSELS' headline, although of more interest to readers may have been its revelation that the Spice Girls were 'true Thatcherites' who 'could NEVER vote for Tony Blair's party'.[97] Such an automatic anti-Labour skew contrasted inversely with the way the *Mirror* had reported how 'Posh Spice' had 'hit the right note' for a band divided in their political loyalties by branding John Major a 'boring pillock'.[98] The *Sun* also proved the most negative of the Tory tabloids in response to Labour's far-reaching pledge in January 1997 not to raise direct taxation in the lifetime of the next parliament (see below, pp. 136–7). Readers were simply urged, 'don't fall for this con trick'.[99] Further coverage unequivocally called on readers to 'VOTE TORY TO SAVE THE POUND' and juxtaposed a choice between Blair, 'the man with flexible convictions', and Major, who 'sticks to his convictions despite trendy ridicule'. Using the same argument that the *Telegraph* later used to endorse its chosen party, the *Sun* asked, 'Why trust imitation Tories more than the real ones?' This stance peaked in mid-February in an attack on 'the hollowness of Labour's carping' which wondered, 'if even Europe agrees that Britain's economy is in good shape thanks to the Tories, why put it at risk?'[100] Just two weeks before its endorsement of Labour, the paper was reminding readers that they were 'still Red Flag socialists at heart'. But by this time, according to insiders, Murdoch had already made his decision to support Blair. The paper had recently accused Labour of performing 'the mother of all U-turns' in its political stance. It was now time for the *Sun* to do the same.[101]

The *Sun*'s declaration generated intense media coverage of how Major found himself 'KNOCKED OFF HIS SOAPBOX' (which he had used to favourable publicity in 1992).[102] Hours later Blair declared it was 'not a question of Murdoch being too powerful' and his activities would not be restricted by any legislation. In a mirror-image of previous left-wing allegations, suitably outraged Conservative officials claimed it 'confirmed a private commercial agreement' between Murdoch and the party.[103] But the publicity disguised an unusually murky *Sun* message which, as former leader writer Ronald Spark observed, 'faced more ways than a Chinese contortionist'. As the headline suggested, the paper endorsed Blair's 'vision, purpose and coverage' rather than Labour, about which it retained 'great reservations'. It failed to credit its chosen party with any good ideas apart from those copied from opponents who had 'all the right policies but all the wrong faces'. Blair's leadership would solve this by offering 'hope to those who are disillusioned . . . while promising to do exactly what the Tories have done by keeping down taxes, borrowing and spending'.[104] This partly reflected serious internal opposition to a position imposed by Murdoch against the opposition of four senior executives and the editor and which provoked angry complaints from some readers – including one who fumed, 'I'm so bloody disgusted with your stand I'm gonna go and buy the *Mirror*.'[105]

More fundamentally, it illustrated the *Sun*'s loss of its assured political direction of the 1980s. This was reflected in muted election coverage that did not once lead with an attack against its new 'enemy' and contained nothing to compare with its previous savaging of Labour and Kinnock.[106] This was hardly surprising given that, on Europe, it had far more common ground with its theoretical enemy than with Labour. This generated some interesting contortions, although the paper was met half-way by Blair's increasingly nationalistic declarations in the paper of his 'love for £'.[107] Nevertheless its remarkable shift meant that the *Sun*'s coverage was more pro-Labour than any other paper apart from the *Mirror*, with nearly half of its coverage being positive and just 26 per cent being negative. By contrast, 59 per cent of its coverage of the Conservatives was unfavourable and only 13 per cent favourable.[108] In a spin Neil Kinnock could only have dreamed of, the paper argued that militant teachers planning strikes no longer threatened a new 'Winter of Discontent' but were doing so because Labour 'no longer' held 'the same beliefs as the left wingers'. Even disagreeing – albeit 'respectfully' – with Thatcher, the *Sun* now believed that Labour's changes represented 'bold and courageous decisions to drag itself out of its 1970s mindset'. Tory attacks on Labour U-turns were 'missing the point' because Blair 'had pointed his party in the right way on the economy, unions and privatisation'.[109] Meanwhile Labour slips were ignored as studiously as they had once been highlighted. Gordon Brown's admission that there was a hole in Labour's spending plans was simply an example of 'honest' politics. A Prescott 'gaffe' that the minimum wage could cost jobs was generously relegated to a two-inch paragraph at the bottom of page two, in contrast to the 'storm' he faced over his alleged admittance of 'lies' on the front pages of the *Mail* and *Express*.[110]

It was perhaps no surprise that the *Sun*'s most important contribution came over the question of 'sleaze'. Just as the Conservatives, aided by the *Mail* and the *Telegraph*, were placing Labour on the defensive on the union question, the *Sun* revealed the 'SCANDAL OF TORY MP'S MISTRESS, 17'. In a classic case of tabloid entrapment, five pages of detail and pictures showing how 'married Tory MP Piers Merchant' had been 'having a sordid affair with a 17-year-old blonde Soho nightclub hostess'. The MP brazenly denied the *Sun*'s allegations and, backed by his constituency party, resisted intense pressure from the Conservative leadership to stand down, generating further hostile coverage of Major's leadership. The *Mail*, fully distracted from its union preoccupation, ran four anti-Conservative front pages which ended with the distinctly barbed complement, 'SLEAZE: MAJOR ACTS AT LAST'. The *Sun* more directly viewed the affair as further proof that a 'weak … loser' who 'cannot run his party is in no position to run the country'.[111] This, and further 'sleaze' revelations ensured that the issue dominated newspaper coverage of the election as much as it had the previous parliament.[112]

Despite earlier tensions, Labour was also vigorously supported by the *Mirror* in coverage that showed none of the uncertainty or balance of its rivals and culminated in fifteen pages of polling day propaganda around the strapline: 'You Deserve Better.'[113] Describing itself as 'the paper that's always been loyal to Labour', the *Mirror* conveyed the 'upbeat and optimistic' mood of Labour's campaign to a much greater extent than in previous elections.[114] Anticipating Blair's dramatic '24 hours to save the NHS' eve-of-poll rhetoric, the paper also produced what was undoubtedly the front page of the election. Under the headline – 'READ THIS AND WEEP ... NOW GET ANGRY' – was text devoted entirely to the tear-inducing words of a 'sobbing nurse'. She had phoned the *Mirror* with details of how, after an 18 hour shift, she had comforted a 22-year-old cancer patient until he died in a story that undoubtedly represented 'a devastating indictment' of how the Conservatives had 'destroyed the National Health Service'.[115] In another inversion of previous coverage, it was the *Mirror's* turn to offer a special 'nightmare' prediction of a Conservative victory that would see a 'right wing coup' bring right-winger Michael Portillo to power, 18 per cent VAT on food, financial chaos and privatised hospitals and police forces. More light-hearted coverage also recalled the self-confident humour of the *Sun* in 1992. 'Vote Labour and make Paul Daniels disappear' was how the paper greeted the 'best election news so far' that the comedian had threatened to leave Britain if Labour won.[116]

With the *Star* supporting Labour for the first time in an election, alongside typically limited but balanced coverage, it was left to the *Daily Telegraph*, once Major's bitter opponent, to provide his only wholehearted press backing as it asked readers, 'Why buy the imitation when you can have the original?'[117] Nevertheless, the attention it gave to sleaze and other pro-Labour issues even made its content slightly pro-Labour in bias, a position shared with all other national papers except the *Daily Mail*, which marginally leaned towards the Conservatives.[118] Another analysis concluded that over one-third of Labour's total coverage was favourable, compared with only 16 per cent for the Conservatives, while the Tories suffered an unprecedented 51 per cent of unfavourable coverage as against an even more remarkable just 29 per cent for Labour.[119]

This reversal of traditional newspaper loyalty did not go unchallenged by the loyal right, which accused the tabloids of presenting 'an extremely distorted picture' of the election and questioned whether the *Sun's* well-timed sleaze revelations were part of 'a Labour campaign'. Major's former Director of Communications, Hugh Clover, attacked an 'unfair' and 'out of balance' press that, after years of courting from Labour, had lost sight of its 'simple duty to put the issues in front of the people'.[120] The authors of these strikingly familiar complaints may have changed, but the usual suspect remained the same, the evil Rasputin of Murdoch, who lay behind the 'character assassinations' and 'twisted agenda' of the *Sun*.[121]

The irony of this remarkable Tory conversion to the principles of balanced and ethical reporting also did not go unnoticed by Labour sympathisers who were amused to find Murdoch denounced by precisely those people who had 'hitherto rigged the market to afford him every possible commercial advantage'.[122] Such hypocrisy, however, merely represented an inversion of Labour's new-found warmth to him and the question of what would distinguish the *Sun's* new partisanship 'from the old shameful propaganda' worried *Guardian* journalists rather more than the pragmatic Labour party.[123] Apart from Claire Short's outspoken comments that the *Sun* was 'still revolting', the party remained uneasily silent about a paper which an off-message Cherie Blair had once declared she 'wouldn't have . . . in the house'.[124] In August 1994, Robin Cook had found it 'extraordinary' to see the controversy over Murdoch's political allegiances conducted solely around which party he would support rather than 'about his obligation to provide objective reporting'.[125] He never commented on his party leadership's subsequent failure to raise this question. For, as Simon Jenkins pointed out:

> If a foreign proprietor had taken a Labour icon and turned it Tory there would have been howls of outrage about foreign interference in British politics . . . This time I heard not a peep about proprietorial interference from Labour . . . We can only marvel at the infinite mutability of human affairs.[126]

The moral – or immoral – equivalence of the parties in their press dealings had been never clearer and once more raised the question of who the real 'harlots' were.

Why the press backed Blair

The most important reason for the dramatic rupturing of the 1979–1992 loyalties was the most obvious. The collapse of the Conservative party's electoral support after September 1992 was mirrored as dramatically among newspaper readers. The massive Conservative lead over Labour among *Mail* and *Express* readers declined by 36 and 33 percentage points respectively by the first half of 1994. By this time over half of *Sun* readers were backing Labour and only half again supporting the Tories. Whereas in 1992, two-thirds of middle-market readers backed the Conservatives, by the 1997 election less than half did so, while 52 per cent of *Sun* readers now voted Labour and only 36 per cent supported their opponents.[127] Commercially or politically, newspapers could not continue to preach the virtues of the Conservative party when this did not correspond with the feelings of most readers. It was no coincidence that while the loyalist *Express* lost one-fifth of its circulation between 1992–1997, the *Mail*, which explicitly articulated readership discontent with the Conservatives, increased its by one-quarter. The wider voting shift was most closely mirrored amongst *Sun* readers, whose voting intentions reflect a cross-section of the electorate. Its stance in 1997 was primarily a reflection of its political powerlessness, of the fact that more readers were going to support Labour than any other party regardless of what it said. As Stuart Higgins revealingly put it, if the *Sun* had been on the wrong side after the election, it would have been 'a journalistic and a commercial nightmare, going against everything we think the *Sun* stands for, i.e. popular opinion'.[128]

This again raises the perennial question of whether newspapers were reflecting or shaping this change of opinion. The two most detailed studies suggest at most a marginal press effect, while two others more positively argue that the press, and especially the *Sun*, boosted the size of Labour's majority in 1997.[129] Blair and the Labour high command certainly viewed the change in press behaviour as 'hugely important' and it undoubtedly had a crucial influence on the wider political agenda.[130] Newspapers, for instance, played a large role in ensuring that the 1997 election became about sleaze and Europe. Moreover, their focus on Conservative failings throughout the parliament meant, in the words of the *Sun*'s political editor, that Labour 'got away with murder' and faced far less critical scrutiny of their position than they might have. A more helpful press would also have made much more of the country's economic prosperity, with an ironic contrast between 'feel good' coverage in the 1992 recession and its complete absence in 1997 when Britain 'on every index had the best record of any major European economy'.[131]

This readership pressure for a more anti-Tory line was further reinforced by the changing political agenda of newspapers after 1992. In retrospect, press loyalty to Major between 1990 and 1992 had been artificial. When Major turned out to be an illegitimate successor, lacking Thatcher's leadership and direction, a press which had never really forgiven the Tory party for November 1990 withdrew their support. This backward-looking loyalty to what Norman Lamont called 'the golden decade' of the 1980s was also paradoxically reinforced by a feeling that newspapers had been rather too loyal during this time and should now assert their independence.[132] Commercially the stories of government divisions, rivalry and plotting that engulfed the Tory party made good copy. The enormous contemporary expansion and competition of media news and current affairs outlets also meant that the 'Tory crisis' story was given much more sustained publicity than, for example, the similar difficulties faced by Wilson in the later 1960s.[133] The preoccupation with sleaze partly reflected the traditional newspaper fascination with sex and also tied in with a further 'dumbing down', personalisation or sexualisation of political coverage detected by some commentators.[134] The press's vigorous anti-government line also reflected a new self-confident, high-earning media elite that had developed under Conservative patronage in the 1980s. This had, according to Williams, become 'the most powerful interest group in modern Britain'. Turning on its creators, it now came to relish its role at war with an unpopular government and its apparent power to dictate resignations and policies.[135]

There was also a more personal element to the conflict. Charles Lewington, the Conservative Director of Communications between 1995–1997, concedes that the party should have 'done more to court the press'. But he adds that 'getting John Major and newspaper editors together was one thing: creating a natural chemistry between them was another'.[136] In marked contrast to the warmth of the Thatcher years, newspaper proprietors and the new wave of newspaper editors increasingly appeared to hold the Prime Minister in political and personal contempt. On the latter level, Major was the victim of much the same intellectual snobbery suffered by Kinnock, from what one loyal journalist denounced as the 'snob mob' of editors and columnists. With Brixton-born Major, who had left school at 16, pitted against Fettes and Oxford-educated Tony Blair, this prejudice seemed to even work in Labour's favour. As one editor put it in the election, 'I find Blair so much easier to get along with than Major. I suppose it's a class thing. He's much more like us, isn't he.'[137] And in a popular press drawn to personalities, the bland and beleaguered Major never had the same appeal as his predecessor, while the press were drawn to Blair's apparent personal and political dynamism in a way they never were to Kinnock.

This press hostility was reciprocated. Major, like others before him, would frequently complain to editors about coverage, angrily telling Kelvin MacKenzie on one occasion how he was 'bloody sick of it'. By early 1994 the Prime Minister could 'barely bring himself to speak to journalists he once regarded as friends', commenting, 'I hate them. They make my flesh creep.'[138] Quite how far these conflicts affected press behaviour is debatable. MacKenzie considered that Major 'allowed a personality clash' with Murdoch to cost him the *Sun*'s endorsement. Lewington was less sure, claiming that 'discontent ran so deep amongst newspaper editors that no amount of discreet breakfasts, pre-deadline phone calls and honours could have done anything to reverse it'.[139] Partly this was because the press was simply bored with the Tories and, as in 1963–1964, 'time for a change' was a potent appeal. The tabloids, if not the country, would have been satisfied by Major's replacement as they could and would have rallied more enthusiastically to a new leader than one they had so fiercely criticised in the past. Also important was that, in the paralysing divisions over the party's post-Thatcherite direction, the Conservative press was not a mere observer, but a highly disruptive and partisan participant. Faced with the adoption of a largely centrist approach by their government, the Eurosceptic-right became the Conservative's own 'party within a party' and formed an 'alternative government' that reached right up to the cabinet 'bastards'. Their stance was encouraged by right-wing newspapers that strongly advocated the need for 'clear blue water' between the parties and ensured that what Major called the 'poison' peddled by the right had such a deadly effect.[140]

Labour also played a key part in neutralising tabloid hostility. Partly this was due to what Mandelson called 'a tough, robust and ... sometimes abrasive approach' to news management, as demonstrated by Campbell's standard rebuke to journalists, 'What's that crap you wrote in today's paper?'[141] The Labour high command were also supported by a 200-strong team at the party's new communication centre in Millbank, which operated in conditions compared to the neighbouring MI5 headquarters, with security swipe cards, a ban on visitors and compulsory confidentiality pledges. As important as these human resources was the party's £500,000 *Excalibur* information retrieval computer system, which served as 'an awesome intelligence gathering tool ... media monitoring as Star Wars was to the Home Guard'. It scanned an astonishing 92,000 pages of automatically indexed information per second and meant that the misrepresentations of opponents could now be 'rapidly-rebutted' within seconds rather than hours or days.[142]

The effectiveness of the party's communication strategy was illustrated most notably over tax. In November 1996, the Conservatives issued a hundred-page dossier which claimed that Labour's spending commitments would mean tax rises of £1,200 for every family. It was a carbon copy of their 1992 campaign but the difference in impact and Labour's response could not have been greater. Labour had been alerted by a previous day's *Daily Telegraph* story in which its author, George Jones, claimed that the Conservative figures had been 'approved' by the independent analysis of head-of-the-civil-service, Sir Robin Butler. Before the Conservatives had even formally made their allegations, Shadow Chancellor Gordon Brown had denounced their 'lying'. Labour also asserted that Butler had not approved the document and had protested about the use of civil servants to check the figures, leading the *Evening Standard*'s first edition to conclude: 'Bang Goes Tory Tax Bombshell.' Shortly after, Labour's media advisers staggered to a press conference with bundles of the paper, which they handed out free and then issued a lengthy rebuttal of '89 Tory lies on top of 22 Tory tax increases'. The party was rewarded by press coverage the following day that saw the broadsheets attack a 'ludicrously over the top' 'sign of self-delusion', the *Express* offer a balanced summary while the *Mail*'s headline and story spin reported 'Labour's fury at the "spree that never was"'.[143]

In contrast to Labour's usually effective media management, in the summer of 1995 the Conservatives did not even have anyone detailed to monitor the all-important newspaper first editions. The 'Maples Memorandum', written by the party's vice-chairman, summed up the party's communication failings and strongly stressed the need 'to feed our friends and potential friends in the press with good stories'. Its leaking, and Labour's immediate republishing of *The Maples Report*, aptly symbolised the problem.[144] Hugh Clover was appointed in June 1995, and pledged to rectify these problems. He resigned barely four months later complaining despairingly of the 'public relations disasters' of a party that behaved as if it were 'in office by divine right'.[145] Failure was virtually guaranteed, given a publicly divided and discredited Conservative party that refused to stay 'on message' and proved unable to agree on how to attack the New Labour enemy. As Major told Charles Lewington on one occasion, 'I know I've got a bad job, but I wouldn't want yours for all the world.'[146]

The result was an election campaign that made Labour's 1983 effort look like a model of disciplined communication. The first ten days saw an almost unbelievable catalogue of 'sleaze'-related disasters, with reports of cash given in brown envelopes from the owner of Harrods to two former ministers followed by the Piers Merchant scandal.[147] This competed with news that a leading Scottish Tory MP had resigned after falling in love with 'a married blonde mother of four while attending a clinic for alcoholism' and was then locked up after trying to murder his wife with an axe. It was quickly followed by the resignation of the chairman of the Scottish Tories following rumours circulated by his own party of a previous homosexual relationship.[148] The climax was reached in Neil Hamilton's Tatton constituency as Martin Bell, an 'anti-sleaze' 'WHITE KNIGHT' journalistic war hero, fought a campaign managed by his beautiful blond daughter and aided by the equally photogenic David Soul. On the other side stood the frightening 'Lady Macbeth' figure of Christine Hamilton, whose attitude to the 'corrupt' media was summed up in her line, 'get those greasy reptiles off the church daffodils'. In perhaps the most surreal moment of the campaign, they were joined by their friend, *Coronation Street* actor Bill Roach, who may have done their chances more harm than good by turning up with a Harrods shopping bag.[149] Faced with an undefendable Tory party and a one-sided election, newspapers were more interested in news than propaganda and the main story was clearly the political turmoil within the Conservative party. This was particularly the case as half their candidates publicly announced their disagreement with party policy on Europe and supported a Eurosceptic line savagely dismissed by their Chancellor as 'paranoid nonsense'. As Lewington later recalled, 'I sometimes wonder why it was only a landslide.'[150] On the other side, Labour fought perhaps its most disciplined campaign ever. This reached its climax as what Mandelson claimed was a Tory 'desire to spread fear among the voters' was more than reciprocated in a nasty but effective pre-poll scare story that the Conservatives were planning to abolish state pensions.[151]

It is arguable that Labour's presentational superiority assumed particular importance as policy differences between the two parties were reduced.[152] But it was this second factor, the changing substance rather than the image, that offered the key to explaining Labour's press triumph in 1997. Between 1994–1997 Labour repositioned itself as 'an ideologically transvestite party', audaciously borrowing policies, images and rhetoric that had once been the property of the right.[153] The party's electoral dominance over the Conservatives was paradoxically accompanied by its acceptance of key elements of the Tory 'neo-Liberal consensus' and a general failure to articulate an alternative ideological vision to Thatcherism. Will Hutton, the proponent of the clearest 'big idea' alternative to neo-liberalism in the form the stakeholder society, suggested soon after the 1997 election victory, 'the Tories are governing in a sense through their surrogates, New Labour'.[154]

This was reflected in policy shifts and aggressive right-wing rhetoric on issues of crime, the family and education, all of which played well in the tabloids. But the most important policy change was Labour's momentous decision to abandon its redistributive taxation policy, 'the central modernising task' of the 1992–1997 period and the key to an electoral strategy of 'reassurance, reassurance reassurance'.[155] Labour's success in 'winning the tax war' climaxed spectacularly in a brilliantly orchestrated news operation in January 1997 as Brown first revealed that he would accept the government's spending targets for the next two years. Just 12 hours later, he dramatically announced that the basic and top rates of direct taxation would remain the same throughout the lifetime of the next parliament.[156] It was a coup that left the Conservatives speechless and was summed up by the *Evening Standard* headline, 'Labour fires Tax Exocet'. While the presentation was brilliant, it was the substance, combined with the Tory record since 1992, which won Labour this support. As the *Mail* noted, it was 'as significant an act of exorcism . . . witnessed in the post-war history of British politics'. And because the Conservatives had 'destroyed their own reputation as tax-cutters', they were 'most ill-qualified to mock New Labour's new-found fiscal restraint'.[157] Traditional responses were reversed as centre-left commentators queued up to attack what seemed to signal 'not simply the end of socialism but of social democracy and the whole Croslandite commitment to use public spending and tax to reduce inequality'. It left columnist Alan Watkins with the question, 'What therefore is the point of a Labour government at all? I merely ask.'[158] The view that a Labour victory would merely produce 'a crypto-Conservative administration' even appeared to be shared by a key player in the earlier stage of modernisation, as Roy Hattersley now lamented that a Labour victory would:

> not herald any sort of transformation of British society. . . . More than 30 years ago Harold Wilson said that the party was a crusade or it was nothing. I try not to think about his assertion. The logical conclusions are too painful.[159]

From the reverse perspective, however, it meant less reason for tabloid hostility. Without Labour's policy transformations, they would have diluted their reservations about Major and fought much harder to safeguard the Thatcherite legacy. But now the difference between New Labour and the Conservatives, to invert a favoured justification, seemed to be 'an inch *not* worth fighting for'.[160] And if their heroine could reassure Murdoch that he had little to worry about in supporting Blair, who were the press to disagree?

The press backs Blair again: the 2001 election and after

In many ways the 2001 election saw a continuation of the pattern visible four years previously. Labour's second landslide victory was accompanied by what was, statistically, an even better press. 72 per cent of newspapers supported the party while the Conservatives received their lowest level of support as they were formally endorsed by the *Daily Telegraph* (which accounted for 8 per cent) while the *Mail* was reduced to a negative anti-Labour stance. Yet beneath the surface was a more complicated position. In the first place the endorsement of Labour was again qualified and measured and the Conservatives or William Hague did not face the sustained personal and ideological hostility that the left faced between 1979–1992. Second, Labour's press honeymoon may not have been over, but there were signs of clear strain. An exhaustive content analysis by Echo research of over 4,000 election articles found that 26 per cent of Labour's coverage was favourable, while 39 per cent was unfavourable and 35 per cent was neutral. This was hardly a glowing endorsement, with an increase in unfavourable material and a decrease in favourable coverage compared with 1997. And it represented only a partial advantage against the Conservatives, with 18 per cent of their coverage being favourable, 42 per cent unfavourable and 40 per cent neutral. Both parties suffered a predominantly negative press in 2001; Labour's was merely less bad than the Conservatives.[161]

The more hostile media environment was visible most notably in the relentlessly hostile coverage that had become devoted to government 'spin' (in contrast to earlier media admiration). The subject now became *the* media story about politics and threatened to damage Labour as much as earlier sleaze allegations had damaged the Conservatives, as it fed into wider trends towards disengagement with the political system.[162] By summer 2002, Labour's honeymoon was well and truly over as senior government ministers accused the right-wing press of a campaign of 'character assassinations' against the Blairs in behaviour that was, claimed Home Secretary David Blunkett, 'almost on the edge of insanity'.[163] This illustrated, third, how the popular press had continued to remain more volatile in its coverage of the parties than during the 1979–1992 period. The *Mirror*, for instance, was later to temporarily renounce its pro-Labour tag completely as it embarked on an aggressive (arguably too commercially aggressive) anti-Blair style of coverage that, at times, even outdid the *Mail* in its anti-Blair coverage (for example over the 'Cheriegate' story about the Blairs' purchase of flats in Bristol in December 2002). Meanwhile, the *Daily Express* switched political sides from Conservative to Labour and back again across 1997–2004, while the *Sun* continued in its political volatility. But at the same time, and fourth, the broad right-of-centre ideological position of the bulk of the popular press remained largely unchanged.

The 2001 election – dubbed by the *Telegraph* as 'the one when Prescott hit a man with bad hair' – was widely judged to be one of low popular interest and little excitement given the expected Labour landslide (aside from the above incident and the berating Blair received over health from one angry voter).[164] As usual, the election saw the *Mirror* and the *Mail* occupy the partisan polarities of left and right while the *Sun* offered measured, but far from uncritical, support for Labour. The *Star* once again endorsed Labour while the *Express*, in the most significant election shift, endorsed Labour for the first time in its history.

The one lone anti-Labour voice in the popular press remained the *Daily Mail*, which had eclipsed the *Mirror* as the second-biggest-circulation UK

Table 5.2 Partisanship and circulation of the popular press in 2001 (millions)

Daily Express	0.92	Lab
Daily Mail	2.33	Anti-Lab
Daily Mirror	2.05	Lab
Sun	3.22	Lab
Daily Star	0.58	Lab

Source: Scammell and Harrop, 'A Press Disarmed', in Butler and King (eds), *The British General Election of 1992.*

newspaper and was the only one that was increasing readership in a declining market. The death of the third Lord Rothermere (succeeded by his young son) and David English strengthened Paul Dacre's control of editorial policy. Any past flirtation with New Labour was now ended as the paper proved the government's most persistent critic in the popular press from 1997. Mutual praise gave way to the more traditional mutual hostility. Appearing before a government select committee in March 2003, Dacre accused Campbell, who had recently resigned as government director of communications, of poisoning relations with the press. He in turn denounced a 'vile' paper that played a key role in spreading the press's 'culture of negativity'.[165] During the election the *Mail* showed no sign of what it denounced as 'the sycophancy to New Labour shown by some sections of the media'.[166] One central theme of its coverage was the paper's denunciation of 'an insidious and dangerous demeaning of democracy' that an 'arrogant' culture of spin had created – the Prescott punch was viewed as symptomatic of this. Another theme was a relentless diet of economic bad news as it dwelt heavily on the 'tax blitz' that middle-earners would suffer under another Labour government and the rising cost of petrol prices, insurance contributions and mortgage payments. Indeed the only rise that the *Mail* could not predict was in support for the Conservatives.[167] The paper's longing for a previous era was demonstrated by an adulatory interview with a 'true leader', Thatcher, viewed as the one voice that 'rises above the hubbub of mediocrity to present a vision of what Britain could be'.[168] Such was its lack of confidence in the Tories that the paper took the highly unusual step of relegating its final campaign endorsement to the inside pages. It could not bring itself to positively endorse a Tory party that was 'timid, incoherent, lacking in the vision and confidence' of the 'unstoppable' Thatcher years. They 'haven't done enough to win' it conceded, instead restricting itself to urging readers to vote negatively 'in a way that will prevent Labour having overweening power'.[169] Despite this, the paper's persistent anti-Labour skew and the lower level of persistent hostility it showed to Hague's Tories compared with the Major government in 1997, made it a more useful friend to them than four years previously.

A more confident, but equally relentless, style of propaganda was to be found in the *Mirror*. The paper's relationship with New Labour after it took office had continued to be strained. New Labour's courting of the *Sun*, alongside a commercial need to avoid being perceived as the government's lapdog, determined a more critical style of coverage. A change of tone appeared notable in May 1998 when the paper launched a stinging attack on the 'shame' of Labour's health record and accused 'the self-styled people's premier' of being 'badly out of step with his people'. The *Mirror* even later backed the Conservative Stephen Norris in the election for London Mayor in 2000 in a stance that was opposed by senior executives, readers and its political editor.[170] More within the paper's traditions was the appointment in 1998 of 'the man Number Ten tried to ban' (see below, p. 141), pro-Brown political editor Paul Routledge, who revelled in his 'off-message' reputation in Downing Street.[171] Yet while flexing its critical muscles lest New Labour take it too much for granted, the *Mirror* remained broadly 'on message' in Labour's first term. It temporarily returned to its role as partisan cheerleader in the general election in what editor Piers Morgan freely admitted to be 'absolutely biased and partisan … four-square' support for Labour.[172]

This was demonstrated in its opening and most memorable election front page: 'BRIDGET HAGUE'S DIARY.' This spoofed the popular column and film, *Bridget Jones's Diary*, as Hague's diary recorded: 'Nightmare! Told we're going to be left on shelf AGAIN!! Seems everyone's right. I AM useless. Hear Portillo is bitching behind my back. Plan to have 14 pints and chicken tikka massala to forget. Note to self: Remember inner poise and find proper career. Job prospects v.v. bad.'[173] Predicable and sometimes puerile anti-Tory coverage followed, with Hague remembered as a 'NERD IN AN ANORAK' from his student days, with 76 per cent of its coverage of the Tories being unfavourable. The Labour alternative and record since 1997 was greeted with a more qualified, but still overwhelmingly positive, partisanship, with 58 per cent of stories being favourable.[174]

A more measured degree of political partisanship was to be found in the *Sun*, which proved slightly less critical of the Tories but more critical of Labour than in 1997. The *Sun*'s approach had continued to show considerable diversity during the first Labour administration. A broadly supportive attitude to New Labour was accompanied by several stinging attacks, notably on its pro-Europe policy, while it also veered between contempt and sympathy for William Hague's leadership. This complex picture was visible in its election coverage and was reflected in a MORI poll that demonstrated that 48 per cent of regular *Sun* readers did not know whether their paper was supporting Labour.[175] On the one hand, whereas once it had relished in its power as a political outsider, now it promoted its cosy relationship with the government that made it, to quote BBC political editor Andrew Marr, 'the St James's Gazette of New Labour'.[176] The *Sun* was informed even before the Queen that the election had been postponed from May to June due to the foot and mouth outbreak (a decision that infuriated Piers Morgan when he later discovered the truth after earlier Labour reassurances that this had not been the case). There duly followed several other front page exclusives that correctly revealed key ministerial appointments in the subsequent Labour government. Equally the paper qualified its support as it warned that 'our support – or at least our enthusiasm – for a Blair second term should NOT be taken for granted'. It continued to warn of its 'deeply, even mortally damaging' opposition to joining the euro. This, it menaced, 'would be opposed with the kind of ferocity we reserved for another Labour leader. Neil Kinnock. Don't forget that Tony.'[177] Several editorials also expressed sympathy for Hague – who fought 'for values he holds dear' and 'will be true to his word' – who was treated with a respect never bestowed on previous Labour leaders. Meanwhile Trevor Kavanagh, dubbed 'the most dangerous man in Britain' for his influence, proved distinctly measured in devoting a similar percentage of negative, positive and neutral stories to both Labour and the Conservatives. The qualified endorsement of New Labour was visible in its eve-of-poll warning that Blair would have to properly deliver on his election promises as it urged: 'DON'T LET US DOWN TONY.'[178]

Perhaps the most substantial political change between 1997 and 2001 was the way the *Express* discarded its reluctant but balanced conservatism with a pro-Labour stance. The paper's post-election conversion to Labour also produced a change of editor, with Labour supporter Rosie Boycott installed in April 1998. Such was the apparent shift in political allegiances symbolised by this that Boycott found herself accused a month later of giving in to government pressure and withdrawing the appointment of Paul Routledge as political editor before he was snapped up by the *Mirror*. This change of political allegiance did little to avert – and may have even accelerated – the paper's loss of readers and, in 2000, to the outrage of the paper's journalists, the paper was sold to soft-porn and *Hello* publisher, Richard Desmond. Desmond, a crudely spoken, highly interventionist proprietor, found himself immediately courted by Labour and was later revealed to have donated £100,000 to the party. But his political allegiances failed to prevent the departures of Boycott (who remained to negotiate a £300,000 pay-off) and political editor Anthony Bevins (who more honourably did not). The paper under Desmond seemed more interested in celebrity gossip than political campaigning and ran just two election front pages in 2001 to make it the most apolitical of all the tabloids.

But what political coverage it did feature was notable as it declared on polling day that after '100 years of support for the Conservatives in every general election since 1900 we urge you to vote Labour today'. This was hardly a reflection of the paper's readership, with 43 per cent of its dwindling band of readers voting Tory, while only 33 per cent backed Labour. But the change in the paper since 1992 was demonstrated when, after the *Daily Mail* challenged Blair to answer 12 election questions but refused to print his answers, the *Express* published them instead in the interests of 'fair debate'.[179] Meanwhile the *Express*'s downmarket sister paper, the *Star*, was more interested in profiling the decision of Jordan, its regular page-three model and star of Desmond's adult publications, to stand as MP – 'that's member of Parliament not Massive Pair' it helpfully explained to readers. Her campaign 'for a bigger, better Britain' generated more coverage than the other parties combined, but alongside this preoccupation, the paper did manage to slip in an eve-of-poll endorsement of Blair as 'a safe pair of hands' with a mostly 'capable team of ministers'.[180] However, the *Express*'s flirtation with Labour proved only a temporary affair. An increasingly anti-government stance, and a hardline policy against asylum, culminated in April 2004 with a front page declaration – 'ENOUGH IS ENOUGH, MR BLAIR' – of the paper's return to the Conservative fold.[181]

Conclusion

New Labour's triumph amongst the press in 1997 and 2001 has led some academics and journalists to point to a press 'shift to the left after 1992' to produce a new pro-Labour bias.[182] Yet, while 60 per cent of newspapers backed the party in 1997 and 72 per cent in 2001, this disguises a far more conservative message than during previous high-points of Labour's support. In 1945 and 1964, the party won support and sympathy fighting, to a large extent, on a centre-left agenda. By contrast, it was ultimately not a press realignment leftwards but Labour's shift rightwards that occurred after 1994. As the *Sun*'s political editor argued, 'It's not the *Sun* that's changed. It's the Labour party. They've moved in our direction and a long way.'[183] Indeed, in some respects, Blair's first press triumph was accompanied by a press shift rightwards after 1992, particularly on Europe. The Conservatives would almost certainly have won the support of the *Sun* and a positive endorsement from the *Mail* if they had fought the 1997 election on a more right-wing agenda. The press continued to extol values of individualism, anti-welfarism and anti-unionism throughout 1994–2003.[184] The Blairite project won its support and sympathy because, with the exceptions of Europe and constitutional reform, it seemed to offer limited challenge to, and broad acceptance of, this agenda. So, in 1997, the *Sun* endorsed New Labour simply because it had accepted that 'virtually everything' the Conservatives 'stood for on free enterprise and union reform was right'. Whereas in 1992 the paper evoked the 'NIGHTMARE ON KINNOCK STREET', in 1997 the similarly timed message was a front page story, 'BLAIR KICKS OUT LEFTIES', who would be 'ruthlessly axed' from his first cabinet. The *Sun*'s entire rhetoric still remained structured around its hostility to socialism and a more general right-wing philosophy. It was illustrative of Labour's rightward shift that the paper, despite its difficulties, was able to endorse the party.[185]

It was further illustrative of Labour's centre-right record in government that the paper continued its support. While the *Sun* did offer some temporary social liberalism during David Yelland's editorship – its 'race' coverage after September 11th, for instance was remarkably restrained – there was little change to its underlying philosophy (and its right-wing edge further hardened from January 2003 with the installation of new editor, Rebekah Wade). This was also demonstrated by the paper's political manifesto published just prior to the 2001 election that was 'in almost every respect one that could be published as the Tory manifesto'.[186] Alongside reiterating its anti-European policy, the paper demanded a tougher approach to crime, the immediate physical removal of illegal asylum seekers from a country 'soft on bogus refugees'. It also supported scrapping the New Deal for unemployed because it was too expensive, letting 'private firms take over the ENTIRE running of failing schools' and the return of tuition fees for students in Scotland. But its manifesto highlight was a plan for tax reductions by 20 per cent across the next two Labour administrations so that the UK was on a par with tax rates in 'the world's premier economy', America. William Hague was given an article the following day to outline his party's support for 'many of the *Sun*'s policies' as he argued, 'If *Sun* readers want *Sun* policies they will have to vote Conservative on June 7.' The paper's editorial jokingly attacked Hague for accusing the paper of having 'nicked his ideas', arguing that it was the other way round, but noted how the 'happy coincidence' of this affinity 'shows he's on the right lines with his policies'. It left the editor of the *New Statesman* pointing to the incongruity of a tabloid that supported Blair but remained 'to its core a Tory paper'.[187]

During the election that followed, even the *Daily Mail* was moved to a rare admission on polling day in 2001 that it had 'always found things to admire in New Labour', not least 'Mr Blair's achievement in dumping the rancorous socialist ideology that made his party unelectable'. Similarly *The Times* now endorsed Labour on the basis that it had 'consolidated many elements of Thatcherism', while one *Telegraph* columnist urged electors to 'vote Blair to defeat socialism and save Conservatism'.[188] The stances of the two leading periodicals in 2001 well captured the extent to which Labour had occupied the ideological ground of its enemies. The right-wing *The Economist*'s front page spoofed a Labour poster that dressed William Hague in a Thatcher wig by placing the offending hairdo instead on Blair beside the headline 'Vote Conservative'. Blair was described as 'the only credible conservative currently available who had 'governed to the centre-right on most issues' and had proved more Tory than his predecessors on macroeconomic policy, education and health. Labour's record had been 'better then expected'. Such enthusiasm contrasted with the left-leaning *New Statesman*'s reluctant call to 'take a deep breath, grit your teeth, put on a cheery smile' and re-elect a government that had 'been an outrage to many, decent, liberal-minded people'.

This relates to a more fundamental impact of the press. Notwithstanding an undoubted ideological basis to the modernising project, a response to the climate of right-wing newspaper opinion was undoubtedly a complementary factor in shaping the cautious form it took in opposition and government. In mid-1996, Hugo Young was to accuse the party of 'running scared of the tabloids'. They were encouraging 'reticence and minimalism' across the whole range of Labour policies because the leadership was allowing itself 'to be held hostage by inordinate fear' of newspaper power. Mandelson effectively admitted as much in January 1997 when he argued that the party had to formulate its taxation policy in advance because 'the strength . . . of Tory propaganda' meant that 'many people were believing Tory lies about us on tax and spending'.[189] This demonstrated 'a timidity born of fear' which grossly overestimated the power of the tabloids. It allowed the agenda of policy-making to be dictated by their opponents and most fundamentally entailed an acceptance of 'the Conservative version of social reality'. Such 'neurotic caution', Young had predicted, could result in an enormous loss of opportunity in the form of 'a mandate without substance'.[190] The party's conduct in both the 1997 election and subsequently only seemed to confirm such a conclusion, magnifying the paradox of a party whose huge lead over a disintegrating Conservative party was accompanied by a defensive acceptance of their economic and social agenda.[191]

Whether Labour could have won in 1997 and 2001 with fewer tabloids and a more radical agenda remains an open question.[192] Instead the party's victory in the electoral battle was accompanied by a surrender of large parts of the ideological battlefield to the Conservatives. On the rare occasions in 1997 when the Conservative party managed to direct its fire outwards, it was met by further shifts rightward. Blair's response to attacks on the party's modest industrial proposals was to water them down still further. Under Labour, he was at pains to stress, British law would still remain 'the most restrictive on trade unions in the western world' and there would be 'no return' to the 'appalling abuses of union power' in the 1970s. The leadership preached in tabloid stereotypes that under inoffensive good new Labour, there would be no going back to the bad 'Old Labour' days, with their stock-evils of robber baron trade union leaders, winters of discontent and 'tax and spend' policies. Or, as the *Sun* put it, Blair was a man who 'recognised there was no turning back to the old ways that didn't work', who 'wouldn't budge one inch' to the demands of the 'union dinosaurs', and considered that 'if privatisation works for Britain, it's fine for me'.[193]

How far New Labour veered from its position after it took office is a matter of debate. Some have argued that it produced a broadly Thatcherite 'continuity' government that accepted much of the neo-liberal agenda and in which 'the *Daily Mail* and the *Sun* too often drove the agenda'. The result was a situation in which social democracy had been ideologically 'left in the wilderness' by the government. Others have less pessimistically suggested that New Labour merely talked right-wing but governed from the centre-left. It is certainly important to acknowledge the complex and at times contradictory nature of New Labour that cannot simply be wedged into a 'Thatcherism Mark 2' pigeonhole.[194] But numerous commentators have noted the extent to which the New Labour administrations have sought to govern largely within rather than seek to transcend or re-shape the

Thatcherite political terrain. Stuart Hall has characterised the Labour administrations as politically hybrid, composed of a dominant neo-liberal strand characterised by a creeping marketisation of every sphere of government, but also a subordinate social democratic strand as well.[195]

The extent to which the right still controlled key parts of the political agenda was visible in the response to Peter Hain's embryonic suggestion, in June 2003, that there should be a debate about whether those 'at the very top of the scale' should pay more tax. As a *Guardian* editorial noted, two things happened: 'First, the media exploded as though Mr Hain had said something totally outrageous and utterly revolutionary. Then the government erupted in the same way too.'[196] Both Blair and Brown made their anger clear and Hain was ordered into a humiliating climb-down that saw him tour the studios to recant his position. His planned speech was now changed to include a pledge that there was 'no going back to the old days of punitive tax rates to fund reckless spending' and a boast that income tax had fallen under Labour compared with under the Tories.

One reason for the government's response was because of the feared reaction from the right-wing media – a subject much discussed when determining policy among the high command – and the damage that might do to its reputation for fiscal conservatism. The *Mail* accused the 'ambitious and slithery' Hain of 'lurching back to the bad old days' of a 'rancorous old socialist policy of income tax rises to soak the "rich"'. The *Sun* called on Blair to sack a 'backstabbing rat' who had 'pushed Labour back to the Red Flag days of Kinnock' with a policy that would satisfy the militants and 'Labour diehards' but would not wash with the electorate. A series of readers' letters reinforced the latter argument as they urged Hain to 'shut up over tax rates' as they denounced his 'ridiculous', 'silly' and 'outrageous' 'tax hike' plan. Similarly the *Star* considered that Hain had 'plunged the Government into crisis', while an *Express* report of the 'OUTCRY AT TAX RISES' was supported by an editorial arguing that Blair had been 'quite right to slap him down'.[197] It left Hain condemning the 'frenzied media climate' that made it impossible to discuss questions about the nation's future. But the *Guardian* chose to blame the continued 'intellectual and moral capitulation' of his party leadership to a right-wing agenda that meant that 'after six years of Labour government, it is still the *Daily Mail* ... that defines Labour's limits of acceptable political debate'.[198] It suggested that the political and media agenda had in some areas even shifted to the right since 1992, when redistributive taxation was at least a subject for legitimate discussion.

Hain's forced recantation that there would be 'no going back to the old days' also symbolised the New Labour project that involved 'not just a rupture with the past but a rejection of it'. But it was not merely this, but a conscious distortion. The modernisers effectively conspired with the press to present a historical picture of their party in which 'accuracy was sacrificed not to enhance but to belittle the original'. At its most extreme, it consigned Labour's entire hundred-year existence 'to the garbage heap'.[199] At its least it merely abandoned the 1970s to the spin of the right-wing press and the Tory party. It was a strategy that sought to demonstrate how the 'new' party had learned from its past and could be trusted again. Yet, by defining its project primarily as a negative repudiation of its own outdated heritage, it also risked confirming 'in the popular mind the view of the Labour party as seen from Tory Central Office and the tabloids'.[200] New Labour seemed at times to accept a memory implant courtesy of the Tory tabloids as its attitude now appeared to be: 'if you can't beat the press propaganda, utilise it'. This might overstate the complexity of the New Labour project, and its relationship with its own history.[201] But the party's near-Stalinist denunciations of its past ideological leanings did reflect the right-wing shift in British politics that had taken place by 1997 and remains, despite some nudges to the left, the case in 2004. The *Express* summed up the condensed version on polling day in 1997 when it ran a front page with a picture of Thatcher under the headline: 'And the real winner is . . .'[202] The Lady, for the tabloids at least, still ruled supreme.

6 Conclusions

> The press is free when it does not depend on either the power of government or the power of money.
>
> (Albert Camus)[1]

Depoliticisation or politicisation?

Recent years have seen much academic and popular discussion about a perceived 'crisis of democracy' that is shaped by media coverage that entertains and trivialises and promotes a cynical and negative 'all politicians are crooks' style of journalism.[2] This can sometimes include a narrative of declining standards from a time when the media played a more positive role in fostering informed debate, a knowledgeable public and a healthy democratic system. Popular complaints about a depoliticised contemporary popular press obsessed with trivia and entertainment contrast this with a past era of highly politicised, crusading tabloid journalism. This is supported by perhaps the most important and influential press historian of recent years, James Curran, who suggests that the post-war history of the press in Britain is characterised by 'deradicalisation' and 'depoliticisation'.[3] Leaving aside for a moment the first trend (discussed below, pp. 155–8), the second rests precariously on an apparent politicised high-point during the Second World War for a popular press that consisted of just eight-to-ten pages. The example often used to illustrate wartime politicisation, the *Daily Mirror*, is as Chapter 1 notes, a questionable one. More generally the evidence for depoliticisation remains inconclusive and ignores other trends. Arguably the key change predated 1945 and came with the very birth of the popular press, as overt political coverage became relegated in importance as the press became independent from political parties for the first time. Certainly attacks on a society 'levelled down' by press trivia have existed even before Northcliffe invented what Conservative minister Lord Derby disdainfully dismissed as one paper for those who could read but not think and another for those that could see but not read.[4]

There is very little in contemporary critiques of the popular press that has not been said about previous, supposedly more enlightened eras of

journalism. Jeremy Tunstall's pioneering work on newspaper political journalism has expressed scepticism towards 'the traditional journalists' grum-
bling assumption that there was a golden age of journalism about 25–30
years ago ... London journalists around 1900 believed there had been a
golden age in the 1870s.'[5] In the 1950s, for instance, the popular press were
denounced for their 'river of pornography and crime, and accused of 'a disgraceful lowering of values' and a pandering to 'baser instincts'. Richard
Hoggart's *Uses of Literacy* denounced a sensational, sex and entertainment-
obsessed popular press for its part in destroying a serious working-class
culture sustained by the 'old broad-sheets'. 'Working people' were being
'culturally robbed' and lulled into an unquestioning 'passive acceptance' of
the status quo and the result was 'a democracy whose working people are
exchanging their birth-right for a mass of pin-ups'.[6] The old *Mirror*, often
seen to embody a past serious, politicised popular press, was frequently
accused of a style of political coverage that was 'often inadequate and tended
to emphasise sensational rather than important news'.[7] In the 1950 election,
for instance, the paper was 'prepared to go to great lengths' to keep election
coverage off its pages and it was easy for the reader to avoid the 'sparsely'
placed coverage and 'exist in a world without an election'.[8]

Quantitative surveys that might be expected to provide more precise data
in this area have offered differing conclusions. Two content analyses of the
popular press in the post-war era came to conclusions that could hardly have
been more different. One found little evidence of tabloidisation, with a
doubling of the percentage space about political news and a contemporary
average story length that in 1997 was no less than in the 1950s and 1960s.
But another detected such a marked fall in the percentage space devoted to
public affairs in the *Mirror* and the *Sun* between 1968–1998 that the author
felt that they no longer qualified as newspapers.[9] Looking at the proportion
of newspaper front pages devoted to election coverage across the post-war
period, there is certainly no clear pattern of depoliticisation (with the possible exception of recent trends at the *Daily Express*). As Table 6.1 demonstrates, there is a more persuasive case for arguing for politicisation of
election campaigning, with the *Mail*, *Express* and *Mirror* carrying a significantly higher number of election front pages in the more recent era. Even
taking into account longer, contemporary campaigns, the percentage of election front page headlines in the popular press was still greater in the 1980s
and 1990s than in the 1940s and 1950s and shows little sign of fundamental variation since the 1970s.

It is also questionable whether the total amount of political news within
each paper has decreased since the apparent high-point of politicisation in
1945. Given the enormous increase in newspaper size between 1945–2001 –
from ten to 59 pages at the *Mirror*, for example – it remains to be explored
whether this has produced depoliticisation, or merely diversification into
other news and feature areas while still retaining the same (or more) total
political coverage. The evidence for depoliticisation is also, at best, partial if

Table 6.1 Election front pages 1951–2001 (Total number and (in brackets) election front pages as a percentage of total front pages)

	1951	1955	1970	1974	1974	1979	1983	1987	1992	1997	2001
Daily Mail	5 (29)	4 (25)	9 (56)	16 (89)	13 (72)	14 (67)	19(82)	15 (68)	18 (72)	14 (51)	9 (43)
Daily Express	9 (53)	5 (31)	9 (56)	16 (89)	15 (83)	14 (67)	20 (88)	18 (82)	19 (76)	14 (51)	2 (10)
Daily Mirror	4 (23)	4 (25)	6 (37)	13 (72)	11 (61)	12 (57)	14 (61)	9 (41)	13 (52)	13 (48)	12 (57)
Daily Sketch/Graphic	4 (23)	3 (19)	5 (31)	–	–	–	–	–	–	–	–
Daily Herald/Sun	6 (35)	3 (19)	6 (38)	12 (67)	15 (83)	12 (57)	5 (22)	11 (50)	9 (36)	6 (22)	9 (43)
News Chronicle	3 (18)	3 (19)	–	–	–	–	–	–	–	–	–
Star	–	–	–	–	–	3 (14)	7 (30)	3 (14)	5 (20)	1 (4)	4 (19)

Sources: Birch, Campbell and Lucas, 'The Popular Press', *Political Studies* 1956; *British General Election of . . .* studies 1945–2001.

we examine changes in space devoted to election coverage since 1945 (where evidence exists). The total amount of election coverage within all papers has increased, being almost double in 1987 compared to the low-key election of 1955. Partly this could be attributed not just to the low 1955 base but also the greater length of contemporary campaigns (although this still means that readers receive more election news than ever before). If we calculate a daily average column inch, the low average in 1955 is followed by results across 1966–1987 that are flatter and, with fluctuations on either side, betrays little evidence of rise or fall. It is unclear whether the sharp rise in 1987 has been sustained, although the impressionistic evidence suggests that it might have been.

Popular attitudes, as Table 6.3 illustrates, also betray little sign of a demand for more political coverage during election time, with only tiny proportions demanding more coverage in recent elections. The most common complaint, of too much coverage, was particularly strong in the elections of 1987 and 1992 while, interestingly, people seemed more satisfied than before with coverage in the 2001 election. However, 16 per cent still wanted to ban all newspaper election coverage! Another MORI poll in 1996 found that by far the most popular reason for buying a newspaper was to get the TV listings, with 42 per cent saying they were 'very interested' in reading this. By contrast, reporting of parliamentary news or analysis of current affairs failed to reach even the Top 20 of the 59 topics people were given to pick from.[10]

Changes in power, circulation and trust

Having suggested a broad pattern of continuity rather than change in the level of political coverage since 1945, it is also clear that there have been several key changes in the popular press since 1945. The first is the most obvious: the decline in its power and circulation. This is true indirectly with the increased dominance of television as the main source of news, complemented more recently by the enormous growth in the amount of broadcast news available plus the emergence of the Internet and other news sources. In 1955, for example, a Gallup poll asked people what they thought was the best way of getting information about politics. 47 per cent specified newspapers, compared with 32 per cent who said radio and 15 per cent who relied on television.[11] By contrast regular polls throughout the 1970s illustrated the overwhelming, and continued, dominance of television as the most important source of news. One 2002 poll stated that television was the main source of news for 65 per cent of the electorate, with newspapers (15 per cent) even relegated to third place just behind radio.[12]

This partly reflects the fact that national newspapers, and especially the tabloid press, are not highly trusted by the electorate. In 2002 newspapers were trusted by just 20 per cent of the UK population, less than half the European average of 46 per cent. Another 2002 poll noted distinct varia-

Table 6.2 Total amount of election coverage 1945–1987 (column inches (daily average column inches in brackets))

	1955	1966	1970	Oct. 1974	1983	1987
Mirror	1,500 (63)	4,126 (217)	3,316 (207)	3,995 (190)	4,075 (177)	5,859 (266)
Mail	2,878 (119)	3,997 (210)	2,397 (150)	5,023 (239)	5,171 (224)	7,400 (336)
Express	1,582 (66)	4,637 (244)	2,837 (177)	5,233 (249)	6,701 (291)	7,985 (362)
Herald/Sun	2,790 (116)	4,161 (219)	4,280 (267)	4,302 (204)	3,896 (169)	4,973 (226)
Sketch	2,590 (107)	2,334 (123)	2,393 (150)	–	–	–
News Chronicle	4,025 (167)	–	–	–	–	–
Star	–	–	–	–	3,258 (141)	4,743 (216)
Total	15,365	19,255	15,223	18,553	19,843	30,960

Sources: Birch, Campbell and Lucas, 'The Popular Press', *Political Studies* 1956; *British General Election of* . . . studies 1945–2001

Table 6.3 How do you feel about the amount of coverage given to the election campaign?

Newspapers	1983	1987	1992	1997	2001
Too much	36	52	56	41	37
About the right amount	46	35	32	41	48
Too little	4	3	1	2	4

Source: MORI.

tions in popular faith in the honesty of journalists, with those on red-top newspapers being trusted by 14 per cent, even less than government ministers (25 per cent). Mid-market papers like the *Mail* did less badly on 38 per cent, but still trailed well behind broadsheet journalists on 65 per cent. A similar poll in the early 1990s asked people to give news sources a believability rating out of five. While TV news scored 4.1 and the broadsheet press 3.7, the middle-market papers trailed behind at 2.9 while the *Mirror* scored 2.5. The *Sun* (at 1.4) was even believed less than party political broadcasts.[13] This decline is also reflected in the reduced circulation figures for the popular press, down by over one-third from its high-point in the 1950s and 1960s. In 1964 it had a collective circulation of about 14 million, with 40 million readers (this includes those reading more than one paper). By 2001 the total circulation of the popular press had fallen to 9.2 million with a total readership of nearly 25 million. Newspapers are bought most days by only about half of the electorate and studies in Britain, America and Europe have all pointed to the worrying phenomena of 'the vanishing younger reader'. In 2002 in the UK 39 per cent of 16–34 year olds said that they bought newspapers daily, compared with 64 per cent of those over 55.[14]

On a more positive side, the high readership of the past can in part be explained by multiple-purchase of very thin, ration-restricted newspapers. Today's newspapers are read less, but they are six times the size of those produced in 1945.[15] Equally it is important not to discount the power of the press because it is trusted far less than television. Surveys suggest that readers in the contemporary era continue to rely on their papers for political guidance in what to think and how to vote, a role that television, with its statutory commitment to balance and impartiality, cannot for the most part compete with.[16] The confident quantitative conclusions about lack of trust need to be qualified by two points. Those who use a media source are more likely to trust it than those who do not. While 11 per cent of people in 2002 said that they trusted the *Sun* to tell the truth, the figure doubled when they were confined just to readers of the paper. More importantly, quantitative findings of lack of trust are partly contradicted by qualitative evidence of how people talk about and use popular newspapers. One study, for example, revealingly demonstrated how people would dismiss the tabloids as 'full of lies', thereby asserting their critical independence from them. But at the same time their talk illustrated that they had absorbed the information that they claimed not to believe.[17]

There have also been several structural changes in the nature of the popular press since the war. The last 30 years has witnessed a polarisation of the press between 'qualities' and 'tabloids' in political coverage and the gradual disappearance of what David English in 1989 called 'the old post-war middle ground with a lot of respectable papers in it'. First, the press's economic dependence on advertising biased towards either a small and wealthy or very large, low-income readership had reduced its diversity by eliminating those papers, such as the *News Chronicle* and the *Daily Herald*, with a million-plus readership that fell between these stools.[18] Second, and just as important, was the move from broadsheet to tabloid format that occurred for the *Mail* and the *Express* during the 1970s. Another change has been the way press ownership shifted in the post-war period to large capitalist conglomerates, which meant that the press, rather than having other business interests, has in fact 'become a subsidiary of other industries'.[19]

From good news from politicians to bad news from journalists

These changes have been accompanied by several inter-linked changes in the nature of press coverage. The first has been the shift from positive propaganda of the paper's favoured party to more negative coverage of opponents, a point that confirms the wider arguments about the contemporary increase in negative 'attack journalism'. In the immediate post-war period, virtually all the papers adopted a positive bias that involved giving around three-quarters of space to reporting their chosen party. By 1979 this had changed to a more negative 'knocking copy' style in which, on average, two-thirds of political coverage in the popular press attacked opponents rather than supported friends. A second key trend is a shift to what Daniel Hallin, writing about American television, has called a more mediated style of political coverage, with a more proactive style in which the words of journalists dominate over those of politicians.[20] Press coverage for the first half of the post-war era tended to be relatively passive, with large chunks of media content being devoted to outlining and repeating the words of politicians, predominantly those the paper supported. For example, in 1963 the *Express* allocated three broadsheet pages to an almost word-for-word regurgitation of the Profumo debate. The well-documented decline in press reporting of parliamentary debates is arguably part of this more general trend to more journalist-centred news.

Even very hostile reports were, to some extent, textually counterbalanced in the relatively straight coverage they could sometimes report direct from the mouths of their political opponents. Given that the full horrors of the concentration camps had just been revealed, the *Daily Express*'s headline description of Labour as 'THE NATIONAL SOCIALISTS' in the 1945 election must rank as one of the most unpleasantly partisan stories against the party ever produced. Yet examining the accompanying page 1, text, it is interesting, from a contemporary perspective, how straight a report it offered of Attlee's response to Churchill's 'Gestapo' allegations (see Chapter 1). The sub-heading, 'We reflect the main streams of the country's life', offers one illustration of this. An opening paragraph provides the only anti-Labour content to a 400-word story as it rather mildly accuses Attlee in his radio broadcast of having 'decked out the familiar goods of his party's policy in the election shop window'. This accounted for 7 per cent of the words in the report but the remainder simply consists of quotations from Attlee's rebuttal of Churchill's allegations (which take up 85 per cent of the story's total number of words), or straight paraphrasing of the Labour leader's response. Such textual generosity was, to some extent, undermined by an accompanying story to its left that consisted of old, allegedly anti-democratic comments from Attlee and Cripps. But it does illustrate how, even during very hostile anti-Labour coverage, newspapers adopted a style of coverage that gave far more space to the words of politicians, and even sometimes opposing politicians, than contemporary styles. In the latter, it is journalists rather than politicians who dominate coverage and even political friends struggle for much direct quotation of their words.

Whether this is a good or a bad thing is more debatable. Certainly contemporary coverage is more analytical, less reactive and quite possibly more interesting for the reader. But it also produces stories that are inherently more homogenous in their message and gives un-elected journalists and media corporations more power to communicate politics to people than democratically elected politicians. While political reporting has become more mediated, it has also become more synonymous with entertainment, especially in the red-top tabloids, as the *Sun*'s coverage most obviously demonstrates. Equally the emergence of a more personalised and cruder style of coverage was well illustrated by the vicious tabloid attacks on Labour leaders during the 1980s, and even some Tory leaders later. Attached to this has also been a coarsening of the language of political debate and attack, in which the *Sun* was again a prime cultural reflector and shaper. Also visible has been a routine personalisation and sexualisation of political coverage.[21] For example, when Marcia Williams was serving as a highly controversial adviser to Harold Wilson, she had two illegitimate children, news of which was never revealed despite being common knowledge in Fleet Street (the father was the reporter Walter Terry) and some high-profile press campaigns against her (see Chapter 3). By contrast, Peter Mandelson found his sexuality quickly 'exposed' by the *News of the World* in the 1987 election.

There are many explanations for these trends, from the impact of Rupert Murdoch to more underlying cultural and media developments. These include the emergence of a less deferential, allegedly more politically disengaged electorate brought up on 'soundbites', 'newssnacks' and 'the three minute culture'.[22] The result, in broadsheets as well as tabloids, has been

shorter reports, bigger photographs and headlines. A wider shift from positive to negative news in media coverage has also been recorded elsewhere,
while the politicisation of issues and subjects that were once thought to be
confined to the private sphere also fed into some of the above processes.[23]
The emergence of television as the pre-eminent news medium was also of
key importance in encouraging the popular press to refocus further towards
opinion, personality and entertainment. In the midst of declining sales there
was also an economic case to be made against balanced news coverage. As
journalist Ian Jack put it, 'comment is cheap, but facts are rather
expensive'.[24]

The tabloidisation of a once largely broadsheet popular press also had an
important effect. It is noticeable that the tabloid newspapers in the 1940s
and 1950s, notably the *Mirror*, contained the most negative and the most
journalist-centred political coverage. The change in format of the *Mail* and
Express in the 1970s was accompanied by a shift away from balanced reporting, positive, politician-centred propaganda to a more negative, journalist-
dominated approach. Popular tabloid newspapers are also arguably
inherently more suited than broadsheets to a straightforward and more
negative propaganda message, to one-story front pages, screaming headlines
and short, punchy campaigning prose at the expense of more detailed text or
long quotations from politicians. In this sense the tabloid medium certainly
has affected the message, and has arguably impacted not just on the popular
press but the wider reporting culture as well.

A right-wing shift

But the most important shift has been what Curran has identified as the
'deradicalisation' of the popular press, even if the extent of the popular
press's radicalism in the 1940s should not be overstated (see Chapter 1). The
dominance of what Albert Camus called 'the power of money' effectively
meant that, for most of the post-war period, the popular press was tilted to
the right of the political instincts of its readership. Until 1997 the Conservatives always enjoyed a newspaper circulation advantage over Labour and a
level of press support that was always greater than the level of popular
support it achieved. Yet, for the first 35 years from 1940, the popular press
was rather more politically balanced, or at least centrist, than left-wing
critics would allow. The Northcliffe revolution initially produced a strongly
anti-socialist press but its expansion to reach a working-class market ensured
the emergence of the *Daily Mirror* as the key Labour-supporting newspaper
after 1945. This, combined with the labour movement's funding for the
Daily Herald, meant that, between 1945–1970, Labour achieved substantial
newspaper representation. In statistical terms this averaged 10–15 per cent
behind that gained by the Conservatives and so remained a handicap in the
electoral battle. But, on key occasions, such as 1945 and 1964, Labour's
press support or sympathy was greater in quality if not quantity than that of

Table 6.4 Party support in the press 1945–2001

	1945	1955	1964	1974(1)	1974(2)	1979	1992	1997	2001
Cons	52	52	57	71	47	67	64	35	28
Lab	35	40	43	32	29	27	27	60	72
Lib	13	9	0	5	26	–	5	5	1

Sources: Seymour-Ure, *British Press and Broadcasting Since 1945*; *British General Election of . . .* studies 1945–2001

its opponents. During its lifetime, the *News Chronicle* also acted as a force further enhancing press diversity and giving much needed representation of liberal sentiments to a popular market.

By the 1960s, however, the harsh commercial logic of the structure of the British newspaper industry once more conspired against the left. The reliance on advertising revenue squeezed out those papers – the *News Chronicle, Daily Herald* and the *Daily Sketch* – with readers who were neither numerous enough nor rich enough to attract enough advertisers. The fact that these papers were predominantly left-of-centre led, as the second Royal Commission on the press observed, to 'a significant loss in diversity of . . . political outlook'.[25] The continued rise in the *Mirror*'s circulation, and the initial rebirth of the *Herald* as the left-leaning *Sun*, meant that this was not immediately apparent. The precarious nature of Labour's position was subsequently demonstrated by Murdoch's gradual transformation from 1975 onwards of the *Sun* into a virulently anti-socialist best-selling newspaper. This tipped the press balance decisively against the party. Its impact, combined with the emergence of television and other cultural changes, further encouraged a reorientation of the middle-market newspapers towards propaganda and opinion. The rise of the *Sun* also eroded the *Mirror*'s dominance that had gone such a long way to giving Labour substantial press representation since 1945.

Looking at newspaper affiliations between 1945–2001, it is again clear that press partisanship was at its strongest between 1979–1992 when, with the exception of the *Sun*, the three main popular newspapers were composed of readerships in which two-thirds supported their paper's party. This contrasts with the early post-war years where the more centrist and less right-wing message of the *Mail* and the *Express*, for example, brought a readership in which a majority of readers did not share their paper's affiliations. Meanwhile, the greater partisanship of the tabloid *Mirror* might explain the greater continuity in its readership's politics. As the last column of Table 6.5 also illustrates (where data is available), in one sense the real losers in post-war press coverage have been the Liberals/Liberal Democrats, who have found themselves virtually ignored in the focus on the adversarial battle between the two main contenders for government.

In an ideal world the operation of democracy requires a level playing

Table 6.5 Support for parties among newspaper readers 1947–2001

	Year	Con	Lab	Lib
Express	1947*	48	28	5
	1964	46	40	10
	1974	48	29	N.A.
	1979	65	2	10
	1992	67	15	14
	2001	43	33	19
Mail	1947	51	26	6
	1964	49	33	14
	1974	45	24	N.A.
	1979	67	23	9
	1992	65	15	18
	2001	55	24	13
Mirror	1947	15	58	2
	1964	22	64	10
	1974	19	54	N.A.
	1979	21	64	9
	1992	20	64	14
	2001	11	71	13
Herald/Sun	1947	7	81	2
	1964	13	77	8
	1974	16	57	N.A.
	1979	38	52	9
	1992	45	36	14
	2001	30	52	12

Sources: MORI/Kellner and Worcester, 'Electoral Perceptions of Media Stance', in Worcester and Harrop (eds), *Political Communications*; Mass-Observation, *The Press and its Readers*; Butler and King, *British General Elections of . . .*

Note
*The 1947 figures should be viewed with some caution as they are drawn from M-O and do not have the same statistical validity of later figures. They are also skewed by high percentages of 'don't knows'.

field.[26] While the press field has never been equal, between 1945–1951 newspaper players on both sides went some way to balancing each other. In a 20-year period of relative consensus after 1951, both sides gravitated towards the sidelines and took much more of an impartial 'spectator' approach. Gradually, from 1974, however, the press rejoined the field in a third stage of post-war press behaviour. On the Conservatives side, the key 1945–1951 supporters, the *Mail* and the more unpredictable *Express*, emerged as more committed, active and reliable participants than in this earlier era. As importantly, they had acquired a new brutally effective player in the form of the *Sun*. Labour now had only the ageing *Mirror*, reduced in its potency and power, to counter their aggression – and the absence of any

independent, effective referee to regulate the game was all the more noticeable. As the 1991 *Hansard Commission on Election Campaigns* noted, the result
was a situation in which the press gave 'an unreasonable advantage to the
Conservative party in the main battle for government'.[27]

Not that there were many complaints from Labour when the situation
appeared to be reversed by 1997. This demonstrated vividly how the party's
complaints have often amounted to little more than the grievance that the
other side possessed a greater number of biased newspapers than they did – a
clear case of self-interest masquerading as principle. This continued
hypocrisy was ultimately the result of the party's efforts to work within
rather than attempt to structurally reform a system of capitalist press ownership inherently skewed towards conservative and right-wing politics. It is
beyond the scope of this book to assess the practicality of various proposals
for media reform advanced by the party in the 1980s, as well as more long-
standing academic suggestions.[28] But it is worth noting that the juxtaposi-
tion frequently made between either a 'free (free-market) press' on the one
side or a state-controlled media on the other is a false one, as the independent regulation of commercial television and other public bodies illustrates.
Regulation of the press in the contemporary era also existed through the
successor to the Press Council, the Press Complaints Commission, which
effectively sees the industry police itself. Its 'hands off' approach to newspaper felonies can be illustrated by its utterly ineffectual code of conduct
which stipulates that 'newspapers, while free to be partisan, should distinguish clearly between comment, conjecture and fact' and 'should take care
not to publish inaccurate, misleading or distorted material'.[29] It is difficult
to see how certain statutory legislation could do anything other than
improve press freedom, if defined as the right of the readers of both left- and
right-wing newspapers to have access to a plurality of viewpoints.

Certainly there is evidence that this is what readers want from their
papers. One 1979 poll (unfortunately never repeated) asking readers to rate
the political affiliations of their own paper, and then the political affiliations
of their ideal paper, was particularly revealing of the divergence between
coverage readers were given and coverage they wanted. Across all popular
newspapers, a consistent 50 per cent of their readers wanted a less partisan
approach than the one that they, for the most part, recognised they were
getting from their paper (the confusion of *Sun* readers reflected the fact that
their paper's politics had recently changed and, by 1991, 64 per cent recognised that their paper was a Conservative one). Even over one-third of
Conservative supporters and nearly one-half of Labour supporters saw their
ideal paper as one that was not politically aligned.

From fourth estate to fifth column

In media mythology the press has often been presented as an independent
'fourth estate', acting as a sword of freedom in scrutinising the behaviour of

Table 6.6 Political affiliations of 'own' paper and 'ideal' paper

Readers of	Own newspaper			'Ideal' newspaper		
	Pro-Conservative	Neither	Pro-Labour	Pro-Conservative	Neither	Pro-Labour
Express	55	22	5	36	48	10
Mail	60	34	5	46	50	4
Mirror	10	26	62	19	50	31
Sun	7	45	48	19	53	29
Conservative identifiers	47	31	19	59	36	3
Labour identifiers	9	32	57	4	48	48

Source: Kellner and Worcester, 'Electoral Perceptions of Media's Stance', in Worcester and Harrop (eds), *Political Communications*, 1979.

parliament and parties.[30] Less grandly, the fundamental prerequisite for the adequate functioning of any pluralistic society must be that, even if people cannot be fully politically informed, they are at least not deliberately misled. While very far from perfect, for much of the post-war period, the free-market system of press ownership, either collectively or individually, went some way to meeting this requirement. But between 1979–1992 the above myth, never true, became inverted. The popular press now functioned as a fifth column rather than a fourth estate as they actively and persistently sought to distort the democratic process.

Most crucially, the uniquely hostile attitude of the press to Labour during this time relates to the way in which the Northcliffe and Thatcher revolutions, although 80 years apart, went hand-in-hand. Ever since its birth, the popular press has 'bolstered capitalism by encouraging acquisitive, materialist and individualistic values'.[31] The entertainment message of the press has an essentially reactionary ideological subtext that has promoted a naturalised view of the world centred around the personal experiences of the individual. It has emphasised consumerism, affluence, the unrestricted possibilities for self-advancement and the negative consequences of excessive state intervention. It has been plausibly suggested that this entertainment coverage has probably had a greater impact on attitudes than overtly political propaganda.[32] Yet, whatever the influence, the reality of the post-1945 political settlement at least partly contradicted this – as demonstrated by the frequent laments of the *Express* against the 'neo-socialists' in the Conservative party. Whoever ruled, the landscape remained at least partly social democratic and collectivist and the Tory press were always fighting an ideological battle that they could never totally win.

Then came the breakdown of this settlement and the emergence of an 'authoritarian populist' Thatcherite project. It involved an unadulterated celebration of popular capitalism. It emphasised individualism, enterprise, consumerism, affluence, property, near-xenophobic patriotism, an almost anti-political 'common sense' rhetoric, and the importance of the 'private' world at the expense of the evil of state engineering.[33] Such a vision fitted almost perfectly with the above values and political coverage now became one seamless element to the wider ideological message of the popular press.[34] On a practical level, the liberation of the press from the pre-1979 constraints was demonstrated by the way Thatcherism facilitated a fundamental shift in the balance of power in favour of capital at the expense of labour in the industry (as more generally). Perhaps the surprising thing in this situation was not that Labour did so badly in popular press coverage, but that it managed to gain any support at all. This was particularly the case in the midst of the apparent terminal social and political decline of 'labourism', to which the party's only initial answer was a more anti-capitalist vision than at any time for 50 years. On this occasion it was the eccentricities of the baronial form of press ownership, as more than personified in Robert Maxwell's complex personality, that acted as the party's saving grace.[35]

As this demonstrates, the press were far from passive observers in the battle for ideological hegemony, but key participants – its elite fighting force – dedicated to ensuring its success by any propaganda means available.[36] The electoral and intellectual triumph of the right over the left in the 1980s was symbolised on a popular level by the obliteration of the left-wing image of 'the hungry 1930s' with their more recent right-wing memory of the 'Winter of Discontent'. In a way, nothing better illustrated or legitimised the replacement of the Attlee with the Thatcher settlement. The myth of Jarrow, a noble symbol of labourite collectivism deprived of work by an inefficient free-enterprise system, now became inverted into a nightmare picture of a socialist state form which so oppressed the individual that *even* the dead could not be buried.

But this is not to exaggerate the success of the New Right's ideological battle to win people's 'hearts and minds'. Numerous studies during the 1980s demonstrated clear, even increasing, electoral support for social-democratic values.[37] The same is true in microcosm if we examine the popular press. At the *Sun*, supposedly the embodiment of Thatcherism, no more than 45 per cent of its readers ever voted Conservative between 1979–1992, much less for the distinctive brand offered by the paper's heroine. Contrary to common misconception, the paper's transformation in the late 1970s took place despite, rather than because of, readership attitudes. There can be no doubt that subsequently the paper captured the political mood of the era and made itself a part of it. But readers were at most only half-convinced or even half-listening.

The fact that large numbers do not pay any attention to their paper's political urgings seems, on the one hand, a clear illustration of the limits of press power. Pluralist theories suggest that the broad shape of any newspaper's politics is ultimately determined by readers rather than imposed by proprietors. As Seymour-Ure points out, 'a paper cannot afford to move too far away from the attitudes of readers without risk to its circulation', a point demonstrated clearly by press behaviour after 1992.[38] Nevertheless these assessments underplay the extent of a paper's political autonomy, as the poll about 'ideal' newspapers above illustrates. It also ignores their potential power over at least some readers, especially the undecided and uninformed. The fact that newspapers are often bought for reasons that are not primarily related to their political coverage in turn gives owners and journalists more power than readers in shaping the political stance of their paper.[39] Few *Sun* readers, for example, tend to purchase it for its overt politics and, as Chapters 3 and 4 suggest, while many remained unmoved by their paper's stance, significant minorities were influenced. There is plenty of evidence to suggest that the popular press can sometimes have important effects on voting behaviour, particularly in evenly balanced political situations, and can be even more important in shaping as well as reflecting the wider political and media agenda. But newspaper power remains finite and in no sense can a hostile press automatically ensure that Labour 'must lose'.

A Tory press wot won it?

Not that this was a line of argument that the architects of New Labour had much time for. The experiences of Macmillan, Wilson and Kinnock suggest that the press can often have as much impact on politicians as on the public. Ironically, it is the myth of massive press power over the electorate that is more important in its impact on politicians than the more complex reality. And this myth, in turn, gives the press real power to influence elite political agendas. It was in its impact on the Labour leadership that the attempt by the right and their press supporters to impose a new political agenda had its most striking success. New Labour is above all synonymous in the public mind with its mastery over 'spin'. Yet, as with Thatcherism earlier, it was not the spin but the substance of the project that ultimately won it press support. For the party's acute concern to avoid alienating the Tory press and repeating the apparently electorally damaging partisanship of the 1980s played a key role in shaping the nature of the New Labour project, both in opposition and government. To invert the spin argument, it was 'New Labour' that appeared to embrace the message of the Tory tabloids rather than the other way round, as the party appeared to accept that there really was 'no (or only limited) alternative' to the values of the Thatcher revolution. Just as they had done in 1945, the press had helped forge a new political settlement. But now, inverting 1951, it was the 'neo-liberals' who ruled. David Hill, erstwhile Labour spin doctor since the 1980s, suggested in late 1998 that, while there remained distinctive social democratic policies that provoked press opposition, 'there is a closer conjunction of opinion between Labour and the tabloids than ever before . . . so in that sense the tabloids have got what they wanted'.[40]

The most apt symbol of this reduction of the ideological gap between Labour and the capitalist press came in the aftermath of Labour's landslide victory of 1997. Lord Rothermere announced his intention to sit on the Labour benches in the House of Lords and was soon joined by the *Express* in his political conversion. From the dark days of the 1980s, Labour had constructed (albeit temporarily) a catch-all coalition embracing every popular newspaper. It was a feat made all the more astonishing given that it had never before even been achieved by the Conservatives. Yet it was a victory that was, in the final analysis, the result of Labour's moderation of its own philosophy rather than any real change in the press's position. The defection of the nephew of Lord Northcliffe to New Labour suggested that, after a century of conflict, the party had finally won the popular press. But it also symbolised that, in both 1997 and 2001, it was the Tory press 'wot had largely won it' in a rather more fundamental way.

Notes

Introduction

1 *Sun*, 11 April 1992; *The Times*, 4 April 1992; throughout this book, the names of daily newspapers have been abbreviated to omit the first word in order to save space.
2 *Telegraph*, 12, 19 April 1992.
3 *Sun*, 11 April 1992; quoted in M. Linton, *Was it the Sun Wot Won It?*, Seventh Guardian Lecture (Oxford: Nuffield College, 1995), p. 3.
4 *Independent*, 14 April 1992; quoted in M. Daly, '"Anti-Tabloid Paranoia"? The Sun, Labour and the 1992 General Election', May Day Lecture (Nottingham: University of Nottingham, 1992), p. 5.
5 B. Franklin, *Packaging Politics* (London: Edward Arnold, 1994), p. 152; *Sun*, 15 April 1992; *Guardian* (eds), 14, 18 April 1992, 14; *Independent* (ed.), 14 April 1992; M. Leapman, 'Right, Left, and Read All Over', *Independent*, 19 April 1992; R. Greenslade, 'Partial Reasons', *Guardian*, 13 April 1992.
6 J. Tulloch, 'The Eternal Recurrence of New Journalism', in C. Sparks and J. Tulloch (eds), *Tabloid Tales: Global Debates Over Media Standards* (Lanham MD: Rowman & Littlefield, 2000), p. 133; see also J. Curran and C. Sparks, 'Press and Popular Culture', *Media, Culture and Society*, 13, 2, 1991, 215–37.
7 See J. Curran, A. Douglas, and G. Whannel, 'The Political Economy of the Human-Interest Story', in A. Smith (ed.), *Newspapers and Democracy: International Essays on a Changing Medium* (Massachusetts: MIT Press, 1980).
8 D. Morley, *Television, Audiences and Cultural Studies* (London: Routledge, 1992); A. Ruddock, *Understanding Audiences: Theory and Method* (London: Sage, 2001); for a summary of recent trends in the field, see J. Curran, *Media and Power* (London: Routledge, 2002), pp. 107–26.
9 For example, J. Blumler and M. Gurevitch, *The Crisis of Public Communication* (London: Routledge, 1995); J. Tunstall, *The Westminster Lobby Correspondents: a Sociological Study of National Political Journalism* (London: Routledge & Kegan, 1970); A. Hetherington, *News, Newspapers and Television* (London: Macmillan, 1985).
10 Curran, *Media and Power*, p. 3, C. Seymour-Ure, 'Why Not More Press History?', in P. Catterall, C. Seymour-Ure and A. Smith (eds), *Northcliffe's Legacy: Aspects of the British Popular Press, 1896–1996* (London: Macmillan, 2000), pp. 1–5.
11 I. Hargreaves and J. Thomas, *New News, Old News* (London: ITC/BSC, 2002), p. 48.
12 T. O'Malley, 'Media History and Media Studies: Aspects of the Development of the Study of Media History in the UK 1945–2000', *Media History*, 8, 2, 2002, 155–73.

13 Seymour-Ure, 'Why Not More Press History?', pp. 1–5.
14 With the exception of 1945 and 1950, all other *The British General Election of . . .* have been written or co-written by David Butler and published by Macmillan.
15 For example, I. Crewe and M. Harrop, *Political Communications: the British General Election Campaign of 1987* (Cambridge: Cambridge University Press, 1989); I. Crewe and B. Gosschalk (eds), *Political Communications: the General Election Campaign of 1992* (Cambridge: Cambridge University Press, 1995); I. Crewe, B. Gosschalk and J. Bartle (eds), *Why Labour Won: the General Election of 1997* (London: Frank Cass, 1998); for the latter, see M. Harrop, 'The Press and Post-War Elections', in Crewe and Harrop (eds), *Political Communications: Election Campaign of 1983* (Cambridge: Cambridge University Press, 1986), pp. 137–49; J. Tunstall, *Newspaper Power: the New National Press in Britain* (Oxford: Clarendon, 1997), pp. 240–55.
16 Curran, *Media and Power*, pp. 159–60.
17 J. Kitzinger, 'A Sociology of Media Power: Key Issues in Audience Research', in G. Philo (ed.), *Message Received* (London: Longman, 1999), pp. 3–20.
18 D. Gauntlett, *Moving Experiences: Understanding Television's Influences and Effects* (London: John Libby, 1995), p. 120. J. Curtice and H. Semetko, 'Does It Matter What the Papers Say?', in A. Heath, R. Jowell and J. Curtice (eds), *Labour's Last Chance: the 1992 Election and Beyond* (Aldershot: Dartmouth, 1994), pp. 43–64; J. Curtice, 'Is the Sun Shining on Tony Blair?: the Electoral Influence of British Newspapers', *Harvard International Journal of Press/Politics*, 2, 2, 1997, 9–23; P. Norris, D. Sanders, M. Scammell and H. Semetko, *On Message: Communicating the Campaign* (London: Sage, 1999), pp. 152–69.
19 S. Iyengar, 'Overview: the Effect of News on the Audience: Minimal or Maximal Consequences', in S. Iyengar and R. Reeves (eds), *Do the Media Govern?: Politicians, Voters and Reporters in America* (Thousand Oaks: Sage, 1997), pp. 215–16.
20 See, among others, J. Kitzenger, ' "Impacts and Influences": Media Influence Revisited: an Introduction to the "New Effects Research" ', in A. Briggs and P. Cobley, *The Media: an Introduction* (Harlow: Longman, 2002), pp. 272–81; J. Beniger, 'Toward an Old New Paradigm: the Half Century Flirtation with Mass Society', *Public Opinion Quarterly*, 51, 1987, 46–66; G. Philo, *Seeing and Believing* (Routledge, 1990); G. Philo (ed.), *Message Received* (London: Longman, 1999); J. Thomas, *Diana's Mourning: A People's History* (Cardiff: University of Wales Press, 2002), pp. 153–81.
21 See K. Newton and M. Brynin, 'The National Press and Party Voting in the UK', *Political Studies*, 49, 2, 2001, 265–85; W. Miller, *Media and Voters: the Audience, Content, and Influence of Press and Television at the 1987 General Election* (Oxford: Clarendon Press, 1991); Linton, *Was It the Sun?*; M. Brynin and K. Newton, 'The National Press and Voting Turnout: British General Elections of 1992 and 1997', *Political Communication*, 20, 2003, 59–73; R. Webber, 'The 1992 Election: Constituency Results and Local Patterns of National Newspaper Readership', in D. Denver, P. Norris, D. Broughton and C. Rallings, *British Parties and Elections Yearbook 1993* (Hemel Hempstead: Harvester, 1993), pp. 205–15; R. Entman, 'How the Media Affect What People Think: an Information Processing Approach', *Journal of Politics*, 51, 2, 1989, 347–70; K. Newton, 'Do People Read Everything They Believe in the Newspapers?: Newspapers and Voters in the 1983 and 1987 Elections', in I. Crewe and P. Norris (eds), *British Parties and Elections Yearbook* (London: Simon & Schuster, 1991), pp. 51–73; P. Dunleavy and C. Husbands, *British Democracy at the Crossroads* (London: George Allen & Unwin, 1985), pp. 113–15.
22 Brynin and Newton, 'The National Press and Voting Turnout', p. 73.
23 Harrop, cited in J. Curran and J. Seaton, *Power Without Responsibility* (London: Routledge, 1995), p. 275.

24 N. Garnham, *Emancipation, the Media and Modernity* (Oxford: Oxford University Press, 2000), p. 15.
25 Philo (ed.), *Message Received.*
26 For introductory discussions of these themes, see B. Franklin, *Newszak and News Media* (London: Arnold, 1998), pp. 35–7; R. Negrine, *Politics and the Mass Media in Britain* (London: Routledge, 1994), pp. 8–9.
27 T. Baistow, *Fourth-Rate Estate* (London: Comedia, 1985), p. 58; see Article 19, Universal Declaration of Human Rights, quoted in J. Keane, *The Media and Democracy* (Cambridge: Polity Press, 1991), p. 136.
28 For a brief summary of this debate, see D. L. LeMahieu, *A Culture for Democracy* (Oxford: Clarendon, 1988), pp. 14–19; Curran, *Media and Power*, pp. 127–55.

1 'Vote for them': the popular press and the 1945 general election

1 For surveys of the inter-war press, see C. Seymour-Ure, 'The Press and the Party System Between the Wars', in G. Peele and C. Cook, *The Politics of Reappraisal* (London: Macmillan, 1975); G. Boyce, 'Crusaders Without Chains: Power and the Press Barons 1896–1951', in J. Curran, A. Smith and P. Wingate (eds), *Impacts and Influences: Essays on Media Power in the Twentieth Century* (London: Methuen, 1987), pp. 97–112; S. Koss, *The Rise and Fall of the Political Press in Britain* (London: Fontana, 1990).
2 A. Cummings, quoted in Labour Party, *The Power of the Press* (London: Labour Publications, 1936), p. 4.
3 N. Blewitt, *The Peers, the Parties and the People: the British General Elections of 1910* (London: Macmillan, 1972), p. 308; A. Russell, *Liberal Landslide: the General Election Campaign of 1906* (Newton Abbot: David & Charles, 1973), pp. 137–9.
4 *Mail*, 17, 18 January 1906.
5 *Mail*, 2 December, 15, 6 January 1910; Koss, *Rise*, pp. 568, 594–6.
6 A. Cummings, *The Press and a Changing Civilisation* (London: John Lane, 1936), pp. 79–80.
7 S. Taylor, *The Great Outsiders: Northcliffe, Rothermere and the Daily Mail* (London: Weidenfeld & Nicolson, 1996), pp. 244–5, 312–13; R. Bourne, *Lords of Fleet Street: the Harmsworth Dynasty* (London: Unwin Hyman, 1990), pp. 128–9; Viscount Rothermere, 'Keep Out the Socialists', *Mail*, 29 May 1929.
8 Rothermere to Beaverbrook, 2 June 1925, Papers of Lord Beaverbrook, House of Lords Record Office (henceforth: BBK), C/283; *Mail*, 25 October 1925; 'Letter to a Correspondent from Lord Rothermere', *Sunday Pictorial*, 9 December 1928; Rothermere to Mosley, 14 July 1934, printed in *Mail*, 19 July 1934; Viscount Rothermere, 'Hurrah for the Blackshirts', *Mail*, 15 January 1934.
9 *Mail*, 1 November–15 December 1922; *Mail*, 1–13 December 1923.
10 The many studies of Beaverbrook include: A. Chisholm and M. Davie, *Beaverbrook: A Life* (London: Pimlico, 1993); A. Taylor, *Beaverbrook* (London: Hamish Hamilton, 1972); A. Christiansen, *Headlines All My Life* (London: Heinemann, 1961); A. Wood, *The True History of Lord Beaverbrook* (London: William Heinemann, 1965); R. Edwards, *Goodbye Fleet Street* (London: Coronet, 1988); L. Gourlay (ed.), *The Beaverbrook I Knew* (London: Quartet, 1984).
11 Taylor, *Beaverbrook*, p. 2.
12 *Express*, 29 November 1923.
13 *Herald*, 6 December 1923; *Mail*, 8 December 1923, 14 January 1924.

14 See R. Lyman, *The First Labour Government* (London: Chapman & Hall, 1957); D. Marquand, *Ramsay MacDonald* (London: Jonathan Cape, 1977), pp. 311–12; C. Cook, *The Age of Alignment: Electoral Politics in Britain 1922–1929* (London: Macmillan, 1975); T. Jeffery and K. McKelland, 'A World Fit to Live in: the Daily Mail and the Middle Classes 1918–1939', in Curran, Smith and Wingate (eds), *Impacts*, pp. 27–52.

15 *Mail*, 16, 17, 15 October 1924.

16 L. Chester, S. Fay and H. Young, *The Zinoviev Letter* (London: Heinemann, 1967), p. 3.

17 *Mail*, 25 October 1924.

18 G. Bennett, 'A Most Extraordinary and Mysterious Business': the Zinoviev Letter of 1924, Foreign and Commonwealth Office History Notes, No. 14 (London: HMSO, 1999), pp. 45–7; Chester, Fay and Young, *Zinoviev*, pp. 94–109; MacDonald diary, quoted in Marquand, *Ramsay MacDonald*, p. 384.

19 *Observer*, 4 March 1928.

20 *Express*, 25, 27, 28 October 1924.

21 *Mirror*, 29 October 1924.

22 For the forgery argument, see Chester, Fay and Young, *Zinoviev*; for its likely genuineness, see C. Andrew, *Secret Service: The Making of the British Intelligence Services* (London: Sceptre, 1986), pp. 430–45; for the Foreign Office's 'best guess' verdict that it was a forgery, see Bennett, *A Most Extraordinary*, pp. 91–2.

23 *Mail, Mirror*, 25 October 1924.

24 A. Thorpe, *The British General Election of 1931* (Oxford: Clarendon, 1991), p. 195.

25 Viscount Rothermere, 'History's Warning, AD419–AD1931', *Mail*, 24 October 1931.

26 *Mail*, 2, 16, 24, 16 October 1931.

27 *Mail*, 24, 14 October 1931; *Herald*, 20 October 1924.

28 Rothermere, 'History's Warning'.

29 *Express*, 8, 14 October 1931.

30 Quoted in Wood, *True History*, p. 196.

31 *Express*, 10, 23 October 1931.

32 *Mail*, 25, 26 October 1931; *Express*, 27 October 1931.

33 Thorpe, *Election of 1931*, p. 205; quoted in Chisholm and Davie, *Beaverbrook*, p. 309.

34 D. Hopkin, 'The Labour Party Press', in K. Brown (ed.), *The First Labour Party 1906–1914* (London: Croom Helm, 1985), pp. 105–28; S. Berger, *The British Labour Party and the German Social Democrats 1900–1931* (Oxford: Clarendon, 1994), pp. 103–11.

35 S. Macintyre, 'British Labour, Marxism and Working Class Apathy', *Historical Journal*, 20, 2, 1977, 479–83; Norman Angell, quoted in Independent Labour Party Information Committee, *The Capitalist Press: Who Owns It and Why* (London: ILP, 1923), p. 5.

36 K. Williams, *Get Me a Murder a Day* (London: Arnold, 1998), pp. 28–47.

37 R. Holton, 'Daily Herald v. Daily Citizen, 1912–15: The Struggle for a Labour Daily in Relation to "The Labour Unrest"', *International Review of Social History*, 19, 1974, 347–76; H. Richards, *The Bloody Circus: the Daily Herald and the Left* (London: Pluto, 1998).

38 'Our purpose' statement, *Daily Citizen*, 8 October 1912; see also T. Ichikawa, 'The Daily Citizen 1912–15: a Study of the First Labour Daily Newspaper in Britain', University of Aberystwyth, MA, 1985.

39 H. Fyfe, *My Seven Selves* (London: George Allen & Unwin, 1935), pp. 257–9.

40 *Herald*, 20–31 October 1924; quoted in Richards, *Bloody*, p. 72.

41 Richards, *Bloody*, p. 138.

42 Richards, *Bloody*, pp. 144–7; D. LeMahieu, *A Culture for Democracy*, p. 258.

43 Richards, *Bloody*, p. 147; Jeffery and McCelland, 'A World Fit to Live In', pp. 33–4.

44 Adrian Smith, 'The Fall and Fall of the Third Daily Herald 1930–1964', in Catterall, Seymour-Ure and Smith (eds), *Northcliffe's Legacy*, p. 173.

45 Labour party, *Power of the Press*, pp. 1, 16–17; *Herald*, 27 October 1931.

46 Richards, *Bloody*, pp. 149–54.

47 Tom Harrison Mass-Observation Archive, University of Sussex (henceforth: MO-A), Mass-Observation File Report (Henceforth: FR), A11 'Newspaper Reading', December 1938, pp. 17, 13.

48 D. Hubback, *No Ordinary Press Baron: a Life of Walter Layton* (London: Weidenfeld & Nicolson, 1985), p. 129; Arthur Henderson to A. G. Gardiner, Papers of A. G. Gardiner, London School of Economics, 1/17; *Daily News*, 27 November, 2 December 1918, 22 October 1924; *Daily Chronicle*, 29 October 1924.

49 *(News) Chronicle*, 1–27 October 1931.

50 T. Clarke, *My Lloyd George Diary* (London: Methuen, 1939); K. von Stutterheim, *The Press in England* (London: George Allen, 1934), p. 138.

51 Hubback, *No Ordinary*, pp. 135, 138; G. Cox, 'The Editor Who Made Love – and Great News', *British Journalism Review*, 7, 3, 1996, 16–24.

52 Papers of Sir Walter Layton, Trinity College, Cambridge (henceforth: Layton papers), Vallance to Henry Cadbury, 27 November 1934, Box 86. Pearson to Cadbury, 21, 11 June, 7, 26 July 1934, Box 88; Notes of News Chronicle Trustees Meeting, 16 January 1935, Box 88; for a summary, see Koss, *Rise*, pp. 957–68.

53 Vallance to Henry Cadbury, 27 November 1934, Layton papers, Box 86.

54 *Chronicle*, 13 November 1935; Hubback, *No Ordinary*, p. 138.

55 Hubback, *No Ordinary*, p. 138; Cox, 'The Editor', pp. 18–19.

56 See T. Stannage, *Baldwin Thwarts the Opposition; the British General Election of 1935* (London: Croom Helm, 1980), pp. 190–216.

57 Macintyre, 'British Labour', p. 482; Labour party, *Power of the Press*, pp. 8–9; Rothermere to Beaverbrook, 10 November 1924; Beaverbrook to Rothermere, 30 October 1924, BBK C/283.

58 Cook, *Age of Alignment*, pp. 310–33; J. Stevenson and C. Cook, *Britain in the Depression: Society and Politics 1929–39* (London: Longman, 1994), pp. 110–29.

59 Political and Economic Planning (PEP), *Report on the British Press* (London, PEP, 1938), pp. 247–53; Curran and Seaton, *Power Without Responsibility*, pp. 65–8.

60 Christiansen, *Headlines*, p. 144.

61 R. McCallam and A. Readman, *The British General Election of 1945* (London: Oxford University Press, 1947), p. 206.

62 A. Smith, with E. Immirzi and T. Blackwell, *Paper Voices: the Popular Press and Social Change 1935–1965* (London: Chatto & Windus, 1965), p. 27; for their friendship, see K. Young, *Churchill and Beaverbrook: a Study in Friendship and Politics* (London: Eyre & Spottiswoode, 1966).

63 *Express*, 5 June 1945.

64 *Express*, 6 June 1945; Royal Commission on the Press, 1947–49, *Minutes of Oral Evidence* (henceforth: RCP/OE), *Express* newspapers, q. 5053; see Chapter 6 for a detailed discussion of this text.

65 Smith, *Paper*, pp. 24–5.

66 B. Pimlott (ed.), *The Political Diary of Hugh Dalton 1918–40, 1945–60* (London: Jonathan Cape, 1986), p. 357; Christiansen, *Headlines*, p. 240.

67 *Express*, 16, 19, 20, 22 June 1945; *Evening Standard*, 22 June 1945; Laski later lost the libel case; for further details of the Laski coverage, see Smith, *Paper*, pp. 34–51.

68 Smith, *Paper*, p. 26; quoted in Taylor, *Beaverbrook*, p. 553.
69 Christiansen to Beaverbrook, 13 April 1945; Beaverbrook to Christiansen, 16 April 1945, BBK, H/115; Christiansen, *Headlines*, p. 219; Smith, *Paper*, pp. 52–3; *Express*, 23 June–4 July 1945.
70 Taylor, *Beaverbrook*, p. 566; Beaverbrook to Churchill, 20 January 1944, BBK D/421; Beaverbrook to Churchill 25 May 1945, Churchill to Beaverbrook, 28 May 1945, BBK D/423.
71 Christiansen, *Headlines*, pp. 238–40; Christiansen to Beaverbrook, 6 July 1945, BBK H/115.
72 RCP/OE, *Express* newspapers, qs. 4833–4838; Royal Commission on the Press, 1947–49, *Memoranda of Evidence* (henceforth: RCP/ME), Vol. 3, *Express* newspapers, p. 124; RCP/OE, Lord Beaverbrook, qs. 5094, 8700.
73 Royal Commission on the Press, *Final Report* (chairman: Sir William Ross) (London: HMSO, 1949) (henceforth: RCP/FR), p. 42; RCP/OE, *Express* newspapers, qs. 5038, 5054.
74 *Express*, 21 June 1945; quoted in McCallum and Readman, *Election of 1945*, p. 149; M. Gilbert, *Never Despair: Winston S. Churchill* (London: Minerva, 1990), pp. 32–7.
75 *Express*, 16 January 1946; Beaverbrook to Churchill, 20 January 1944, BBK, D/241; P. Addison, *Churchill on the Home Front* (London: Cape, 1992).
76 M-OA, FR 2270A, 'A Report on the General Election June–July 1945', October 1945, p. 85; *Express*, 9 June–5 July 1945.
77 For the consensus debate see, among others, P. Addison, *The Road to 1945: British Politics and the Second World War* (London: Quartet, 1977); and K. Jefferys, *The Churchill Coalition and Wartime Politics 1940–1945* (Manchester: Manchester University Press, 1991).
78 S. Taylor, *The Reluctant Press Lord: Esmond Rothermere and the Daily Mail* (London: Weidenfeld & Nicolson, 1998), pp. 15–16; RCP/OE, Rothermere, qs. 10449–10750.
79 *Mail*, 6, 11, 21, 25 June–4 July 1945; McCallum and Readman, *Election of 1945*, p. 190; *Tribune*, 22 February 1946.
80 D. Hart-Davies, *The House the Berry's Built: Inside the Telegraph 1928–1966* (London: Stoddart, 1990), pp. 84, 120; Lord Hartwell, *William Camrose: Giant of Fleet Street* (London: Weidenfeld & Nicolson, 1992), pp. 187–8; M. Muggeridge, *Chronicles of Wasted Time, Part 2, The Infernal Grove* (London: Collins, 1973), pp. 260–1; *Telegraph*, 8 June–5 July 1945.
81 Michael Hartwell to the author, 17 February 1994; RCP/OE, Kemsley, qs. 12003, 12001, 12190.
82 D. Hamilton, *Editor in Chief: the Fleet Street Memoirs of Sir Denis Hamilton* (London: Hamilton, 1989); pp. 59, 71, 58; *Sunday Times*, 14 April 1946; Hartwell, *William Camrose*, p. 319.
83 *Sketch*, 1 June–5 July 1945.
84 Viscount Kemsley, 'My Reply to the Lord President', *Western Mail*, 10 July 1946.
85 *Herald*, 26, 19, 5 June, 3, 5 July 1945; *Daily Worker*, 12 June 1945; RCP/OE, J. W. Dunbar (editorial director, Odhams Press), and Percy Cudlipp (editor), qs. 9050, 9067; McCallum and Readman, *Election of 1945*, p. 180.
86 *Herald*, 6, 8, 27 June, 2, 3, 5 July 1945.
87 MO-A, FR 2270C 'Newspaper Reading in the General Election', July 1945, pp. 1–2; M-OA, FR 3005, 'Report on Reading of the Daily Herald', June 1948.
88 Morgan Phillips, 'Dear Colleague' letter, August 1945, Labour Party Archive, National Museum of Labour History, Manchester (henceforth: LPA), Daily Herald file GS/DH/58; W. Fienburgh, *25 Momentous Years: A 25th Anniversary*

in the History of the Daily Herald (London: Odhams, 1955), pp. 159–61; Viscount Camrose, *British Newspapers and their Controllers* (London: Cassell, 1947), p. 45.

89 Gerald Barry, 'Draft Autobiography', Papers of Sir Gerald Barry, London School of Economics (henceforth: Barry papers), Box 57, draft autobiography, p. 3; 'Notes on Policy Conference', No. 1, 17 June 1936, Layton papers, Box 89.

90 'Notes on Policy Conference', No. 5, 17 June 1938, Layton papers, Box 89; Koss, *Rise*, p. 1059; Hubback, *No Ordinary*, p. 163; Wintour, *Rise and Fall*, p. 74.

91 Gerald Barry, 'Draft Autobiography', pp. 3–4, Barry papers, Box 57.

92 Hubback, *No Ordinary*, pp. 196–7; Wintour, *Rise and Fall*, pp. 74–5; R. Davies and L. Ottaway, *Vicky* (London: Secker & Warburg, 1987), pp. 37–67.

93 Hubback, *No Ordinary*, pp. 197–8; Wintour, *Rise and Fall*, p. 72; RCP/OE, News Chronicle, q. 8193; Barry, 'Draft Autobiography', Barry papers, p. 4.

94 M-OA, FR 2557, 'Attitude to Daily Newspapers', January 1948, p. 12.

95 *Chronicle*, 5 July, 14, 11 June, 2, 5 July 1945.

96 *Chronicle*, 26 June 1945; for other similar examples, see 6, 20, 22 June 1945.

97 T. Benson, 'Low and Lord Beaverbrook: the Case of a Cartoonist's Autonomy', University of Kent, PhD, 1998, pp. 221–8; *Manchester Guardian*, 27 June 1945; see also 8, 28 June 1945; reprinted in McCallum and Readman, *Election of 1945*, p. 189; for Low and Vicky, see also A. Smith, 'Cartoonist and the General Elections of 1945 and 1983', *Historian*, autumn 1984, 12–15.

98 *Manchester Guardian*, 3–5 July 1945; Ayerst, *Guardian*, pp. 560–3.

99 Smith, *Paper*, p. 62.

100 See H. Cudlipp, *Publish and be Damned! The Astonishing Story of the 'Daily Mirror'* (London: Dakers, 1953); M. Edelman, *The Mirror: a Political History* (London: Hamish Hamilton, 1966); H. Cudlipp, 'The Godfather of the British Tabloids', *British Journalism Review*, 6, 3, 1995, 34–44; W. Conner, *Cassandra: Reflections in a Mirror* (London: Cassell, 1969), pp. 24–40; C. King, *Strictly Personal* (London: Weidenfeld and Nicolson, 1969), p. 101.

101 C. King, *The Future of the Press* (London: MacGibbon & Kee, 1967), pp. 59–60; C. King, *Strictly Personal* (London: Weidenfeld and Nicolson, 1969), p. 101; Edelman, *Mirror*, pp. 38–40, 46; Cudlipp, *Walking*, pp. 64, 66; Cudlipp, *Publish*, p. 236.

102 A. Taylor, *English History 1914–1945* (London: Penguin, 1975), p. 666; Cudlipp, *Publish*, p. 253.

103 A. Smith, with E. Immirzi and T. Blackwell. *Paper Voices: the Popular Press and Social Change 1935–1965* (London: Chatto & Windus, 1975), pp. 62–142.

104 J. Curran, 'Advertising as a Patronage System', in Harry Christian (ed.), *The Sociology of Journalism and the Press*, Sociological Review Monograph 29 (Keele: University of Keele, 1980), pp. 86–7, 94; see also M. Pugh, 'The Daily Mirror and the Revival of Labour 1935–1945', *Twentieth Century British History*, 9, 3, 1998, 420–38.

105 J. Thomas, 'Reflections on a Broken Mirror: the Rise and Fall of Radical Journalism Reconsidered', *Media History*, 9, 2, 2003, 103–21; M. Bromley, 'Was it the Mirror Wot Won It? The Development of the Tabloid Press During the Second World War', in N. Hayes and J. Hill (eds), *'Millions Like Us'? British Culture in the Second World War* (Liverpool: Liverpool University Press, 1999), pp. 93–124.

106 MO-A, FR, 1173, 'Warning to the Daily Mirror', March 1942.

107 Papers of Hugh Cudlipp, Cardiff School of Journalism, Media and Cultural Studies (henceforth HC), King to Cudlipp, 16 December 1943, HC 2/1.

108 *Mirror*, 29 January 1943; Mass-Observation, *The Press and its Readers* (London: Arts & Technics, 1949), p. 124.

109 *Mirror*, 19–22 February 1943.
110 MO-A, Topic Collections (henceforth: TC), Newspaper Reading 1937–62, Box 53; MO-A, FR 1173, 'Warning to the Daily Mirror', March 1942, p. 3; FR 743, 'The Public and the Press', June 1941, pp. 1–2; M-OA, FR 1231, 'Daily Mirror Warning and News Belief', April 1942, p. 1; M-OA, FR 283, 'Report on Press Prestige', July 1940, p. 3.
111 Mass-Observation, *Press and its Readers*, p. 126.
112 MO-A, FR 1173, 'Warning to Daily Mirror', p. 3.
113 *Mirror*, 17 July 1944.
114 *Mirror*, 23 February 1945.
115 Classic assertions of this position include A. Calder, *The People's War* (London: Jonathan Cape, 1969); R. Milliband, *Parliamentary Socialism: a Study in the Politics of Labour* (London: Merlin, 1961), pp. 272–4.
116 S. Fielding, 'What Did "the People" Want? The Meaning of the 1945 General Election', *Historical Journal*, 35, 3, 1992, 623–39; T. Mason and P. Thompson, 'Reflections on a Revolution? The Political Mood in Wartime Britain', in N. Tiratsoo (ed.), *The Attlee Years* (London: Pinter, 1991), pp. 54–70.
117 Smith, *Paper Voices*, p. 140.
118 J. Curran and J. Seaton, *Power Without Responsibility* (London: Routledge, 1997), pp. 93–5.
119 *Mirror*, 29 October 1942; Public Record Office, INF 1/292, Home Intelligence Weekly Reports, No. 77, 24 March 1942, 'Appendix: Home Made Socialism'; see also Addison, *Road*, pp. 162–3.
120 *Mirror*, 25 May 1942, 18 June 1943, 14 September 1942.
121 *Mirror*, 7 June 1943.
122 HC, King to Cudlipp, 4 September 1944, 2/1.
123 S. Fielding, 'The Second World War and Popular Radicalism: The Significance of the "Movement away from Party"', *History*, 80, 2, 1995, 38–57; S. McCulloch, 'Labour, the Left and the British General Election of 1945', *Journal of British Studies*, 21, 1, 1995, 465–89; *Mirror*, 9 February, 16 June 1943.
124 *Mirror*, 6 November, 23 March 1943.
125 Fielding, 'The Second World War', p. 54; *Mirror*, 7 September 1942.
126 *Mirror*, 19 October 1942, 7 September 1942, 3 January 1945.
127 *Mirror*, 19 May 1945.
128 Fielding, 'What did the People', p. 629; King, *With Malice*, p. 296.
129 King, *With Malice*, p. 266; King, *Strictly Personal*, p. 118; M. Baines, 'The Liberal Party and the 1945 General Election', *Contemporary Record*, 9, 1, 1995, 48–61.
130 *Mirror*, 2 February 1945; 18 June 1945; *News Chronicle*, 2–5 July 1945; *Manchester Guardian*, 3–5 July 1945.
131 *Mirror*, 1–19 June 1945.
132 *Sunday Pictorial*, 3 June, 1 July 1945.
133 McCallum and Readman, *Election of 1945*, p. 212; *Mirror*, 18 May, 5, 6, 19, 22 June, 3, 5 July 1945.
134 Koss, *Rise*, pp. 1063–4; Pugh, 'The Daily Mirror', pp. 434–5; for the pro-Labour voting intention of Liberals, see M-O, 'Report on the General Election', p. 116; Fielding, 'What did the People', p. 631.
135 M-O, 'Report on the General Election', pp. 10–11.
136 M-O, 'Report on the General Election', pp. 10–11, 84–6; see also *Chronicle*, 23 June 1945.
137 M-O, 'Newspaper Reading in the General Election', p. 2; M-O, 'General Election: Voting Patterns', 2265, July 1945, p. 21.
138 J. A. Plummer to Robertson (June 1945), BBK H/114.

139 Taylor, *Beaverbrook*, p. 566.
140 K. Young (ed.), *The Diaries of Sir Robert Bruce Lockhart* (London: Macmillan, 1980), pp. 449–50, 457; *Chronicle*, 8 June 1945; Lord Moran, *Winston Churchill: the Struggle for Survival* (London: Constable, 1966), p. 286; Robertson to Beaverbrook, report of defeated Conservative candidates conference, October 1945, BBK H/117.
141 Quoted in Addison, *Road to 1945*, p. 266.
142 *Mirror*, 1 July 1945.
143 M-O, 'Report on the General Election', p. 18; S. Brooke, 'The Labour Party and the 1945 General Election', *Contemporary Record*, 9, 1, 1995, 9–10.
144 Cudlipp, *Publish*, p. 234; *The Economist*, 4 August 1945, 154.
145 A. Purdue, 'The Myth of Jarrow', *New Society*, 8 July 1982, 50–1; Stevenson and Cook, *Britain During the Depression*; *Mirror*, 19 June 1945.
146 Addison, *Road to 1945*, pp. 267–8.
147 See J. Baxendale and C. Rawling, *Narrating the Thirties – a Decade in the Making: 1930 to the Present* (London: Macmillan, 1996), pp. 116–39; polling evidence suggests that the Conservatives increased their support in the campaign, see Addison, *Road to 1945*, p. 266.
148 D. Jay, *Change and Fortune* (London: Hutchinson, 1980), p. 126; S. Orwell and I. Angus (eds), *The Collected Essays, Journalism and Letters of George Orwell* (London: Penguin, 1970), p. 137.
149 Assheton to Beaverbrook, 25 January 1946, BBK H/117; R. Cockett, 'The Government, the Press and Politics 1937–1945', University of London, PhD, 1988, pp. 223–37.
150 M-O, 'Newspaper Reading and Voting', p. 1; M-O, *Press and its Readers*, pp. 88, 125, 91–3.
151 A. Aldgate and J. Richards, *Britain Can Take It: the British Cinema in the Second World War* (London: Basil Blackwell, 1994); Baxendale and Pawling, *Narrating the Thirties*, pp. 116–39; Williams, *Get Me a Murder*, pp. 130–50.
152 *The Times*, 17 May 1948, 21 February 1950; *Chronicle*, 12 October 1951; H. Shawcross, *Life Sentence: the Memoirs of Lord Shawcross* (London: Constable, 1995), pp. 146–8; *The Times*, 20, 21 July, 9 August 1945.
153 F. Williams, *Nothing so Strange* (London: Cassell, 1970), pp. 215–18; Margach, *Abuse*, pp. 86–90; B. Donoughue and G. Jones, *Herbert Morrison: Portrait of a Politician* (London: Weidenfeld and Nicolson, 1973), p. 359.
154 *The Times*, 9 July 1946; Kemsley, 'My Reply to the Lord President'.
155 *The Times*, 17, 23 July 1946; Donoughue and Jones, *Herbert Morrison*, p. 359; T. O'Malley, 'Labour and the 1947–9 Royal Commission on the Press', in M. Bromley and T. O'Malley (eds), *A Journalism Reader* (London: Routledge, 1997), pp. 126–55.
156 RCP/ME, Vol. 3, Express newspapers, p. 124, Associated newspapers, pp. 39–40, Kemsley newspapers, pp. 104–5; RCP/OE, Odhams newspapers, q. 9050.
157 RCP/FR, pp. 274–359, 150.
158 RCP/FR, pp. 118, 354, 358; RCP/OE, Kemsley, qs. 12041–12044.
159 M. Foot, 'Lord Kemsley Spills the Beans', *Tribune*, 3 September 1948.
160 *House of Commons Parliamentary Debates*, Fifth Series, 467, 28 July 1949, cols. 2710–11; RCP/FR, p. 107.
161 RCP/FR, pp. 354, 331, 314; *Herald*, 24 November 1946; RCP/OE, Hannen Swaffer, qs. 632, 634; RCP/OE, Michael Foot, qs. 1947, 1949–50, 1738.
162 H. Nicholas, *The British General Election of 1950* (London: Macmillan, 1951), p. 145; D. Butler, *The British General Election of 1951* (London: Macmillan, 1952), p. 136; S. White, 'British Press Stoops to Conquer', *New York Herald Tribune*, 7 March 1950.
163 *Mail*, 25, 5 October 1951.

164   *Graphic*, 14 February 1950; Gilbert, *Never Despair*, p. 514.

165   Morgan Phillips, 'General Election Campaign 1951: General Secretary's Report', LPA, NEC, 7 November 1951; *Annual Conference Report of the Labour Party*, 1952, p. 31; Morgan Phillips to Percy Cudlipp, 6 March 1950; LPA, *Daily Herald* file, GS/DH/145.

166   RCP/FR, pp. 347, 358, 317, 301.

167   A. Cummings, *Chronicle*, 24 October 1951; *Mirror*, 9–25 October 1951; Butler, *Election of 1951*, pp. 133–4; H. Macmillan, *Tides of Fortune: 1945–1955* (London: Macmillan, 1969), pp. 559–60.

168   Ayerst, *Guardian*, pp. 606–7; *Manchester Guardian*, 22 October 1951; Christiansen to Beaverbrook (undated), BBK H/148.

169   *Chronicle*, 8 February 1950; Laurence Cadbury to Layton, 28 January 1946, Layton papers, Box 90; Henry Cadbury to Layton, 28 February 1950, Layton papers, Box 91.

170   'Our Editorial Policy' memorandum, 1952, Layton papers, Box 91; *Chronicle*, 22 October 1951.

171   Taylor, *Beaverbrook*, p. 570, 579–81.

172   RCP/OE, Beaverbrook, q. 8703; Robertson to Beaverbrook, 11 February 1947, BBK, H/122; Brian Chapman, resignation letter to Christiansen, February 1947, BBK H/122.

173   Christiansen to Beaverbrook, 27 January 1950, BBK, H/141; *Express*, 16, 17, 25, 28 January 1950.

174   *Express, Mail*, 27 January 1950; Christiansen to Beaverbrook, 27 January and 2 February 1950, BBK, H/141; for details, see D. Hughes, 'The Spivs', in M. Sissons and P. French (eds), *The Age of Austerity 1945–51* (London: Penguin, 1964), pp. 86–91.

175   *Express*, 4, 20 February 1950; Beaverbrook to Christiansen, July 1950, BBK, H/141.

176   Christiansen to Beaverbrook, 2 February 1950, BBK H/141; Christiansen to Beaverbrook, 10 October 1951, including memorandum from J. E. Sewell, BBK H/148; for Bevan, see J. Campbell, *Nye Bevan: a Biography* (London: Hodder & Stoughton, 1994) and M. Foot, *Aneurin Bevan, Vol. II, 1945–1960* (Herts: Paladin, 1975).

177   Butler, *Election of 1951*, p. 131; *Sunday Express*, 7 October 1951, *Express*, 21, 25, 29 September, 9, 6 October 1951.

178   *Express*, 12, 18 October 1951; quoted in Christiansen to Beaverbrook, 22 February 1952, BBK H/148.

179   Quoted in Chisholm and Davie, *Beaverbrook*, p. 524; quoted in Taylor, *Beaverbrook*, p. 584.

180   *Standard*, 2 March 1950; for earlier attacks on Strachey as Minister of Food, see M. Newman, *John Strachey* (Manchester: Manchester University Press, 1989), pp. 108–18.

181   H. Thomas, *John Strachey* (London: Eyre Methuen, 1973), p. 260; statement, March 1950, papers of John Strachey, Mrs Elizabeth Quadhi (henceforth: Strachey papers), Box 9; *Standard*, 3, 4, 6 March 1950.

182   *Guardian*, 4 March 1950; Wadsworth to Strachey, 7 March 1950, Strachey papers, Box 9; for this, see RCP/OE, Beaverbrook, q. 8744.

183   J. Cameron, *Point of Departure* (London: Grafton, 1969), pp. 87–92; Cameron, letter to *The Times*, 11 March 1950; Cameron to Strachey, 15 March 1950, Strachey papers, Box 12.

184   Quoted in Christiansen to Beaverbrook, 3 March 1950, BBK, H/141.

185   M. Foot, 'Lower than Kemsley', *Tribune*, 10 March 1950.

186   Taylor, *Beaverbrook*, p. 598; Robertson to Beaverbrook, 15 December 1950 and 2 July 1951, BBK H/144.

187 Assheton to Beaverbrook, 25 January 1946, Beaverbrook to Assheton, 1 February 1946, BBK H/117.
188 RCP/OE, Beaverbrook, qs. 8656, 8749; see also RCP/OE, *Express* newspapers, qs. 4830–5094.
189 Taylor, *Beaverbrook*, pp. 581–2; RCP/OE, Robertson, q. 5045; quoted in Robertson to Beaverbrook, 11 February 1947, BBK, H/122; RCP/OE, Robertson, q. 5045; see Benson, 'Low and Lord Beaverbrook' for the limitations to Low's much-hyped journalistic freedom.
190 RCP/OE, Trevor Evans, q. 11206; RCP/FR, pp. 286, 328, 331.
191 Beaverbrook to Blackburn, 9 February 1947, H/119; Robertson to Beaverbrook, 10 January 1947, H/122; Gordon to Beaverbrook, October 1947, H/121.
192 Christiansen to Beaverbrook, 7 February 1947, 31 January 1947, 10 January 1947, H/120; Christiansen to Beaverbrook, 8 December 1950, H/141.
193 Beaverbrook to Churchill, 8 March 1944, BBK, D/421; Taylor, *Beaverbrook*, p. 569; *Express*, 12, 13, 15 May 1947.
194 Thompson to Beaverbrook, 13 May 1947, BBK H/119; Christiansen to Beaverbrook, 19 May 1947, BBK H/120.
195 R. Cockett (ed.), *My Dear Max: the Letters of Brendan Bracken to Lord Beaverbrook 1925–1938* (London: Historians Press, 1990), pp. 7, 31, 58; for example, policy statement, *Express*, 30 November 1950.
196 *Express*, 10, 12 October 1950; A. Wood, 'The Beaverbrook Bombshell', *Picture Post*, 29 October 1949; Shawcross, *Life*, p. 212.
197 Robertson to Beaverbrook 12 and 20 January 1950, BBK H/143, Gordon to Beaverbrook, 20 January 1950, BBK H/138.
198 BBK H/141, Christiansen to Beaverbrook, 27 January 1950, 2 February 1950.
199 *Express*, 9, 21, 23 February 1950; *Express*, 3, 17 February, 25, 11 January 1950.
200 *Express*, 8–25 October 1951; Taylor, *Beaverbrook*, pp. 601–2.
201 *Labour Year Book 1925* (London: Labour Publications, 1925), p. 352; this phrase is C. Seymour-Ure's, see *The Political Impact of Mass Media*, pp. 156–201.
202 RCP/FR pp. 152, 154.

2 'George the Third – or time for a change?' The popular press and the 1964 general election

1 A. Beith, 'The Press', in D. Butler and A. King (eds), *The British General Election of 1964* (London: Macmillan, 1965), p. 203.
2 See A. Birch, P. Campbell and P. Lucas, 'The Popular Press and the British General Election of 1955', *Political Studies*, 4, 3, 1956, 297–306; D. Butler, *The British General Election of 1955* (London: Macmillan, 1955).
3 Daily Herald directors, 'The Daily Herald and the General Election', p. 6, LPA, General Secretary Papers, Daily Herald File, Box B, GS/DH/200–301; J. Morgan (ed.), *The Backbench Diaries of Richard Crossman, 1951–1964* (London: Hamish Hamilton, 1981) (henceforth: RCD), p. 418.
4 *Mirror*, 17 May 1955; *Observer*, 16 May 1955; Butler, *Election of 1955*, p. 103.
5 H. Cudlipp, *Walking On The Water*, p. 209; Butler, *Election of 1955*, p. 209.
6 *Mirror*, 6, 5, 10 May 1955.
7 *Mirror*, 24, 25, 26 May 1955.
8 *Mirror*, 12 September–3 October 1959; D. Butler and R. Rose, *The British General Election of 1959* (London: Macmillan, 1960), p. 115; *Mirror*, 3 October 1959.

9 H. Cudlipp, *At Your Peril* (London: Weidenfeld & Nicolson, 1962), p. 226; RCD, pp. 747, 772–3, 798; F. Williams, 'Shattered Mirror', *New Statesman*, 17 October 1959, 496; *Mirror*, 12–20 October 1959; *Observer*, 1 November 1959.

10 *Herald*, 1–25 May 1955.

11 NEC, Memorandum, undated, 'The Daily Herald', p. 1; NEC, 'Comparison Between Front Page of "Daily Herald" During 1951 and 1955 General Election Campaigns', pp. 1–2; LPA, General Secretary's Papers, Daily Herald file, Box B, GS/DH/200–301.

12 See, for instance, *Mail*, 25, 26 May 1955; Birch, Campbell and Lucas, 'The Popular Press', p. 305.

13 Beaverbrook to Bracken, 19 April 1955, BBK C/58.

14 Butler, *Election of 1955*, p. 180.

15 *Express*, 9, 16 May 1955.

16 Birch, Campbell and Lucas, 'The Popular Press'; see, for example, *Express*, 9, 3 May 1955; *Express*, 12, 19 September 1959.

17 Birch, Campbell and Lucas, 'The Popular Press', p. 305; *Chronicle*, 26 May 1955.

18 *Sketch*, 24, 25 May 1955; *New Statesman*, 49, 28 May 1955, 736; *Sketch*, 1, 2 October 1959.

19 Royal Commission On the Press, *1961–62 Report* (Chairman: Lord Shawcross) (London: HMSO, 1962), p. 18.

20 H. Evans, *Downing Street Diary: the Macmillan Years, 1957–1963* (London: Hodder & Stoughton, 1981), p. 153.

21 K. Alderman, 'Harold Macmillan's "Night Of The Long Knives"', *Contemporary Record*, 6, 2, 1992, 260–2, 256–7; A. Horne, *Macmillan, Vol. II, 1957–1986* (London: Macmillan, 1989), p. 343; J. Ramsden, *The Winds of Change: Macmillan to Heath, 1957–1975* (London: Longman, 1996), 166–7.

22 See Horne, *Macmillan*, pp. 462–3, for differing accounts of Galbraith's resignation.

23 Horne, *Macmillan*, p. 463; *House of Commons Parliamentary Debates*, Fifth Series, 667, 14 November 1962, Col. 401; Evans, *Downing Street*, pp. 229, 227.

24 *Report Of The Tribunal Appointed To Inquire Into The Vassall Case* (Chairman: Lord Radcliffe) (London: HMSO, 1962), pp. 64–86; W. Deedes, *Dear Bill: W. F. Deedes Reports* (London: Pan, 1997), p. 162; F. Williams, 'The Honour of the Press', *New Statesman*, 65, 29 March 1963, 450; F. Williams, 'Curbing Press Freedom', *New Statesman*, 65, 15 March 1963, 366.

25 *House of Commons, Parliamentary Debates*, Fifth Series, 667, Col. 409, Col. 40, 14 November 1962; Horne, *Macmillan*, p. 464.

26 H. Macmillan, *At The End Of The Day* (London: Macmillan, 1973), p. 465.

27 Williams, 'Honour of the Press', pp. 450–2; H. Massingham, 'The Boil is Lanced', *Sunday Telegraph*, 24 March 1963.

28 P. Johnson, 'London Diary', *New Statesman*, 65, 22 March 1963, 417.

29 R. Lamb, *The Macmillan Years: the Emerging Truth* (London: John Murray, 1995), p. 456.

30 Deedes, *Dear Bill*, p. 169.

31 *Express*, 15 March 1963; *Lord Denning's Report* (London: HMSO, 1963), p. 52.

32 Aitken to Beaverbrook, 22 March 1963, BBK H/226; *Denning Report*, pp. 65–72.

33 Evans, *Downing*, p. 69; *Denning Report*, pp. 101–13; *The Times*, 11 June 1963; Horne, *Macmillan*, pp. 263–4; *Express*, 5 June 1963; *Mirror*, 13 June 1963.

34 S. Somerfield, *Banner Headlines* (London: Scan Books, 1979), p. 139.

35 *The Times*, 11 June 1963; Horne, *Macmillan*, pp. 263–4; for the best depiction of this mood, see C. Booker, *The Neophiliacs: the Revolution in English Life in the Fifties and Sixties* (London: Pimlico, 1992), pp. 189–210.

36 Macmillan, *At the End*, p. 442; Horne, *Macmillan*, p. 491.
37 Macmillan, *At the End*, p. 438; Lord Carrington, *Reflections on Things Past* (London: Fontana, 1989) p. 173; Ramsden, *Winds*, p. 184.
38 *Express*, 25 May 1964; Aitken to Beaverbrook, 25 April 1963, BBK H/226.
39 This is overwhelmingly the most dominant subject of Beaverbrook's correspondence during this time, see BBK H/225.
40 George Malcolm Thompson to Beaverbrook, 8 October 1962, BBK H/225.
41 C. Vines, *A Little Nut-Brown Man* (London: L. Trewin, 1968), pp. 146–8.
42 Beaverbrook to Gaitskell, 6 December 1962, BBK C/139; *Express*, 30 January 1963.
43 For King's personal support for Macmillan on this issue, see Macmillan, *At the End*, p. 14.
44 Beaverbrook to John Paul, 10 February 1962, BBK C/269.
45 Junor to Beaverbrook, 31 May 1963, BBK H/229; J. Junor, *Memoirs: Listening For A Midnight Train* (London: Pan, 1990), p. 123; Beaverbrook to Junor, 24 May 1963. In the event, Junor, who was forced to work out the remaining six months of his contract, was saved by Macmillan's own resignation and remained as editor.
46 Beaverbrook to Tony Lampton, 21 March 1963, BBK H/227; Horne, *Macmillan*, p. 262.
47 Butler and Stokes, *Political Change*, pp. 235–6.
48 Beaverbrook to Lampton, 21 March 1963, BBK H/227; Beaverbrook to Pickering, undated, BBK H/230.
49 Beaverbrook to Edwards, 30 May 1963, BBK H/227.
50 Edwards to Beaverbrook, 5 June 1963, BBK H/227; Christopher Nicholson to Beaverbrook, 5 June 1963, BBK H/330.
51 Beaverbrook to Thompson, 16 April 1963, BBK H/230; *Express*, 11 April 1963.
52 Thompson to Beaverbrook, 16 April 1963, BBK H/230.
53 Beaverbrook to Pickering, 17 May 1962, BBK H/225; Beaverbrook to Edwards (undated), BBK H/220.
54 For a brilliant portrayal of this aspect to Beaverbrook's personality in his later life, see Vines, *A Little Brown*; Chisholm and Davie, *Beaverbrook*, p. 516.
55 *Express*, 16 October 1963; *Sunday Express*, 14 October 1963; Junor, *Memoirs*, pp. 129–35; Dorothy Shaw (repeating points made to her by Beaverbrook) to Edwards, 16 October 1963, BBK H/226.
56 Vines, *A Little Brown*, p. 235; A. Watkins, *Brief Lives: With Some Memoirs* (London: Hamilton, 1982), p. 10.
57 *Express*, 1 January 1964.
58 Beaverbrook to Edwards, 7 October 1963, BBK H/226.
59 J. Campbell, *Edward Heath* (London: Pimlico, 1994), pp. 150–4; D. Jay, *Change and Fortune*, p. 294.
60 *Express*, 15, 16 January, 17 February, 25, 9, 30, 26 March 1964.
61 Quoted in A. Watkins, 'Lapsed Calvinist', in L. Gourley (ed.), *The Beaverbrook I Knew*, p. 238; *Express*, 9 April, 11 March 1964.
62 Beaverbrook to Junor, 27 March 1963, BBK H/229.
63 *Express*, 10 February, 18 April, 27 May 1964.
64 *Mail*, 16, 17 January 1964; *Mail, Express*, June–August 1964.
65 D. Butler and D. Stokes, *Political Change In Modern Britain: Forces Shaping Electoral Choice* (London: Macmillan, 1969), pp. 222, 229, 218–19; J. Blumler and D. McQuail, *Television In Politics: its Uses and Influences* (London: Faber & Faber, 1968), pp. 32–43.
66 A. Briggs, *A History of Broadcasting, Vol. 5, Competition* (Oxford: Oxford University Press, 1995), p. 451.

67 See Briggs, *A History of Broadcasting*, pp. 157, 448; B. Sendall, *Independent Television in Britain, Vol. 2, Expansion and Change 1958–68* (London: Macmillan, 1983), p. 230.

68 Beith, 'Press', pp. 189–90, 197; the *Mirror*'s circulation topped five million on 9 June 1964.

69 King and Cudlipp, *Minutes of Oral Evidence, Vol. 1* (London: HMSO, 1962), pp. 189–91; T. Matthews, *The Sugar Pill: an Essay on Newspapers* (London: Victor Gollancz, 1957), pp. 65–9.

70 Quoted in Edelman, *The Mirror*, p. 41; H. Cudlipp, 'The Humble Seeker After Knowledge', in V. Brodzky (ed.), *Fleet Street: The Inside Story of Journalism* (London: Macdonald, 1966), pp. 52, 56.

71 Quoted in R. Williams, *Communications* (London: Chatto & Windus, 1966), p. 97; C. King, *Future Of The Press*, p. 89; Cudlipp, *Walking*, p. 218.

72 H. Cudlipp, *At Your Peril* (London: Weidenfeld & Nicolson, 1962), pp. 128–9; H. Cudlipp, 'End the Bevan Myth', *Sunday Pictorial*, 28 September 1952.

73 King, *Strictly Personal*, p. 130; Cudlipp, *Walking*, p. 212; Cudlipp, *At Your Peril*, pp. 220–43

74 Deedes, *Dear Bill*, pp. 189–90; RCD, p. 997; C. King, *The Cecil King Diary: 1965–70* (London: Cape, 1972) (henceforth: CKD), p. 12.

75 CKD, p. 30.

76 Wilson to King, 4 October 1963, HC 3/3/1.

77 H. Cudlipp, 'Whose Finger on the Voters?', *British Journalism Review*, 7, 4, 1996, 33.

78 Quoted in T. Benn, *Out of the Wilderness: Diaries 1963–67* (London: Arrow, 1988), p. 133; CKD, p. 11; quoted in 'Alice Through the Looking Glass', *Spectator*, 23 September 1964.

79 CKD, p. 11.

80 *Mirror*, 12 September 1964; John Beavan to Cudlipp, 27 July 1964, HC 3/3/1; A. Howard and R. West, *The Making Of A Prime Minister* (London: Cape, 1965), p. 133; Cudlipp wrote the opening and closing paragraphs.

81 *Mirror*, 28 September 1964; for the full text, see Smith, *Paper*, pp. 181–2.

82 *Mirror*, 1, 12 October, 24 September 1964; Cudlipp, 'Whose Fingers on the Voters?', p. 35.

83 *Mirror*, 15 October 1964.

84 CKD, p. 62; Smith, *Paper Voices*, pp. 179–81.

85 K. Jefferys, 'British Politics and the Road to 1964', *Contemporary Record*, 9, 1, 1995, 120–46.

86 *Mirror*, 14 October 1964.

87 S. Fielding, 'White Heat and White Collars: the Evolution of "Wilsonism"', in R. Coopey, S. Fielding and N. Tiratsoo (eds), *The Wilson Governments* (Pinter: New York, 1993), pp. 36–7; R. West, 'Campaign Journal', *Encounter*, December 1964, 19.

88 B. Pimlott, *Harold Wilson* (London: HarperCollins, 1993), pp. 315–16; Howard and West, *Making*, pp. 191–3; *Mirror*, 7, 8, 9, 11 October 1964.

89 For this point, see Smith, *Paper*, p. 178; R. Williams, 'The Face Behind the Mirror', *Observer*, 29 April 1962.

90 I. Waller, 'The Left-Wing Press', in Kaufman, G. (ed.) The Left: a Symposium (London: Blond, 1966), p. 83; *Election Campaigning: the New Marketing of Politics* (Oxford: Blackwell, 1995), p. 81; Butler and King, *Election of 1964*, pp. 150–2.

91 Butler and King, *Election of 1964*, p. 151; *Mirror*, 13 October, 30, 29 September 1964.

92 Williams, *Hugh Gaitskell*, p. 668; Cudlipp, *Walking*, p. 248.

93 Richards, *Bloody*, pp. 177–9; *Sun*, 15 September 1964.

94 M. Abrams, *The Newspaper Reading Public of Tomorrow* (London: Odhams Press, 1964), p. 73.
95 B. Grundy, *The Press Inside Out* (London: W. H. Allen, 1976), p. 93; Benn, *Out of the Wilderness*, p. 141.
96 *Sun*, 5, 6, 7 October, 16 September 1964.
97 *Sun*, 15, 18 September 1964; C. King, 'Wanted: More Skill at the Top' and 'The Menace of the Old-boy Network', *Sun*, 23, 30 September 1964; F. Williams, 'Fleet Street', *New Statesman*, 68, 23 October 1964, 602; *Sun*, 1–9 October 1964.
98 West, 'Campaign Journal', p. 19.
99 Beith, 'Press', p. 185; *Express*, for example, 25, 26 September, 9 October 1964.
100 *Express*, 12 October 1964.
101 Edwards, *Goodbye*, p. 152; Robert Edwards to the author, 11 August 1997.
102 Junor, *Memoirs*, p. 96.
103 Edwards, *Goodbye*, pp. 150–2; Edwards to the author.
104 Edwards, *Goodbye*, p. 153; interview, Terry Lancaster, 31 August 1997.
105 Interview, Lancaster; Edwards to the author.
106 *Express*, 12, 18 September 1964.
107 *Express*, 5 October 1964; Smith, *Paper*, p. 172.
108 *Express*, 7, 1, 10 October 1964.
109 *Express*, 7 October 1964.
110 P. Paterson, *Tired and Emotional: the Life of Lord George-Brown* (London: Chatto & Windus, 1993), p. 151.
111 *Sunday Express*, 28 September 1964; Howard and West, *Making*, pp. 164–5.
112 *Express*, 28, 29 September 1964; Howard and West, *Making*, pp. 163–5; *Observer*, 4 October 1964.
113 Smith, *Paper*, p. 169.
114 Howard and West, *Making*, p. 176.
115 A. Douglas Home, *The Way the Wind Blows* (London: Collins, 1976), p. 213.
116 *Mail, Sun, Mirror*, 1 October 1964.
117 *Express*, 1 October 1964.
118 Interview, Lancaster.
119 *Express*, 9 October 1964.
120 *Express*, 9 October 1964; Edwards, *Goodbye*, pp. 154–5.
121 A. Howard, *RAB: the Life of R. A. Butler* (London: Cape, 1987), pp. 334–5; D. Thorpe, *Alec Douglas Home* (London: Sinclair Stevenson, 1996), p. 369; K. Young, *Sir Alec Douglas-Home* (London: Dent, 1970), p. 214.
122 *Express*, 15 October 1964; Edwards to the author; Edwards, *Goodbye*, p. 155.
123 S. Taylor, *The Reluctant Press Lord: Esmond Rothermere and the Daily Mail* (London: Weidenfeld & Nicolson, 1998), pp. 105–6, 145–6; R. Bourne, *Lords of Fleet Street*, pp. 190–1.
124 M. Randall, *The Funny Side of the Street* (London: Bloomsbury, 1988), pp. 75–83.
125 Bourne, *Lords*, pp. 174–5; H. Macmillan, *Pointing the Way* (London: Macmillan, 1972), p. 258.
126 Bourne, *Lords*, p. 175; Evans, *Downing Street*, p. 152; A. Watkins, 'Far from a Buccaneer', *Spectator*, 11 April 1998, p. 35.
127 Randall's internal publication, 'Why, Why, Why', quoted in D. McLachlan, 'How Lord Rothermere Lost his Nerve', *Spectator*, 162, 30 December 1966, 835–6; M. Turnstille, 'The Mail Affair', *New Statesman*, 72, 23 December 1966, 929; Taylor, *Reluctant*, pp. 152–3.
128 Randall, *Funny*, p. 6; Taylor, *Reluctant*, p. 162.
129 Randall, *Funny*, p. 6.
130 Bourne, *Lords*, p. 179; Randall, *Funny*, p. 6; for Murray, see L. Andrews and H.

Taylor, *Lords and Labourers of the British Press* (Carbonale and Edwardsville: South Illinois University Press, 1970), pp. 243–55.
131 Beith, 'Press', p. 187; *Mail*, 2–14 October 1964.
132 Beith, 'Press', p. 188, 202; *Mail*, 1 October 1964.
133 Beith, 'Press', p. 189; *Mail*, 1 October 1964.
134 *Mail*, 12, 18, 19, 21, 22, 25 September 1964.
135 *Mail*, 17, 30 September, 14 October 1964.
136 *Mail*, 5, 7, 9, 12 October 1964.
137 *Mail*, 18 September 1964.
138 Booker, *Neophiliacs*, pp. 120–1, 135; Taylor, *Reluctant*, p. 15; Randall, *Funny*, p. 7.
139 Randall, *Funny*, p. 8.
140 Bernard Levin, 'Don't Know No More', *Mail*, 15 October 1964.
141 Randall, *Funny*, p. 10; see also M. Randall, 'Did Bernard Levin Let Labour In?', *The Times*, 28 May 1983.
142 Taylor, *Reluctant*, pp. 175, 201; quoted in Edwards, *Goodbye*, p. 202.
143 *Sketch*, 12, 28, 30 September 1964.
144 *Sketch*, 7–14 October 1964.
145 *Sketch*, 12, 15 October 1964.
146 Beith, 'Press', pp. 193–8.
147 C. Seymour-Ure, *The Press, Politics and the Public* (London: Methuen, 1968), pp. 48–50.
148 King, *Future*, p. 65; J. Tunstall, *The Media in Britain* (London: Constable, 1983), p. 83; M. Leapman, *Treacherous Estate: The Press After Fleet Street* (London: Hodder & Stoughton, 1992), p. 34.
149 *The Law and the Press* (chairman, Lord Shawcross) (International Press Institute, 1965), p. 33; F. Williams, *Communications*, p. 46; Beith, 'Press', p. 203.
150 Seymour Ure, *British Press*, p. 221.
151 Beith, 'Press', p. 197; Waller, 'Left-Wing Press', p. 78.
152 Beaverbrook to Thompson, 16 April 1963, BBK H/230.
153 Butler and King, *Election of 1964*, p. 155; *Express*, 12, 18 September 1964.
154 M. Williams, *Inside Number 10* (Weidenfeld & Nicolson, 1972), p. 218; Johnson, 'London Diary', p. 417.
155 Pickering to Beaverbrook, 27 February 1963, BBK H/230.
156 R. Butt, 'Labour in the Looking Glass', *The Times*, 9 April 1987; interview, Lancaster; interview, Anthony Howard, 16 September 1997.
157 Pimlott, *Harold Wilson*, pp. 303–5; interview, Howard; B. Ingham, *Kill the Messenger* (London, HarperCollins, 1991), p. 65.
158 RCD, pp. 989–90; see also Pimlott, *Wilson*, p. 288.
159 A. Howard, 'Press Barons and Power: From the Age of Deference to the Eve of Mogul Power', Radio 4, Part 2, 26 July 1998; A. Goodman, *Tell Them I'm On My Way* (London: Chapmans, 1993), p. 213; interview, Howard; D. Watt, 'When Press Relations Turn Sour', *Financial Times*, 26 January 1968.
160 'Voters and the 1964 General Election', Report Prepared for The Thompson Organisation Ltd, Vol. 1, p. 47, Conservative Central Office Papers (CCO), Conservative Party Archive, Bodleian Library, Oxford (henceforth: CPA), CCO 180/11/2/1.
161 *Mirror*, 15 October 1963; Cudlipp, *Walking*, pp. 216–17; *Mirror*, 19 October 1963.
162 *Telegraph*, *Mail*, 18 October 1963; *Express*, 18,19 October 1963.
163 Michael Fraser, 'Thoughts on a Close Election', CPA, Conservative Research Department (CRD), memorandum, 23 October 1964, p. 4, CRD 2/48/85; see also Butler and King, *Election of 1964*, pp. 94–5; Jefferys, 'Road to 1964', p. 139.

164 West, 'Campaign Journal', p. 19; Williams, *Inside*, p. 218; Pimlott, *Harold Wilson*, pp. 312–14; Howard and West, *Making*, pp. 198–9.

165 *Express*, 14 October 1964; *Mail*, 12 October 1964; see also Pimlott, *Harold Wilson*, pp. 315–16.

166 *Mail*, 12 October 1964; Williams, *Inside*, pp. 220–1; Howard and West, *Making*, p. 227.

167 Butler and King, *Election of 1964*, p. 147; interview, Lancaster; although, as noted earlier, the Labour campaign was for the most part less than focused.

168 For the classic argument, see A. Sampson, *The Anatomy of Britain* (London: Hodder & Stoughton, 1962), pp. 637–8.

169 Jefferys, 'Road to 1964', p. 121; Michael Fraser, quoted in R. Rhodes James, 'Here's to the Class of '59', *The Times*, 14 March 1992.

170 King, *Strictly Personal*, p. 132; Cudlipp, *Walking*, p. 218; CKD, p. 12.

171 Jay, *Change*, p. 295; Butler and Stokes, ibid.; 'Voters and the 1964 General Election', Vol. 1, p. 22, Vol. 2, Table 25, CPA, CCO 180/11/2/1.

172 Butler and Stokes, *Political Change*, pp. 234–9; D. Porter, 'Downhill All the Way: Thirteen Tory Years 1951–64', in Fielding, Coopey and Tiratsoo (eds), *Wilson Governments*, p. 10.

173 Quoted in H. Berrington, 'The British General Election of 1964', *Journal of Royal Statistical Society*, 129, 1, 1965, 56.

174 Quoted in Butler and King, *Election of 1964*, p. 145; Butler and King, ibid., p. 300. There were, of course, key differences, notably the intellectual mood and the credibility and popularity of the respective Labour leaders.

175 *The Gallup International Public Opinion Polls 1937–1975* (New York: Random House), pp. 763–5; NOP poll, quoted in *Mail*, 24 September 1964; General Election, 1964, 'Final Report by the General Secretary', LPA, NEC minutes, 25 November 1964. The above figures are very similar to those blamed for Labour's defeat in 1992.

176 The *Express* (3, 14 October 1964) covered this theme in two notably detached and balanced reports.

3 Towards the 'Winter of Discontent': the popular press and the road to 1979

1 C. Seymour-Ure, 'The Press', in D. Butler and A. King, *The British General Election of 1966* (London: Macmillan, 1966), p. 149.

2 *Mail*, 30 March 1966; Butler and King, *Election of 1966*, pp. 108–10; *Mail*, 14 March 1966.

3 Seymour-Ure, 'Press', p. 164; *Express*, 14, 29, 19 March 1966; *Mail*, 30, 18 March 1966.

4 *Express*, 18, 19 March 1966; Butler and King, *Election of 1966*, pp. 110–14, 103, 92.

5 Beaverbrook to Aitken, 19 January 1962, BBK H/221; H. Evans, 'How Holy Writ Hampers Express', *Sunday Times*, 20 March 1966; Seymour-Ure, 'Press', p. 160; Butler and King, *Election of 1966*, p. 119; *The Times*, 10 March 1964; *Mirror*, 11 March 1966; *Express*, 12 March 1966.

6 Seymour Ure, 'Press', pp. 156–7; *Sun*, 18, 25 March 1966.

7 H. Evans, 'Why the Daily Mirror is Playing Cool with Labour', *Sunday Times*, 13 March 1966; CKD, p. 61.

8 J. Wells, 'Mirror, Mirror on the Wall', *Spectator*, 25 March 1966, 351–2; *Mirror*, for example, 3 December, 9 August, 10, 17, 29 September 1965; CKD, pp. 64, 14, 30–4, 36, 43.

9 M. Turnstile, 'King v. Wilson', *New Statesman*, 25 March 1966, 420; *Mirror*, 7, 8, 11, 17 March 1966; CKD, p. 62.

10 *Mirror*, 23, 28, 30, 31 March 1966; CKD, pp. 64–6.

11 J. Wells, 'The Mechanical Man', *Spectator*, 1 April 1966, 395; Williams, *Inside No. 10*, pp. 225–6; interview, Anthony Howard, 16 September 1997; Pimlott, *Harold Wilson*, p. 443.

12 *Report of the Committee of Privy Councillors Appointed to Enquire into 'D' Notice Matters* (London: HMSO, 1967), pp. 1–8, 71–4; C. Pincher, *Inside Story: a Documentary on the Pursuit of Power* (London: Book Club Associates, 1978), pp. 233–4; *Express*, 21 February 1967.

13 H. Wilson, *The Labour Government 1964–1970: a Personal Record* (London: Weidenfeld & Nicolson, 1971), pp. 374–5; *House of Commons Parliamentary Debates*, Fifth Series, 471, 21 February 1967, Col. 1432.

14 *Report*, pp. 11, 19, 26–7.

15 CKD, p. 129; *Mail, Express, Mirror*, 14 June–7 July 1967.

16 B. Castle, *The Castle Diaries, 1964–70* (London: Weidenfeld & Nicolson, 1984), pp. 254, 268; Wilson, *Labour*, p. 373; Williams, *Inside*, pp. 195–6, 184–5.

17 P. Jenkins, 'Bad PM or Bad Press', *Guardian*, 27 May 1969; D. Watt, 'When Press Relations Turn Sour', *Financial Times*, 26 January 1968; R. Butt, 'Why the "Honeymoon" Went Wrong', *The Times*, 22 May 1969.

18 Watt, 'When Press Relations'; N. Tunstall, *The Westminster Lobby Correspondents*, pp. 104–7.

19 Pimlott, *Wilson*, pp. 447–8.

20 *Mail*, 11 May 1968; *Express*, 15, 16, 20 January 1968; Cudlipp, *Walking*, pp. 308–10.

21 CKD, pp. 71–4, 84, 96, 114–15, 143.

22 See Cudlipp, *Walking*, pp. 302–5; King's entire 1965–70 diary is underpinned by this mood.

23 *Mirror*, 18 July 1966; 25, 27, 28 September 1967.

24 P. Jenkins, 'Mr King's Power Politics', *Guardian*, 22 February 1967; Cudlipp, *Walking*, p. 317; *Mirror*, 1,2 January 1968.

25 T. Benn, *Office Without Power: Dairies 1968–72* (London: Hutchinson, 1988), pp. 29–31.

26 Cudlipp, *Walking*, pp. 318–22; G. Gale, 'The Monumental Gnat', *Spectator*, 2 December 1972, pp. 882–3.

27 Cudlipp, *Walking*, pp. 296, 319

28 'C. King talks to Robin Day', *Listener*, 4 April 1968, pp. 435–6; *Mirror*, 1 April 1968.

29 P. Wright, *Spycatcher* (Richmond: Heinemann, 1987), p. 369; S. Dorril and R. Ramsay, *Smear: Wilson and the Secret State* (London: Grafton, 1992), pp. 173–82; H. Cudlipp, 'The So-Called "Military Coup" of 1968', *Encounter*, September 1981, pp. 11–21.

30 C. King, 'Enough is Enough', *Mirror, Sun*, 10 May 1968; C. King, 'Why I Spoke Out', *Sunday Mirror*, 12 May 1968; Cudlipp, *Walking*, p. 341; *Observer*, 12 May 1968; 'One Pair of Press Lords', *Listener*, 79, 23 May 1968, 667–9.

31 *Guardian*, 11 May 1968; *The Times*, 13 May 1968; Cudlipp, *Walking*, pp. 337, 348–51; CKD, p. 198.

32 R. Perrott, 'Why Cecil King lost faith in Wilson', *Observer*, 12 May 1968; CKD, pp. 75, 27, 144–5, 154; W. Terry, 'Whose Hand on the Dagger?', *Mail*, 31 May 1968; Cudlipp, *Walking*, pp. 314–16.

33 *Sunday Times*, 2 June 1968.

34 P. Brendon, *The Life and Death of the Press Barons*, p. 213; *Guardian*, 31 May 1968; CKD, p. 198; *Mirror*, 24 July 1968.

35 'All Done by Mirrors', profile: Hugh Cudlipp, *New Statesman*, 15 November 1968, 660–1; *Mirror*, 19 July, 12, 14 August, 18 October 1968.

36 *Mirror*, 14, 18 May 1969; *Guardian*, 15 May 1969; *The Times*, 9 December 1969; *Mirror*, 10, 11, 12 December 1969.

37 *The Times*, 12 March, 21 May 1969; *People and the Press*, 16th Annual Report of the Press Council, 1969, p. 85, *People and the Press*, 17th Annual Report of the Press Council, 1970, p. 85.

38 C. Seymour-Ure, 'Fleet Street' (henceforth: 'Fleet Street' (1970)), in D. Butler and M. Pinto-Duschinsky (eds), *The British General Election of 1970* (London: Macmillan, 1970), pp. 246–7.

39 *Sketch, Mail, Express*, 18 May–17 June 1970.

40 *Mirror*, 1–17 June 1970; Zeigler, *Wilson*, pp. 348–51.

41 *The Times*, 20 July 1970.

42 C. Seymour-Ure, 'The Press' (henceforth: 'Press' (1974)), in D. Butler and D. Kavanagh, *The British General Election of February 1974* (London: Macmillan, 1974), pp. 170–2.

43 *Mirror*, 8 February 1974; 'Harold's Favourite Tycoon', profile: Sir Don Ryder, *New Statesman*, 1 November 1974, 610–11; C. Adam, 'A Press for One Party', *New Statesman*, 15 February 1974, 216.

44 'Evidence of Mirror Group Newspapers to the Third Royal Commission on the Press', 9E2 (London: The Commission, 1975); C. Adam, 'A Press'; P. Ackroyd, 'The Press and the Election', *Spectator*, 2 March 1974, 264; interview, Mike Molloy, 18 January 1999.

45 Interview, Joe Haines, 10 September 1998; Margach, *Abuse of Power*, p. 168; *Mirror*, 9–28 February 1974.

46 *Express*, 8 February 1974; *Mail*, 13 February 1974.

47 Taylor, *Reluctant Press Lord*, pp. 201–2; Bourne, *Harmsworth Dynasty*, pp. 208–10; '*Mail* Heir', profile: Vere Rothermere, *New Statesman*, 4 October 1974, 462–3.

48 N. Coleridge, *Paper Tigers: the Latest, Greatest Newspaper Tycoons and How They Won the World* (London: William Heinemann, 1993), pp. 272–3.

49 For profiles of English, see Taylor, *Reluctant Press Lord*, pp. 116–28, 169–75; R. Greenslade, 'The English Patient', *Guardian*, 21 April 1997; 'Machiavelli or Prince?', *UK Press Gazette*, 8 July 1991; D. Hill, 'Major's Knight Editor', *Guardian*, 11 March 1992; 'The Tories' Favourite Editor', *Observer*, 10 May 1992.

50 *Mail, Express*, 13 February 1974.

51 *Mirror*, 1–10 October 1974; C. Seymour-Ure, 'Fleet Street' (henceforth: 'Fleet Street'(1974)), in D. Butler and D. Kavanagh (eds), *The British General Election of October 1974* (London: Macmillan, 1975), pp. 171–2.

52 *Mail*, 25 September–9 October 1974; *Express*, 25 September–10 October 1974.

53 *Mail*, 28 September 1974; *Express*, 28 September, 7 October 1974.

54 Pimlott, *Wilson*, pp. 625–8.

55 *Mail, Express*, 3–10 April 1974; M. Falklander, *Downing Street in Perspective* (London: Weidenfeld & Nicolson, 1983), pp. 138–9; Harold Wilson, 'Evidence Submitted to Royal Commission on the Press', 242 E1 (London: The Commission 1977), reprinted in *The Times*, 14 May 1977.

56 *The Times*, 4 April 1974; *Mail*, 10 April 1974; J. Haines, *The Politics of Power* (London: Cape, 1977), p. 202.

57 *Express, Mail*, 5 October 1974; *Sun*, 28 September 1974.

58 *Express*, 20, 21 September 1974; Haines, *Politics*, p. 203.

59 Wilson, 'Evidence to Royal Commission'.

60 B. Donoughue, *Prime Minister: the Conduct of Policy under Harold Wilson and James Callaghan* (London: Jonathan Cape, 1987), p. 41; Haines, *Politics*, p. 202.

61 Seymour-Ure, 'Press' (1974), p. 200; Seymour-Ure, 'Fleet Street' (1974), p. 186.
62 Seymour-Ure, 'Press' (1974), pp. 186–9, 198–200.
63 Seymour-Ure, 'Press' (1974), p. 174; *Express*, 12, 20, 15 February 1974.
64 *Mail, Express*, 22, 25, 26 February 1974.
65 *Express*, 1–10 October 1974.
66 J. Torode, 'Will the Real Ted Stand Up', *New Statesman*, 12 June 1970, 824; Ball and Seldon (eds), *The Heath Government*, pp. 368–9; Ackroyd, 'Press and the Election', p. 264.
67 'Machiavelli or Prince'; *Mail*, 26 February 1974; B. Grundy, 'The Press and the Election', *Spectator*, 5 October 1974, 431.
68 Howard, 'The Press and the Election', *New Statesman*, 11 October 1974, 492.
69 Wilson, 'Evidence to Royal Commission'; Wright, *Spycatcher*, p. 369; Pincher, *Inside*, p. 48; Dorril and Ramsay, *Smear*, pp. 271–2; *Sunday Times*, 6 October 1974, also reported campaign rumours to this effect.
70 Falklander, *Downing*, p. 134; A. Watkins, 'Labour and the Press', *New Statesman*, 26 April 1974, 566.
71 B. Levin, 'Why the Press has Refused to be Silent This Time', *The Times*, 9 April 1974; *The Freedom of the Press*, Granada Guildhall Lectures (London: Hart-Davies, MacGibbon, 1974).
72 Insight, 'Wilson and the Tory Press'; Haines, *Politics*, pp. 201–3; interview, Joe Haines, 10 September 1998; *Mail*, 10 April 1974.
73 Insight, 'Wilson and the Tory Press'; see also English's comments, *Mail*, 10 April 1974.
74 Watkins, 'Labour and the Press', p. 566.
75 Howard, 'Press and the Election', p. 492.
76 S. Regan, *Rupert Murdoch: a Business Biography* (London; Angus & Robertson, 1975), p. 164; R. Grose, *The Sunsation: Behind the Scenes of Britain's Best-Selling Newspaper* (London: Angus & Robertson, 1989), p. 13; T. Baistow, 'Jumbo and the Mouse', *New Statesman*, 19 December 1969, 886.
77 W. Shawcross, *Rupert Murdoch: Ringmaster of the Information Circus* (London: Chatto & Windus, 1992), pp. 67, 78; Cudlipp, *Walking*, p. 203; Regan, *Rupert Murdoch*, p. 102; G. Munter, *Murdoch: A Paper Prince* (London: Penguin, 1985), pp. 135–6; C. Horrie and P. Chippendale, *Stick It Up Your Punter: the Uncut Story of the Sun Newspaper* (London: Pocket, 1999), pp. 50–1.
78 *Sun*, 17 May 1970.
79 Seymour-Ure, 'Fleet Street' (1970), pp. 244, 247; Horrie and Chippendale, *Stick It*, pp. 3, 36–7.
80 J. Tunstall, 'The Media: Lapdogs for Thatcher?', *Contemporary Record*, 4, 2, 1990, 6; Harrop, 'Press and Post-War Elections', pp. 140–1.
81 Seymour-Ure, 'Press' (1974), pp. 195, 186–7; *Sun*, 9 February 1974; C. Adam and R. West, 'Orchestrating the Press', *New Statesman*, 87, 18 January 1974, 74–5.
82 *Sun*, 15, 21, 27 February 1974.
83 *Sun*, 8 October 1974.
84 *Sun*, 3, 1 October 1974; *Mail*, 1 October 1974; *Sun*, 21 September 1974.
85 *Sun*, 8 October, 28 September 1974.
86 Regan, *Rupert Murdoch*, p. 102; the *Sun*'s readership profile in 1974 was almost identical to the *Mirror*'s, with both reaching a greater number of C2 readers than any other paper, see Seymour-Ure, 'Fleet Street' (1974), p. 166.
87 Horrie and Chippendale, *Stick It*, pp. 55–6; H. Young, *One of Us* (London: Pan, 1993), p. 74; *Sun*, 3, 5 February 1975.
88 *Sun*, 21, 28 June, 9 October, 21 June, 28 July 1975.
89 *Sun*, 8 October, 19, 16 July 1975.

90 *Attitudes to the Press: A Report by Social and Community Planning Research* (London: Royal Commission on the Press, 1977), pp. 69–70, 74.

91 *Sun*, 16, 6 December 1976.

92 *Sun*, for instance, 3 December, 3 April, 29 September, 16 July, 30 December 1976.

93 Labour Party, Oral/Written Evidence to the Royal Commission on the Press, 83OE1, 83E1 (London: The Commission, 1975), pp. 3, 10.

94 *Mail*, 19 May 1977; *Guardian*, 20 May 1977.

95 *Guardian*, 21, 23, 24 May 1977.

96 *Mail*, 21 May 1977; Bourne, *Lords of Fleet Street*, p. 218.

97 *House of Commons Parliamentary Debates*, Fifth Series, 932, 24 May 1977, cols. 1182–3; *Guardian*, 27, 23 May 1977; *Mail*, 23, 24 May 1977; *The Times*, 25 May 1977.

98 *Royal Commission on the Press: Final Report* (Chairman: O. R. McGregor) (London: HMSO, 1977), pp. 98–9, 107.

99 *Royal Commission on the Press: Minority Report* (reprinted by the Labour Party, 1977), pp. 6–8.

100 *Sun*, 24, 14 March, 16 June 1977; *Sun*, 25, 26 July, 11 October 1977.

101 Grundy, *The Press Inside Out*, p. 25; *Sun*, 1, 4 March 1978.

102 Lamb, quoted in M. Hollingsworth, *The Ultimate Spindoctor: the Life and Fast Times of Tim Bell* (London: Coronet, 1997), p. 70; R. Cockett, 'The Party, Publicity and the Media', in A. Seldon and S. Ball (eds), *The Conservative Party Since 1900* (Oxford: Oxford University Press, 1994), pp. 573–4.

103 Horrie and Chippendale, *Stick It*, p. 56; Grose, *The Sunsation*, p. 37.

104 Lamb, *Sunrise*, p. 160; quoted in Grose, *The Sunsation*, p. 37; P. Rose, 'A Place in the Sun', Paper to ICBH 'Century of the Popular Press' conference, London, September 1996.

105 J. Tuccille, *Murdoch* (London: Piatkus, 1989), pp. 24, 39; Shawcross, *Murdoch*; pp. 171–3; R. Belfield, C. Hird and S. Kelly, *Murdoch: the Great Escape* (London: Warner, 1994), pp. 29–30.

106 Shawcross, *Murdoch*, p. 211; Lamb, *Sunrise*, pp. 222, 224; R. Spark, 'On Being One of the Men Who Took You to Your Leader', *Spectator*, 17 July 1999.

107 Hollingsworth, *Ultimate*, p. 71; Lamb, *Sunrise*, p. 165; *Sun*, 8 September, 2, 12, 14 November, 7, 19 December 1978.

108 Quoted in M. Hollingsworth, *The Press and Political Dissent* (London: Pluto, 1985), p. 53.

109 Greenslade, 'The English Patient'; N. Tiratsoo, 'You've Never Had it so Bad', in N. Tiratsoo (ed.), *From Blitz to Blair: a New History of Britain since 1939* (London: Phoenix, 1998), pp. 187–9.

110 Hollingsworth, *Press*, p. 33; *Mail*, 14 November 1980; quoted in S. Jenkins, *The Market for Glory: Fleet Street Ownership in the 20th Century* (London: Faber & Faber, 1986), pp. 127–9.

111 Quoted in B. Whitaker, *News Limited: Why You Can't Read All About It* (London: Minority Press Group, 1981), p. 58; D. Jameson, *Last of the Hot Metal Men: from Fleet Street to Showbiz* (London: Ebery, 1990), p. 41.

112 *Mail*, 8, 18 January 1979; *Express*, 15, 16 January 1979; *Sun*, 8, 23 January 1979; for general assessments, see 'Symposium: the Winter of Discontent', *Contemporary Record*, 1, 3, 1987, 34–43; K. Morgan, *Callaghan: A Life* (Oxford: Oxford University Press), pp. 653–76.

113 *Sun*, 20, 22 January 1979; *Mail*, 12 January 1979; *Mail*, 11, 9, 8 January, *Sun*, 8, 9 January 1979; the irony of the former image is that the strikes were actually the result of the failure of the central union leadership to control their rank-and-file activists.

114 *Sun*, 11, 16 January 1979; *Express*, 11 January 1979; *Mail*, 8 January 1979. Callaghan's actual words were, 'I don't think that other people in the world would share the view that there is mounting chaos' although he accepted that the headline accurately conveyed his tone, see Morgan, *Callaghan*, p. 662.

115 P. Whitehead, 'The Writing on the Wall: Britain in the Seventies (London: Michael Joseph, 1985), 281; Tom McNally, quoted in C4, 'Secret History: The Winter of Discontent', 13 June 1998 and Cockerell, *Live*, p. 243.

116 *Sun*, 7, 8 February 1979; *Express*, 8 February 1979.

117 *Mail*, 1 February 1979; *Mail, Express, Sun*, 20 January 1979.

118 *Mail*, 23 January 1979; *Telegraph, Mail*, 1 February 1979.

119 *Express*, 9 February 1979; *Sun*, 8, 10 February 1979; *Mail*, 2 February 1979.

120 *Guardian*, 25 January 1979; *Express, Mail, Sun*, 25, 26 January 1979.

121 Trades Union Media Working Group, *A Cause for Concern: Media Coverage of Industrial Disputes, January and February 1979* (London: TUC, 1979).

122 N. Fountain, 'A Long, Hot Winter', *Guardian*, 25 September 1993, p. 26.

123 Speaking on 'Secret History: The Winter of Discontent'; *Telegraph, Sun*, 1 February 1979.

124 *Sun*, 12, 15 January 1979.

125 'Blame the Bosses too', *Economist*, 3 February 1979, 68; Tiratsoo, 'You've Never Had it', p. 182; W. Brown, 'Industrial Relations', in M. Artis and D. Cobham (eds), *Labour's Economic Policies 1974–1979* (London: Macmillan, 1985), pp. 215, 224.

126 *Mail*, 18 January 1979; C. Hitchens, 'The Daily Mail Does it Again', *New Statesman*, 97, 2 February 1979, 136; A. Coate, 'Strike Havoc Probe', *New Statesman*, 26 January 1979, 107; *Mail*, 6 February 1979; C. Hitchens, 'Ghost Writing at the Daily Mail', *New Statesman*, 97, 9 February 1979, 172.

127 W. Rodgers, 'Government Under Stress: Britain's Winter of Discontent 1979', *Political Quarterly*, 54, 1984, 178; A. King, 'Politics, Economics and Trade Unions', in H. Pennimann (ed.), *Britain at the Polls 1979: a Study of the General Election* (Washington: American Enterprise Institute for Public Policy Research, 1981), p. 82; Morgan, *Callaghan*, p. 664.

128 Quoted in 'Secret History: Winter of Discontent'; P. Jenkins, *Mrs Thatcher's Revolution: the Ending of the Socialist Era* (London: Cape, 1987), pp. 23, 27.

129 Donoughue, *Prime Minister*, p. 165; Morgan, *Callaghan*, p. 665; J. Callaghan, *Time and Chance* (London: Collins, 1987), p. 537.

130 R. Taylor, 'The Trade Union "Problem" in the Age of Consensus', in B. Pimlott and C. Cook (eds), *The Trade Union Question in British Politics: Government and Unions Since 1945* (London: Longman, 1991), p. 174; J. Seaton, 'Trades Unions and the Media', in B. Pimlott and C. Cook, *The Trade Union Question*, pp. 256–73; Glasgow University Media Group, *Bad News* (London: Routledge and Kegan, 1976).

131 P. Kellner and R. Worcester, 'Electoral Perceptions of Media Stance', in R. Worcester and M. Harrop (eds), *Political Communications: The General Election Campaign of 1979* (London: George Allen & Unwin, 1982), pp. 58–9.

132 *Mirror*, 30 January 1979; *Sunday Mirror*, 28 January 1979; *Guardian*, 29, 30 January 1979; TUC, *Cause for Concern*, p. 27; *Mail*, 29, 30 January 1979; *Express*, 30 January 1979; *Sun*, 30 January 1979.

133 For assessments of its role, see D. Butler and D. Kavanagh, *The British General Election of 1979* (London: Macmillan, 1980), pp. 344, 377; I. Crewe, 'How to Win a Landslide Without Really Trying', in Pennimann (ed.), *Britain*, pp. 265–9.

134 See also C. Hay, 'Narrating Crisis: The Discursive Construction of the "Winter of Discontent"', *Sociology*, 30, 2, 1996, 253–77.

135 Jenkins, *Mrs Thatcher's*, p. 28.

136 Hay, 'Narrating Crisis', p. 261.

137 *Express*, 10, 11, 27 April 1979; *Mail*, 7, 10 April 1979.
138 Jameson, *Last*, p. 41.
139 *Express*, 26 April 1979.
140 *Express*, 11 April 1979.
141 *Express*, 6, 11, 27 April, 2 May 1979; Jameson, *Last*, p. 55.
142 Jameson, *Last*, p. 136; *Express*, 3 May 1979.
143 T. Baistow, 'Forget the Facts, Push the Story', *Guardian*, 23 April 1979; *Mail*, 19 April 1979.
144 *Mail*, 10, 9, 12 April, 2 May 1979; *Express*, 12, 17 April, 2 May 1979.
145 *Express*, 9 April 1979; *Mail*, 9 April 1979; *Telegraph*, 9 April 1979; A. Howard, 'Not Many Don't Knows Left in Fleet Street', *Observer*, 22 April 1979; P. Paterson, 'Telegraphing the Leader', *Spectator*, 28 April 1979, p. 20.
146 M. Bilton and S. Himelfarb, 'Fleet Street', in Butler and Kavanagh (eds), *Election of 1979*, p. 245; D. Hart-Davies, *The House the Berrys Built: Inside the Telegraph 1928–1986*, pp. 255–6; Deedes, *Dear Bill*, pp. 271–3.
147 *Telegraph, Express, Mail*, 12, 21 April 1979.
148 Howard, 'Touch-and-Go for Sunday Allegiance', *Observer*, 29 April 1979, *Mail*, 26 April 1979; Press Release, Angus Maude, Statement 'Labour Lies', 25 April 1979, CPA, GE, 696/79.
149 G. Howe, *Conflict of Loyalty* (London: Macmillan, 1994), pp. 115–16; R. Hattersley, 'The Guilty Editors', *The Times*, 29 January 1992; Butler and Kavanagh, *Election of 1979*, p. 191; A. Bevins, 'Cometh the Election, Cometh the Smear', *Independent*, 3 February 1992.
150 Butler and Kavanagh, *1979*, p. 132; interview, Molloy.
151 Interview, Molloy; *Mirror*, 17, 19, 7 April 1979.
152 *Mirror*, 3 May 1979.
153 Figures derived from content analysis, presented in P. Foot, 'It Depends on Which Facts are Sacred', *New Statesman*, 4 May 1979, p. 631; for a 1974 comparison, see Insight, 'The Headline War', *Sunday Times*, 29 September 1974; Seymour-Ure, 'Press' (1974), pp. 184–5.
154 *Sun*, 30 March 1979; Butler and Kavanagh, *1979*, p. 201; *Mirror*, 2 April 1979.
155 *Sun*, 3 April 1979; A. Howard, 'Fleet St. Gets its Snout in the Trough', *Observer*, 15 April 1979.
156 *Sun*, 9, 24 April 1979; Bilton and Himelfrab, 'Fleet Street', p. 224.
157 *Sun*, 30 April 1979; Lamb, *Sunrise*, p. 159.
158 Hollingsworth, *Ultimate*, p. 71; Lamb, *Sunrise*, p. 165; *Sun*, 12, 26, 30 April 1979.
159 A. Howard, 'The Favourite of Fleet Street', *Observer*, 6 May 1979; Lamb, *Sunrise*, pp. 154–8; M. Engel, *Tickle the Public: One Hundred Years of the Popular Press* (London: Indigo, 1997), p. 226; *Sun*, 3 May 1979.
160 Horrie and Chippendale, *Stick It*, p. 61; Kellner and Worcester, 'Electoral Perceptions', pp. 59–62.
161 Howard, 'Favourite of Fleet Street'; Kellner and Worcester, 'Electoral Perceptions', p. 62; for the full figures, see Chapter 6, Table 6.5.
162 Kellner and Worcester, 'Electoral Perceptions', pp. 63–5; R. Worcester and P. Kellner, 'A Rival for Television', *New Statesman*, 4 May 1979, p. 632; Tunstall, *Media in Britain*, pp. 161–5.
163 Crewe, 'Why the Conservatives Won', pp. 278–9; Lamb, *Sunrise*, pp. 161–2; Hollingsworth, *Ultimate*, p. 71.
164 Kellner and Worcester, 'Electoral Perceptions', pp. 59–61; W. Miller, *Media and Voters: The Audience, Content, and Influence of Press and Television at the 1987 General Election* (Oxford: Clarendon Press, 1991).
165 Quoted in Howard, 'Fleet Street gets its Snout'.

166 *Royal Commission, Minority Report*, p. 8.
167 See, for example, Butler and Kavanagh, *1979*, pp. 320–1, 326–8, 333; Callaghan, quoted in Donoughue, *Prime Minister*, p. 191.

4 A 'Nightmare on Kinnock Street': Labour and the Tory tabloids 1979–1992

1 *Sun*, 9 April 1992.
2 This was demonstrated, for example, by strongly pro-Thatcherite coverage of the *Mail*, *Express* and *Sun* during serious internal conflicts of November 1980/1981.
3 *Mail*, 16, 17 May 1983; C. Wintour, 'Not Many Marks for Fleet Street', *Observer*, 5 June 1983.
4 *People and the Media*, 29th/30th Annual Report of the Press Council, 1983, p. 132; *Mail*, 4 June, 24 May 1983.
5 B. Castle, 'Buying Power with Monopoly Money', *The Times*, 23 May 1983; P. Johnson, 'Napping a One-Horse Race', *Spectator*, 21 May 1983, p. 19.
6 M. Linton, 'Fleet Street', *Guardian*, 25 May 1983; C. Ward, 'Apres Moi, le Wet Weekend in Skegness' and 'Trying the Scargill Muzzle for Size', *The Times*, 27 May, 9 June 1983; T. Baistow, 'Monkey Business as Usual for the Tabloids', *Guardian*, 30 May 1983.
7 *Express*, 10, 17 May 1983.
8 *Express*, 6 May 1983; Hollingsworth, *Press*, pp. 222–4; *People and the Press*, 1983, pp. 93–4.
9 M. Engel, *Tickle the Public: One Hundred Years of the Popular Press*, p. 268; D. Jameson, *Last of the Hot Metal Men: from Fleet Street to Showbiz*, p. 71.
10 Hollingsworth, *Press*, pp. 230–2.
11 *Star*, 7 April 1979–3 May 1979; Bilton and Himelfrab, 'Fleet Street', p. 234.
12 Hollingsworth, *Press*, pp. 232–3; J. Stevens, 'Where Victor Went Wrong', *UK Press Gazette*, 28 October 1985; *Star*, 5, 11 November 1980.
13 See, for instance, *Star*, 28 January, 3 March 1980; Hollingsworth, *Press*, p. 233.
14 Stevens, 'Where Victor Went Wrong'.
15 *Star*, 10 May–8 June 1983.
16 M. Leapman, *Treacherous Estate: the Press after Fleet Street*, p. 63; C. Horrie and P. Chippendale, *Stick It Up Your Punter: the Uncut Story of the Sun Newspaper*, pp. 128–32; R. Harris, *Gotcha! the Media, the Government and the Falklands Crisis* (London: Faber & Faber, 1983), pp. 38–55.
17 For assessments of press coverage, see Hollingsworth, *Press*, pp. 140–69; P. Tatchell, *The Battle for Bermondsey* (London: Heretic Books, 1983); Horrie and Chippendale, *Stick It*, pp. 132–8; M. von Hattern, 'How Not to Win an Election', *Financial Times*, 23 February 1983; H. Macpherson, 'Bermondsey: An Abuse of Media Power', *Tribune*, 3 March 1983.
18 M. Harrop, 'Press', in D. Butler and D. Kavanagh (eds), *The British General Election of 1983* (London: Macmillan, 1984), p. 180; *Sun*, 10 May–8 June 1983.
19 *Sun*, 10 May 1983; *Mail*, 20 May 1983.
20 *Sun*, 7 June 1983.
21 *Express*, 2 June 1983; Hollingsworth, *Press*, pp. 228–30.
22 *People and the Media*, 31st Annual Report of the Press Council, 1984, pp. 48–9.
23 Harrop, 'Press', pp. 206–8; Hollingsworth, *Press*, pp. 236–9.
24 Quoted in Horrie and Chippendale, *Stick It*, p. 140.
25 *Sun*, *Mail*, 9, 10 November 1981; Mervyn Jones, *Michael Foot*, p. 476.

26 *Sun*, 22 May, 2 June 1983; *Mail*, 8 June 1983.

27 *Express*, 7 June 1983; quoted in Harrop, 'Press', p. 208.

28 *Express*, 10, 23 May 1983; Harrop, 'Press', p. 207.

29 *Mail*, *Sun*, *Express*, 9 June 1983.

30 *Mirror*, 20 November 1981; *The Times*, 20 November 1981; interview, Goodman; interview, Haines; interview, Molloy; Harrop, 'Press', pp. 183, 189.

31 Harrop, 'Press', pp. 177–9, 193–4.

32 Harrop, 'Press', p. 198.

33 D. Healey, 'The 1983 General Election', undated NEC paper, LPA, NEC minutes, July 1983; Gwyneth Dynwoody to Jim Mortimer, 18 July 1983, LPA, NEC minutes.

34 MORI report on the election, quoted in M. Foot, *Another Heart and Other Pulses: the Alternative to the Thatcher Society* (London: Collins, 1984), p. 158.

35 *Sunday People*, 15 May 1983.

36 *Express*, *Mail*, 26 May 1983; *Mail*, 28 May 1983; Foot, *Another Heart*, pp. 79, 83–4.

37 *Express*, *Mail*, *Sun*, 27 May, 2, 3, 7 June 1983; Ranney (ed.), *Britain at the Polls 1983*, pp. 158–61; M. Jones, *Michael Foot* (London: Victor Gollancz, 1994), pp. 449–50.

38 M. Linton, 'Disaster Snatched from the Jaws of Defeat', *Guardian*, 30 June 1983; Dennis Howell to Jim Mortimer, 'General Election 1983', 8 July 1983; Sam McCluskie, 'Report on the General Election', 6 July 1983, LPA, NEC Minutes; J. Innes, 'The Inside Story of Labour's Press Machine', *Journalist*, July 1983; F. Beckett, 'Paper Tigers', *Guardian*, 15 June 1984.

39 John Reid to Kinnock, June 1983, KNNK, Box 89; *Sun*, 21 June, 21 September, 6 July, 3 October 1983; see also *Mail*, 6 July, 8 August, 3 October 1983.

40 P. Gould, 'Communications Review' (December 1985), p. 51, KNNK, Box 218; N. Wood, 'Labour Attacks "Distortion" in Press Reports', *The Times*, 23 December 1986.

41 M. Leapman, *Kinnock* (London: Unwin Hyman, 1987), pp. 180–2; *Mail*, 22 December 1986; Kinnock to Roy Schrieber, 26 January 1987, KNNK, Box 224.

42 Goldsmith College Media Research Group, *Media Coverage of London Councils*, *Revised Interim Report* (April 1987); see also G. Oakley, 'Media Madness Stifles an Informed Debate', *Listener*, 17 March 1988, 8–9.

43 Goldsmith College Media Group, *Media Coverage of London Councils, Final Report* (June 1987), pp. 117–30; *Sun*, 16 February 1987.

44 *Mail*, 24, 28 February 1987; Sigmund Sternberg to the *Sun*, 18 February 1987, KNNK, Box 229; *Sun*, 12 February 1987.

45 *Sun*, 20, 21 February 1987; *Express*, *Mail*, 20 February 1987; Goldsmiths Media Group, *Interim Report*, pp. 8–9.

46 A. McSmith, *Faces of Labour* (London: Verso, 1996), p. 58.

47 'Briefing Note – Greenwich by-election', February 1987, KNNK, Box 253; *Mail*, 2 February 1987; *News of the World*, 15, 22 February 1987; *Sun*, 23, 26 February 1987.

48 *Express*, *Sun*, 15 February 1984; the latter quote featured in tabloid coverage of Kinnock's visit to the USSR in November 1984.

49 Leapman, *Kinnock*, pp. 159–60; quoted in C. Brown, 'Liberals Worry Over Labour Nuclear Policy', *Independent*, 4 December 1986.

50 Brown, 'Liberals Worry'; *Mail*, 2, 4, 6 December 1986; *Express*, 2, 3, 6 December 1986; *Sun*, 4 December 1986.

51 Patricia Ramsay, 'Report of December Trip to US', 17 December 1986, KNNK, Box 244.

52 'Visit to the USA: Options', undated, unauthored (Patricia Hewitt?), KNNK, Box 224.

53 *Guardian*, 25 March 1987; P. Pringle, *Independent*, 28 March 1987.
54 *Mail*, 24, 26, 27 March 1987; *Sun*, *Express*, 26 March 1987.
55 *Telegraph*, 31 March 1987; A. Campbell, 'You Guys Are the Pits', *New States-man*, 3 April 1987, 20.
56 Campbell, 'You Guys'; G. Smith, *Reagan and Thatcher* (London: Bodley Head, 1990), p. 228; D. Blindy, 'Kinnock "Walked into a White House Trap"', *Sunday Telegraph*, 29 March 1987; *Sunday Times*, 29 March 1987; 'Dear Ray' letter from Patricia Hewitt to US administration, 31 March 1987, KNNK, Box 225.
57 *Express, Today, Star, Mail, Sun*, 28 March 1987.
58 Hewitt to the US administration; Patricia Ramsay to Hewitt, 9 April 1987, KNNK, Box 225.
59 *Mirror*, 30 March 1987; Campbell, 'You Guys'.
60 *Star, Express, Today, Mail, Sun*, 30 March 1987; *Independent*, 2 April 1987; S. Jenkins, 'Kinnock is Press Ganged Unfairly', *Sunday Times*, 5 April 1987; as usual the *Mirror*'s coverage provided the alternative skew, 27, 28, 30 March 1987.
61 D. Hughes and P. Wintour, *Labour Rebuilt: the New Model Party* (London: Fourth Estate, 1990), p. 24; MacShane to Hewitt, 10 April 1987, KNNK, Box 229.
62 M. Harrop, 'Press' (henceforth, 'Press' (1987)) in D. Butler and D. Kavanagh (eds), *The British General Election of 1987* (London: Macmillan, 1987), pp. 166–8.
63 *Sun*, 26 March 1987; T. Benn, *The End of an Era: Diaries 1980–90*, p. 499.
64 Hollingsworth, *Press*, pp. 77–105; J. Curran, 'The Boomerang Effect: the Press and the Battle for London 1981–6' in Curran, Smith and Wingate (eds), *Impacts and Influences*, pp. 113–40; Harrop, 'Press' (1987), p. 169.
65 Harrop, 'Press' (1987), p. 171; *Express*, 22, 23 May 1987; *Independent*, 23 May 1987.
66 *Mail*, 29–30 May 1987.
67 *Sun*, 22 May, 10 June 1987.
68 *Mail*, 28 May 1987; *Sun*, 8–9 June 1987; *Star*, 11 June 1987; *Mail*, 30 May 1987.
69 George Gale, *Sunday Express*, 31 May 1987; quoted in Harrop, 'Press' (1987), p. 170; *Express*, 8 May 1987; libel writ, 10 June 1987, KNNK, Box 47.
70 Gould, 'Communications Review', p. 15; B. Gould, *Goodbye To All That* (London: Macmillan, 1995), p. 246; P. Mandelson, 'Marketing Labour', *Contemporary Record*, 1, 4, 1988, 13; for confirmation, see Brendan Bruce, Conservative Communications Director 1989–1991, quoted in N. Jones, *Soundbites and Spin Doctors: How Politicians Manipulate the Mass Media – and Vice Versa* (London: Cassell, 1995), p. 195.
71 P. Gould, P. Herd and C. Powell, 'The Labour Party's Campaign Communica-tions', in I. Crewe and M. Harrop (eds), *Political Communications: The British General Election Campaign of 1987* (Cambridge: Cambridge University Press, 1989), p. 74; Butler and Kavanagh, *Election of 1987*, pp. 102, 153–5; *Mail*, 23, 25 May 1987; *Express*, 22 May 1987.
72 P. Forbes, 'Sticking to the Issues Nearly Comes Unstuck', *New Statesman*, 5 June 1987, 18–20; *Express*, 25, 27, 30 May 1987; *Mail*, 26, 27, 28 May 1987; *Sun*, 29 May 1987.
73 Miller, *Media and Voters*, pp. 177–8.
74 W. Miller, H. Clarke, L. Leduc and P. Whitely, *How Voters Change: the 1987 British General Election in Perspective* (Oxford: Clarendon, 1990), p. 187; Butler and Kavanagh, *Election of 1987*, pp. 106–7.
75 M. Harrison, 'Broadcasting', in Butler and Kavanagh, *1987*, p. 147; *Mirror*, 5

June 1987; R. Tyler, *Campaign: the Selling of the Prime Minister* (London: Grafton, 1987), p. 215.

76 *Sun, Mail, Express, Telegraph*, 5 June 1987.

77 *Mail on Sunday, Sunday Express*, 7 June 1987; *Star*, 10 June 1987.

78 *Sun*, 9 June 1987; D. Healey, *The Time of My Life* (London: Penguin, 1990), p. 535; *Sun, Guardian, Express, Mail*, 10 June 1987; memo from Mark Dowdney to Joe Haines, 10 August 1987, p. 2, KNNK, Box 373.

79 Mandelson and Hewitt, 'The Labour Campaign', p. 53; Butler and Kavanagh, *Election of 1987*, pp. 146–7, 183; Miller, Clarke, Leduc and Whitely, *How Voters*, pp. 60–4, 138.

80 N. Jones, *Election '92* (London: BBC Books, 1992), pp. 48, 92, 108.

81 A. Howard, 'Poison Pens Prove Write Off for the Tabloids', and 'Despairing Columnists Distance Themselves from Major's Tories', *Guardian*, 7, 3 April 1992; C. Wintour, 'Fleet Street', *The Times*, 7 April 1992; M. White, 'Bombshell Too Far Gives Tories the Blues', *Guardian*, 2 April 1992; Jones, *Election '92*, pp. 85–6, 77; I. Hargreaves, 'Tabloids Suffer Pollsters Droop', *Financial Times*, 5 April 1992; I. Dawney, 'True Blue Loyalty Wearing Thin', *Financial Times*, 7 April 1992; B. MacArthur, 'Minders Foil the Tabloids', *Sunday Times*, 5 April 1992.

82 See, for example, M. Harrop and M. Scammell, 'A Tabloid War', in D. Butler and D. Kavanagh (eds), *The British General Election Of 1992* (London: Macmillan, 1992), pp. 180–210; D. McKie, 'Fact is Free but Comment is Sacred, or Was it the Sun Wot Won It?', in I. Crewe and B. Gosschalk (eds), *Political Communications: the General Election Campaign of 1992* (Cambridge: Cambridge University Press, 1995); for an earlier version of this chapter's argument, see J. Thomas, 'Labour, the Tabloids, and the British General Election of 1992', *Contemporary British History*, 12, 3, 1998, 80–104.

83 *Sunday Telegraph*, 12 April 1992.

84 Butler and Kavanagh, *1992*, pp. 105–6, *Express, Sun, Star*, 17 March 1992.

85 M. Leapman, 'Middle Market Male', interview: D. English, *Independent on Sunday*, 22 March 1992; *Mail*, 17 March 1992.

86 *Express*, 25–26 March 1992; *Mail* 26–27 March 1992; *Sun*, 26 March 1992.

87 K. Newton, 'Caring and Competence: the Long Campaign', in A. King (ed.), *Britain at the Polls* (New York: Chatham, 1992), pp. 147–8; *Guardian*, 26 March 1992.

88 Jones, *Election '92*, p. 153.

89 Jones, *Election '92*, p. 153; D. Hare, *Asking Around* (London: Faber & Faber, 1993), p. 222; *Mail, Express, Sun*, 7, 8 April 1992.

90 B. MacArthur, 'Perhaps It Was the Sun Wot Won It', *Sunday Times*, 12 April 1992; see also MacArthur, 'Did the Sun sink Kinnock? Yes and No', *Sunday Times*, 26 April 1992; 'General Secretary's Report, 1992', p. 10

91 MacArthur, 'Perhaps It Was'; Harrop and Scammell, 'A Tabloid War', p. 209.

92 R. Worcester, 'The Media in the General Election', *British Journalism Review*, 3, 3, 1992, 24; for similar figures for 1987, see 'The Electoral Impact of the Partisan Press', *Social Studies Review*, November 1987, 60; then only 41 per cent of *Sun* readers voted Conservative, while 40 per cent of *Mail* readers failed to vote Tory.

93 Worcester, 'Media in the General Election', p. 24.

94 D. Hill, 'The Labour Party's Strategy', in Crewe and Gosschalk (eds), *Political Communications*, p. 40; D. Hill, 'General Election Campaign: Some Observations', KNNK, Box 180; *The Times*, 14 April 1992; J. Gibson, 'A Man Exposed', interview: Rupert Murdoch, *Guardian*, 9 November 1998.

95 Linton, *Was It the Sun?*, pp. 28–9; J. Curtice and H. Semetko, 'Does It Matter What the Papers Say?', pp. 43–64; for Linton's critique, see *Was It the Sun?*, p. 8.

96 Newton and Brynin, 'The National Press and Party Voting', p. 280.
97 Newton and Brynin, 'The National Press and Party Voting', pp. 265–85. Brynin and Newton, 'The National Press and Voting Turnout', pp. 59–73.
98 Hill, quoted in Leapman, 'Did the Tabloids Destroy Neil Kinnock?', *Independent*, 14 April 1992.
99 Robin Cook, 'The Labour Campaign', in Crewe and Gosschalk (eds), *Political Communications*, p. 16.
100 *Express, Mail*, 6 January 1992.
101 *Mail*, 25 January 1992; P. Wintour, 'Tories Prime Mail for Shots at Labour', *Guardian*, 29 January 1992; S. Baxter, 'For Election Coverage "the best is yet to come"', *New Statesman*, 31 January 1992, 22; W. Hutton, 'Big Brother Bites on Labour's Heals', *Guardian*, 27 January 1992.
102 *Mail*, 23 January 1992; Wintour, 'Tories Prime Mail'; R. Hattersley, 'The Guilty Editors', *The Times*, 29 January 1992.
103 H. Semetko, M. Scammell and T. Nossiter, 'The Media's Coverage of the Campaign', in Heath, Jowell and Curtice (eds), *Labour's Last Chance*, pp. 28, 30; *Mail*, 13 March–9 April 1992.
104 Interview, Hill; quoted on *Newsnight*, 14 March 1996; *Sun*, 31 March, 8 April 1992; Jones, *Election '92*, pp. 85–6; *Mail*, 7 April 1992; *Express*, 9 April 1992.
105 D. Sanders, 'Why the Conservatives Won Again', in King (ed.), *Britain*, pp. 205–7.
106 *Mail*, 13 March 1992; *Guardian*, 18 April 1992; B. Castle, *Fighting All the Way* (London: Macmillan, 1993), p. 590; Cook, 'The Labour Campaign', pp. 16–17; 'General Secretary's Report, 1992', Section 6.
107 P. Mosley, 'Popularity Functions and the Role of the Media: A Pilot Study of the Popular Press', *British Journal of Political Science*, 14, 1984, 117; see also D. Sanders, D. Marsh and H. Ward, 'The Electoral Impact of Press Coverage of the British Economy', *British Journal of Political Science*, 23, 1993, 175–210.
108 K. Newton, 'Economic Voting in the 1992 General Election', in D. Denver, P. Norris, D. Broughton and C. Rallings (eds), *British Elections and Parties Yearbook 1993* (London: Harvester Wheatsheaf, 1994), p. 161; Sanders, 'Why the Conservatives', p. 207.
109 Sanders, 'Why the Conservatives', p. 208.
110 G. Brown, 'First the Good News', *Guardian*, 18 February 1992.
111 *Express*, 3 April 1992; *Star*, 7 April 1992; *Mail*, 8 April 1992; E. Pearce, *Election Rides* (London: Faber & Faber, 1992), p. 159.
112 A. Lansley, 'Accentuating the Negative to Win Again', *Observer*, 3 September 1995; *Express*, 7 April 1992; *Mail*, 2 April 1992; *Sun*, 4 April 1992.
113 C. Soley, 'Time To Tame These Paper Tigers', *Guardian*, 20 April 1992; C. Smith, 'Tabloids Aren't the Only Threat', *Tribune*, 17 April 1992; N. Kinnock, 'Reforming the Labour Party', *Contemporary Record*, 8, 3, 1994, 553; M. Billig and P. Golding, 'The Hidden Factor: Race, the News Media and the 1992 Election', *Representation*, 131, 114, 1992, 36–8.
114 Interview, Hill; 'General Secretary's Report, 1992', p. 10.
115 For the argument that this was the case in 1992, see A. Heath, R. Jowell, J. Curtice and P. Clifford, 'False Trails and Faulty Expectations', in D. Denver, P. Norris, D. Broughton and C. Rallings, *British Elections and Parties Yearbook 1993*, pp. 116–28.
116 Linton, *Was It the Sun?*, pp. 28, 20–1; see also, W. Miller, 'I Am What I Read', *New Statesman*, 24 April 1992, 17.
117 Miller, *Media and Voters*, pp. 188–99.
118 See, for instance, Hollingsworth, *Press*; Horrie and Chippendale, *Stick It*; C. Searle, *Your Daily Dose: Racism and the Sun* (London: CPBF, 1989); T. Van Dijk, *Racism and the Press* (London: Routledge, 1991); B. Franklin (ed.), *Social*

Policy, the Media and Misrepresentation (London: Routledge, 1999); Philo (ed.), *Message Received.*

119 Miller, *Media and Voters*, pp. 191–2.
120 R. Webber, 'The 1992 Election: Constituency Results and Local Patterns of National Newspaper Readership', in Denver, Norris, Broughton and Rallings (eds), *British Parties and Elections Yearbook 1993*, pp. 205–15; B. MacArthur, 'Sunshine for the Tories', *British Journalism Review*, 3, 2, 1992, 74–7.
121 Medhurst, 'Soaraway Sunsations', *Marxism Today*, November 1989, 40–1; M. Pursehouse, 'Reading the Sun: Conflict in the Popular', University of Birmingham, MPhil, 1989; for a summary, see Pursehouse, 'Looking at the Sun into the Nineties with a Tabloid and its Readers', *Cultural Studies from Birmingham*, 1, 1991, 88–153.
122 R. Taylor, *Film Propaganda: Soviet Russia and Nazi Germany* (London: Tauris, 1998), p. 146; Semetko, Scammell and Nossiter, 'Media's Coverage', p. 27; *Sun*, 1 June 1987.
123 *Sun*, 8 April, 12, 20 March, 9 April 1992; M. Lawson, 'Kinnock Lays His Ghosts to Rest', *Independent*, 9 April 1992; C. Seymour-Ure, 'Characters and Assassinations: Portrayals of John Major and Neil Kinnock in the Daily Mirror and the Sun', in Crewe and Gosschalk (eds), *Political Communications*, p. 144.
124 For the former point, see Harrop and Scammell, 'A Tabloid War', pp. 182, 184; for the latter suggestion, see Linton, 'Press Ganged', p. 41; and more generally, Pursehouse, 'Reading the Sun', p. 112; Medhurst, 'Soaraway Sunsations', p. 41.
125 Semetko, Scammell and Nossiter, 'The Media's Coverage of the Campaign', pp. 30–1.
126 *Sun*, 26 March, 8 April 1992.
127 R. Harris, 'Spare a Thought For A Good Man Treated Badly', *Sunday Times*, 12 April 1992; Hattersley, quoted in A. Howard, 'Press Barons and Power', Part 3, 2 August 1998.
128 J. McGinnis, *The Selling of the President* (London: Deutsch, 1969), p. 222; Hare, *Asking*, p. 227; Hughes and Wintour, *Labour Rebuilt*, p. 26.
129 J. Brown, 'The Major Effect: Changes in Party Leadership and Party Popularity', *Parliamentary Affairs*, 45, 4, 1992, 561; King (ed.), *Britain*, pp. 151, 193. It has been argued that Kinnock was merely used by voters as shorthand for more fundamental reasons, which he symbolised, for not voting Labour, while Smith's assumption of the leadership had no effect on the party's popularity.
130 T. Johnson, *The Perfidious Welshman* (London, 1910), pp. 8–10; B. Gilbert, *David Lloyd George: A Political Life: The Architect Of Change 1863–1912* (London: Batsford, 1987), p. 12; *Mail*, 29 March 1992.
131 *Sun*, 14 March 1986; see J. Thomas, 'Taffy was a Welshman, Taffy was a Thief: Anti-Welshness, the Press and Neil Kinnock', *Llafur*, 7, 2, 1997, 95–108.
132 D. Hill, *Out For The Count: Politicians and the People, Election 1992* (London: Macmillan, 1992), p. 240; Castle, *Fighting All The Way*, p. 583; Butler and Kavanagh, *Election of 1992*, pp. 128–9.
133 *Mail*, 2 April 1992; *Sun*, 6 April, 23 January 1992; *Sunday Telegraph*, 5 April 1992; *Mail*, 9 April 1992.
134 For example, J. Paxman, *The English: a Portrait of a People* (London: Michael Joseph, 1998), p. 49; for others, see Thomas, 'Taffy', p. 98.
135 J. Sopel, *Tony Blair: The Moderniser* (London: Michael Joseph, 1995), p. 130.
136 J. Smith, *The Welsh Image*, Institute of Welsh Affairs, Gregynog Papers, 1, 4, 1998, 2–16; Thomas, 'Taffy', pp. 104–8.
137 *Mail on Sunday*, 29 March 1992; Hughes and Wintour, *Labour Rebuilt*

(London: Fourth Estate, 1990), pp. 24, 26; Jones, *Soundbites*, pp. 72–3; S. Berry, 'Labour's Strategy and the Media: the Failure of Labour's 1992 Election Campaign', *Parliamentary Affairs*, 45, 4, 1992, 565–81.

138   D. Hill, quoted in M. Scammell, *Designer Politics: How Elections Are Won* (London: Macmillan, 1995), p. 276; quoted in Hare, *Asking Around*, p. 221; 'General Secretary's Report, 1992', Section 6, 'Assessment of Media Campaign', KNNK, Box 180.

139   See, for example, *Guardian*, 27, 28 March 1992; *Independent on Sunday*, 22 March 1992; Berry, 'Labour's Strategy', p. 575.

140   D. Hare, *The Absence of War* (London: Faber & Faber, 1993), p. 92.

141   *Mail*, 6, 7 April 1992; *Sun*, 3 April 1992.

142   See, for instance, *Standard*, 24 March 1992; *Express*, 6, 8 April 1992; *Mail*, 16, 30 March 1992; *Sun*, 3, 4 April 1992.

143   M. Lawson, 'Tabloids Gun for the Man in the Mask', *Independent*, 21 March 1992.

144   Newton, 'Caring and Competence', p. 157; see also R. McKibbin, 'Labour Blues', *London Review of Books*, 11 February 1993, p. 13.

145   Hare, *Asking*, pp. 169–70; for an example, see P. Kellner, 'Mr Kinnock's Taxing Time with Punctuation', *Independent*, 22 June 1990.

146   Interview, Kinnock; Hare, *Asking*, p. 235; B. Woffinden, 'Left Out', *Listener*, 29 September 1988, pp. 6–7.

147   Julie Hall, quoted in Hare, *Asking*, p. 227.

148   A. Campbell, 'Change of Tune that Doesn't Ring True', *Today*, 21 July 1994; for similar comments, see V. Grove, 'The Man Who Pipes Up For Blair', interview: Campbell, *Sunday Times*, 9 September 1994.

149   D. MacShane, 'Columnists For Kinnock', *New Statesman*, 15 May 1987, 13; Leapman, *Kinnock* p. 181; G. Drover, *Neil Kinnock: the Path to Leadership* (London: Weidenfeld & Nicolson, 1984), p. 63; R. Hattersley, *Who Goes Home?*, pp. 285–6; R. Harris, *The Making of Neil Kinnock* (London: Faber & Faber, 1984), pp. 233–4.

150   M. Foley, *The Rise of the British Presidency* (Manchester: Manchester University Press, 1993), p. 228; *Express*, *Mail*, 16, 17 November 1991; *Sun*, *Star*, 17 November 1991; D. Macintyre, 'Kinnock: How the Man Became the Issue', *Independent on Sunday*, 22 September 1991.

151   Interview, Kinnock; Castle, *Fighting*, p. 563; Hattersley, *Who Goes*, pp. 285–6; Campbell, 'Change of Tune'.

152   See Curtice and Stead, 'The Results Analysed', in Butler and Kavanagh (eds), *Election of 1992*, pp. 322–51, for how a result so decisive in popular support could be so close in seats.

153   'General Secretary's Report to the NEC on the General Election', 21 June 1992; Jack Cunningham, article written for *The Times*; David Hill, 'General Election Campaign: Some Observations', NEC, 24 June 1992, KNNK, Box 180; interview, Kinnock; D. Hill, 'Watching and Hoping For the Worms to Turn', *Independent*, 28 April 1993; G. Kaufman, 'Comrades, Keep it Clean', *Guardian*, 8 May 1992.

154   Newton, 'Economic Voting', p. 169; R. Hattersley, 'Labour Must Start to Set Out its Tax Stall Now', *Guardian*, 13 March 1995.

155   P. Mandelson, 'Why Labour Lost', *Fabian Review*, 4, 3, 1992, 6; P. Hewitt, 'What Went Wrong', *Fabian Review*, 104, 3, 1992, 4.

156   'General Secretary's Report, 1992', Section 6.

157   Gould, *Goodbye*, pp. 211–12, 238–9; N. Wapshott, 'Labour's Top Men Twice Tried to Oust Kinnock', *Observer*, 21 June 1992; for general assessments of his leadership, see the special *Contemporary Record*, 8, 3, 1994, 555–601; M. Westlake, *Kinnock* (London: Little Brown, 2001). The term 'The Kinnock Factor'

was coined in a *Times* editorial (16 September 1991) which described it as an alleged 'lack of brain . . . and gravitas'.

158 Interview, Hill; *Express, Sun, Mail,* 8 April 1992.

159 Interview, Kinnock.

160 *Express,* 13 March 1992; *Sunday Express,* 'Lest we Forget' series, March–April 1992; *Mail,* 9 April 1992; *Sun,* 8 April 1992.

161 Interview, Hill; Hill, 'The Labour Party's Strategy', p. 38.

162 Tiratsoo, 'Never Had It So Bad', pp. 163–90; Morgan, *Callaghan: A Life,* pp. 469–676; Artis and Cobham, *Labour's Economic Policies.*

163 M. Smith, *Britain and 1940: history, Myth and Popular Memory* (London: Routledge, 1999), p. 6.

164 Anthony Clare interview, Neil Kinnock, ITV, 10 September 1995.

165 S. McAnulla, 'The Post-Thatcher Era', in D. Marsh, J. Buller, C. Hay, *et al., Postwar British Politics in Perspective* (Cambridge: Polity, 1999), p. 195.

166 J. Lewis, *Constructing Public Opinion: How Political Elites Do What They Like and Why We Seem To Go Along With It* (New York: Columbia University Press, 2001).

167 Miller, *Media and Voters,* p. 4; Entman, 'How the Media Effect What People Think', pp. 347–70; Linton, *Was It the Sun?,* pp. 17–21; for similar findings for the 1987 and 1983 elections, see Miller, *Media and Votes,* pp. 171–7; Newton, 'Do People Read Everything They Believe in the Newspapers?', pp. 51–73; Dunleavy and Husbands, *British Democracy at the Crossroads,* pp. 113–15.

168 Labour Party, 'Campaign Plan', 30 January 1992, KNNK, Box 51; Sanders, 'Why the Conservatives', p. 200; John Underwood, 'Campaign Strategy Paper', prepared for NEC, 27 March 1991, KNNK, Box 48; for assessments of the government's economic record from 1979, see N. Healey, *Britain's Economic Miracle: Myth or Reality?* (London: Routledge, 1993); Newton, 'Economic Voting', pp. 158–9.

169 *Financial Times,* 17 March 1992.

170 *Mail,* 12 March 1992; Newton, 'Economic Voting', pp. 173–4; *Mirror,* 6, 2, April, 21, 23 March 1992.

171 D. Butler and D. Kavanagh, *The British General Election of 1979,* pp. 323, 137, 165–6, 68; *Economist,* 28 April 1979, 23, 5 May 1979, 13; Morgan, *Callaghan: A Life,* p. 516. This was also partly the case because Callaghan refused pressure to attack Thatcher in the way the Conservatives later did with Kinnock; see Kavanagh, *Election Campaigning,* pp. 86–8.

172 See also Harrop, cited in Curran and Seaton, *Power,* pp., 274–5.

173 Lewis, *Constructing Public Opinion,* p. 201.

174 F. Hayward and B. Langdon-Davies, *Democracy and the Press* (London: National Labour Press, 1919), p. 4.

175 *Sunday Times,* 2 February 1979; *Guardian,* 3 February 1992; see also R. Norton-Taylor, 'History of Red-Herrings', *Guardian,* 3 February 1992; I. Aitken, 'Learning the Tricks of the Tirade', *Guardian,* 10 February 1992; *Daily News,* 13 December 1923.

176 W. Miller, 'Sun Burned, Star Struck', *New Statesman,* 17 February 1992, 29–30; C. Sparks, 'Popular Journalism: Theory and Practice', in C. Sparks and P. Dahlgren (eds), *Journalism and Popular Culture* (London: Sage, 1992), p. 37.

177 D. MacShane, 'Media Policy and the Left', in Seaton and Pimlott (eds), *The Media,* pp. 215–35; J. Curran, 'Reconstructing the Mass Media', in J. Curran (ed.), *The Future of the Left* (Oxford: Polity Press, 1984), pp. 150–8.

178 An early illustration was the publication, Labour party, *The Media and the People* (1974); and the reprinting of the 1977 Minority Report; see also the resolutions carried by the two conference debates on the media; Labour party,

Annual Conference Report, 1982, pp. 238–43 and *Annual Conference Report, 1983*, pp. 204–6.

179   Lord Macarthy, *The Feasibility of Establishing a New Labour Movement Daily* (TUC, 1983); *Labour Daily? Ins and Outs of a New Labour Daily and other Media Alternatives* (London: CPBF, 1984); P. Chippendale and C. Horrie, *Disaster! The Rise and Fall of News On Sunday* (London: Sphere, 1988).

180   Labour Party, *The Right of Reply* (1982); *Britain Will Win* (1987), p. 14; *Meet the Challenge, Make the Change* (1987), p. 60; *Arts and Media: Our Cultural Future* (1991), pp. 31–2; *Opportunity Britain* (1991), p. 45; *It's Time to get Britain Moving Again* (1992), p. 24; M. Leapman, 'Labour's Self-Appointed Ombudsman', interview: Roy Hattersley, *Independent*, 27 June 1990.

181   Shawcross, *Rupert Murdoch*, p. 542.

182   Interview, Kavanagh; E. Pearce, 'It's Time for Kinnock to Go', and 'At Best a Mere Supporting Actor', *Guardian*, 4, 11 December 1991.

183   Kinnock to Roy Schreiber, 26 January 1987, KNNK, Box 224; Straw, 'Why Neil Has Plenty to Boast About'; W. Ellis, *The Oxbridge Conspiracy* (London: Michael Joseph, 1996), pp. 176–80; for the overwhelmingly Oxbridge/London background of newspaper journalists, see also Tunstall, *Newspaper Power*, pp. 151–2.

184   Hattersley, *Who Goes*, p. 287; *Sun*, 9 June 1987; McSmith, *Faces of Labour*, p. 11; R. Johnson, 'Loss Leader', *New Statesman*, 28 July 1989, p. 24; H. Young, 'The Unbearable Lightness of Being Kinnock', *Guardian*, 16 June 1988.

185   Interview, Julia Langdon, 15 September 1997; interview, Trevor Kavanagh, 23 September 1997; B. Bruce, *Images of Power* (London: Kogan Page, 1992), pp. 110–11; Hughes and Wintour, *Labour Rebuilt*, p. 167.

186   R. Harris, 'Labour's Siege Mentality', *Observer*, 6 March 1987; D. English, 'Diary', *Spectator*, 7 October 1995, 9; Jones, *Soundbites*, p. 72; D. Macshane, 'Columnists for Kinnock'; Leapman, *Kinnock*, pp. 181–2; N. Williamson, 'Campaign on a Knife Edge', *The Times*, 16 March 1992.

187   R. Greenslade, 'The English Patient', interview: David English, *Guardian*, 21 April 1992; Stewart Steven, letter to the *Guardian*, 16 April 1992; *Sun*, 14 April 1992.

188   *Sun*, 23, 24 April 1987; Glenys Kinnock later noted how the press attacks on her were a 'very effective' way of getting to Kinnock, Radio 4, *Desert Island Discs*, 25 November 1994.

189   Interview, Hill; Charles Clarke, quoted in P. Gould, *The Unfinished Revolution: How the Modernisers Saved the Labour Party*, p. 112; interview, Kavanagh.

190   Seymour-Ure, *The British Press and Broadcasting Since 1945*, p. 201; for a summary of challenges to the consensus politics argument, see H. Jones, 'The Postwar Consensus in Britain: Thesis, Antithesis, Synthesis?', in B. Brivati, J. Buxton and A. Seldon (eds), *The Contemporary History Handbook* (Manchester: Manchester University Press, 1996), pp. 41–9.

191   See, for example, G. Murdock and P. Golding, 'The Structure, Ownership and Control of the Press, 1914–76', in Boyce, Curran and Wingate (eds), *Newspaper History*, pp. 136–46; J. Tunstall, 'The British Press in the Age of Television', in Christian (ed.), *The Sociology of Journalism*, pp. 28–31; Royal Commission on the Press, 1977, *Final Report*, p. 149.

192   A. Bevins, 'The Crippling of the Scribes', *British Journalism Review*, 1, 2, 1990, 13; G. Williams, *Britain's Media: How They Are Related* (London: CPBF, 1994), p. 34.

193   Leapman, *Treacherous Estate*, p. 69; Tunstall, *Newspaper Power*, p. 248.

194   Lamb, *Sunrise*, p. 161.

195   I. Gilmour, *Dancing with Dogma* (London: Simon and Schuster, 1993), p. 2.

196   B. Ingham, *Kill the Messenger* (London: HarperCollins, 1991), p. 170; N. Lawson,

The View from No. 11: Memoirs of a Tory Radical (London: Corgi, 1993), p. 467; see also R. Harris, *Good and Faithful Servant: the Unauthorised Biography of Bernard Ingham* (London: Faber & Faber, 1990); for Thatcher's distance from the lobby, alongside her autobiographical ingratitude to her press friends, see P. Riddell, 'Not a Word of Thanks From Mrs T', *British Journalism Review*, 5, 1, 1994, 6–8.

197   For explorations of this relationship, see H. Young, 'A Touch of Fantasy in the Message Parlour', *Guardian*, 8 October 1985; 'The Media Under Mrs Thatcher', *Contemporary Record*, 3, 4, 1990; A. Finney, 'The Truth Comes Between the Lines', *British Journalism Review*, 2, 2, 1990, 40–50; for one illustration of the seductive effects of power, see Nick Lloyd, passage in T. Gray (ed.), *Fleet Street Remembered* (London: Heinemann, 1990), pp. 260–1.

198   J. Junor, *Memoirs: Listening for a Midnight Train*, p. 259.

199   A. Neil, *Full Disclosure* (London: Macmillan, 1996), p. 166; H. Evans, *Good Times, Bad Times* (London: Phoenix, 1994), especially pp. 268–70, 329–32; R. Belfield, C. Hird and S. Kelly, *Murdoch: the Great Escape*, pp. 42–3, 84–5; H. Young, 'Rupert Murdoch and the Sunday Times: A Lamp Goes Out', *Political Quarterly*, 55, 1984, 382–90.

200   Shawcross, *Rupert Murdoch*, p. 210; Charles Douglas-Home, quoted in Belfield, Hird and Kelly (eds), *Murdoch*, pp. 81–2; *Journals of Woodrow Wyatt*, p. 359.

201   K. Ewing and B. Napier, 'The Wapping Dispute and the Labour Law', *Cambridge Law Journal*, July 1986, 285–304; Shawcross, *Murdoch*, pp. 345, 357; P. Kellner, 'Wapping Power of the Tories' Trade Union Laws', *Guardian*, 17 February 1986.

202   Text of Kinnock speech delivered at a 'Wapping' rally, Wembley, March 1986, KNNK, Box, 308; NEC resolution, 29 January 1986, KNNK, Box 265; Leapman, *Kinnock*, pp. 139–40; B. Dean, 'Reflections on Fighting Impossible Odds', *New Statesman*, 13 February 1987, 12; the ban was suspended during the Fulham by-election, while it also appears that informal contact continued despite it; interview, Robin Oakley, 16 September 1997; P. Jenkins, 'The Treason of the Hacks', *Spectator*, 7 March 1986, 18–19.

203   Kinnock to Chris Moncrieff (chairman of the lobby), 29 January 1986, Moncrieff to Kinnock, 29 January 1986, Kinnock to Moncrieff, 1 February 1986, KNNK, Box 265; Leapman, *Kinnock*, p. 140.

204   Shawcross, *Murdoch*, p. 359; interview, Hill; *New Statesman*, 17 April 1992, 7; interview, Kavanagh.

205   Evans, *Good Times*, p. xvii; quoted by John Smith, *House of Commons Parliamentary Debates*, Sixth Series, 119, 6 July 1987, col. 26; Curtis (ed.), *Journals of Woodrow Wyatt*, pp. 371–2, 378, 384–5.

206   Shawcross, *Murdoch*, pp. 233, 381–2; *Independent*, 5, 12, 13, 15 November 1990; *House of Commons, Parliamentary Debates*, Sixth Series, 180, 12 November 1990, cols 347–51, 361–4; Rupert Murdoch, 'Freedom in Broadcasting', MacTaggert Lecture, Edinburgh International Film Festival, August 1989, p. 8.

207   *Express*, 23 November 1990; for coverage, see *Express, Mail, Sun, Star*, 13–26 November 1990.

208   *Express, Mail, Sun*, 12 October, 12 December 1990.

209   See J. Thomas, 'The "Max Factor" – a Mirror Image? Robert Maxwell and the Daily Mirror Tradition', in Catterall, Seymour-Ure and Smith (eds), *Northcliffe's Legacy*, pp. 201–26.

210   *Mirror*, 16, 18 March 1992; interview, Hill; *Mirror*, 8, 9 April 1992.

211   M. Linton, *Money and Votes* (London: Institute for Public Policy Research, 1994), p. 29.

212   Linton, *Money and Votes*, p. 29; Hill, 'The Labour Party's Strategy', p. 40; *Express*, 9 April 1992; *Independent*, 21 June 1994; Labour Research Department, 'Who Paid for the Tory Victory', July 1993, pp. 12–13.

213 *Independent*, 14 April 1992.
214 I. Aitken, 'The Truth and Anything but the Truth', *Guardian*, 20 April 1992.

5 'Vote Conservative – vote Blair': Labour and the popular press 1992–2003

  1 R. Addis. 'A Red Rose Blooms in Blackfriars', *Independent*, 9 June 1997;
     Addis, *Daily Express* editor in 1997, suggested that this was the unwritten
     headline of that election. *The Economist* also used a 'vote conservative' slogan to
     endorse Blair in 2001.
  2 P. Mandelson, 'The Media We Deserve', *Tribune*, 17 March 1995.
  3 H. Margetts and G. Smyth (eds), *Turning Japanese: Britain with a Permanent
     Party of Government* (London: Laurence & Wishart, 1994); A. King, 'The
     Implications of One-Party Government', in A. King (ed.), *Britain at the Polls
     1992*, pp. 223–48; McKie, 'Facts are Free'.
  4 D. Butler and D. Kavanagh, *The British General Election of 1997* (London:
     Macmillan, 1997), p. 244.
  5 D. Denver, 'The Government That Could Do No Right', in A. King (ed.),
     New Labour Triumphs: Britain at the Polls (New Jersey: Chatham, 1998), pp.
     15–48.
  6 P. Norton, 'The Conservative Party', in King, *New Labour Triumphs*, pp.
     79–80.
  7 D. MacKie, 'Nightmare on Norm Street', in Margetts and Smyth, *Turning
     Japanese*, p. 138; for instance, *Sun*, 30 July 1992.
  8 A. Seldon, *John Major: A Political Life* (London: Weidenfeld & Nicolson,
     1997), pp. 323–4, 300.
  9 P. Stephens, *Politics and the Pound: the Conservatives' Struggle with Sterling*
     (London: Macmillan, 1996), pp. 245–55.
 10 K. MacKenzie, speaking on A. Howard, 'Press Barons and Power', Radio 4, 9
     August 1998; B. MacArthur, 'Editors Snipe at Party Leadership', *The Times*, 2
     October 1992; *Sun*, 17 September 1992.
 11 MacArthur, 'Editors Snipe'; R. Greenslade, 'Mail Man Delivers', *Guardian*, 3
     April 1995.
 12 A. Seldon, *John Major*, p. 326; MacArthur, 'Editors Snipe'; *Sun*, 13 October
     1992.
 13 R. Negrine, 'The "Gravest Political Crisis Since Suez": the Press, the Govern-
     ment and the Pit Closures Announcement of 1992', *Parliamentary Affairs*, 8, 1,
     1995, 40–56.
 14 J. Daley, 'No Poodle, this Rottweiler', *Telegraph*, 20 October 1992.
 15 *Mail*, 14 October 1992.
 16 *Sun*, 28, 20 October 1992.
 17 B. MacArthur, 'Major Wakes Up to Black Sunday', *The Times*, 19 October 1992.
 18 N. Jones, *Soundbites*, pp. 205–6; McKie, 'Nightmare', p. 140; *Sun*, *Mail*, 18
     March 1993; S. Bates, 'Savage U-turn by the Tabloids', *Guardian*, 18 March
     1993.
 19 Seldon, *John Major*, pp. 398, 402–3; H. Williams, *Guilty Men* (London:
     Aurum, 1998), pp. 47–8; N. Jones, 'Goldfish Among the Piranhas', *Guardian*,
     17 January 1994.
 20 *News of the World*, 26 December 1993.
 21 R. Littlejohn, *Sun*, 6 January 1994.
 22 Seldon, *John Major*, pp. 431–2.
 23 *Mail*, 11 January 1994; *Telegraph*, 10 January 1994; Deedes, quoted in 'It's
     War', *Guardian*, 17 January 1994.
 24 Quoted in 'It's War'.

25 *Sun*, 14 January 1994.
26 S. Bates, 'Shell-shocked Tories Mutter Paranoid Allegations of Press Conspiracies', *Guardian*, 14 February 1994; Stewart Steven, quoted in 'It's War'.
27 A. Neil, 'The Press and Mr Major', *Sunday Times*, 23 January 1994.
28 *Mail*, 4 July 1995; *Sun*, 3–4 July 1995; *Telegraph*, 3 July 1995.
29 For this point, see P. Cowley, '111 Not Out: The Press and the 1995 Conservative Leadership Contest', *Talking Politics*, 8, 3, 1996, 187–90; J. Johnson, 'Biting the Hand That Spins', *British Journalism Review*, 6, 3, 1995, 68–9; S. Hogg and J. Hill, *Too Close to Call: Power and Politics – John Major in No. 10* (London: Warner Books, 1996), p. 281; Seldon, *John Major*, pp. 585–6.
30 I. Katz, 'Monty the Merciless', *Guardian*, 14 March 1994; W. Ellis, 'Monty: a Press Baron to Trust', *Sunday Times*, 30 January 1994; G. Gall, 'Looking in the Mirror: a Case Study of Industrial Relations in a National Newspaper', in M. Bromley and T. O'Malley (eds), *A Journalism Reader*, pp. 233–46; *Socialist Worker*, 31 October 1992; M. Prescott and R. Hunt, 'Smith goes into Battle to Save the Mirror's Political Soul for Labour', *Sunday Times*, 21 February 1993; J. Diamond, 'Mirror, Mirror, Off the Wall', *Guardian*, 22 February 1993.
31 J. Langdon, 'High Noon at Holborn Oasis', *Guardian*, 18 February 1993; Diamond, 'Mirror, Mirror'; J. Pilger, *Hidden Agendas*, p. 436.
32 *Guardian*, 17, 18 February 1993; see also P. Anderson, 'Through a Glass Darkly', *Tribune*, 26 February 1993.
33 R. Greenslade, 'A Vote for Trivia', *Guardian*, 10 May 1993.
34 Diamond, 'Mirror, Mirror'; see also A. Alderson and R. Syal, 'Labour Leaders Desert Mirror as Sales Plummet to New Low', *Sunday Times*, 28 November 1993; *Guardian* (ed.), 22 February 1993.
35 I. Katz, 'Chimera Down the Lift Shaft', *Guardian*, 18 April 1994; *Mirror*, 5, 6 May 1994; interview, David Hill, 18 December 1998; A. McSmith, 'Charmer Blair Tries Wooing the Press with a Red Rose Valentine', *Observer*, 2 February 1997.
36 'It's War'; D. McKie, 'The Sun Rises in Tarzan's Jungle', *Guardian*, 7 March 1994.
37 *Sun*, 4, 6 May 1994.
38 *Sun*, 9 June 1994.
39 *Sun*, 14 May 1994; *Express*, 13 May 1994; *Mail*, 13 May 1994; B. Franklin and G. Larsen, 'Kingmaking in the Labour Leadership Contest', *British Journalism Review*, 5, 4, 1994, 63–70; D. McKie, 'Dewy-eyed Over Bambie', *Guardian*, 23 May 1994.
40 *Tribune* (ed.), 20 May 1994; *New Statesman and Society*, 20 May 1994, 3, 8; A. Campbell, *Tribune*, 3 June 1994.
41 P. Routledge, *Gordon Brown: the Biography* (London: Pocket Books, 1998), p. 201.
42 *Mail*, *Sun*, 22 July 1994.
43 D. McKie, 'Blue Views on Bambi', *Guardian*, 25 July 1994; Franklin and Larsen, 'Kingmaking', pp. 66–7; *Mail*, *Star*, *Express*, *Sun*, 22 July 1994.
44 Quoted in Jones, *Soundbites*, p. 171.
45 N. Lloyd, 'Blair's Subtle Seduction of the Tory Press', *The Times*, 23 October 1996; Jones, *Soundbites*, p. 171.
46 English, 'Diary', *Spectator*, 7 October 1995, 9.
47 McKie, 'A Beastly Reminder', *Guardian*, 10 October 1994.
48 English, 'Diary', p. 9.
49 *Guardian*, 10 August 1994.
50 N. Timmins, 'Populist Blair Uses Tabloid Tactics on Tax Propaganda War', *Independent*, 29 August 1994; N. Jones, 'Taking Tony to the People', *Guardian*, 1 June 1995.

51 Neil, *Full Disclosure*, p. 170.
52 *House of Commons Parliamentary Debates*, Sixth Series, 20 July 1994, col. 445; P. Wintour, 'Mowlam Presses for Easing of TV Ownership Rules', *Guardian*, 10 August 1994.
53 G. Kaufman, 'Superhighway Labour Should Ride Not Avoid', *Guardian*, 29 September 1994; M. Mowlam, 'Paper Tigers', *New Statesman*, 9 September 1994, 24; Wintour, 'Mowlam Presses'.
54 Quoted in H. Porter, 'The Murdoch Wooing Game', *Guardian*, 26 September 1994; 'No Deal Mr Murdoch', *Tribune* (ed.), 19 August 1994.
55 Neil, *Full Disclosure*, p. 170; *Independent*, 17 July 1995.
56 Clive Soley, letter to *Tribune*, 11 August 1995; T. Blair, 'Left With No Option', *Guardian*, 27 July 1995.
57 J. Johnson, 'Rupert's Grip?', *British Journalism Review*, 9, 1, 1998, 14.
58 Neil, *Full Disclosure*, pp. 169–70; H. Porter, 'The Murdoch Wooing Game'; R. Williams, 'Murdoch Woos Blair with Clandestine Dinner', *Independent*, 30 December 1994; S. Castle, 'How They Wooed and Won the Sun', *Independent on Sunday*, 23 March 1997; McSmith, 'Charmer Blair Tires Wooing'.
59 Quoted in *Guardian*, 21 May 1995; Michael Grade, letter to *Guardian*, 22 May 1995.
60 'The View from Canary Wharf', Conrad Black interview, *British Journalism Review*, 9, 2, 1998, 10.
61 R. Murdoch, 'Cross? You Bet!', *Guardian*, 15 May 1995; *Guardian*, 15 April 1996; Pilger, *Hidden Agendas*, p. 469.
62 Oglivy and Mather, 'The Devil's in the Details', quoted in *Guardian*, 28 October 1996.
63 C. Horrie and P. Chippendale, *Stick It*, pp. 206–8; Seldon, *John Major*, p. 711.
64 R. Greenslade, 'Nice One Sun, Says Tony', interview: S. Higgins, *Guardian*, 19 May 1997; quoted in P. Wintour, 'Thatcher Advised Murdoch to Back Labour', *Observer*, 28 September 1997.
65 Lloyd, 'Blair's Subtle Seduction'; Neil, *Full Disclosure*, pp. 170, 166; K. MacKenzie, 'Hair Yesterday, Gone Tomorrow', *Spectator*, 19 July 1997, pp. 13–14.
66 A. Culf, 'Tory Papers Salute Blair as Prime Minister in Waiting', *Guardian*, 6 October 1994; *Mail, Express, Today*, 5 October 1994.
67 D. McKie, 'A Beastly Reminder'; *Express, Mail*, 7 October 1994.
68 David Blunkett, quoted in N. Timmins, 'Murdoch Says He Could Imagine Backing Blair', *Independent*, 9 August 1994; *Sun*, 3, 4, 5, 7 October 1994; Franklin and Larsen, 'Kingmaking', pp. 69–70.
69 *Express*, 7 October 1994; *Mail*, 1 May 1995; D. McKie, 'The Tory Line', *Guardian*, 8 May 1995; *Sun*, 29 April 1995; R. Greenslade, 'Finding the Right Tone', *Guardian*, 8 May 1995.
70 *Mail*, 4, 5 July 1995; *Sun*, 4, 5 July 1995.
71 *Sun*, 9 November 1995, 3 July 1996; P. Davies, *This England* (London: Abacus, 1998), p. 15.
72 *Sun*, 4 October 1995.
73 *Sun*, 3, 6, 4 October, 13 September 1995, 12 August, 28 September 1994, 3 October 1996.
74 *Sun*, 14 June 1996.
75 D. Deacon, P. Golding and M. Billig, 'Between Fear and Loathing: National Press Coverage of the 1997 British General Election', paper to EPOP Conference, 'Assessing the 1997 Election: Voters, Parties and the Media', University of Essex, September 1997.
76 R. Greenslade, 'Mail Regresses in Struggle with Political Identity Crisis', *Guardian*, 4 April 1997.
77 *Mail*, 4 April 1997.

78 Quoted in S. Castle, 'More Tory Newspapers Abandon the Cause in Favour of Labour', *Independent*, 23 March 1997; S. Miller, '18 Years of Certainty, 16 Days of Doubt', *Guardian*, 17 May 1997; D. McKie, 'Swingers, Clingers, Waverers and Quaverers: the Tabloid Press in the 1997 General Election', in I. Crewe, B. Gosschalk and J. Bartle (eds), *Political Communications: Why Labour Won the General Election of 1997* (London: Frank Cass, 1998), p. 124.

79 M. White, 'Right-wing Press Baron to Support Labour', *Guardian*, 23 May 1997; Miller, '18 years of certainty'.

80 For the *Mail*'s editorial focus on this theme, see C. Seymour-Ure, 'Editorial Opinion in the National Press', *Parliamentary Affairs*, 50, 4, 1997, 595; *Mail*, 25, 26 March 1997.

81 *Mail*, 3, 16, 23, 7 April 1997.

82 *Mail*, 9, 7, 10 April 1997; *Mail*, 9, 7, 4, 12 April 1997.

83 Gould, *The Unfinished*, pp. 364–6; Seldon, *John Major*, p. 720; *Mail*, 8, 9 April 1997.

84 M. Scammell and M. Harrop, 'The Press', in Butler and Kavanagh (eds), *Election of 1997*, p. 168; *Mail*, 18,30 April 1997; Carma International, *The Power of the Press: the 1997 UK General Election* (1997), pp. 20–1; Seymour-Ure, 'Editorial Opinion', p. 602.

85 *Mail*, 15, 16, 17 April 1997; *The Times* and the *Telegraph* also published similar lists.

86 Carma, *The Power*, p. 13; *Mail*, 30 April 1997; P. Norris, 'The Battle for the Campaign Agenda', in King (ed.), *Britain*, p. 123.

87 Williams, *Guilty Men*, p. 184; A. Bevins, 'Cometh the Election Cometh the Smear', *Independent*, 3 February 1992; Seldon, *John Major*, pp. 436, 587, 595; Prescott, quoted in *Guardian*, 7 October 1995.

88 M. Brown, 'Could the Sun Swing it for Blair?', *The Times*, 16 October 1996; Seldon, *John Major*, p. 712; R. Greenslade, 'An Express Takeover?', *Guardian*, 6 May 1996.

89 T. Rubython, 'Hollick Moves to Swing Express Behind Labour', *Sunday Business*, 27 October 1996; J. Lloyd, 'Couch Moralists and Paper Tigers', *New Statesman*, 4 April 1997, p. 19; interview: Lord Hollick, *New Statesman*, 24 January 1997, pp. 18–19.

90 Greenslade, 'An Express Takeover?'; Seldon, *John Major*, p. 712; M. Brown, 'A Peer and a Paradox', interview: Lord Hollick, *Guardian*, 16 September 1996; Brown, 'Could the Sun Swing?'; interview: Hollick, *New Statesman*.

91 Brown, 'Could the Sun Swing?'.

92 Seldon, *John Major*, p. 712; Addis, 'A Red Rose Blooms'.

93 Scammell and Harrop, 'The Press', p. 166; Carma, *Power*, pp. 18, 20; J. Lloyd, 'Couch Moralists', pp. 18–19; for example, *Express*, 10, 20, 26, 28 April 1997.

94 T. Burns, 'The Impact of the National Press on Voters in 1997', paper delivered to EPOP conference, '1997 Election', p. 3; Seymour-Ure, 'Editorial Opinion', pp. 595–605; *Express*, 17 March–1 May 1997.

95 *Express*, 1 May 1997; Addis, 'A Red Rose Blooms'.

96 *Sun*, 18 March 1997, 2, 6 December 1996.

97 *Sun*, 10, 16 December 1996, D. Macintyre, 'What the Sun Says About Blair and Europe', *Independent*, 17 December 1996; in the 2001 election Geri Halliwell publicly endorsed Labour before it was quickly revealed that she had not registered to vote.

98 M. Linton, 'It's Still Up to You, my Sun', *Guardian*, 6 January 1997; *Sun*, 10, 13 December 1997; *Mirror*, 10, 13 December 1997.

99 *Sun*, 21, 22 January 1997.

100 *Sun*, 24, 25 January 1997; *Sun*, 13, 16, 8, 15 February 1997.

101 *Sun*, 6 March 1997; A. Bosheff, 'Sun Shines for Blair but Casts a Shadow of Unease', *Telegraph*, 18 March 1997; *Sun*, 8 February 1997.

102 *Mail*, 18 March 1997; the story made the front page, opinion and comment columns of the *Telegraph*, *The Times*, *Financial Times* and *Guardian*.

103 Interview: Tony Blair, *New Statesman*, 21 March 1997, 12; *Financial Times*, 20 March 1997.

104 R. Spark, 'It's Rupert Murdoch Wot Done It', *Telegraph*, 18 March 1997; *Sun*, 18 March 1997; Greenslade, 'Nice One Sun'.

105 A. McSmith and J. Arlidge, 'Sun Chiefs Tried to Defy Murdoch', *Observer*, 23 March 1997; Bosheff, 'Sun Shines for Blair'; Greenslade, 'Nice One Sun'.

106 Harrop and Scammell, 'The Press', pp. 160–4; C. Seymour-Ure, 'Leaders and Leading Articles', pp. 7–9; H. Young, 'Murdoch Chameleons Look Very Unhappy', *Guardian*, 24 April 1997; University of Loughborough Communication Research Centre, '1997 Election Study for the Guardian', Report No. 5, Post Election Review, p. 8.

107 *Sun*, 17, 11, 15 March 1997.

108 Burns, 'The Impact', p. 3; Carma, *The Power*, p. 19.

109 *Sun*, 1, 2, 5 April 1997.

110 Scammell and Harrop, 'The Press', p. 160; *Sun, Express, Mail*, 14 April 1997; C. Brown, *Fighting Talk: the biography of John Prescott* (London: Simon & Schuster, 1997), pp. 361–2.

111 *Sun*, 27 March 1997; *Express, Mail, Sun*, 28, 29, 31 March, 1 April 1997.

112 Loughborough Communication Centre, 'Election Study', Reports No. 1–2; Carma, *The Power*, p. 9; Scammell and Harrop, 'The Press', p. 175; Deacon, Golding and Billig, 'Between Fear', pp. 7, 10.

113 Deacon, Golding and Billig, 'Between Fear', p. 11; Carma, *Power*, pp. 18, 20; Burns, 'The Impact' p. 3; Loughborough Communication Centre, 'Election Study', Report No. 5, p. 8; *Mirror*, 1 May 1997.

114 *Mirror*, 18 March 1997; Scammell and Harrop, 'The Press', p. 166.

115 *Mirror*, 18 April 1997.

116 *Mirror*, 28 April, 19 March, 11 April 1997.

117 For the *Star*'s attitude, see Scammell and Harrop, 'The Press', p. 169; *Telegraph*, 30 April 1997.

118 Burns, 'The Impact', pp. 2–3.

119 Carma, *The Power*, p. 7.

120 C. Moore, 'The Right Way to Tell It', *Guardian*, 14 April 1997; J. Daley, 'The Sleaze-to-Order Election', and 'Press v People – the Real Contest', *Telegraph*, 1, 8 April 1997; W. Rees Mogg, 'The Sleaze Campaign Discredits Labour too', *The Times*, 31 March 1997; H. Clover, 'Press for Self-Destruct', *Guardian*, 28 March 1997.

121 P. Johnson, 'The Media Candidate', *Telegraph*, 8 April 1997; Daley, 'The Sleaze-to-Order'; Rees-Mogg, 'The Sleaze Campaign'; Clover, 'Press for Self-Destruct'.

122 *Telegraph*, 30 April 1997.

123 C. Bennett, 'Prodigal Sun Gives Fatted Calf to Blair', *Guardian*, 19 March 1997.

124 *Independent on Sunday*, 23 March 1997; quoted in S. Glover, 'The Tories were Uncooperative, New Labour Wasn't – but Blair Will Lose his Place in the Sun', *Spectator*, 22 March 1997, 34.

125 A. McSmith, 'Prince in Waiting Ponders Success', *Observer*, 14 August 1994.

126 S. Jenkins, 'It's the Voters Wot Won It', *The Times*, 19 March 1997.

127 R. Worcester, 'Index of Partisanship: a Methodology for Determining Change in the Political Bias of Newspaper Readers', paper to Asia-Pacific Rim Conference, Sydney, Australia, July 1994, pp. 24–5, 32; Scammell and Harrop, 'The Press', p. 161.

128 Greenslade, 'Nice One Sun'.
129 J. Curtice, 'Is the Sun Shining on Tony Blair?: the Electoral Influence of British Newspapers', *Harvard International Journal of Press/Politics*, 2, 2, 1997, 9–23; P. Norris, D. Sanders, M. Scammell and H. Semetko, *On Message: Communicating the Campaign* (London: Sage, 1999), pp. 152–69; Newton and Brynin, 'The National Press and Party Voting', pp. 265–85; Burns, 'The Impact', pp. 1–7.
130 Blair, cited in *Guardian*, 30 October 1997; interview, Hill.
131 P. Vallery, 'Clever Trevor', interview: Trevor Kavanagh, *Independent*, 10 March 1997; Butler and Kavanagh, *Election of 1997*, p. 103.
132 Quoted in Seldon, *John Major*, p. 555; Neil, 'The Press and Mr Major'; Tunstall, *Newspaper Power*, p. 254; interview, Robin Oakley, 16 September 1997.
133 S. Richards, 'One Brewed-Up Story, One Headache', *Independent*, 8 June 1994.
134 For interesting analyses, see J. Seaton (ed.), *Politics and the Media: Harlots and Prerogatives at the Turn of the Millennium* (Oxford: Blackwell, 1998); C. Sparks and J. Tulloch (eds), *Tabloid Tales: Global Debates Over Media Standards* (Lanham, MD: Rowman & Littlefield, 2000).
135 Williams, *Guilty Men*, pp. 14–20; G. Walden, *The New Elites: Making a Career in the Masses* (London: Penguin, 2001), pp. 169–87; G. Wheatcroft, 'Government by Columnist', *Independent on Sunday*, 6 February 1994.
136 Lewington, 'The Conservatives' Media Strategy', paper delivered to EPOP conference, '1997 Election'.
137 J. Craig, quoted in *Guardian*, 25 April 1994; A. McElvey, 'Making (If Necessary Faking), a Prime Minister', *Spectator*, 26 April 1997, 11.
138 MacKenzie, 'Hair Yesterday', pp. 13–14; Williams, *Guilty Men*, p. 20; quoted in S. Bates, 'Shell-Shocked Tories'.
139 MacKenzie, 'Hair Yesterday', p. 14; Lewington, 'The Conservatives' Media Strategy'.
140 J. Critchley, 'The Party's Over for Top Tories', *Independent*, 21 November 1996; quoted in Seldon, *John Major*, pp. 708–9, 390.
141 P. Mandelson, 'Out of the Darkness', *Guardian*, 28 September 1996; D. Hencke, 'How High Priests of Spin Keep Order', *Guardian*, 8 August 1998.
142 N. Jones, *Campaign: 1997: How the General Election was Won and Lost* (London: Indigo, 1997), pp. 15, 20–3; Gould, *The Unfinished*, pp. 302–3; M. Prescott, 'Cry Spin and Let Slip the Dogs of War', *Sunday Times*, 23 March 1997; S. Bayley, *Labour Camp: the Failure of Style over Substance* (London: Batsford, 1998), pp. 18–19.
143 *Standard*, 20 November 1996; Jones, *Campaign*, p. 79: *The Times, Independent, Guardian, Express, Mail*, 21 November 1996.
144 *Financial Times*, 21 November 1994.
145 R. Greenslade, 'Light the Blue Touchpaper', *Guardian*, 26 June 1995; H. Clover, 'Why Do Tories Always Snatch Defeat from the Jaws of Victory?', *Sun*, 9 November 1995.
146 Lewington, 'The Conservatives Media Strategy'; see also T. Bale and K. Sanders, '"Playing by the Book": Success and Failure in John Major's Approach to Prime Ministerial Media Management', *Contemporary British History*, 15, 4, 2001, 93–110.
147 *Sun*, 27 March 1997.
148 *Express, Mail, Express*, 31 March 1997.
149 *Express*, 7 April 1997; J. Sweeney, *Purple Homicide: Fear and Loathing on Knutsford Heath* (London: Bloomsbury, 1997).
150 *Observer*, 20 April 1997; interview: C. Lewington, *Sunday Telegraph*, 8 June 1997; Lewington, 'The Conservatives' Media Strategy'.
151 S. Fielding, 'The Labour Campaign', in A. Geddes and J. Tongue (eds),

Labour's Landslide, p. 32; Gould, *Unfinished*, pp. 380–1; P. Mandelson, 'Hold on Tight, We're in for a Bumpy Ride', *Guardian*, 14 April 1997; Jones, *Campaign*, pp. 244–6.

152   D. Deacon, P. Golding and M. Billig, 'Losing Face or Loss of Faith?', *The Bulletin of the European Institute for the Media*, 14, 2, 1997, 8; Jones, *Campaign*.

153   M. Lawson, 'Dog Days for Labour', *Guardian*, 16 April 1997.

154   C. Crouch, 'The Terms of the Neo-Liberal Consensus', *Political Quarterly*, 68, 1997, 352–60; C. Hay, 'Blajorism: Towards a One-Vision Polity', in ibid., pp. 372–8; *Marxism Today*, November/December 1998; D. Coates, 'Placing New Labour', in B. Jones (ed.), *Political Issues in Britain Today* (Manchester: Manchester University Press, 1999), pp. 346–66; W. Hutton, *The State We're In* (London: Jonathan Cape, 1995).

155   Gould, *The Unfinished*, pp. 284, 283.

156   Jones, *Campaign*, pp. 87–99; P. Wintour, 'The Death of Tax and Spend', *Observer*, 26 January 1997.

157   Gould, *The Unfinished*, p. 290; *Standard*, 20 January 1997; *Mail*, 21 January 1997.

158   Wintour, 'Death of Tax'; W. Hutton, 'Equality is a Casualty of the Drive for Power', *Observer*, 26 January 1997; H. Young, 'Realistic it May Be, But in the End it's Puny', *Guardian*, 21 January 1997; A. Watkins, 'All Too Eager to do the Government's Job for Them', *Independent on Sunday*, 26 January 1997.

159   M. Jacques and S. Hall, 'Tony Blair: the Greatest Tory Since Thatcher?', *Observer*, 13 April 1997; R. Hattersley, 'Own Goals Make Life Easy for Blair', *Guardian*, 18 April 1997.

160   The original quote appears to be that of Richard Neville, with reference to the Australian Labor government, quoted in Cohen, *Cruel Brittania*, p. 59; Labour MP Anthony Wright has also used the same phrase; see Coates, 'Placing New Labour', p. 361.

161   Echo Research, *The 2001 UK General Election: Media Content Analysis of UK, US and French Press* (Echo Research, London, 2001), pp. 7–25.

162   M. Scammell, 'The Media and Media Management', in A. Seldon (ed.), *The Blair Effect* (London: Little Brown, 2001), pp. 509–33; N. Jones, *The Control Freaks* (London: Politico, 2001).

163   K. Macguire, A. Travis and M. White, 'Blunkett Leads Attack on Press "Insanity"', *Guardian*, 20 June 2002; P. Wintour, 'Straw Joins Call for New Approach by Media', *Guardian*, 21 June 2002.

164   *Telegraph*, 24 May 2001.

165   *Independent*, 12 May 2003.

166   *Mail*, 12 May 2001.

167   *Mail*, 2 May–6 June 2001.

168   *Mail*, 23 May 2001.

169   *Mail*, 6 June 2001.

170   M. Jones, 'Mirror, Mirror, Who is the Most Disloyal Paper of Them All?', *Sunday Times*, 31 May 1998; *Mirror*, 3, 5 May 2000; K Macguire, 'Gott im Himmel: the Mirror Says Vote Tory', *Guardian*, 8 May 2000; P. Morgan, 'I Thought Norris Would be Better', *Guardian*, 8 May 2000.

171   R. Greenslade, 'Labour's Lost our Love', *Guardian*, 1 June 1998.

172   *The Times*, 16 May 2001

173   *Mirror*, 9 May 2001.

174   *Mirror*, 30 May 2001; Echo Research, *2001 Election*, p. 25.

175   Scammell and Harrop, 'Press Disarmed', p. 163.

176   A. Marr, 'Blair Shows his Hand Before Re-shuffle', *Telegraph*, 29 May 2001.

177   *Sun*, 19 March, 29 May, 19 March 2001.

178   *Sun*, 10 May, 5 June 2001; J. Silver, 'Is This the Most Dangerous Man in

Britain?', *Evening Standard*, 14 March 2001; Echo Research *2001 General Election*, p. 33.

179 *Express*, 6 June, 16 May 2001.

180 *Star*, 23 May, 6 June 2001.

181 *Express*, 23 April 2004.

182 B. McNair, *News and Journalism in the UK* (London: Routledge, 1999), p. 216; see also *The Economist*, 2 June 2001.

183 Interview, Trevor Kavanagh; Paul Vallery, 'Clever Trevor'.

184 I. Aitken, 'A Win for the Right', *New Statesman*, 7 July 1995, 14; for Stuart Higgins's suggestion of this, see Greenslade, 'Nice One Tony'; Deacon, Golding and Billig, 'Fear and Loathing', p. 20.

185 *Sun*, 29 April 1997.

186 P. Wilby, 'A Tory Tabloid says "Vote Labour"', *Independent*, 15 May 2001.

187 *Sun*, 9, 10 May 2001; Wilby, 'A Tory Tabloid'.

188 *The Times*, 5 June 2001; *Telegraph*, 2 June 2001.

189 H. Young, 'Running Scared of the Tabloids', *Guardian*, 25 June 1996; interview: P. Mandelson, *New Statesman*, 24 January 1997, 14.

190 R. McKibbin, 'Very Old Labour', *London Review of Books*, 3 April 1997, 3–6; Young, 'Running Scared'.

191 McKibbin, 'Very Old Labour', pp. 3–6; Jacques and Hall, 'Tony Blair'.

192 For the argument that the Conservatives had effectively lost the election before Blair became Labour leader, see R. Worcester and R. Mortimer, *Explaining Labour's Landslide* (London: Politico, 1999).

193 T. Blair, 'We Won't Look Back to the 1970s', *The Times*, 31 March 1997; *Sun*, 2, 14, 7, 28 April 1997.

194 P. Toynbee and D. Walker, *Did Things Get Better?* (London: Penguin, 2001), p. 237; N. Thompson, *Left in the Wilderness: the Political Economy of British Democratic Socialism Since 1979* (London: Acumen, 2002); For useful overviews and discussions, see S. Fielding, *The Labour Party: Continuity and Change in the Making of 'New' Labour* (London: Palgrave, 2003); S. Ludlam and M. Smith (eds) *New Labour in Government* (London: Macmillan, 2001).

195 S. Hall, 'New Labour Has Picked Up Where Thatcherism Left Off', *Guardian*, 6 August 2003.

196 *Guardian*, 21 June 2003.

197 *Mail*, 21 June, *Sun*, 21, 22 June, *Star*, 22 June, *Express* 21 June 2003.

198 *Guardian*, 21 June 2003

199 Jacques and Hall, 'Tony Blair'; E. Shaw, *The Labour Party Since 1945*, p. 217; I. Aitken, 'Enemy of the Old', *Guardian*, 24 December 1998.

200 McKibbin, 'Very Old Labour', p. 3.

201 S. Fielding, 'New Labour and the Past', in D. Tanner, P. Thane and N. Tiratsoo, *Labour's First Century* (Cambridge: Cambridge University Press, 2000), pp. 367–87.

202 *Sun*, 29 April 1997; *Express*, 1 May 1997.

6 Conclusions

1 Quoted in J. Keane, *The Media and Democracy*, p. 150.

2 For a summary, see P. Norris, *A Virtuous Circle: Political Communications in Postindustrial Societies* (Cambridge: Cambridge University Press, 2000).

3 J. Curran and J. Seaton, *Power Without Responsibility* (London: Routledge, 2003), pp. 87–93.

4 G. Gissing, quoted in J. Carey, *The Intellectuals and the Masses: Pride and Prejudice Among the Literary Intelligentsia, 1880–1939* (London: Faber & Faber, 1992), pp.

93, 6–8; T. S. Matthews, *The Sugar Pill: an Essay on Newspapers* (London: Victor Gollanz, 1957), p. 48.

5 J. Tunstall, 'Failing to Look Beyond the Lobby', *Times Higher Education Supplement*, 2 November 2001; see also his 'Trends in News Media and Political Journalism', in R. Kuhn and E. Nevue (eds), *Political Journalism: New Challenges, New Practices* (London: Routledge/ECPR, 2002), pp. 227–41; A. Lee, *The Origins of the Popular Press in England 1855–1914* (London: Croom Helm, 1976).

6 R. Hoggart, *The Uses of Literacy* (London: Penguin, 1957/1992), pp. 206–45.

7 *Royal Commission on the Press* (1949), p. 358; Thomas, 'Reflections', pp. 112–13.

8 Nicholas, *General Election of 1950*, pp. 163, 180.

9 S. McLachlan and P. Golding, 'Tabloidization in the British Press: a Quantitative Investigation into Changes in British Newspapers, 1952–1997', in Sparks and Tulloch (eds), *Tabloid Tales*, 75–89; D. Rooney, 'Thirty Years of Competition in the British Tabloid Press: the *Mirror* and the *Sun* 1968–1998', in Sparks and Tulloch (eds), *Tabloid Tales*, pp. 91–109; see also Thomas, 'Reflections', pp. 105–7.

10 R. Mortimore, S. Atkinson and G. Skinner, 'What the Papers Say: Do Readers Believe What the Editors Want Them To?', paper presented to EPOP conference, Edinburgh, 8–10 September 2000; http://www.mori.com/mrr/2000/c001006.shtml, accessed 14 June 2004.

11 *News Chronicle*, 23 May 1955.

12 Hargreaves and Thomas, *New News*, p. 45.

13 Eurobarometer poll, quoted in I. Black, 'British Newspapers Least Trusted in Europe'. *Guardian*, 24 April 2002; P. Preston, 'Should You Believe What You Read?', *Observer*, 23 March 2003; S. Barnett, 'Slipping Down the Slippery Slope', *British Journalism Review*, 4, 1, 1993, 69.

14 Beith, 'The Press', p. 197; Scammell and Harrop, 'A Press Disarmed', pp. 158–9; Pew Research Centre for the People and the Press, 'Public Habits Little Changed since September 11', June 2002, http://people-press.org/reports, accessed 14 June 2004; E. Lauf, 'The Vanishing Younger Reader: SocioDeterminants of Newspaper Use as a Source of Political Information in Europe 1980–98', *European Journal of Communication*, 16, 2, 2001, 233–43; information derived from quantitative survey for Hargreaves and Thomas, *New News, Old News*.

15 Tunstall, *Newspaper Power*, p. 32.

16 Kellner and Worcester, 'Electoral Perceptions of Media Stance', pp. 63–5; Tunstall, *Media in Britain*, pp. 161–5; W. Miller, *Media and Voters*, pp. 169–99.

17 Information derived from quantitative survey for Hargreaves and Thomas, *New News, Old News*; M. Billig, *Talking of the Royal Family* (London: Routledge, 1997), pp. 144–71.

18 J. Curran, 'Advertising as a Patronage System', in H. Christian (ed.), *The Sociology of Journalism and the Press*, Sociological Review Monograph (University of Keele, 1980), pp. 71–120.

19 See, for example, G. Murdock and P. Golding, 'The Structure, Ownership and Control of the Press, 1914–76', in Boyce, Curran and Wingate (eds), *Newspaper History*, pp. 136–46; J. Tunstall, 'The British Press in the Age of Television', in Christian (ed.), *The Sociology of Journalism*, pp. 28–31; Royal Commission on the Press, 1977, *Final Report*, p. 149.

20 D. Hallin, *We Keep America on Top of the World: Television Journalism and the Public Sphere* (London: Routledge, 1994), pp. 136–47.

21 Quoted in Leapman, *Treacherous Estate*, p. 180; M. Harrop, 'The Press and Post-War Elections', in I. Crewe and M. Harrop (eds), *Political Communications: The General Election Campaign of 1983* (Cambridge: Cambridge University Press, 1986), pp. 137–49.

22 B. MacArthur, 'New Readers, New Times', *Times*, 3 February 1997 and 'From Soundbites to NewsSnacks', *British Journalism Review*, 4, 2, 1993, 68; P. Dorey,

British Politics Since 1945 (Oxford, Blackwell, 1995), pp. 61–2, 160–1; P. Stothard, 'The Times They Aren't Changing', *Guardian*, 16 June 1997; for the reduction in the reporting of parliament, see J. Straw, 'Democracy on the Spike', *British Journalism Review*, 4, 4, 1993, 45–51; B. Franklin, *Newszak and News Media* (London: Arnold, 1997), pp. 232–49.

23 For a discussion, see M. Macdonald, *Understanding Media Discourse* (London: Arnold, 2003), pp. 53–102.

24 Jack, 'Introduction', in *The Granta Book of Reportage* (London: Granta, 1998), p. viii.

25 Royal Commission on the Press, *1961–62 Report*, pp. 106–7.

26 John Rawls, quoted in M. Linton, *Money and Votes*, p. 4.

27 *Agenda for Change: The Report of the Hansard Society Commission on Election Campaigns* (London: Hansard Society for Parliamentary Government, 1991), p. 49.

28 See, for example, Linton, *Was It the Sun?*, pp. 38–9; J. Curran and J. Seaton, *Power Without Responsibility*, pp. 335–47; and for further suggestions and criticisms, see D. MacShane, 'Media Policy and the Left', in J. Seaton and B. Pimlott (eds), *Media in British Politics*, pp. 215–35.

29 *Review of Press Self-Regulation* (Chairman: David Calcutt) (London: HMSO, 1993), p. 79; for a negative assessment of the Press Council, see G. Robinson, *People Against the Press* (London: Quartet, 1983); T. O'Malley and C. Soley, *Regulating the Press* (London: Pluto, 2000); for competing views on its successor, see O'Malley and Soley, *Regulating the Press*, and R. Shannon, *A Press Free and Responsible: Self-Regulation and the Press Complaints Commission 1991–2001* (London: John Murray, 2001).

30 For a critique, see G. Boyce, 'The Fourth Estate: the Reappraisal of a Concept', in Boyce, Curran and Wingate (eds), *Newspaper History*, pp. 19–40.

31 C. Seymour-Ure, 'Northcliffe's Legacy', in Seymour-Ure, Smith and Catterall, *Northcliffe's Legacy*, p. 23.

32 C. Sparks, 'Popular Journalism: Theories and Practice', in C. Sparks and P. Dahlgren, *Journalism and Popular Culture* (London: Sage, 1992), pp. 24–44; J. Curran, A. Douglas and G. Whannel, 'The Political Economy of the Human-Interest Story', in A. Smith (ed.), *Newspapers and Democracy: International Essays on a Changing Medium* (Massachusetts: MIT Press, 1980), pp. 288–347; J. Chalaby, *Journalism: the Invention of a Tradition*, p. 191; J. Seaton and B. Pimlott (ed.), *The Media in British Politics*, p. x.

33 See, for example, S. Hall, *The Hard Road to Renewal: Thatcherism and the Crisis of the Left* (London: Verso, 1988); C. Leadbeater, 'Power to the Person', *Marxism Today*, October 1988, 14–19; A. Gamble, *The Free Economy and the Strong State: the Politics of Thatcherism* (London: Macmillan, 1994); B. Jessop, K. Bonnett, S. Bromley and T. Ling, *Thatcherism: a Tale of Two Nations* (London: Polity, 1988).

34 J. Seabrook, 'What the Papers Show', *New Society*, 5 June 1987, 16–18.

35 See Thomas, 'The Max Factor', pp. 201–26.

36 S. Hall, 'Thatcherism and the Interpretation of Culture', in C. Nelson and L. Grossberg, *Marxism and the Interpretation of Culture* (London: Macmillan, 1988), pp. 47, 63; Gamble, *Free Economy*, p. 222.

37 See, for instance, I. Crewe, 'Has the Electorate Become Thatcherite?', in R. Skidelsky (ed.), *Thatcherism* (London: Chatto & Windus, 1988), pp. 25–49.

38 J. Whale, *The Politics of the Media* (Glasgow: Fontana, 1977), p. 85; Seymour Ure, 'Northcliffe's Legacy', p. 18; for critiques of this theory, see, for instance, J. Keane, *Media and Democracy*; J. Curran, 'Mass Media and Democracy: a Reappraisal', in J. Curran and M. Gurevitch (eds), *Mass Media and Society* (London: Edward Arnold, 1991), pp. 84–97.

39 Newton and Brynin, 'The National Press and Party Voting', pp. 269–70.

40 Interview, David Hill, 18 December 1998.

Select bibliography

More detailed references can be found in the footnotes. All publications are London unless otherwise stated.

Manuscript sources

Gerald Barry papers (London School of Economics).
Lord Beaverbrook papers (House of Lords Records Office, London).
Conservative party archive (Bodleian Library, Oxford).
Hugh Cudlipp papers (Cardiff School of Journalism, Cardiff).
Michael Foot papers (National Museum of Labour History, Manchester).
A. G. Gardiner papers (London School of Economics).
Neil Kinnock papers (Churchill College, Cambridge).
Labour party archive (National Museum of Labour History, Manchester).
Walter Layton papers (Trinity College, Cambridge).
John Strachey papers (Mrs Elizabeth Quadhi, London).

Newspapers and periodicals

Daily Chronicle; *Daily Citizen*; *Daily Express*; *Daily Graphic*; *Daily Herald*; *Daily Mail*; *Daily Mirror*; *Daily News*; *Daily Sketch*; *Daily Star*; *Daily Telegraph*; *Daily Worker/Morning Star*; *The Economist*; *Encounter*; *Financial Times*; *Guardian/Manchester Guardian*; *Independent*; *Independent on Sunday*; *Labour Leader*; *Listener*; *Mail on Sunday*; *News Chronicle*; *New Leader*; *New Statesman*; *News of the World*; *Observer*; *Reynolds News*; *Spectator*; *Sun*; *Sunday Express*; *Sunday Pictorial/Sunday Mirror*; *Sunday Telegraph*; *Sunday Times*; *The Times*; *Today*; *Tribune*; *Western Mail*; *Westminster Gazette*.

Interviews

Geoffrey Goodman, 19 January 1999; Joe Haines, 10 September 1998; Anthony Howard, 16 September 1997; David Hill, 3 November 1994, 18 December 1998; Trevor Kavanagh, 23 September 1997; Neil Kinnock, 24 November 1994; Terry Lancaster, 31 August 1997; Julia Langdon, 15 September 1997; Michael Molloy, 18 January 1999; Robin Oakley, 16 September 1997; Richard Stott, 11 September 1998.

Correspondence

Robert Edwards, 11 August 1997; Michael Hartwell, 17 February 1994; Neil Kinnock, 11 November 1997.

Published official reports

Bennett, G., 'A Most Extraordinary and Mysterious Business': the Zinoviev Letter of 1924, Foreign and Commonwealth History Notes, No. 14 (HMSO, 1999).
Lord Denning's Report (HMSO, 1963).
House of Commons Parliamentary Debates, Fifth/Sixth Series.
Report of the Committee of Privy Councillors Appointed to Enquire into 'D' Notice Matters (HMSO, 1967).
Report of the Tribunal Appointed to Enquire into the Vassall Case (chairman: Lord Radcliffe) (HMSO, 1962).
Review of Press Self-Regulation (chairman: David Calcutt) (HMSO, 1993).
Royal Commission on the Press, *1947–49 Report* (chairman: Sir William Ross) (HMSO, 1949).
Royal Commission on the Press, 1947–49, *Minutes of Oral Evidence*, Vols 1–48 (HMSO, 1949).
Royal Commission on the Press, 1947–49, *Memoranda of Evidence*, Vols 1–3 (HMSO, 1949).
Royal Commission on the Press, *1961–62 Report* (chairman: Lord Shawcross) (HMSO, 1962).
Royal Commission on the Press, 1962, *Minutes of Oral Evidence*, Vols 1–3 (HMSO, 1962).
Royal Commission on the Press, 1977, *Final Report* (chairman: O. R. McGregor) (London: HMSO, 1977).
Royal Commission on the Press, 1977, *Minority Report* (reprinted by the Labour party, 1977).
Royal Commission on the Press, 1977, *Minutes of Evidence* (The Commission, 1975, 1977).

Other published reports

Agenda for Change: the Report of the Hansard Society on Election Campaigns (Hansard Society, 1991).
Annual Conference Reports of the Labour party.
Mass-Observation File Reports, 1938–1951.
People and the Press: Annual Reports of the Press Council.

General works

Brendan, P., *The Life and Death of the Press Barons* (Secker & Warburg, 1982).
Bromley, M. and O'Malley, T. (eds), *A Journalism Reader* (Routledge, 1997).
Catterall, P., Seymour-Ure, C. and Smith, A. *Northcliffe's Legacy: Aspects of the Popular Press, 1896–1996* (Macmillan, 2000).
Conboy, M., *The Press and Popular Culture* (Sage, 2001).
Curran, J., *Media and Power* (Routledge, 2002).

Curran, J. and Gurevitch, M. (eds), *Mass Media and Society* (Arnold, 2000).

Curran, J. and Seaton, J., *Power Without Responsibility: the British Press and Broadcasting in Britain* (Methuen, 1985).

Curran, J., Smith, A. and Wingate, P. (eds), *Impacts and Influences: Essays on Media Power in the Twentieth Century* (Methuen, 1987).

Franklin, B., *Packaging Politics* (Edward Arnold, 1995).

Franklin, B., *Newszak and News Media* (Arnold, 1997).

Griffiths, Dennis (ed.), *The Encyclopedia of the British Press 1422–1992* (Macmillan, 1992).

Harrop, M., 'The Press and Post-War Elections', in Crewe and Harrop (eds), *Political Communications: the British General Election Campaign of 1983*.

Koss, S., *The Rise and Fall of the Political Press* (Fontana, 1990).

Kuhn, R. and Nevue, E., *Political Journalism: New Challenges, New Practices* (Routledge, 2002).

McNair, B., *News and Journalism in the UK* (Routledge, 1999).

McNair, B., *Journalism and Democracy: an Evaluation of the Political Sphere* (Routledge, 2000).

Media History, *The Daily Mirror*, 9, 2, 2003.

Negrine, R., *Politics and the Mass Media in Britain* (Routledge, 1994).

Norris, P., *A Virtuous Circle: Political Communications in Postindustrial Societies* (Cambridge, Cambridge University Press, 2000).

Richards, H., *The Bloody Circus: the Daily Herald and the Left* (Pluto, 1997).

Ruddock, A., *Understanding Audiences: Theory and Method* (Sage, 2001).

Seaton, J. (ed.), *Politics and the Media: Harlots and Prerogatives at the Turn of the Millennium* (Oxford: Blackwell, 1998).

Seaton, J. and Pimlott, B. (eds), *The Media in British Politics* (Aldershot: Avebury, 1987).

Seymour-Ure, C., *The British Press and Broadcasting Since 1945* (Oxford: Blackwell, 1996)

Smith, A. C. H., *Paper Voices: the Popular Press and Social Change 1935–1965* (Chatto & Windus, 1965).

Sparks, C. and Tulloch, J. (eds), *Tabloid Tales: Global Debates Over Media Standards* (Lanham MD: Rowman & Littlefield, 2000).

Street, J. *Mass Media, Politics and Democracy* (Palgrave, 2001).

Tunstall, J., *The Media in Britain* (Constable, 1983).

Tunstall, J., *Newspaper Power: the New National Press in Britain* (Oxford: Clarendon, 1997).

Williams, K., *Get Me a Murder a Day* (Arnold, 1998).

The British General Election of... published after every election since 1945 and written or co-written by D. Butler since 1950, all contain important surveys of press coverage.

Published biographies, autobiographies, memoirs, diaries.

Andrews, L. and Taylor, H. A., *Lords and Labourers of the British Press* (Carbonale and Edwardsville: South Illinois University Press, 1970).

Belfield, R., Hird, C. and Kelly, S., *Murdoch: the Great Escape* (Warner, 1994).

Bourne, R., *Lords of Fleet Street: the Harmsworth Dynasty* (Unwin Hyman, 1990).

Brodsky, V. (ed.), *Fleet Street: the Inside Story of Journalism* (Macdonald, 1966).

Cameron, J., *Point of Departure* (Grafron, 1969).

Viscount Camrose, *British Newspapers and their Controllers* (Cassell, 1947).

Christiansen, A., *Headlines All My Life* (Heinemann, 1961).

Cockett, R. (ed.), *My Dear Max: the Letters of Brendan Bracken to Lord Beaverbrook 1925–1958* (Historians Press, 1990).

Conner, R., *Reflections in a Mirror* (Cassell, 1969).

Cudlipp, H., *Publish and Be Damned! The Astonishing Story of the 'Daily Mirror'* (Dakers, 1953).

Cudlipp, H., *At Your Peril* (Weidenfeld & Nicolson, 1962).

Cudlipp, H., *Walking on the Water* (Bodley Head, 1976).

Cudlipp, H., 'Whose Finger on the Voters?', *British Journalism Review*, 7, 4, 1996.

Curtis, S. (ed.), *The Journals of Woodrow Wyatt: Vol. I* (Macmillan, 1998).

Davies, R. and Ottoway, L., *Vicky* (Secker & Warburg, 1987).

Donoughue, B., *Prime Minister: the Conduct of Policy Under Harold Wilson and James Callaghan* (Jonathan Cape, 1987).

Driberg, T., *Beaverbrook: a Study in Power and Frustration* (Weidenfeld & Nicolson, 1956).

Drover, G., *Kinnock* (Publishing Corporation, 1994).

Edelman, M., *The Mirror: a Political History* (Hamish Hamilton, 1966).

Edwards, R., *Goodbye Fleet Street* (Coronet, 1988).

Edwards, R. D., *Newspapermen: Hugh Cudlipp, Cecil Harmsworth King and the Glory Days of Fleet Street* (Secker & Warburg, 2003).

Evans, H., *Downing Street Diary: the Macmillan Years, 1957–1963* (Hodder & Stoughton, 1981).

Evans, H., *Good Times, Bad Times* (Phoenix, 1994).

Feinbach, W., *25 Momentous Years: a 25th Anniversary in the History of the Daily Herald* (Odhams, 1955).

Ferris, P., *The House of Northcliffe: the Harmsworths of Fleet Street* (Weidenfeld & Nicolson, 1971).

Foot, M., *Another Heart and Other Pulses: the Alternative to the Thatcher Society* (Collins, 1984).

Giles, F., *Sundry Times* (John Murray, 1986).

Gilmour, I., *Dancing With Dogma* (Simon & Schuster, 1993).

Gould, P., *The Unfinished Revolution: How the Modernisers Saved the Labour Party* (Little Brown, 1998).

Gourlay, L. (ed.), *The Beaverbrook I Knew* (Quartet, 1984).

Gray, T. (ed.), *Fleet Street Remembered* (Heinemann, 1990).

Grose, R., *The Sunsation: Behind the Scenes of Britain's Best-Selling Newspaper* (Angus & Robertson, 1989).

Haines, J., *The Politics of Power* (Cape, 1977).

Hamilton, D., *Editor in Chief: the Fleet Street Memoirs of Sir Denis Hamilton* (Hamilton, 1989).

Hare, D., *Asking Around* (Faber & Faber, 1993).

Harris, R., *Good and Faithful Servant: the Unauthorised Biography of Bernard Ingham* (Faber & Faber, 1990).

Hill, D., 'The Labour Party's Strategy', in Crewe, I. and Gosschalk, B. (eds), *Political Communications: the British General Election Campaign of 1992* (Cambridge University Press, 1995).

Hollingsworth, M., *The Ultimate Spin Doctor: the Life and Fast Times of Tim Bell* (Coronet, 1997).

Horne, A., *Macmillan, 1957–1986* (Macmillan, 1989).

Horrie, C. and Chippendale, P., *Stick It Up Your Punter: the Uncut Story of the Sun Newspaper* (Pocket, 1999).

Howard, A., *RAB: the Life of R. A. Butler* (Jonathan Cape, 1987).

Hubback, D., *No Ordinary Press Baron: a Life of Walter Layton* (Weidenfeld & Nicolson, 1985).

Ingham, B., *Kill the Messenger* (HarperCollins, 1991).

Jameson, D., *Last of the Hot Metal Men: from Fleet Street to Showbiz* (Ebery, 1990).

Jones, M., *Michael Foot* (Victor Gollancz, 1994).

Jones, N., *Election '92* (BBC Books, 1992).

Jones, N., *Soundbites and Spin Doctors: How Politicians Manipulate the Media – and Vice Versa* (Cassell, 1995).

Jones, N., *Campaign 1997: How the General Election was Won and Lost* (Indigo, 1997).

Junor, J., *Memoirs: Listening for a Midnight Train* (Pan, 1990).

King, C., *The Future of the Press* (MacGibbon & Kee, 1967).

King, C., *Strictly Personal* (Weidenfeld & Nicolson, 1969).

King, C., *With Malice Towards None: a War Diary* (Sidgewick & Jackson, 1970).

King, C., *The Cecil King Diary: 1965–70* (Jonathan Cape, 1972).

Lamb, L., *Sunrise: the Remarkable Rise and Rise of the Best-Selling Soaraway Sun* (Papermac, 1989).

Leapman, M., *Kinnock* (Unwin Hyman, 1987).

Macmillan, H., *At the End of the Day* (Macmillan, 1973).

Mandelson, P. and Hewitt, P., 'The Labour Campaign', in Crewe, I. and Gosschalk, B. (eds), *Political Communications: the British General Election Campaign of 1987* (Cambridge University Press, 1989).

Margach, J., *The Abuse of Power: the War Between Downing Street and the Media* (Star, 1979).

Marquand, D., *Ramsay MacDonald* (Jonathan Cape, 1977).

Munter, G., *Murdoch: a Paper Prince* (Penguin, 1985).

Neil, A., *Full Disclosure* (Macmillan, 1996).

Pilger, J., *Hidden Agendas* (Vintage, 1998).

Pimlott, B., *Harold Wilson* (HarperCollins, 1993).

Pincher, C., *Inside Story: a Documentary on the Pursuit of Power* (Book Club Associates, 1978).

Pound, R. and Harmsworth, G., *Northcliffe* (Cassell, 1989).

Randall, M., *The Funny Side of the Street* (Bloomsbury, 1988).

Regan, S., *Rupert Murdoch: a Business Biography* (Angus & Robertson, 1976).

Riddell, P., 'Not a Word of Thanks from Mrs T', *British Journalism Review*, 5, 1, 1994.

Rodgers, W., 'Government Under Stress: Britain's Winter of Discontent 1979', *Political Quarterly*, April/June, 1984.

Seldon, A., *John Major: a Political Life* (Weidenfeld & Nicolson, 1997).

Shawcross, H., *Life Sentence: the Memoirs of Lord Shawcross* (Constable, 1995).

Shawcross, W., *Rupert Murdoch: Ringmaster of the Information Circus* (Chatto & Windus, 1992).

Sommerfield, S., *Banner Headlines* (Scan Books, 1979).

Tatchell, P., *The Battle for Bermondsey* (Heretic Books, 1983).

Taylor, A., *Beaverbrook* (Hamish Hamilton, 1972).

Taylor, S., *The Great Outsiders: Northcliffe, Rothermere and the Daily Mail* (Weidenfeld & Nicolson, 1996).

Taylor, S., *The Reluctant Press Lord: Esmond Rothermere and the Daily Mail* (Weidenfeld & Nicolson, 1998).

Thorpe, D., *Sir Alec Douglas-Home* (Sinclair Stevenson, 1996).

Tucille, J., *Murdoch* (Piatkus, 1989).

Vines, C., *A Little Brown Nut Man: My Three Years with Lord Beaverbrook* (L. Trewin, 1968).

Watkins, A., *Brief Lives: with Some Memoirs* (Hamilton, 1982).

Westlake, M., *Kinnock: the Biography* (Little Brown, 2002).

Williams, F., *Nothing So Strange: an Autobiography* (Cassell, 1970).

Williams, H., *Guilty Men* (Aurum, 1998).

Williams, M., *Inside Number Ten* (Weidenfeld & Nicolson, 1972).

Williams, M., *Downing Street in Perspective* (Weidenfeld & Nicolson, 1983).

Wilson, H., *The Labour Government 1964–1970: a Personal Record* (Weidenfeld & Nicolson, 1971).

Wood, A., *The True History of Lord Beaverbrook* (William Heinemann, 1965).

Ziegler, P., *Wilson: the Authorised Life of Lord Wilson of Rievaulx* (HarperCollins, 1995).

Other published works

Abrams, M., *The Newspaper Reading Public of Tomorrow* (Odhams Press, 1964).

Addison, P., *The Road to 1945: British Politics and the Second World War* (Quartet, 1977).

Alderman, K., 'Harold Macmillan's "Night of the Long Knives"', *Contemporary Record*, 6, 2, 1992.

Angell, N., *The Press and the Organisation of Society* (Cambridge: Gordon Fraser, 1933).

Attitudes to the Press: a Report by Social and Community Planning Research (HMSO, 1977).

Baistow, T., *Fourth-Rate Estate* (Comedia, 1985).

Ball, S. and Seldon, A. (eds), *The Heath Government* (Longman, 1996).

Baxendale, J. and Pawling, C., *Narrating the Thirties – a Decade in the Making: 1930 to the Present Day* (Macmillan, 1996).

Beniger, J., 'Toward an Old New Paradigm: the Half Century Flirtation with Mass Society', *Public Opinion Quarterly*, 51, 1987, 46–66.

Benson, T., 'Low and Lord Beaverbrook: the Case of a Cartoonist's Autonomy', University of Kent, PhD, 1998.

Berry, S., 'Labour's Strategy and the Media: the Failure of Labour's 1992 Election Campaign', *Parliamentary Affairs*, 45, 4, 1992.

Billig, M., *Talking of the Royal Family* (Routledge: 1997).

Birch, A., Campbell, P. and Lucas, P., 'The Popular Press and the British General Election of 1955', *Political Studies*, 4, 3, 1956.

Blewitt, N., *The Peers, the Parties and the People: the British General Election of 1910* (Macmillan, 1972).

Blumler, J. and McQuail, D., *Television in Politics: its Uses and Influences* (Faber & Faber, 1968).

Booker, C., *The Neophiliacs: the Revolution in English Life in the Fifties and Sixties* (Pimlico, 1992).

Boyce, G., Curran, J. and Wingate, P. (eds), *Newspaper History: from the 17th Century to the Present Day* (Constable, 1978).

Brenton, H. and Hare, D., *Pravda: a Fleet Street Comedy* (Methuen, 1985).

Bromley, M., 'Was it the *Mirror* Wot Won It? The Development of the Tabloid Press During the Second World War', in Hayes, Nick and Hill, Jeff (eds), *'Millions Like Us'? British Culture in the Second World War* (Liverpool: Liverpool University Press, 1999), pp. 93–124.

Burns, T., 'The Impact of the National Press on Voters in 1997', paper to EPOP 'Assessing the 1997 Election: Voters, Parties, Polls and the Media' conference, University of Essex, September 1997.

Butler, D. and Stokes, D., *Political Change in Modern Britain: Forces Shaping Electoral Choice* (Macmillan, 1969).

Carey, J., *The Intellectuals and the Masses: Pride and Prejudice Among the Literary Intelligentsia 1880–1939* (Faber & Faber, 1992).

Carma International, *The Power of the Press: the 1997 UK General Election* (Carma, 1997).

Chalaby, J., *The Invention of Journalism* (Macmillan, 1998).

Chester, Lewis, Fay, S. and Young, H., *The Zinoviev Letter* (Heinemann, 1967).

Chisholm, Anne and Davie, M., *Beaverbrook: a Life* (Pimlico, 1993).

Christian, H. (ed.), *The Sociology of Journalism and the Press*, Sociological Review Monograph 29 (University of Keele, 1980).

Cockerell, M., *Live from Number 10: the Inside Story of Prime Ministers and Television* (Faber & Faber, 1989).

Cockerell, M., Hennessy, P. and Walker, D., *Sources Close to the Prime Minister* (Macmillan, 1984).

Cockett, R., 'The Government, the Press and Politics 1937–1945', University of London, PhD, 1988.

Cockett, R., 'The Party, Publicity and the Media', in Seldon, A. and Ball, S. (eds), *The Conservative Party Since 1900* (Oxford: Oxford University Press, 1994).

Cohen, N., *Cruel Britannia: Reflections on the Sinister and the Preposterous* (Verso, 1999).

Cole, H., *Socialism and the Press* (Victor Gollancz, 1952).

Coleridge, N., *Paper Tigers: the Latest, Greatest Newspaper Tycoons and How They Won the World* (William Heinemann, 1993).

Cook, C., *The Age of Alignment: Electoral Politics in Britain 1922–1929* (Macmillan, 1975).

Crewe, I. and Gosschalk, B. (eds), *Political Communications: the General Election Campaign of 1992* (Cambridge: Cambridge University Press, 1995).

Crewe, I., Gosschalk, B. and Bartle, J. (eds) *Why Labour Won: the General Election of 1997* (Frank Cass, 1998).

Crewe, I. and Harrop, M., *Political Communications: the British General Election Campaign of 1987* (Cambridge: Cambridge University Press, 1989).

Cudlipp, H., *The Prerogative of the Harlot: Press Barons and Power* (Bodley Head, 1980).

Cummings, A., *The Press and a Changing Civilisation* (John Lane, 1936).

Curran, J., Douglas, A. and Whannel, G., 'The Political Economy of the Human-Interest Story', in Smith, A. (ed.), *Newspapers and Democracy: International Essays on a Changing Medium* (Massachusetts: MIT Press, 1980).

Curtice, J., 'Is the Sun Shining on Tony Blair?: the Electoral Influence of British Newspapers', *Harvard International Journal of Press/Politics*, 2, 2, Spring 1997.

Curtice, J. and Semetko, H., 'Does it Matter What the Papers Say?', in Heath, A., Jowell, R. and Curtice, J. (eds), *Labour's Last Chance: the 1992 General Election and Beyond* (Dartmouth, 1994).

Daly, M., '"Anti-Tabloid Paranoia"? The Sun, Labour and the 1992 General Election', May Day Lecture, University of Nottingham, 1992.

Denver, D., Norris, P., Broughton, D. and Rallings, C. (eds), *British Elections and Parties Yearbook 1993* (Harvester Wheatsheaf, 1993).

Driver, S. and Martell, L., *New Labour: Politics After Thatcherism* (Cambridge: Polity Press, 1998).

Engel, M., *Tickle the Public: One Hundred Years of the Popular Press* (Indigo, 1997).

Entman, R., 'How the Media Affect What People Think: an Information Processing Approach', *Journal of Politics*, 52, 2, 1989.

Evans, H., 'The Half-Free Press', in *The Freedom of the Press*, Granada Guildhall Lectures (Hart Davie, MacGibbon, 1974).

Fielding, S., Thompson, P. and Tiratsoo, N., *'England Arise!': the Labour Party and Popular Politics in 1940s Britain* (Manchester: Manchester University Press, 1995).

Finney, A., 'The Truth Comes Between the Lines', *British Journalism Review*, 2, 2, 1990.

Foley, M., *The Rise of the British Presidency* (Manchester: Manchester University Press, 1993).

Franklin, B. (ed.), *Social Policy, the Media and Misrepresentation* (London: Routledge, 1999).

Franklin, B. and Larsen, G., 'Kingmaking in the Labour Leadership Contest', *British Journalism Review*, 5, 4, 1994.

Geddes, A. and Tongue, J. (eds), *Labour's Landslide: the British General Election 1997* (Manchester: Manchester University Press, 1997).

Glasgow University Media Group, *Bad News*; *More Bad News*; *Really Bad News* (Routledge & Kegan, 1976, 1980, 1982).

Goldsmith College Media Research Group, *Media Coverage of London Councils, Final Report* (June 1987).

Grundy, Bill, *The Press Inside Out* (W. H. Allen, 1976).

Hargreaves, I. and Thomas, J., *New News, Old News* (ITC/BSC, 2002).

Hay, C., 'Narrating Crisis: the Discursive Construction of the "Winter of Discontent"', *Sociology*, 30, 2, 1996.

Heath, A., Jowell, R. and Curtice, J. (eds), *Labour's Last Chance: the 1992 General Election and Beyond* (Aldershot: Dartmouth, 1994).

Hennessy, P., *Never Again: Britain 1945–1951* (Vintage, 1993).

Hetherington, A., *News, Newspapers and Television* (Macmillan, 1985).

Hinton, J., '1945 and the apathy school', *History Workshop Journal*, 43, 1997.

Hoggart, R., *The Uses of Literacy* (Chatto & Windus, 1957).

Hollingsworth, M., *The Press and Political Dissent* (Pluto, 1986).

Hopkin, D., 'The Labour Party Press', in Brown, K. D. (ed.), *The First Labour Party 1906–1914* (Croom Helm, 1985).

Howard, A., 'Press Barons and Power: From the Age of Deference to the Eve of Mogul Power', Radio 4, Parts 1–4, July/August 1998.

Howard, A. and West, R., *The Making of the Prime Minister* (Cape, 1965).

Hughes, D. and Wintour, P., *Labour Rebuilt: the New Model Party* (Fourth Estate, 1990).

Jefferys, K., *The Churchill Coalition and Wartime Politics* (Manchester: Manchester University Press, 1991).

Jefferys, K., 'British Politics and the Road to 1964', *Contemporary Record*, 9, 1, 1995.

Jenkins, P., *Mrs Thatcher's Revolution: the Ending of the Socialist Era* (Cape, 1987).

Jenkins, S., *The Market for Glory: Fleet Street Ownership in the 20th Century* (Faber & Faber, 1986).

Johnson, J., 'Rupert's Grip?', *British Journalism Review*, 9, 1, 1998.

Kavanagh, D., *Thatcherism and British Politics: the End of Consensus?* (Oxford: Oxford University Press, 1990).

Kavanagh, D., *Election Campaigning: the New Marketing of Politics* (Blackwell, 1995).

Kavanagh, D. and Seldon, A. (eds), *The Thatcher Effect* (Oxford: Oxford University Press, 1989).

Kavanagh, D. and Seldon, A. (eds), *The Major Effect* (Papermac, 1994).

Keane, J., *The Media and Democracy* (Cambridge: Blackwell, 1991).

Kellner, P. and Worcester, R., 'Electoral Perceptions of Media Stance', in Worcester, R. and Harrop, M. (eds), *Political Communications: the General Election Campaign of 1979* (George Allen & Unwin, 1982).

King, A. (ed.), *Britain at the Polls* (New Jersey: Chatham, 1992).

King, A. (ed.), *New Labour Triumphs: Britain at the Polls* (New York: Chatham, 1998).

Labour Party, *The Power of the Press* (Labour Publications, 1936).

Labour Party, *The People and the Media* (Labour Party, 1974).

Leapman, M., *Treacherous Estate: the Press After Fleet Street* (Hodder & Stoughton, 1992).

LeMahieu, D., *A Culture for Democracy* (Oxford: Clarendon, 1988).

Lewis, J., *Constructing Public Opinion: How Political Elites Do What They Like And Why We Seem To Go Along With It* (New York, Columbia University Press, 2001).

Linton, M., 'Press Ganged at the Polls', in Linton, M. (ed.), *Guardian Guide to the House of Commons* (Fourth Estate, 1992).

Linton, M., *Money and Votes* (Institute of Public Policy Research, 1994).

Linton, M., *Was It the Sun Wot Won It?*, Seventh Guardian Lecture, Nuffield College, Oxford, 1995.

Lyman, R. W., *The First Labour Government* (Chapman & Hall, 1957).

MacArthur, B., 'The National Press', in Crewe, I. and Harrop, M. (eds), *Political Communications: the British General Election Campaign of 1987* (Cambridge University Press, 1989).

McCallum, R. and Readman, A., *The British General Election of 1945* (Oxford, Oxford University Press, 1947).

McKie, D., 'Fact is Free but Comment is Sacred', or Was It the Sun Wot Won It?', in Crewe, I. and Gosschalk, B. (eds), *Political Communications: the British General Election of 1992* (Cambridge University Press, 1995).

McKie, D., 'Nightmare on Norm Street', in Margetts, H. and Smyth, G. (eds), *Turning Japanese: Britain with a Permanent State of One-Party Government* (Laurence & Wishart, 1994).

McKie, D., 'Swingers, Clingers, Waverers and Quaverers: the Tabloid Press in the 1997 General Election', in Crewe, I., Gosschalk, B. and Bartle, J. (eds), *Why Labour Won: the General Election of 1997* (Frank Cass, 1998).

Marquand, D., *The Progressive Dilemma* (Heinemann, 1992).

Marxism Today, November/December 1998.

Mass-Observation, *The Press and its Readers* (Arts & Technics, 1949).

Matthews, T., *The Sugar Pill: an Essay on Newspapers* (Victor Gollancz, 1957).

Miller, W., *Media and Voters: the Audience, Content and Influence of Press and Television at the 1987 General Election* (Oxford: Clarendon, 1991).

Morgan, K., *The People's Peace: British History 1945–1990* (Oxford: Oxford University Press, 1992).

Morgan, K., *Callaghan: A Life* (Oxford: Oxford University Press, 1997).

Morley, D., *Television, Audiences and Cultural Studies* (Routledge, 1992).

Negrine, R., 'The "Gravest Political Crisis Since Suez": the Press, the Government and the Pit Closures Announcement of 1992', *Parliamentary Affairs*, 8, 1, 1995.

Newton, K., 'Do People Read Everything They Believe in the Newspapers?: Newspapers and Voting in the 1983 and 1987 Elections', in Crewe, I. and Norris, Pippa (eds), *British Parties and Elections Yearbook* (Simon & Schuster, 1991).

Noelle-Neumann, E., *The Spiral of Silence* (Chicago: University of Chicago Press, 1993).

Norris, P., Sanders, D., Scammell, M. and Semetko, H., *On Message: Communicating the Campaign* (Sage, 1999).

Pattie, C., Denver, D., Fisher, J. and Ludlam, S. (eds), *British Parties and Elections Review* (Frank Cass, 1997).

Philo, G., *Seeing and Believing* (Routledge, 1990).

Philo, G. (ed.), *Message Received* (Longman, 1999).

Political and Economic Planning, *Report on the British Press* (PEP, 1938).

Pugh, M., 'The Daily Mirror and the Revival of Labour 1935–1945', *Twentieth Century British History*, 9, 3, 1998.

Pursehouse, M., 'Looking at the Sun into the Nineties with a Tabloid and its Readers', *Cultural Studies from Birmingham*, 1, 1991, 88–153.

Rallings, C., Farrell, D., Denver, D. and Broughton, D. (eds), *British Parties and Elections Yearbook 1995* (Frank Cass, 1996).

Ramsden, J., *The Winds of Change: Macmillan to Heath, 1957–1975* (Longman, 1996).

Richards, H., '"Constriction, Conformity and Control": the Taming of the Daily Herald 1921–30', Open University, PhD, 1993.

Robertson, G., *People Against the Press* (Quartet, 1993).

Rosenbaum, M., *From Soapbox to Soundbite: Party Political Campaigning in Britain Since 1945* (Macmillan, 1997).

Russell, A. K., *Liberal Landslide: the General Election Campaign of 1906* (Newton Abbot: David & Charles, 1973).

Scammell, M., *Designer Politics: How Elections are Won* (Macmillan, 1995).

'Secret History: the Winter of Discontent', Channel 4, 13 June 1998.

Semetko, H., Scammell, M. and Nossiter, T., 'The Media's Coverage of the Campaign', in Heath, A., Jowell, R. and Curtice, J. (eds), *Labour's Last Chance: the 1992 Election and Beyond* (Dartmouth, 1994).

Seymour-Ure, C., *The Press, Politics and the Public* (Methuen, 1968).

Seymour-Ure, C., *The Political Impact of Mass Media* (Constable, 1974).

Seymour-Ure, C., 'The Press and the Party System Between the Wars', in Peele, G. and Cook, C. (eds), *The Politics of Reappraisal* (Macmillan, 1975).

Seymour-Ure, C., 'National Daily Papers and the Party System', in Boyd-Barrett, Oliver, Seymour-Ure, C. and Tunstall, J. (eds), *Studies on the Press*, Royal Commission on the Press, Working Paper No. 3 (HMSO, 1977).

Seymour-Ure, C., 'Characters and Assassinations: Portrayals of John Major and Neil Kinnock in the Daily Mirror and the Sun', in Crewe, I. and Gosschalk, B. (eds) *Political Communications: the British General Election Campaign of 1992* (Cambridge University Press, 1995).

Seymour-Ure, C., 'Editorial Opinion in the National Press', *Parliamentary Affairs*, 50, 4, 1997.

Shaw, E., *The Labour Party Since 1945: Old Labour, New Labour* (Oxford: Blackwell, 1996).

Smith, M., *Britain and 1940: History, Myth and Popular Memory* (Routledge, 2000).

Snoody, R., *The Good, the Bad, and the Unacceptable: the Hard News about the British Press* (Faber & Faber, 1992).

Stannage, T., *Baldwin Thwarts the Opposition: the British General Election of 1935* (Croom Helm, 1980).

Stevenson, J. and Cook, C., *Britain in the Depression: Society and Politics 1929–39* (Longman, 1994).

Symposium: 'The Winter of Discontent', *Contemporary Record*, 1, 3, 1987.

Thomas, J., ' "Taffy was a Welshman, Taffy was a Thief": Anti-Welshness, the Press and Neil Kinnock', *Llafur: Journal of Welsh Labour History*, 7, 2, 1997.

Thomas, J., 'Labour, the Tabloids, and the 1992 General Election', *Contemporary Record*, 12, 2, 1998.

Thomas, J., 'The "Max Factor" – a Mirror Image? Robert Maxwell and the Daily Mirror Tradition', in Catterall, P., Seymour-Ure, C. and Smith, A. (eds), *Northcliffe's Legacy: Aspects of the Popular Press, 1896–1996* (Macmillan, 2000).

Thomas, J., *Diana's Mourning: A People's History* (Cardiff: University of Wales Press, 2002).

Thomas, J., 'Reflections on the Broken Mirror: the Rise and Fall of Radical Journalism Re-considered', *Media History*, 9, 2, 2003.

Thorpe, A., *The British General Election of 1931* (Clarendon, 1991).

Tiratsoo, N. (ed.), *From Blitz to Blair: a New History of Britain Since 1939* (Phoenix, 1998).

Trade Union Media Working Group, *A Cause for Concern: Media Coverage of the Industrial Disputes, January and February 1979* (TUC, 1979).

Tunstall, J., *The Westminster Lobby Correspondents: a Sociological Study of National Political Journalism* (Routledge & Kegan, 1970).

Tunstall, J., 'The Media: Lapdogs for Thatcher?', *Contemporary Record*, 4, 2, 1990.

Waller, I., 'The Left Wing Press', in Kaufman, G. (ed.), *The Left: a Symposium* (Blond, 1966).

Whale, J., *The Politics of the Media* (Glasgow: Fontana, 1977).

Whitaker, B., *News Limited: Why You Can't Read All About It* (Minority Press Group, 1981).

Whitehead, P., *The Writing on the Wall: Britain in the Seventies* (Michael Joseph, 1985).

Williams, F., *Dangerous Estate* (Readers Union, 1958).

Williams, G., *Britain's Media: How They Are Related* (Campaign for Press and Broadcasting Freedom, 1994).

Wintour, C., *The Rise and Fall of Fleet Street* (Hutchinson, 1989).

Worcester, R., 'Index of Partisanship: a Methodology for Determining Change in the Political Bias of Newspaper Readers', Paper to Asia-Pacific Rim Conference, Sydney, Australia, July 1994.

Young, H., 'Rupert Murdoch and the Sunday Times: a Lamp Goes Out', *Political Quarterly*, 55, 1984.

Young, H., 'The Media Under Mrs Thatcher', *Contemporary Record*, 3, 4, 1990.

Index